DIRECTORY
OF
HISTORIC
AMERICAN
THEATRES

DIRECTORY OF HISTORIC AMERICAN THEATRES

Edited by
John W. Frick
and Carlton Ward

*For the League
of Historic American Theatres*

Historic American Theatres Data Base,
created by John B. Heil

Greenwood Press
New York • Westport, Connecticut • London

Library of Congress Cataloging-in-Publication Data

Directory of historic American theatres.

"Historic American Theatres Data Base, created by
John B. Heil"-T.p.
  Bibliography: p.
  Includes index.
  1. Theaters—United States—Directories.
2. Theater—United States—History—Sources.
I. Frick, John W. II. Ward, Carlton. III. Heil,
John B. IV. League of Historic American Theatres
(Washington, D.C.)
PN2289.D57 1987   792′.025′73   87-10709
ISBN 0-313-24868-0 (lib. bdg. : alk. paper)

Library of Congress Catalog Card Number: 87-10709
ISBN: 0-313-24868-0

First published in 1987

Greenwood Press, Inc.
88 Post Road West, Westport, Connecticut 06881

Printed in the United States of America

The paper used in this book complies with the
Permanent Paper Standard issued by the National
Information Standards Organization (Z39.48-1984).

10 9 8 7 6 5 4 3 2 1

Contents

Illustrations #41 through #80   *following page 199*

List of Illustrations

Following Page 199

Foreword

In the late 1960s I wrote a book called *The American Playhouse in the Eighteenth Century*, a brief architectural history of the earliest theatres built in this country. I began my research believing that no more than a dozen theatres had been built here before 1800; I wound up with a list of more than seventy. As a result, I was able to piece together a fair picture of theatre building in America before the turn of the eighteenth century.

Thus emboldened—as writers used to say—I decided to tackle the nineteenth century. I gave up within a few months, totally intimidated by the explosion of theatre building that had taken place in this country after 1800. I came to realize that literally thousands of theatres had been built before the new century came to an end. The task of tracing their development, as I had with the eighteenth-century buildings, seemed far too big.

Now such tasks are no longer too big to handle. The new *Directory of Historic American Theatres* will provide scholars with a base of raw material that will make detailed comparative studies of our nineteenth- and early twentieth-century theatres really viable for the first time. It is the very best sort of raw material—information about *surviving* buildings, almost 900 of them in all, which can be visited and studied and surveyed. The book is a rare gift to theatre scholars, to architectural and urban historians, and to all those interested in historic American buildings. The givers of this gift—John Frick and Carlton Ward—deserve our gratitude for completing a monumental piece of editorial work. Their reward, I am sure, will be a new surge of scholarship in a field where they have been pioneers.

I can only add my personal thanks for their efforts and the thanks of the League of Historic American Theaters, which sponsored the project. It has never been said in so many words, but all of us involved with the *Directory* know that it is dedicated to the memory of the League's first president, Gene

Chesley, whose deep concern for America's historic theatres ultimately led to this work.

Brooks McNamara
New York University

Preface

The Directory of Historic American Theatres owes its genesis to the pioneering work of the late Gene Chesley of the University of California at Davis, who, in 1970, began compiling data on extant theatres, opera houses and halls built in the United States before 1915. Lists of the historic theatres which he discovered and documented were published between 1975-1979 by the League of Historic American Theatres, the sponsor of this Directory. At the time of his death in 1981, Chesley was in the process of preparing an updated list for publication, a task that was subsequently completed in 1983 by Carlton Ward of Jacksonville State University in Alabama. Chesley's extensive collection of materials on historic theatres was donated by his widow to the Princeton University Theatre Collection. Currently the Gene Chesley Collection, which contains not only materials accumulated by Chesley, but information gathered for this volume, is available to scholars and other qualified researchers by appointment.

The objective of this directory is to record in one volume all available vital data about theatres built in the United States before 1915. For the purposes of this directory, the word theatre refers to any building which had as one of its central functions the housing of live performance, including drama, musical comedy, concerts, vaudeville, magic shows, burlesque, minstrel shows, lectures, medicine shows, opera, Chautauquas, circuses, or similar events.

Theatres included in this volume all meet the following criteria: they were built before 1915; they were designed for the presentation of live entertainment or a combination of live entertainment and movies, with live performance as the principal attraction; and they are extant, although not necessarily used for their original purpose. In the case of theatres which presented both vaudeville and film, every attempt has been made to determine which was actually the principal entertainment form. Theatres which were <u>primarily</u> motion picture houses have been excluded; those which were <u>primarily</u> for vaudeville appear in this volume. When a clear determination about use could not be made, this fact has been noted in the entry for that theatre.

The choice of 1915 as the cutoff date for this directory should not be considered to be a judgment about the importance of later buildings. In the first place, 1915 was the date which Gene Chesley had adopted as he prepared the 1983 list of theatres. In addition, the date enabled us to restrict the scope and scale of our study by eliminating the large number of theatres built in the late teens and 1920s. Otherwise, a multivolume work would have been necessary to survey theatres nationwide. It is hoped that later editions of <u>The Directory</u> will be able to include legitimate and vaudeville theatres erected since 1915 as well as all those erected solely for motion picture exhibition since the turn of the century.

In keeping with Chesley's framework, only <u>extant</u> theatres are included in this study. Interpretation of this word was rather liberal, including theatres which are still operating and virtually unchanged since they first opened, buildings for which only the shell remains, and theatres such as Old Musical Fund Hall in Philadelphia where just the facade remains -- in this case attached to a recently-built condominium.

To collect data for this study, questionnaires were sent to more than 5,000 local and county historical societies throughout the country; to nearly 1,200 theatres which were reported to be extant; to some 500 public libraries; and to individuals interested in historic preservation or historic theatres. This survey was augmented by research conducted at the Billy Rose Theatre Collection of the New York Public Library at Lincoln Center, the Harvard Theatre Collection, the Theatre Collection of the Philadelphia Free Library, the Theatre Collection of the Princeton University Library, the Shubert Archives, the Theatre Collection of the Museum of the City of New York, and the Theatre Historical Society Archives in Chicago. Followup consisted of three --in some cases four--additional letters of inquiry sent to known theatres and, in certain cases, telephone calls to theatre managers.

In compiling our study, every attempt was made to document each theatre as thoroughly as possible, regardless of size, location or historic significance. Thus information was solicited from small, second-floor opera houses and giant multi-auditoria performing arts centers alike.

The directory is divided into two sections. Both are arranged alphabetically by state and then by city, with

theatres recorded alphabetically within each city. The first
section presents data about those theatres that have been
documented, even partially, on the basis of responses to
questionnaires, supplemented where possible by additional
research by the editors.   In some cases, the information
provided by a theatre owner or another interested respondent
was minimal. On the other end of the scale, some respondents
included more information than it was possible to print. All
of the data provided by respondents can be consulted at the
Chesley Collection.

The second section, "Theatres Reported/Confirmed," lists
those buildings for which no questionnaire was returned and
no information could be found in other sources. Theatres in
this section have been labeled [R], which indicates that a
theatre has been reported but that its existence has not been
confirmed, or [C], indicating that the existence of the
theatre has been confirmed but that little or no information
has been provided.

To assist the reader, two separate indexes have been
provided. The first is an index of theatres which lists
buildings, not only by their principal names, but also by
earlier or alternate names. The second index includes all
other subjects including names of performers, architects,
theatre owners, plays, operas, and films. Photographs
representing the wide range of theatres in the Directory were
selected from the Chesley Collection and from those donated
by theatre owners and local historical societies and appear
in two separate sections of the book.

In compiling this directory, we have attempted to
recreate a sense of each building as a theatre. It was felt
that simply describing a space which had been stripped of its
theatrical equipment and trappings would be of little use to
the reader. Therefore, in those cases where information was
minimal, historical sources such as Julius Cahn's Official
Theatrical Guide, published in the late 19th and early 20th
centuries as a "thesaurus of statistics both to members of
the dramatic profession and to travelling men," were used to
supplement information provided on the questionnaire. The
use of one of Cahn's guides for stage dimensions or other
technical information is indicated by the symbol *. Its use
signifies that all of the information that follows was taken
from that source. If seating capacity was derived from Cahn,
an asterisk appears there as well. Of course, information
from Cahn is no longer current and is given only to help
reestablish the original dimensions of a theatre.

Since certain structural features of a theatre such as
seating capacity, levels of seating, and stage dimensions
changed with time, several sets of data may exist in various
sources. Where space permitted, all of this information has
been recorded; where selection was necessary, however, only

the most current figures were used. Original dimensions and capacities of a theatre, when furnished by respondents, are identified as such in the text.

Certain editorial decisions were dictated by space considerations. It was sometimes necessary, for example, to limit the section on stars who appeared at a theatre, and selection was unavoidable. The choice of language in an entry was also dependent on available space. Consequently, such terms as "Dance," "Drama," and "Concerts" have been employed to encompass wide ranges of activities. "Dance," for example, includes such forms as ballet, jazz, modern, ballroom, tap, ethnic, and folk dance; "Drama" refers to any play, regardless of genre; and "Concerts" run the gamut from solo recitals to symphony orchestras, from classical music to jazz and pop.

The process of compiling such a directory is not without its inherent problems. In many cases, records of small-town theatres no longer exist or are so fragmented as to be of little use. The problem of sources is exacerbated by the fact that many historic theatres ceased operation as theatres years ago. Often they were converted to commercial use and their original function has been forgotten.

Possibly the most significant problem was the necessity of having to rely on "the kindness of strangers" in order to obtain information. While the reliability of the data furnished by the vast majority of local historians, librarians and theatre managers is high, exceptions invariably do exist. Furthermore, some owners or managers failed to return our questionnaires; consequently their theatres appear in the "Theatres Reported/Confirmed" section of the book instead of the documented portion. For these reasons and because of the sheer size of the project, the information recorded in this volume is the best data available to us at the time the entry was made. The volume is by no means comprehensive, but it represents, we believe, an important first step in solving a major historical problem.

The process of discovering and documenting historic theatres -- which theatre restoration consultant Craig Morrison compares to archeology-- is an ongoing one. Each day a forgotten theatre is discovered, and more state and city governments are becoming aware of the valuable resource that exists, uninhabited, above the drug store or behind recently installed paneling in the local movie theatre. In the quest to identify and save America's historic theatres, however, the best single resource remains the interested individual who, for example, may know of a forgotten 1871 second-floor opera house that is now being used as a furniture warehouse.

Although 886 theatres are already included in this

directory and 102   previously   unreported   theatres   were
"discovered" during its preparation,   one   of   the   principal
goals of this   volume   is   to   stimulate   others   to   become
involved in the   process   of   discovering   this   country's
historic theatres.   The editors   and   the   League of Historic
American Theatres would greatly appreciate information   about
historic theatres for   future   editions   of   The Directory of
Historic   American   Theatres.   Information   can   be sent to the
editors, c/o The League of   Historic American   Theatres, 1600
H Street, N. W., Washington,   DC 20006.

The editors   wish   to thank the many people who have made
the Directory of Historic   American   Theatres possible.   First,
thanks are due   to   Brooks McNamara   and   to   the   League   of
Historic American Theatres for giving us the   opportunity   to
conduct this study and for providing advice and encouragement
while the project was under way.

We are   indebted   to the following archivists who devoted
their time and   efforts   to   unearthing   valuable   research
materials: Mary Ann Jensen, Michelle McIntyre   and   the staff
at the Princeton   Theatre Collection; Geraldine Duclow at the
Theatre Collection of the Philadelphia   Free   Library; Jeanne
Newlin and Martha   Mahard at the Harvard Theatre   Collection;
Dorothy Swerdlove and   the   staff   of   the Billy Rose Theatre
Collection, New York Public Library;   Brigitte   Kueppers   and
Reagan Fletcher at the Shubert Archives; William Benedict and
the staff of   the   Theatre Historical Society Archives;   Judy
Resop at the   University   of Wisconsin – Fond du Lac Library;
and the Reference Department at   the   Fond   du Lac, Wisconsin
Public Library.

For giving   freely   of   their   expertise   and   furnishing
crucial information that   otherwise   might   not   have   been
available to us, we wish to thank   the following scholars and
regional experts: Ted Van Arsdol, Irvin R. Glazer,   George B.
Bryan, Mary C.   Henderson,   Don   B.   Wilmeth, Craig Morrison,
Gene Gladson, Stephen Burge Johnson,   Steve Vallillo, Barbara
Parisi, Jack Neeson, Joe Rosenberg, Donald R.   Streibig, Tony
Rivenbark, Russell Collins, Maureen Patton, Nadine Salonites,
Robert Murray, Marilyn Bacon, Kenneth Thomas, Frank Hildy, W.
J. Davenport, and C. V. March.

We also   wish to thank Jean Huberty, Sue Byerly, Sue Last
and Thom Homburg at the University of Wisconsin – Fond du Lac
for their help in preparing the   mailings and the final manu-
script; Tom Clausen   for "rescuing" many of the   photographs;
Ramona Silipo and   Debbie   Mikula   at   the League of Historic
Theatres offices for their ongoing   logistical   support;   and
Jack Heil, Chairman of the Computer Science Department of the
University of Wisconsin   Centers, for creating   the   computer
programs and data   base   that   allowed   us to reduce the work
period by years.

Finally, we wish to express our indebtedness to the unsung heroes of this directory, the countless city and county historical societies, local librarians and individual theatre owners without whose contributions this directory would not exist and to our wives, Marsha and Sharon, for their patience and encouragement during the course of this project.

THEATRES DOCUMENTED

Theatres included in this section of the directory have been documented using information provided on questionnaires, augmented in some cases with dimensions or statistics from historical sources like <u>Julius</u> <u>Cahn's</u> <u>Official</u> <u>Theatrical</u> <u>Guide</u>, the latter signified by the use of the symbol *. With the exception of cases where the data was obviously incorrect, information has been presented as it was provided by the respondents.

Throughout the directory, we have attempted to use standard theatrical terms. Consequently, auditorium seating levels are labeled "tiers" and terms like "family circle" and "dress circle," which have multiple meanings, have been avoided.

In compiling this directory, the following codes were used. When a theatre did not fit neatly into any of the "types," we selected the closest category.

<u>CODES</u>

<u>Type</u> <u>of</u> <u>Theatre</u>:

   a. A theatre or opera house built originally as a single use performance space, having a proscenium and with the stage area equipped for theatrical performance.

   b. Theatre or opera house within a multiple use structure. Often an "upstairs" house. Sometimes related to lodge use or as a performance space in a town hall or commercial building.

   c. All other performance spaces - e.g., rooms in churches, converted rooms, rooms in bars.

Degree of Restoration:

    a.   Restored

    b.   Restoration planned as of July 1, 1985

    c.   Unrestored

    d.   Restoration not necessary - currently in use

Alabama

Birmingham, AL

LYRIC THEATRE, 319 18th Street North
  OPENING DATE: 1912
  STYLE OF ARCHITECTURE: Commercial   TYPE OF BUILDING:
    Movie theatre   FACADE: Stone   TYPE OF THEATRE: (a)
  DEGREE OF RESTORATION: (c)   CLOSING DATE: 1960
  CURRENT USE: Vacant   PERFORMANCE SPACES IN BUILDING: 1
  LOCATION OF AUDITORIUM: First floor
  MAJOR TYPES OF ENTERTAINMENT: Drama, vaudeville, movies
  MAJOR STARS WHO APPEARED AT THEATRE: Will Rogers, Sophie
    Tucker
  ADDITIONAL INFORMATION: Theatre has been vacant since early
    1960s and is in poor condition.

Decatur, AL

COTACO OPERA HOUSE (other names: Price's Opera House,
    Masonic), DeBank Street
  OPENING DATE: 1890
  ARCHITECTS: Morris and Morris
  STYLE OF ARCHITECTURE: Commercial Victorian
  TYPE OF BUILDING: Masonic Lodge   FACADE: Stone
  TYPE OF THEATRE: (a)   DEGREE OF RESTORATION: (c)
  CURRENT USE: Vacant   PERFORMANCE SPACES IN BUILDING: 1
  LOCATION OF AUDITORIUM: First floor
  STAGE DIMENSIONS AND EQUIPMENT: Height and width of
    proscenium, 24ft x 32ft; Distance from edge of stage to
    back wall of stage, 36ft; Distance from edge of stage to
    curtain line, 5ft; Distance between side walls of stage,
    45ft 2in; Distance from stage floor to fly loft, 57ft;
    Depth under stage, 8ft; Stage floor, flat; Trap doors, 1
  DIMENSIONS OF AUDITORIUM: Distance between side walls of
    auditorium, 55ft; Distance stage to back wall of
    auditorium, 76ft; Capacity of orchestra pit, 10
  SEATING (3 levels): 1st level, 400; 2nd level, 250;
    3rd level, 200

SHAPE OF THE AUDITORIUM: Rectangular
MAJOR TYPES OF ENTERTAINMENT: Drama, vaudeville, concerts
ADDITIONAL INFORMATION: Little evidence of the theatre
  remains after alterations by the Masons. Interior
  measurements from Julius Cahn's Official Theatrical Guide
  (1910) verified by comparison with recent blueprint.

Dothan, AL

DOTHAN OPERA HOUSE (other name: City Auditorium), North and
  Andrews Streets
OPENING DATE: October 8, 1915
OPENING SHOW: The Winning of Barbara Worth
STYLE OF ARCHITECTURE: Victorian   FACADE: Brick and stone
TYPE OF THEATRE: (a)   DEGREE OF RESTORATION: (a)
CURRENT USE: Theatre   PERFORMANCE SPACES IN BUILDING: 1
LOCATION OF AUDITORIUM: First floor
STAGE DIMENSIONS AND EQUIPMENT: Height and width of
  proscenium, 14ft 9in x 31ft 6in; Shape of proscenium
  arch, square; Distance from edge of stage to back wall of
  stage; 30ft; Distance from edge of stage to curtain line,
  3ft; Distance between side walls of stage, 52ft; Stage
  floor, flat; Dressing rooms, 2 (basement)
SEATING (3 levels): 1st level, 260; 2nd level, 150; 3rd
  level, 90
SHAPE OF THE AUDITORIUM: U-shaped
MAJOR TYPES OF ENTERTAINMENT: Vaudeville, burlesque
MAJOR STARS WHO APPEARED AT THEATRE: Al G. Fields, Silas
  Green

Fort Payne, AL

FORT PAYNE OPERA HOUSE (other name: Rice's Opera House),
  510 Gault Avenue North
OPENING DATE: September 10, 1890
OPENING SHOW: Hoyt's A Tin Soldier
STYLE OF ARCHITECTURE: Victorian   TYPE OF BUILDING:
  Theatre, storage   FACADE: Brick and wood (maroon, red)
TYPE OF THEATRE: (b)   DEGREE OF RESTORATION: (a)
CURRENT USE: Community theatre   PERFORMANCE SPACES IN
BUILDING: 1   LOCATION OF AUDITORIUM: Ground floor
STAGE DIMENSIONS AND EQUIPMENT: Height and width of
  proscenium, 17ft 6in x 29ft; Shape of proscenium arch,
  arched; Distance from edge of stage to back wall of
  stage, 39ft 6in; Distance from edge of stage to curtain
  line, 11ft 6in; Distance between side walls of stage,
  47ft 10in; Distance from stage floor to fly loft, 18ft
  6in; Depth under stage, 4ft 6in; Stage floor, flat;
  Dressing rooms, 2
DIMENSIONS OF AUDITORIUM: Distance between side walls of
  auditorium, 47ft 2in; Distance stage to back wall of
  auditorium, 51ft; Orchestra pit, none
SEATING (3 levels): 1st level, 290; 2nd level, 160;
  3rd level, 12

SHAPE OF THE AUDITORIUM: Rectangular
MAJOR TYPES OF ENTERTAINMENT: Drama, concerts
MAJOR STARS WHO APPEARED AT THEATRE: Jimmy Rodgers (1932)
   and Alabama in 1970s (Fort Payne is their home town)
ADDITIONAL INFORMATION: The theatre was restored in 1970
   as a community theatre and auditorium. The theatre was
   damaged by fire in 1981, but has reopened. Auditorium is
   lighted by "circle of lights" attached to the ceiling.

Greensboro, AL

GREENSBORO OPERA HOUSE (other name: Blunt Opera House),
   Main Street
OPENING DATE: 1903   TYPE OF BUILDING: Church
CLOSING DATE: 1948   CURRENT USE: Vacant
PERFORMANCE SPACES IN BUILDING: 1
LOCATION OF AUDITORIUM: Second floor
STAGE DIMENSIONS AND EQUIPMENT: Height and width of
   proscenium, 12ft x 30ft; Shape of proscenium arch,
   square; Distance from edge of stage to back wall of
   stage, 22ft; Distance from edge of stage to curtain line,
   4ft; Distance from stage floor to fly loft, 12ft; Stage
   floor, flat; Dressing rooms, 4
DIMENSIONS OF AUDITORIUM: Distance between side walls
   of auditorium, 54ft; Distance stage to back wall of
   auditorium, 54ft; Orchestra pit, none
SEATING (2 levels): 1st level, 250; 2nd level, 80
SHAPE OF THE AUDITORIUM: Square
MAJOR TYPES OF ENTERTAINMENT: Drama
ADDITIONAL INFORMATION: Originally erected in 1897, the
   theatre burned in 1902 and was rebuilt the following
   year. It was converted to movies in 1910 and is
   currently part of Greensboro Historic District.

Jacksonville, AL

JACKSONVILLE OPERA HOUSE, Public Square
OPENING DATE: 1902
OPENING SHOW: Walter Camp's Alabama Greater Minstrels
STYLE OF ARCHITECTURE: Commercial "Arts and Crafts"
TYPE OF BUILDING: Storage   FACADE: Brick
TYPE OF THEATRE: (b)   DEGREE OF RESTORATION: (c)
CLOSING DATE: 1915   CURRENT USE: Vacant
PERFORMANCE SPACES IN BUILDING: 1
LOCATION OF AUDITORIUM: Second floor
DIMENSIONS OF AUDITORIUM: Distance between side walls
   of auditorium, 30ft; Distance stage to back wall of
   auditorium, 50ft; Orchestra pit, none
SEATING (1 level)
SHAPE OF THE AUDITORIUM: Rectangular
MAJOR TYPES OF ENTERTAINMENT: Drama, vaudeville, minstrel
   shows, movies
ADDITIONAL INFORMATION: The theatre was rebuilt after a
   fire in 1897 and was used for local theatricals until

1915 when a movie house opened nearby. Second floor
auditorium seated about 200 and was lighted by kerosene
until 1910.

Mobile, AL

SEAMAN'S BETHEL THEATRE, University of South Alabama
    STYLE OF ARCHITECTURE: Gothic Revival
    TYPE OF BUILDING: Seamen's Bethel   FACADE: Reddish brown
        brick   TYPE OF THEATRE: (c)   DEGREE OF RESTORATION: (a)
    CLOSING DATE: 1984   CURRENT USE: Rehearsals, dances
    PERFORMANCE SPACES IN BUILDING: 1
    LOCATION OF AUDITORIUM: First floor
    SHAPE OF THE AUDITORIUM: U-shaped with 19' x 25' thrust
    MAJOR TYPES OF ENTERTAINMENT: Drama, small musicals
    ADDITIONAL INFORMATION: The building served as a
        bethel until 1923 when it became the Little Theatre, a
        forerunner of the Joe Jefferson Players. The structure
        was removed from its original site and placed on
        university property in 1968.

Montgomery, AL

MONTGOMERY THEATRE, Dexter Avenue
    OPENING DATE: 1860
    STYLE OF ARCHITECTURE: Commercial   TYPE OF BUILDING:
        Commercial   FACADE: Brick   TYPE OF THEATRE: (b)
    DEGREE OF RESTORATION: (c)   CLOSING DATE: c.1900
    CURRENT USE: Store   PERFORMANCE SPACES IN BUILDING: 1
    LOCATION OF AUDITORIUM: Second floor
    SHAPE OF THE AUDITORIUM: Rectangular
    MAJOR TYPES OF ENTERTAINMENT: Drama, concerts, minstrel
        shows
    ADDITIONAL INFORMATION: The song Dixie was supposedly
        first played here and the music was scored on the wall
        with charcoal.

Talledega, AL

CHAMBERS OPERA HOUSE, Battle and Court Streets
    OPENING DATE: 1887
    ARCHITECT: George Weatherley Chambers, builder
    STYLE OF ARCHITECTURE: Commercial   TYPE OF BUILDING:
        Commercial   FACADE: Brick   TYPE OF THEATRE: (b)
    DEGREE OF RESTORATION: (c)   CLOSING DATE: 1905
    CURRENT USE: Furniture store
    LOCATION OF AUDITORIUM: Second floor
    MAJOR TYPES OF ENTERTAINMENT: Drama, vaudeville
    ADDITIONAL INFORMATION: Theatre space is a conversion of a
        pre-1860 building that housed a grocery store and a
        factory where rifles were made for the Confederate Army.

Talledega, AL

ELK'S THEATRE, East Street
  OPENING DATE: 1905
  STYLE OF ARCHITECTURE: Victorian
  TYPE OF BUILDING: Commercial   FACADE: Red brick
  TYPE OF THEATRE: (a)   DEGREE OF RESTORATION: (c)
  CLOSING DATE: 1928   CURRENT USE: Service station
  LOCATION OF AUDITORIUM: First floor
  STAGE DIMENSIONS AND EQUIPMENT: Width of proscenium,
    30ft; Distance from edge of stage to back wall of
    stage, 29ft; Distance from edge of stage to curtain
    line, 5ft; Distance between side walls of stage, 57ft;
    Distance from stage floor to fly loft, 45ft; Depth under
    stage, 4ft; Trap doors, 1; Scenery storage rooms, 1
  DIMENSIONS OF AUDITORIUM: Capacity of orchestra pit, one
    piano
  SEATING (3 levels)
  MAJOR TYPES OF ENTERTAINMENT: Drama, movies
  MAJOR STARS WHO APPEARED AT THEATRE: William Jennings
    Bryan
  ADDITIONAL INFORMATION: Portions of the theatre are
    reported to be intact.

Union Springs, AL

ELEY OPERA HOUSE, 212 North Prairie Street
  OPENING DATE: 1897
  STYLE OF ARCHITECTURE: Neo-Classical   TYPE OF BUILDING:
    Bank   FACADE: Brick   TYPE OF THEATRE: (b)
  DEGREE OF RESTORATION: (c)   CURRENT USE: Bank
  PERFORMANCE SPACES IN BUILDING: 1
  LOCATION OF AUDITORIUM: Second floor
  MAJOR TYPES OF ENTERTAINMENT: Drama, concerts
  ADDITIONAL INFORMATION: Bank's accounting department now
    occupies stage space and all traces of theatre have been
    removed. A town librarian reports that a large scenic
    drop still exists somewhere in the town.

Wetumpka, AL

JOE MACON HOME, 206 West Tuskeena Street
  OPENING DATE: c. 1830
  TYPE OF BUILDING: Residence   FACADE: Painted wood
  TYPE OF THEATRE: (a)   DEGREE OF RESTORATION: (a)
  CURRENT USE: Residence
  LOCATION OF AUDITORIUM: First floor
  ADDITIONAL INFORMATION: This is a well-restored structure
    which was originally erected as a theatre. The owner has
    restored it as faithfully as possible. Platforms at the
    end of the theatre space (a large, empty room) may have
    served as a stage. The building was moved from its
    original site across the river.

Arizona

Prescott, AZ

YAVAPAI COLLEGE COMMUNITY THEATRE (other name: Elks Opera
   House), 115 East Gurley Street
   OPENING DATE: February 17, 1905
   OPENING SHOW: Marta of the Lowland
   ARCHITECT: John R. Minor   STYLE OF ARCHITECTURE:
   Commercial   TYPE OF BUILDING: Office building
   FACADE: Granite and brick   TYPE OF THEATRE: (a)
   DEGREE OF RESTORATION: (d)   CURRENT USE: College
   productions and rentals   PERFORMANCE SPACES IN
   BUILDING: 1   LOCATION OF AUDITORIUM: Ground floor
   STAGE DIMENSIONS AND EQUIPMENT: Height and width of
   proscenium, 19ft 3in x 29ft 5in; Shape of proscenium
   arch, rectangular; Distance from edge of stage to back
   wall of stage, 28ft 6in; Distance from edge of stage to
   curtain line, 5ft 6in; Distance stage floor to fly loft,
   40ft; Depth under stage, 10ft; Scenery storage rooms, 2
   (beneath stage); Dressing rooms, 4 (basement, beneath
   stage)
   DIMENSIONS OF AUDITORIUM: Distance between side walls of
   auditorium, 58ft; Distance from stage to back wall of
   auditorium, 69ft; Capacity of orchestra pit, 30
   SHAPE OF AUDITORIUM: 1st and 3rd levels, rectangular; 2nd
   level, horseshoe-shaped
   SEATING (3 levels): 1st level, 450; 2nd level, 150; 3rd
   level, 50

Tombstone, AZ

BIRD CAGE THEATRE, Allen Street
   OPENING DATE: September 23, 1881
   STYLE OF ARCHITECTURE: Western
   TYPE OF BUILDING: Bar   FACADE: Adobe
   TYPE OF THEATRE: (b)   DEGREE OF RESTORATION: (a)
   CURRENT USE: Museum   PERFORMANCE SPACES IN BUILDING: 1
   LOCATION OF AUDITORIUM: Ground floor

MAJOR TYPES OF ENTERTAINMENT: Local and touring
    productions
ADDITIONAL INFORMATION: This adobe building, now a
    theatrical museum, is a remnant of a once-rowdy
    western tradition.

Tombstone, AZ

SCHIEFFELIN HALL, Fremont Street
    OPENING DATE: March 17, 1881
    OPENING SHOW: Irish League Ball
    TYPE OF BUILDING: Museum   FACADE: Adobe brick
    TYPE OF THEATRE: (a)   DEGREE OF RESTORATION: (a)
    CURRENT USE: Museum   PERFORMANCE SPACES IN BUILDING: 1
    STAGE DIMENSIONS AND EQUIPMENT: Height and width of
        proscenium, 20ft x 34ft; Distance from edge of stage to
        back wall of stage, 30ft; Distance from edge of stage to
        curtain line, 4ft 6in; Depth under stage, 8ft; Trap
        doors, 3
    SEATING (2 levels): 1st level, 500; 2nd level, 200
    ADDITIONAL INFORMATION: The theatre hosts a dramatic
        presentation, The Town Too Tough to Die.

Arkansas

Van Buren, AR

KING OPERA HOUSE, 427 Main Street
 OPENING DATE: 1901
 STYLE OF ARCHITECTURE: Victorian
 TYPE OF BUILDING: Commercial   FACADE: Red Brick
 TYPE OF THEATRE: (c)   DEGREE OF RESTORATION: (b)
 CURRENT USE: Civic auditorium
 LOCATION OF AUDITORIUM: First floor
 STAGE DIMENSIONS AND EQUIPMENT: Height and width of
   proscenium, 18ft x 30ft 2in; Shape of proscenium,
   rectangular; Distance from edge of stage to back wall
   of stage, 39ft 3in; Distance between side walls of stage,
   48ft 2in; Distance from stage floor to fly loft, 39ft
   3in; Depth under stage, 8ft 5in; Stage floor, flat; Trap
   doors, 4
 DIMENSIONS OF AUDITORIUM: Distance between side walls of
   auditorium, 48ft 2in; Distance from Stage to back wall of
   auditorium, 48ft 8in
 SHAPE OF AUDITORIUM: Rectangular
 SEATING (2 levels): 1st level, 230; 2nd level, 140
 MAJOR TYPES OF ENTERTAINMENT: Vaudeville, burlesque and
   drama in the early 1900s; movies beginning in the 1920s
 MAJOR STARS WHO APPEARED AT THEATRE: William Jennings
   Bryan, Sousa and his band, and Illuno, "The Electric
   Wonder," who walked a charged tightwire wearing a helmet
   which lit up
 ADDITIONAL INFORMATION: The theatre is part of a Main
   Street Historic District. Restoration is in progress.
   "King Opera House" is inscribed on the facade.

California

Berkeley, CA

HEARST GREEK THEATRE, U.C.B. Campus
    OPENING DATE: 1903   OPENING SHOW: The Birds
    ARCHITECT: John Galen Howard   STYLE OF ARCHITECTURE: Greek
    TYPE OF BUILDING: Concert hall   TYPE OF THEATRE: (a)
    DEGREE OF RESTORATION: (d)   CURRENT USE: Theatre
    LOCATION OF AUDITORIUM: First floor
    STAGE DIMENSIONS AND EQUIPMENT: Distance from edge of stage
        to back wall of stage, 28ft; Distance between side walls
        of stage, 133ft
    SHAPE OF THE AUDITORIUM: Semicircular
    MAJOR TYPES OF ENTERTAINMENT: Theatre, opera, dance, and
        student rallies
    MAJOR STARS WHO APPEARED AT THEATRE: Presidents Theodore
        Roosevelt, Taft, and Wilson; Ben Greet Players, Sarah
        Bernhardt, General Pershing, and Nehru
    ADDITIONAL INFORMATION: William Randolph Hearst financed
        construction of the theatre which was influenced by the
        ancient theatres at Epidaurus and Pompeii.

Berkeley, CA

HISTORIC FINNISH HALL (other name: Toveri Tupa), 1819
        Tenth Street
    OPENING DATE: 1909   TYPE OF BUILDING: Cultural center
    TYPE OF THEATRE: (b)   DEGREE OF RESTORATION: (a)
    CURRENT USE: Civic functions
    PERFORMANCE SPACES IN BUILDING: 1
    LOCATION OF AUDITORIUM: Second floor
    STAGE DIMENSIONS AND EQUIPMENT: Height and width of
        proscenium, 14ft 4in x 27ft 6in; Shape of proscenium
        arch, rectangular; Distance from edge of stage to back
        wall of stage, 28ft; Distance between side walls of
        stage, 48ft; Distance from stage floor to fly loft,
        28ft; Depth under stage, 7ft 6in; Stage floor, raked;
        Trap doors, 1; Dressing rooms, 1 (side of stage)

DIMENSIONS OF AUDITORIUM: Distance between side walls
   of auditorium, 48ft; Distance stage to back wall of
   auditorium, 55ft
SEATING (2 levels)
SHAPE OF THE AUDITORIUM: Rectangular
MAJOR TYPES OF ENTERTAINMENT: Drama, vaudeville, concerts

Columbia, CA

FALLON THEATRE, Washington and Broadway
   OPENING DATE: 1886
   STYLE OF ARCHITECTURE: Wood Vernacular
   TYPE OF BUILDING: Hotel, bar, dance hall
   FACADE: brick and wood   TYPE OF THEATRE: (b)
   DEGREE OF RESTORATION: (a)   CURRENT USE: Theatre
   PERFORMANCE SPACES IN BUILDING: 1
   LOCATION OF AUDITORIUM: Ground floor
   STAGE DIMENSIONS AND EQUIPMENT: Stage floor, flat
   DIMENSIONS OF AUDITORIUM: Orchestra pit, none
   SEATING (2 levels): 1st level, 200; 2nd level, 30
   MAJOR TYPES OF ENTERTAINMENT: Drama, opera, rallies,
      vaudeville
   ADDITIONAL INFORMATION: Originally a dance hall. Produces
      in repertory in summer.

Los Angeles, CA

MERCED THEATRE (other name: Wood's Opera House), 418 North
   Main Street
   OPENING DATE: December 31, 1870
   OPENING SHOW: Fanchon The Cricket
   ARCHITECT: E.F. Kysor   STYLE OF ARCHITECTURE: Spanish
   TYPE OF BUILDING: Armory; commercial   FACADE: brick
   TYPE OF THEATRE: (B) DEGREE OF RESTORATION: (C)
   CURRENT USE: Part of public park
   LOCATION OF AUDITORIUM: Second floor
   STAGE DIMENSIONS AND EQUIPMENT: Distance from edge of stage
      to back wall of stage, 25ft; Distance between side walls
      of stage, 35ft; Dressing rooms, 2
   DIMENSIONS OF AUDITORIUM: Distance between side walls
      of auditorium, 35ft; Distance stage to back wall of
      auditorium, 75ft
   SHAPE OF THE AUDITORIUM: Rectangular
   MAJOR TYPES OF ENTERTAINMENT: Vaudeville, drama, variety
   ADDITIONAL INFORMATION: Theatre is in a State Park and
      exterior has been restored. No theatre elements remain.

Monterey, CA

CALIFORNIA'S FIRST THEATRE, Pacific and Scott Streets
   OPENING DATE: 1846
   STYLE OF ARCHITECTURE: Vernacular   TYPE OF BUILDING:
      Whaling station, bar, drug store   FACADE: Stone

TYPE OF THEATRE: (c)   DEGREE OF RESTORATION: (a)
CURRENT USE: Museum   LOCATION OF AUDITORIUM: First floor
STAGE DIMENSIONS AND EQUIPMENT: Dressing rooms, 2 (ladies',
    stage right; mens', in attic)
DIMENSIONS OF AUDITORIUM: Capacity of orchestra pit, 4
SEATING (3 levels)
SHAPE OF THE AUDITORIUM: Rectangular
MAJOR TYPES OF ENTERTAINMENT: Local productions
ADDITIONAL INFORMATION: Restored theatre that was built
    as a saloon and sailors' boarding house. Plays were
    performed here by soldiers from 1847 to 1849.

Napa, CA

NAPA OPERA HOUSE (other name: Crowley's Opera House),
    1010-1028 Main Street
OPENING DATE: 1879
ARCHITECTS: Joseph and Samuel Newsom
STYLE OF ARCHITECTURE: Italianate   TYPE OF BUILDING:
    Commercial   FACADE: Brick   TYPE OF THEATRE: (b)
DEGREE OF RESTORATION: (c)   CLOSING DATE: 1909
CURRENT USE: Vacant   PERFORMANCE SPACES IN BUILDING: 1
LOCATION OF AUDITORIUM: Second floor
STAGE DIMENSIONS AND EQUIPMENT: Height and width of
    proscenium, 20ft x 27ft 6in; Distance from edge of
    stage to back wall of stage, 30ft; Distance from edge
    of stage to curtain line, 6ft; Distance between side
    walls of stage, 65ft; Distance from stage floor to fly
    loft, 22ft; Depth under stage, 8ft; Stage floor, raked;
    Trap doors, 4; Scenery storage rooms, 1
SHAPE OF THE AUDITORIUM: Horseshoe-shaped
MAJOR TYPES OF ENTERTAINMENT: Drama, vaudeville, burlesque,
    opera

National City, CA

GRANGER MUSIC HALL, 1700 East Fourth Street
OPENING DATE: 1898
ARCHITECT: Irving Gill   TYPE OF BUILDING: Music hall
FACADE: Cedar Shingle   DEGREE OF RESTORATION: (a)
CURRENT USE: Community events
LOCATION OF AUDITORIUM: Ground floor
STAGE DIMENSIONS AND EQUIPMENT: Distance between side walls
    of stage, 32ft
DIMENSIONS OF AUDITORIUM: Distance between side walls
    of auditorium, 32ft; Distance stage to back wall of
    auditorium, 80ft
SEATING (1 level)
SHAPE OF THE AUDITORIUM: Rectangular
ADDITIONAL INFORMATION: Irving Gill was a student of Adler
    and Sullivan. A 1,060-pipe organ is located behind the
    stage. The building is nearly all wood and has excellent
    acoustics. The theatre is not situated on its original
    site.

Nevada, CA

NEVADA THEATRE
OPENING DATE: 1865   OPENING SHOW: Gala Benefit to help
   defray construction costs
STYLE OF ARCHITECTURE: Commercial Spanish
FACADE: Brick   TYPE OF THEATRE: (a)
DEGREE OF RESTORATION: (a)   CURRENT USE: Theatre
PERFORMANCE SPACES IN BUILDING: 1
LOCATION OF AUDITORIUM: First floor
STAGE DIMENSIONS AND EQUIPMENT: Height and width of
   proscenium, 20ft x 30ft; Distance from edge of stage to
   back wall of stage, 28ft; Distance from edge of stage to
   curtain line, 2ft; Distance between side walls of stage,
   45ft; Distance from stage floor to fly loft, 60ft; Depth
   under stage, 8ft; Trap doors, 1
DIMENSIONS OF AUDITORIUM: Distance between side walls
   of auditorium, 45ft; Capacity of orchestra pit, 5
SEATING (3 levels)
MAJOR TYPES OF ENTERTAINMENT: Touring companies, minstrel
   shows
MAJOR STARS WHO APPEARED AT THEATRE: Jack London, Mark
   Twain, Lotta Crabtree, and Emma Nevada
ADDITIONAL INFORMATION: Plays were presented until 1915
   when movies were introduced. Movies continued until 1958
   when theatre was closed. Building is now restored and
   the original facade has been restored. Gene Chesley was
   the theatre consultant for the restoration. The Dutch
   Governor (September 9, 1865) was the first play
   presented.

Pacific Grove, CA

CHAUTAUQUA HALL, 16th and Central Avenues
OPENING DATE: 1881
STYLE OF ARCHITECTURE: Western   TYPE OF BUILDING:
   Civic uses   FACADE: Wood   TYPE OF THEATRE: (c)
DEGREE OF RESTORATION: (d)   CURRENT USE: Community events
LOCATION OF AUDITORIUM: First floor
MAJOR TYPES OF ENTERTAINMENT: Drama, dance, music, and
   lectures
ADDITIONAL INFORMATION: This building claimed to be
   "the largest Chautauqua Hall in the country," but no
   seating capacity is available. The last Chautauqua event
   was held here on August 7, 1926. The building is now
   owned by the City and is still in good condition.

Reedley, CA

REEDLEY OPERA HOUSE, 1720 10th Street
OPENING DATE: 1903
ARCHITECT: Jesse Jansen   STYLE OF ARCHITECTURE:
   Commercial   TYPE OF THEATRE: (b)   DEGREE OF
RESTORATION: (a)   CURRENT USE: Dinner theatre

STAGE DIMENSIONS AND EQUIPMENT: Height and width of
  proscenium, 12ft; Distance from edge of stage to back
  wall of stage, 18ft; Distance between side walls of
  stage, 14ft; Distance from stage floor to fly loft, 12ft;
  Dressing rooms, 1
DIMENSIONS OF AUDITORIUM: Capacity of orchestra pit, 20
SEATING (2 levels)
SHAPE OF THE AUDITORIUM: Horseshoe-shaped balcony
ADDITIONAL INFORMATION: Horseshoe-shaped balcony is intact.
  Renovated in 1984 and converted to a dinner theatre.
  Tables and chairs replace earlier fixed seating.

San Diego, CA

SPRECKLES THEATRE BUILDING, 121 Broadway
  OPENING DATE: 1914
  STYLE OF ARCHITECTURE: Beaux Arts   TYPE OF BUILDING:
    Commercial   FACADE: Stone   TYPE OF THEATRE: (b)
  DEGREE OF RESTORATION: (a)   CURRENT USE: Theatre
  LOCATION OF AUDITORIUM: First floor
  STAGE DIMENSIONS AND EQUIPMENT: Shape of proscenium arch,
    arched; Distance from edge of stage to back wall of
    stage, 52ft; Distance from edge of stage to curtain line,
    6ft; Distance between side walls of stage, 88ft
  DIMENSIONS OF AUDITORIUM: Capacity of orchestra pit, 35
  SEATING (3 levels)
  SHAPE OF THE AUDITORIUM: Rectangular
  MAJOR TYPES OF ENTERTAINMENT: Drama

San Francisco, CA

GEARY THEATRE (other names: Columbia, Wilkes, Lurie),
  415 Geary Street
  OPENING DATE: January 10, 1910
  OPENING SHOW: The Scarlet Woman
  ARCHITECTS: Bliss and Faville   STYLE OF ARCHITECTURE:
    Beaux Arts   FACADE: Terra cotta TYPE OF THEATRE: (a)
  DEGREE OF RESTORATION: (d)   CURRENT USE: Theatre
  LOCATION OF AUDITORIUM: Ground floor
  STAGE DIMENSIONS AND EQUIPMENT: Height and width of
    proscenium, 30ft x 36ft; Shape of proscenium arch,
    rectangular; Distance from edge of stage to back wall of
    stage, 45ft; Distance from edge of stage to curtain line,
    2ft; Distance between side walls of stage, 76ft; Stage
    floor, raked; Trap doors, 1; Scenery storage rooms
    (scene shop); Dressing rooms, 15 (theatre annex)
  DIMENSIONS OF AUDITORIUM: Orchestra pit, yes
  SEATING (3 levels): 1st level, 573; 2nd level, 484;
    3rd level, 399
  MAJOR TYPES OF ENTERTAINMENT: Drama
  MAJOR STARS WHO APPEARED AT THEATRE: Sarah Bernhardt,
    Nazimova, Isadora Duncan
  ADDITIONAL INFORMATION: The theatre is the home of the
    American Conservatory Theatre.

San Francisco, CA

SOUTH SAN FRANCISCO OPERA HOUSE, Third Street
  OPENING DATE: December 1888   OPENING SHOW: Little Puck
    with Frank Daniels and Bessie Mason
  STYLE OF ARCHITECTURE: Renaissance
  TYPE OF BUILDING: Commercial   FACADE: Wood
  TYPE OF THEATRE: (a)   DEGREE OF RESTORATION: (a)
  CURRENT USE: Theatre   LOCATION OF AUDITORIUM: First floor
  ADDITIONAL INFORMATION: Theatre was built by the Masons and
    was the only San Francisco theatre to survive the 1906
    earthquake. Movies were never shown at this theatre.
    Building is owned by the city.

Sonora, CA

OPERA HALL GARAGE (other name: Opera Hall), 258 South
    Washington Street
  OPENING DATE: 1886
  STYLE OF ARCHITECTURE: Vernacular   TYPE OF BUILDING:
    Commercial   FACADE: Stone   TYPE OF THEATRE: (c)
  DEGREE OF RESTORATION: (c)   CLOSING DATE: Pre-1910
  CURRENT USE: Garage   LOCATION OF AUDITORIUM: First floor
  STAGE DIMENSIONS AND EQUIPMENT: Shape of proscenium arch,
    arched
  SEATING (2 levels)
  SHAPE OF THE AUDITORIUM: Rectangular
  MAJOR TYPES OF ENTERTAINMENT: Local and touring productions
  ADDITIONAL INFORMATION: Stone building was built in 1879 as
    a flour mill and burned in 1885. The opera house was
    built within previous walls in 1886. Building has been a
    garage since 1910. Proscenium and balcony remain. Cars
    are now serviced where patrons once sat.

Volcano, CA

ARMORY HALL, Union Square, The Consuolation
  OPENING DATE: 1912
  STYLE OF ARCHITECTURE: Gold Rush Utilitarian
  TYPE OF BUILDING: Town Meeting Hall   FACADE: White
    clapboard, green Trim   TYPE OF THEATRE: (c)
  DEGREE OF RESTORATION: (d)   CURRENT USE: Community events
  STAGE DIMENSIONS AND EQUIPMENT: Height and width of
    proscenium, 9ft x 13ft; Shape of proscenium arch;
    rectangular; Distance from edge of stage to back wall of
    stage, 15ft; Distance from edge of stage to curtain line,
    4ft 8in; Distance between side walls of stage, 13ft;
    Stage floor, flat;   Scenery storage rooms, 2 (stage
    left); Dressing rooms, 2 (stage left)
  DIMENSIONS OF AUDITORIUM: Distance between side walls
    of auditorium, 43ft; Distance stage to back wall of
    auditorium, 49ft 8in; Orchestra pit, none

SEATING (1 level): 1st level, 175
SHAPE OF THE AUDITORIUM: Rectangular
MAJOR TYPES OF ENTERTAINMENT: Vaudeville, musical comedy,
    concerts, dances, "box socials"
ADDITIONAL INFORMATION: The original curtain has been
    preserved.

Weaverville, CA

THOMAS' THEATRE
    OPENING DATE: 1853
    STYLE OF ARCHITECTURE: Western Commercial
    TYPE OF BUILDING: Commercial   TYPE OF THEATRE: (b)
    DEGREE OF RESTORATION: (c)
    ADDITIONAL INFORMATION: When it opened, a portion of
        the building was used as a theatre. The structure
        burned partially soon after opening. It is now Van
        Mastre's store.

Woodland, CA

WOODLAND OPERA HOUSE, Second Street between Main and
    Dead Cat Alley
    OPENING DATE: 1896
    STYLE OF ARCHITECTURE: Vernacular   TYPE OF BUILDING:
        Theatre FACADE: Brick   TYPE OF THEATRE: (a)
    DEGREE OF RESTORATION: (a)   CLOSING DATE: 1913
    CURRENT USE: Theatre and community center
    LOCATION OF AUDITORIUM: First floor
    STAGE DIMENSIONS AND EQUIPMENT: Height and width of
        proscenium, 25ft x 25ft; Shape of proscenium arch,
        square; Distance from edge of stage to back wall of
        stage, 25ft; Distance from edge of stage to curtain line,
        5ft; Distance between side walls of stage, 65ft; Distance
        from stage floor to fly loft, 55ft; Depth under stage,
        10ft; Stage floor, flat; Trap doors, 3; Scenery storage
        rooms, 0; Dressing rooms, 7 (basement)
    DIMENSIONS OF AUDITORIUM: Capacity of orchestra pit, 20
    SEATING: 1st level, 88; 2nd level, 224; 3rd level, 300;
        Boxes, 32
    SHAPE OF THE AUDITORIUM: Rectangular
    MAJOR TYPES OF ENTERTAINMENT: Over 300 companies performed
        here between 1896-1913.
    MAJOR STARS WHO APPEARED AT THEATRE: Louis Davenport, Sousa
        and his band, Walter Huston, Sidney Greenstreet
    ADDITIONAL INFORMATION: Theatre was closed after 1913 due
        to lawsuits which resulted when a patron suffered a
        broken arm when stepping from a side door of the theatre.
        Thereafter, owner enthusiasm declined and in 1913 the
        theatre was boarded up. The building burned partially
        (roof fire) in 1937 and it remained closed until 1976.
        Since then, restoration efforts have revived the theatre
        which is used for a limited performance schedule. The
        theatre is now a State Park.

Colorado

Aspen, CO

WHEELER OPERA HOUSE, 320 East Hyman Avenue
  OPENING DATE: April 23, 1889
  OPENING SHOW: The King's Fool by Adolph Muller
  ARCHITECT: W. J. Edbrook (Denver)
  STYLE OF ARCHITECTURE: Italianate Commercial
  TYPE OF BUILDING: Commercial   FACADE: Native brownstone
  TYPE OF THEATRE: (b)   DEGREE OF RESTORATION: (a)
  CURRENT USE: Community center   PERFORMANCE SPACES IN
  BUILDING: 1   LOCATION OF AUDITORIUM: Third floor
  STAGE DIMENSIONS AND EQUIPMENT: Height and width of
    proscenium, 18ft 3in x 28ft 3in; Shape of proscenium
    arch, arched; Distance from edge of stage to back wall of
    stage, 28ft; Distance from edge of stage to curtain line,
    3ft; Distance between side walls of stage, 70ft 10in;
    Distance from stage floor to fly loft, 19ft; Stage floor,
    flat; Scenery storage rooms, 1 (first floor); Dressing
    rooms, 6 (second floor, pit level, and green room)
  DIMENSIONS OF AUDITORIUM: Distance between side walls
    of auditorium, 75ft; Distance stage to back wall of
    auditorium, 90ft; Orchestra pit, none
  SEATING (2 levels): 1st level, 376; 2nd level, 110
  SHAPE OF THE AUDITORIUM: U-shaped with horseshoe balcony
  MAJOR TYPES OF ENTERTAINMENT: Drama, vaudeville, burlesque,
    opera
  MAJOR STARS WHO APPEARED AT THEATRE: Helena Modjeska, James
    O'Neill, William Harrigan, Patti Rosa
  ADDITIONAL INFORMATION: The theatre is currently used for
    community and professional engagements (concerts, drama,
    dance and a film classics program). The theatre was
    closed for some time, but was reopened in 1984.

Boulder, CO

CHAUTAUQUA AUDITORIUM, Chatauqua Park
  OPENING DATE: July 4, 1898

OPENING SHOW: Henry Wotterson, Kansas City Symphony
ARCHITECTS: Kidder and Rice, Denver   FACADE: Wood
    (light brown with white trim)   TYPE OF THEATRE: (a)
DEGREE OF RESTORATION: (a)   CURRENT USE: Summer theatre
PERFORMANCE SPACES IN BUILDING: 1
LOCATION OF AUDITORIUM: Ground floor
STAGE DIMENSIONS AND EQUIPMENT: Height and width of
    proscenium, 30ft x 65ft; Shape of proscenium arch,
    rectangular; Distance from edge of stage to back wall of
    stage, 35ft; Distance between side walls of stage, 65ft;
    Depth under stage, 3ft; Stage floor, flat; Dressing
    rooms, 1 (stage right)
DIMENSIONS OF AUDITORIUM: Distance between side walls
    of auditorium, 80ft; Distance stage to back wall of
    auditorium, 65ft; Orchestra pit, none
SEATING (1 level): 1st level, 1300
SHAPE OF THE AUDITORIUM: Rectangular
MAJOR TYPES OF ENTERTAINMENT: Chautauqua oratory, readings,
    concerts
MAJOR STARS WHO APPEARED AT THEATRE: William Jennings
    Bryan, John Phillip Sousa, Billy Sunday, Bill Munroe,
    Victor Borge, Dave Brubeck, Jane Adams

Central City, CO

BELVIDERE THEATRE (other names: Armory Hall, Wisebart Variety
    Hall, Montana Theatre)
OPENING DATE: November 1875
STYLE OF ARCHITECTURE: Commercial   TYPE OF BUILDING:
    National Guard Armory   FACADE: Painted brick
TYPE OF THEATRE: (b)   DEGREE OF RESTORATION: (b)
CURRENT USE: Club   PERFORMANCE SPACES IN BUILDING: 1
LOCATION OF AUDITORIUM: Second floor
STAGE DIMENSIONS AND EQUIPMENT: Height and width of
    proscenium, 12ft x 20ft; Shape of proscenium arch,
    rectangular; Distance from edge of stage to back wall of
    stage, 20ft; Distance from edge of stage to curtain line,
    4ft; Distance between side walls of stage, 30ft; Distance
    from stage floor to fly loft, 20ft; Stage floor, flat;
    Dressing rooms, 2 (backstage)
DIMENSIONS OF AUDITORIUM: Distance between side walls of
    stage, 40ft; Distance stage to back wall of auditorium,
    60ft; Capacity of orchestra pit, 12
SEATING (2 levels): 1st level, 200; 2nd level, 50
SHAPE OF THE AUDITORIUM: Rectangular
MAJOR TYPES OF ENTERTAINMENT: Drama, concerts
ADDITIONAL INFORMATION: The theatre opened originally as
    Wisebart Variety Hall in 1862. A fire in 1874 burned
    most of the town and the theatre was damaged severely.
    The theatre was furnished with plain oak chairs, black
    walnut railings, and dressing rooms. It was 55ft long and
    40ft wide. The theatre entrance was located on the right
    side of building.

Central City, CO

CENTRAL CITY OPERA HOUSE, Eureka Street
OPENING DATE: March 4, 1878
OPENING SHOW: Concert of vocal and instrumental music
ARCHITECT: Robert S. Roeschlaub   STYLE OF ARCHITECTURE:
   Eclectic   FACADE: Native stone   TYPE OF THEATRE: (a)
DEGREE OF RESTORATION: (d)   CURRENT USE: Annual opera
   festivals   PERFORMANCE SPACES IN BUILDING: 1
LOCATION OF AUDITORIUM: First floor
STAGE DIMENSIONS AND EQUIPMENT: Height and width of
   proscenium, 17ft 6in x 25ft; Shape of proscenium arch,
   rectangular; Distance from edge of stage to back wall of
   stage, 42ft; Distance from edge of stage to curtain line,
   6ft 11in; Distance between side walls of stage, 50ft 6in;
   Distance from stage floor to fly loft, 34ft; Depth under
   stage, 12ft; Stage floor, flat; Trap doors, 1; Scenery
   storage rooms, 1; Dressing rooms, 4 (adjacent to theatre)
DIMENSIONS OF AUDITORIUM: Distance between side walls of
   auditorium, 50ft 6in; Distance stage to back wall of
   auditorium, 56ft; Capacity of orchestra pit, 75
SEATING (2 levels): 1st level, 477; 2nd level, 276
SHAPE OF THE AUDITORIUM: Rectangular
MAJOR TYPES OF ENTERTAINMENT: Opera
MAJOR STARS WHO APPEARED AT THEATRE: Lillian Gish (1932),
   Mae West (1950), Beverly Sills (1960), Francis Bible
   (1957)
ADDITIONAL INFORMATION: The 1932 restoration of the opera
   house may have been the first theatre restoration in the
   United States. The 1932 Opera Festival was led by
   designer, Robert Edmond Jones, who also designed its
   first production, Camille.

Denver, CO

ELITCH GARDENS THEATRE, 4620 West 38th Avenue
OPENING DATE: 1891   OPENING SHOW: Vaudeville bill
STYLE OF ARCHITECTURE: Victorian Vernacular
FACADE: Wood, painted green   TYPE OF THEATRE: (a)
DEGREE OF RESTORATION: (d)   CURRENT USE: Summer stock
   theatre   LOCATION OF AUDITORIUM: First floor
STAGE DIMENSIONS AND EQUIPMENT: Width of proscenium, 32ft;
   Shape of proscenium arch, rectangular; Distance from
   edge of stage to back wall of stage, 40ft; Distance
   from edge of stage to curtain line, 3ft; Distance
   between side walls of stage, 90ft; Distance from stage
   floor to fly loft, 45ft; Depth under stage, 10ft;
   Stage floor, flat; Scenery storage rooms, 2; Dressing
   rooms, 12 (stage left)
DIMENSIONS OF AUDITORIUM: Capacity of orchestra pit, 10
SEATING (2 levels): 1st level, 950; 2nd level, 469
SHAPE OF THE AUDITORIUM: Octagonal
MAJOR TYPES OF ENTERTAINMENT: Drama
MAJOR STARS WHO APPEARED AT THEATRE: P.T. Barnum and Tom
   Thumb (1890), James O'Neill (1897), Sarah Bernhardt
   (1906), Clark Gable

ADDITIONAL INFORMATION: Possibly the oldest summer theatre
in America in continuous use. Stagehouse was remodeled
in 1950, but wooden auditorium is original. Theatre is
in an historic pleasure garden built by the Elitch
family. Original scenic drop has view of Anne Hathaway's
cottage. Drop was painted by Thompson Scenic Company.

Denver, CO

TIVOLI OPERA HOUSE (other name: West Denver Turnhalle),
    1320-1348 10th Street
    OPENING DATE: 1882
    STYLE OF ARCHITECTURE: Italianate   TYPE OF BUILDING:
    Movie theatre   FACADE: Brick   TYPE OF THEATRE: (b)
    DEGREE OF RESTORATION: (a)   CURRENT USE: Films
    PERFORMANCE SPACES IN BUILDING: 1
    LOCATION OF AUDITORIUM: First floor
    SHAPE OF THE AUDITORIUM: U-shaped
    ADDITIONAL INFORMATION: Attached to Tivoli Brewery.
    Converted to a twelve-screen movie house which opened
    in August 1985. Originally it contained a suspended
    balcony and elaborate proscenium. The owner is Tivoli
    Development Company, 901 Lorimer Street, Denver.

Gunnison, CO

SMITH'S OPERA HOUSE, Boulevard and Tomichi
    OPENING DATE: January 8, 1883
    OPENING SHOW: Turn of the Tide
    ARCHITECT: Frank C. Smith, builder   TYPE OF BUILDING:
    Apartment building   FACADE: Brick
    TYPE OF THEATRE: (b)   DEGREE OF RESTORATION: (c)
    CLOSING DATE: October 3, 1884   CURRENT USE: Apartments
    LOCATION OF AUDITORIUM: Second floor
    DIMENSIONS OF AUDITORIUM: Distance between side walls
    of auditorium, 43ft; Distance stage to back wall of
    auditorium, 55ft
    SEATING (2 levels): 1st level, 375; 2nd level, 125
    SHAPE OF THE AUDITORIUM: Rectangular
    MAJOR TYPES OF ENTERTAINMENT: Drama
    MAJOR STARS WHO APPEARED AT THEATRE: The Chicago Comedy
    Company presented more shows than any other company

La Junta, CO

ROURKE THEATRE (other names: Rourke Opera House, Fox
    Theatre), 11 East Third
    OPENING DATE: March 9, 1914
    OPENING SHOW: Within The Law
    ARCHITECT: George Roe   FACADE: Yellow stucco
    TYPE OF THEATRE: (a)   DEGREE OF RESTORATION: (d)
    CURRENT USE: Movie theatre   PERFORMANCE SPACES IN
    BUILDING: 1   LOCATION OF AUDITORIUM: First floor

DIMENSIONS OF AUDITORIUM: Orchestra pit, none
SEATING (2 levels)
MAJOR TYPES OF ENTERTAINMENT: Drama, vaudeville
ADDITIONAL INFORMATION: Theatre occupies plot of
    land 60ft x 110ft.

Leadville, CO

TABOR OPERA HOUSE (other names: Weston Opera House, Elks
    Opera House), 308 Harrison Avenue
OPENING DATE: November 20, 1879
OPENING SHOW: The Serious Family and Who's Who
ARCHITECT: Builder, J. Thomas Roberts
STYLE OF ARCHITECTURE: Victorian   TYPE OF BUILDING:
    Commercial   FACADE: Red brick   TYPE OF THEATRE: (b)
DEGREE OF RESTORATION: (a)   CURRENT USE: Theatre and store
STAGE DIMENSIONS AND EQUIPMENT: Trap doors, 1; Scenery
    storage rooms, 1; Dressing rooms, 10 (under stage)
DIMENSIONS OF AUDITORIUM: Capacity of orchestra pit, 15
SEATING: (2 levels)
SHAPE OF THE AUDITORIUM: Horeshoe-shaped
MAJOR TYPES OF ENTERTAINMENT: Opera, drama, minstrel
    shows, concerts, lectures
MAJOR STARS WHO APPEARED AT THEATRE: Sousa, Houdini,
    Modjeska, Maude Adams, Oscar Wilde, Harry Lauder

Longmont, CO

DICKENS OPERA HOUSE, Third and Main Streets
OPENING DATE: February 2, 1882
STYLE OF ARCHITECTURE: Generic   TYPE OF BUILDING:
    Commercial   FACADE: Red brick   TYPE OF THEATRE:
    (b)   DEGREE OF RESTORATION: (c)   CLOSING DATE:
    1920   CURRENT USE: Vacant   PERFORMANCE SPACES IN
BUILDING: 1   LOCATION OF AUDITORIUM: Second floor
STAGE DIMENSIONS AND EQUIPMENT: Height and width of
    proscenium, 34ft x 25ft; Distance from edge of stage
    to back wall of stage, 17ft; Distance between side walls
    of stage, 49ft; Distance from stage floor to fly loft,
    34ft
SEATING (1 level): 1st level, 850
MAJOR TYPES OF ENTERTAINMENT: Road shows, local musical
    performances, balls, graduations

Ouray, CO

WRIGHT'S HALL, West Lido at Main
OPENING DATE: 1888
ARCHITECTS: George and Ed White   STYLE OF ARCHITECTURE:
    Romanesque and Greek Revival   TYPE OF BUILDING:
    commercial   FACADE: Cast iron (white)
TYPE OF THEATRE: (b)   DEGREE OF RESTORATION: (c)
CURRENT USE: Summer productions

LOCATION OF AUDITORIUM: Second floor
STAGE DIMENSIONS AND EQUIPMENT: Height and width of
  proscenium, 14ft x 26ft; Distance from edge of stage to
  back wall of stage, 20ft; Distance from edge of stage to
  curtain line, 2ft; Distance between side walls of stage,
  48ft; Depth under stage, 3ft 6in; Trap doors, 1
ADDITIONAL INFORMATION: Theatre has a beautiful white
  cast-iron facade. Building is three stories tall. The
  original stage and painted front curtain remain. The
  theatre now houses the summer presentation, San Juan
  Odyssey.

Telluride, CO

SHERIDAN OPERA HOUSE (other name: Show), 110 North Oak
OPENING DATE: 1914
FACADE: Red brick   TYPE OF THEATRE: (a)
DEGREE OF RESTORATION: (a)   CURRENT USE: Community center
LOCATION OF AUDITORIUM: 1st to 3rd floors
STAGE DIMENSIONS AND EQUIPMENT: Height and width of
  proscenium, 14ft x 21ft; Shape of proscenium arch,
  arched; Distance from edge of stage to back wall of
  stage, 15ft; Distance from edge of stage to curtain
  line, 4ft; Distance between side walls of stage, 30ft;
  Distance from stage floor to fly loft, 24ft; Depth under
  stage, 4ft; Stage floor, flat; Scenery storage rooms, 1
  (stage right), Dressing rooms, 1 (stage left)
DIMENSIONS OF AUDITORIUM: Distance between side walls
  of auditorium, 40ft; Distance stage to back wall of
  auditorium, 35ft; Orchestra pit, none
SEATING (2 levels): 1st level, 190; 2nd level, 60
SHAPE OF THE AUDITORIUM: Rectangular with horseshoe -
  shaped balcony
MAJOR TYPES OF ENTERTAINMENT: Drama, movies, concerts,
  meetings, conventions
MAJOR STARS WHO APPEARED AT THEATRE: Sarah Bernhardt,
  Jack Nicholson, Jimmy Buffet, Gloria Swanson

Trinidad, CO

JAFFA OPERA HOUSE, (other name: Marsman Drug), 100-116
  West Main
STYLE OF ARCHITECTURE: Victorian Italianate
FACADE: Sandstone   TYPE OF THEATRE: (b)
DEGREE OF RESTORATION: (b)   CURRENT USE: Apartments
PERFORMANCE SPACES IN BUILDING: 1
LOCATION OF AUDITORIUM: Second floor
STAGE DIMENSIONS AND EQUIPMENT: Height and width of
  proscenium, 16ft x 22ft; Distance from edge of stage to
  back wall of stage, 20ft; Distance between side walls
  of stage, 45ft; Depth under stage, 3ft 6in; Trap doors, 2
ADDITIONAL INFORMATION: Nothing remains of theatre
  furnishings. The inscription,"Trinidad Opera House -
  1882," appears in the pediment.

Connecticut

Bridgeport, CT

STUDIO THEATRE (other names: Bijou Theater, Rivoli Theater),
275 Fairfield Avenue
OPENING DATE: 1910
STYLE OF ARCHITECTURE: Spanish Colonial Revival
FACADE: Brick   TYPE OF THEATRE: (a)   DEGREE OF
RESTORATION: (d)   CURRENT USE: Movie theatre
PERFORMANCE SPACES IN BUILDING: 1
LOCATION OF AUDITORIUM: Ground floor
ADDITIONAL INFORMATION: The Studio Theatre is Bridgeport's
oldest extant theatre still in operation.

Chester, CT

CHESTER MEETING HOUSE (other name: Old Town Hall), Liberty
Street and Goose Hill Road
OPENING DATE: 1876 (as theatre)
STYLE OF ARCHITECTURE: Colonial   TYPE OF BUILDING: Meeting
House   FACADE: White wood   TYPE OF THEATRE: (c)
DEGREE OF RESTORATION: (a)   CURRENT USE: See ADDITIONAL
INFORMATION   PERFORMANCE SPACES IN BUILDING: 1
LOCATION OF AUDITORIUM: Ground floor
STAGE DIMENSIONS AND EQUIPMENT: Height and width of
proscenium, 11ft x 18ft; Shape of proscenium arch,
arched; Distance from edge of stage to back wall of
stage, 40ft; Distance from edge of stage to curtain
line, 7ft; Stage floor, flat; Trap doors, 0;
Scenery storage rooms, 2 (basement); Dressing rooms,
2 (basement)
DIMENSIONS OF AUDITORIUM: Distance between side walls
of auditorium, 44ft; Distance stage to back wall of
auditorium, 30ft; Orchestra pit, none
SEATING (2 levels): 1st level, 140; 2nd level, 75
SHAPE OF THE AUDITORIUM: Horseshoe-shaped
MAJOR TYPES OF ENTERTAINMENT: Drama, concerts, lectures

MAJOR STARS WHO APPEARED AT THEATRE: General Tom Thumb
ADDITIONAL INFORMATION: The building has been in continuous
    use since 1793 and is still used for town meetings,
    theatrical performances, concerts, and civic receptions.

Derby, CT

STERLING OPERA HOUSE
    OPENING DATE: 1889
    LOCATION OF AUDITORIUM: Second floor
    STAGE DIMENSIONS AND EQUIPMENT: * Height and width of
        proscenium, 30ft x 30ft; Distance from edge of stage to
        back wall of stage, 34ft; Distance from edge of stage to
        curtain line, 4ft; Distance between side walls of stage,
        64ft; Depth under stage, 8ft; Trap doors, 4
    MAJOR TYPES OF ENTERTAINMENT: Drama, vaudeville, concerts,
        movies, wrestling matches
    MAJOR STARS WHO APPEARED AT THEATRE: The Barrymores, Donald
        O'Connor, Houdini

East Haddam, CT

GOODSPEED OPERA HOUSE (other name: Goodspeed's Hall),
    Goodspeed Landing
    OPENING DATE: October 27, 1887
    OPENING SHOWS: Charles II, Box & Cox & Turn Him Out
    ARCHITECTS: Jebez Comstock, General Contractor
    STYLE OF ARCHITECTURE: Victorian with mansard roof
    TYPE OF BUILDING: Offices, general store
    FACADE: White wood   TYPE OF THEATRE: (b)   DEGREE OF
    RESTORATION: (a)   CURRENT USE: LORT Musical Theatre
    PERFORMANCE SPACES IN BUILDING: 1
    LOCATION OF AUDITORIUM: 5th and 6th floors
    STAGE DIMENSIONS AND EQUIPMENT: Height and width of
        proscenium, 16ft x 27ft; Shape of proscenium arch,
        arched; Distance from edge of stage to back wall, 20ft
        4in; Distance between side walls of stage, 42ft 10in;
        Depth under stage, 3ft 7in; Stage floor, flat; Trap
        doors, 0; Scenery storage rooms, (backstage); Dressing
        rooms, 5 (floor under stage level)
    DIMENSIONS OF AUDITORIUM: Distance between side walls of
        auditorium, 42ft 9in; Distance stage to back wall of
        auditorium, 49ft 5in; Capacity of orchestra pit, 15
    SEATING (2 levels): 1st level, 295; 2nd level, 103;
        boxes, 16
    SHAPE OF THE AUDITORIUM: U-shaped
    MAJOR TYPES OF ENTERTAINMENT: Melodrama, vaudeville,
        minstrel shows, lectures, balls
    MAJOR STARS WHO APPEARED AT THEATRE: Henry Ward Beecher,
        Minnie Maddern Fiske, Effie Ellsler, Josh Billings
    ADDITIONAL INFORMATION: The Goodspeed Opera House, which
        bills itself as "The Home of the American Musical
        Theatre," presents a nine-month season of musical
        revivals and new works.

East Hampton, CT

SIEBERT'S OPERA HOUSE, 95 Main Street
   OPENING DATE: c. 1877
   STYLE OF ARCHITECTURE: Victorian   TYPE OF BUILDING: Stores
      on ground floor   FACADE: Wood   TYPE OF THEATRE: (b)
   DEGREE OF RESTORATION: (a)   CURRENT USE: Banquet hall
   LOCATION OF AUDITORIUM: Second floor
   STAGE DIMENSIONS AND EQUIPMENT: Distance from edge of stage
      to back wall of stage, 15ft; Distance from edge of stage
      to curtain line, 3ft; Distance between side walls of
      stage, 20ft; Stage floor, flat
   SEATING (1 level)
   SHAPE OF THE AUDITORIUM: Rectangular

East Windsor, CT

BROADBROOK OPERA HOUSE, 107 Main Street
   OPENING DATE: 1892
   ARCHITECTS: Cook and Hapgood   TYPE OF BUILDING: Social
      hall, store   FACADE: Asbestos siding
   TYPE OF THEATRE: (b)   CURRENT USE: Meetings, parties,
      weddings   LOCATION OF AUDITORIUM: Second floor
   STAGE DIMENSIONS AND EQUIPMENT: Shape of proscenium arch,
      rectangular

Goshen, CT

OLD TOWN HALL, Route 63 North
   OPENING DATE: 1895
   STYLE OF ARCHITECTURE: Colonial Revival   TYPE OF BUILDING:
      Town Offices   FACADE: Clapboard   TYPE OF THEATRE: (b)
   CURRENT USE: Town offices and theatre
   PERFORMANCE SPACES IN BUILDING: 1
   LOCATION OF AUDITORIUM: Ground floor
   ADDITIONAL INFORMATION: The original stage curtain, painted
      by O.L. Story of Somerville, MA, was restored in 1978.
      The original stage is intact. In the 1950s, stairs
      leading to the basement were added to either end of the
      stage. In 1978, the position of the main stairway was
      changed.

Granby, CT

PHELPS HALL, Corner of Mountain Road and North Granby Road
   OPENING DATE: c. 1880
   FACADE: Wood   TYPE OF THEATRE: (c)   DEGREE OF
   RESTORATION: (d)   LOCATION OF AUDITORIUM: Second floor
   MAJOR TYPES OF ENTERTAINMENT: Drama, musical comedy,
      concerts, lectures

Granby, CT

   TOWN HALL (other name: Grange Hall)
   OPENING DATE: c. 1902
   TYPE OF BUILDING: Town Hall   TYPE OF THEATRE: (c)
   DEGREE OF RESTORATION: (d)   CURRENT USE: Town Hall
   MAJOR TYPES OF ENTERTAINMENT: Musical comedy, dramas,
      lectures, concerts

Greenwich, CT

GREENWICH CINEMA
   OPENING DATE: September 2, 1914
   OPENING SHOW: Vaudeville bill
   ARCHITECT: Theodore M. Blake (see ADDITIONAL INFORMATION)
   FACADE: Stucco and brick   TYPE OF THEATRE: (a)
   DEGREE OF RESTORATION: (d)   CURRENT USE: Movie theatre
   PERFORMANCE SPACES IN BUILDING: 1
   LOCATION OF AUDITORIUM: Ground floor
   STAGE DIMENSIONS AND EQUIPMENT: Width of proscenium, 41ft;
      Distance from edge of stage to back wall of stage, 21ft
   DIMENSIONS OF AUDITORIUM; Distance between side walls of
      auditorium, 48ft; Distance stage to back wall of
      auditorium, 118ft
   MAJOR TYPES OF ENTERTAINMENT: Vaudeville, movies
   ADDITIONAL INFORMATION: At the time of the theatre's
      construction, Blake was an architect with the firm of
      Carrere and Hastings.

Hamden, CT

DIXWELL PLAYHOUSE (other name: Dixwell Theatre), 824 Dixwell
      Avenue
   OPENING DATE: c. 1915
   STYLE OF ARCHITECTURE: Art Deco   FACADE: Beige cement
   TYPE OF THEATRE: (a)   DEGREE OF RESTORATION: (c)
   CURRENT USE: Factory
   STAGE DIMENSIONS AND EQUIPMENT: Shape of proscenium arch,
      arched; Stage floor, flat; Scenery storage rooms,
      2 (either side of the stage)
   SHAPE OF THE AUDITORIUM: Rectangular
   MAJOR TYPES OF ENTERTAINMENT: Drama, movies
   MAJOR STARS WHO APPEARED AT THEATRE: Ernest Borgnine
   ADDITIONAL INFORMATION: The current occupant of the
      building maintains that the stage, the ceiling of the
      theatre and a projection booth still exist although
      representatives of the Connecticut Trust for Historic
      Preservation maintain that the interior was gutted.

Hartford, CT

LYRIC HALL
   OPENING DATE: 1890

STYLE OF ARCHITECTURE: 19th Century Commercial Vernacular
FACADE: Brick   TYPE OF THEATRE: (a)
DEGREE OF RESTORATION: (c)   CLOSING DATE: 1979
CURRENT USE: Vacant
PERFORMANCE SPACES IN BUILDING: 1
MAJOR TYPES OF ENTERTAINMENT: Vaudeville, movies, minstrel
    shows
ADDITIONAL INFORMATION: In addition to vaudeville and
    minstrel shows, the theatre has served as a major social
    center. In the late 1970s, Spanish language films were
    shown. The theatre closed in the summer of 1979 after a
    fire damaged the interior.

Middletown, CT

MIDDLESEX OPERA HOUSE (other name: Old Middlesex Theater),
    109-111 College Street
    OPENING DATE: May 26, 1892
    ARCHITECT: Francis H. Kimball
    STYLE OF ARCHITECTURE: Early Art Deco   FACADE: Red brick
    TYPE OF THEATRE: (a)   DEGREE OF RESTORATION: (a)
    CLOSING DATE: 1960   CURRENT USE: Vacant
    LOCATION OF AUDITORIUM: Ground floor
    SEATING (3 levels)
    MAJOR TYPES OF ENTERTAINMENT: Drama, musical comedy,
        concerts, opera, vaudeville, movies
    ADDITIONAL INFORMATION: This elaborately decorated theatre
        was constructed in 1892 "as a contribution to the
        artistic development of Middletown." A few days after
        the opening, a fire destroyed the structure. When it
        reopened, it contained a third-floor lounge for theatre
        patrons, a balcony and gallery, and two tiers of box
        seats. The interior was decorated with plaster relief
        work, mural paintings and artistic panels. The theatre
        burned again in 1926, and when it reopened, the gallery
        and boxes had been removed and a single large balcony
        had been added, which increased the seating capacity to
        1,397.

New Haven, CT

COLLEGE THEATRE (other names: Hyperion Theatre, Carll's Opera
    House), 1026 Chapel Street
    OPENING DATE: 1880
    ARCHITECT: Peter Carll   STYLE OF ARCHITECTURE: Romanesque
    FACADE: Red brick   TYPE OF THEATRE: (a)
    DEGREE OF RESTORATION: (c)   CLOSING DATE: Late 1970s
    CURRENT USE: Vacant
    DIMENSIONS OF AUDITORIUM: Orchestra pit, none
    SEATING (2 levels)
    SHAPE OF THE AUDITORIUM: Wedge-shaped
    MAJOR TYPES OF ENTERTAINMENT: Drama, vaudeville, opera
    MAJOR STARS WHO APPEARED AT THEATRE: Sarah Bernhardt

ADDITIONAL INFORMATION: Theatre was renovated in 1930 by
   Thomas Lamb.

New Haven, CT

SHUBERT PERFORMING ARTS CENTER (other name: Shubert Theatre),
   247 College Street
   OPENING DATE: Dec. 18, 1914
   OPENING SHOW: Belle of Bond Street
   ARCHITECT: Robert Wendler (Renovation)   STYLE OF
   ARCHITECTURE: Classical Revival   TYPE OF THEATRE: (a)
   DEGREE OF RESTORATION: (a)   CURRENT USE: Theatre
   PERFORMANCE SPACES IN BUILDING: 1
   LOCATION OF AUDITORIUM: Ground floor
   STAGE DIMENSIONS AND EQUIPMENT: Height and width of
      proscenium, 30ft x 40ft; Shape of proscenium arch,
      rectangular; Distance from edge of stage to back wall
      of stage, 44ft; Distance from edge of stage to curtain
      line, 5ft; Distance between side walls of stage, 91ft;
      Distance from stage floor to fly loft, 24ft 4in; Stage
      floor, flat; Scenery storage rooms, 0; Dressing
      rooms, 11 (under stage)
   DIMENSIONS OF AUDITORIUM: Capacity of orchestra pit, 45
   SEATING (3 levels): 1st level, 664; 2nd level, 503;
      3rd level, 407
   SHAPE OF THE AUDITORIUM: U-shaped
   MAJOR TYPES OF ENTERTAINMENT: Musical theatre, drama, opera

New London, CT

LYRIC THEATRE (other name: Lyric Hall), 243 Captain's Walk
   OPENING DATE: 1897
   ARCHITECTS: Goldsmith and Hess (builders)   STYLE OF
   ARCHITECTURE: Beaux Arts   TYPE OF BUILDING: Stores,
      restaurant   FACADE: Brick with sandstone trim
   TYPE OF THEATRE: (b)   DEGREE OF RESTORATION: (c)
   CURRENT USE: Commercial
   LOCATION OF AUDITORIUM: Second floor
   DIMENSIONS OF AUDITORIUM: Distance between side walls
      of auditorium, 37ft; Distance stage to back wall of
      auditorium, 60ft; Orchestra pit, none
   SEATING (2 levels)
   SHAPE OF THE AUDITORIUM: Rectangular
   MAJOR TYPES OF ENTERTAINMENT: Drama, concerts, musical
      theatre
   ADDITIONAL INFORMATION: The theatre, at the rear of the
      second floor, is reached via a central stairway. It
      still retains its original features and is regarded as
      operational. During its vaudeville days, it was managed
      by C.M. Brocksieper.

New Milford, CT

BANK STREET THEATRE, 46 Bank Street
  OPENING DATE: 1902
  ARCHITECT: H. Buckingham (1920 renovation)   STYLE OF
  ARCHITECTURE: Art Deco facade over Renaissance Revival
  FACADE: Brick with Carrara glass facade
  TYPE OF THEATRE: (a)   DEGREE OF RESTORATION: (d)
  CURRENT USE: Movie theatre
  PERFORMANCE SPACES IN BUILDING: 1
  STAGE DIMENSIONS AND EQUIPMENT: Width of proscenium, 37ft;
    Distance from edge of stage to back wall of stage, 30ft;
    Distance from edge of stage to curtain line, 9ft 6in;
  DIMENSIONS OF AUDITORIUM:
    Distance between side walls of auditorium, 46ft;
    Distance stage to back wall of auditorium, 120ft
  MAJOR TYPES OF ENTERTAINMENT: Vaudeville, movies
  ADDITIONAL INFORMATION: The lobby once had a terrazzo floor
    which is now covered by carpeting. The auditorium
    contains a stepped ceiling and Art Deco piers which rise
    to the ceiling.

Norfolk, CT

APPLE HOUSE (other names: Opera House; Village Hall),
    Greenwoods Road
  OPENING DATE: 1883
  STYLE OF ARCHITECTURE: Queen Anne   TYPE OF BUILDING: Store
  FACADE: Painted wood   TYPE OF THEATRE: (b)
  DEGREE OF RESTORATION: (c)   CURRENT USE: Store
  PERFORMANCE SPACES IN BUILDING: 1
  LOCATION OF AUDITORIUM: Second floor
  STAGE DIMENSIONS AND EQUIPMENT: Height and width of
    proscenium, 12ft x 15ft; Shape of proscenium arch,
    arched; Distance from edge of stage to back wall of
    stage, 14ft; Distance from edge of stage to curtain line,
    6ft; Depth under stage, 5ft; Stage floor, flat; Trap
    doors, 0; Scenery storage rooms, 0; Dressing rooms,
    2 (sides of stage)
  DIMENSIONS OF AUDITORIUM: Distance between side walls
    of auditorium, 50ft; Distance stage to back wall of
    auditorium, 65ft; Orchestra pit, none
  SEATING (2 levels): 1st level, 135; 2nd level, 40
  SHAPE OF THE AUDITORIUM: Rectangular
  MAJOR TYPES OF ENTERTAINMENT: Vaudeville, minstrel shows,
    lectures, local talent shows, concerts
  ADDITIONAL INFORMATION: The second floor theatre retains
    its balustraded balcony which is 24 feet deep. A painted
    stage curtain and "decorative" proscenium arch also
    remain.

Norfolk, CT

NORFOLK CHAMBER MUSIC FESTIVAL MUSIC SHED, RT. 44

OPENING DATE: 1906
ARCHITECT: E. K. Rossiter
FACADE: California redwood [inside and out]
TYPE OF THEATRE: (a)   DEGREE OF RESTORATION: (d)
CURRENT USE: Summer concerts   PERFORMANCE SPACES IN
BUILDING: 1   LOCATION OF AUDITORIUM: Ground floor
STAGE DIMENSIONS AND EQUIPMENT: Distance between side
  walls of stage, 30ft; Stage floor, flat; Trap doors, 0;
  Scenery storage rooms, 0; Dressing rooms, 0
DIMENSIONS OF AUDITORIUM: Capacity of orchestra pit, 30
SEATING (2 levels)
SHAPE OF THE AUDITORIUM: Rectangular
MAJOR TYPES OF ENTERTAINMENT: Choral concerts, chamber
  music, orchestral concerts
MAJOR STARS WHO APPEARED AT THEATRE: Fritz Kreisler, Sergei
  Rachmaninoff, Efrem Zimbalist, Enrico Caruso, Jan Ignace
  Paderewski, Alma Gluck, Jean Sibelius, Max Bruch, Victor
  Herbert
ADDITIONAL INFORMATION: In addition to the Norfolk Chamber
  Music Festival, the theatre houses the Yale Summer School
  of Music.

Putnam, CT

  IMPERIAL CINEMA (other name: Bradley Theatre), 26 Front
    Street
  OPENING DATE: c. 1905   TYPE OF BUILDING: Commercial
  FACADE: White brick   TYPE OF THEATRE: (a)
  DEGREE OF RESTORATION: (c)   CURRENT USE: Movie theatre
  PERFORMANCE SPACES IN BUILDING: 1
  LOCATION OF AUDITORIUM: First floor
  STAGE DIMENSIONS AND EQUIPMENT: Height and width of
    proscenium, 30ft x 45ft; Shape of proscenium arch,
    arched; Distance from edge of stage to back wall of
    stage, 20ft; Distance from edge of stage to curtain line,
    7ft; Distance between side walls of stage, 30ft; Depth
    under stage, 4ft; Stage floor, raked; Trap doors, 0;
    Scenery storage rooms, 1 (basement); Dressing rooms, 5
  DIMENSIONS OF AUDITORIUM: Distance between side walls
    of auditorium, 60ft; Distance stage to back wall of
    auditorium, 40ft
  SEATING (2 levels): 1st level, 193; 2nd level, 127
  SHAPE OF THE AUDITORIUM: Horseshoe-shaped
  MAJOR TYPES OF ENTERTAINMENT: Vaudeville
  ADDITIONAL INFORMATION: After a fire in 1937, the theatre
    was remodeled. The entry was altered and a bay window
    added to the second floor.

South Norwalk, CT

  HOYT'S THEATRE (other name: Rialto Theatre), 12-130
    Washington Street
  OPENING DATE: c. 1890
  STYLE OF ARCHITECTURE: Second Empire   TYPE OF BUILDING:

Warehouse   FACADE: Brick   TYPE OF THEATRE): (a)
DEGREE OF RESTORATION: (b)   CLOSING DATE: Late 1950s
CURRENT USE: Plumbing warehouse
PERFORMANCE SPACES IN BUILDING: 1
LOCATION OF AUDITORIUM: Ground floor
STAGE DIMENSIONS AND EQUIPMENT: * Height and width of
    proscenium, 28ft x 33ft; Distance from edge of stage to
    back wall of stage, 38ft; Distance from edge of stage to
    curtain line, 2ft; Distance between side walls of stage,
    50ft; Depth under stage, 8ft; Trap doors, 4; Dressing
    rooms, 12
MAJOR TYPES OF ENTERTAINMENT: Drama, vaudeville, movies
ADDITIONAL INFORMATION: Hoyt's Theatre was constructed to
    resemble the Garrick Theater of New York. In 1922, the
    building became a movie house and was renamed the Rialto.

South Norwalk, CT

PALACE PERFORMING ARTS CENTER (other name: Palace Theatre),
    29-33 North Main Street
OPENING DATE: 1914
STYLE OF ARCHITECTURE: Originally Beaux Arts. Remodeled
    in 1930   FACADE: Brick   TYPE OF THEATRE: (a)
DEGREE OF RESTORATION: (a)   CURRENT USE: Performing Arts
    Center   PERFORMANCE SPACES IN BUILDING: 1
LOCATION OF AUDITORIUM: Ground Floor
MAJOR TYPES OF ENTERTAINMENT: Drama, vaudeville, concerts,
    movies, dance
MAJOR STARS WHO APPEARED AT THEATRE: Mae West, Harry
    Houdini, Weber and Fields
ADDITIONAL INFORMATION: In its heydey, the theatre operated
    as a vaudeville house and was known as "the theatre you
    play before you play the Palace in New York." Now the
    home of the Ballet Etudes Repertory Company.

Southington, CT

SOUTHINGTON SHOWKASE (other names: Coleman's Theater,
    Colonial Theater), 51 North Main Street
OPENING DATE: 1911   OPENING SHOW: The Wedding of Tom
    Thumb   STYLE OF ARCHITECTURE: Colonial Revival
TYPE OF BUILDING: Stores, apartments   FACADE: Brick
TYPE OF THEATRE: (a)   CLOSING DATE: October 1981
PERFORMANCE SPACES IN BUILDING: 1
MAJOR TYPES OF ENTERTAINMENT: Drama, movies, minstrel shows

Stafford, CT

MEMORIAL HALL (other name: Spiritualist Hall),
    Orcuttville Road
OPENING DATE: 1867; 1902 as theatre   OPENING SHOW:
    Rip Van Winkle   STYLE OF ARCHITECTURE: Gothic
TYPE OF BUILDING: Meeting hall   FACADE: Wood, blue and

white   TYPE OF THEATRE: (a)   DEGREE OF RESTORATION: (a)
CURRENT USE: Theatre and meeting hall
LOCATION OF AUDITORIUM: Ground floor
STAGE DIMENSIONS AND EQUIPMENT: Height and width of
  proscenium, 15ft 6in x 24ft; Shape of proscenium arch,
  arched; Distance from edge of stage to back wall of
  stage, 21ft; Distance from edge of stage to curtain line,
  2ft 6in; Distance between side walls of stage, 56ft;
  Distance from stage floor to fly loft, 17ft 6in; Depth
  under stage, 3ft 6in; Stage floor, flat; Trap doors, 1;
  Scenery storage rooms, 0; Dressing rooms, 2 (one in each
  wing)
DIMENSIONS OF AUDITORIUM: Distance between side walls
  of auditorium, 35ft; Distance stage to back wall of
  auditorium, 43ft; Orchestra pit, none
SEATING (2 levels): 1st level, 185; 2nd level, 90
SHAPE OF THE AUDITORIUM: Rectangular
MAJOR TYPES OF ENTERTAINMENT: Drama, concerts, lectures,
  operettas
ADDITIONAL INFORMATION: Stage curtains and pink stencilling
  on walls still exist.

Stamford, CT

  HARTMAN THEATRE (other name: Stamford Theatre), 307
    Atlantic Avenue
  OPENING DATE: 1913   OPENING SHOW: Vaudeville bill
  ARCHITECT: J. Sarfield Kennedy   STYLE OF ARCHITECTURE:
    Neo-Classical Revival   FACADE: Brick
  TYPE OF THEATRE: (a)   DEGREE OF RESTORATION: (d)
  CURRENT USE: Theatre   PERFORMANCE SPACES IN BUILDING: 1
  LOCATION OF AUDITORIUM: Ground floor
  STAGE DIMENSIONS AND EQUIPMENT: Height and width of
    proscenium, 24ft x 38ft; Distance from edge of stage to
    back wall of stage, 42ft; Distance between side walls
    of stage, 80ft
  SEATING (2 levels)
  MAJOR TYPES OF ENTERTAINMENT: Vaudeville, movies
  ADDITIONAL INFORMATION: The theatre originally opened as
    a vaudeville house managed by Mrs. Emily Hartley. When
    it was converted into a movie house in the 1930s, the
    marquee was added to the facade. A high relief bust of
    Eleanora Duse and several low relief masks in the theatre
    were carved by noted sculptor, Gutzon Borlum.

Delaware

Dover, DE

CAPITOL THEATRE (other name: Dover Opera House),
   South State and West North Streets
   OPENING DATE: 1902   CURRENT USE: Movies and civic
   functions   LOCATION OF AUDITORIUM: First floor
   STAGE DIMENSIONS AND EQUIPMENT: Height and width of
   proscenium, 21ft 6in x 28ft; Distance from edge of
   stage to back wall of stage, 31ft 6in; Distance from
   edge of stage to curtain line, 4ft; Distance between
   side walls of stage, 52ft; Distance from stage floor to
   fly loft, 21ft; Depth under stage, 7ft; Stage floor,
   flat; Trap doors, 1
   SEATING (3 levels): 1st level, 337; 2nd level, 96;
   3rd level, 147
   MAJOR TYPES OF ENTERTAINMENT: Drama
   ADDITIONAL INFORMATION: The theatre is located in the
   Victorian Dover District. Theatre was remodeled in
   1920s and renamed the Capitol.

Newark, DE

NEWARK OPERA HOUSE
   OPENING DATE: 1891   STYLE OF ARCHITECTURE: Commercial
   Vernacular   TYPE OF BUILDING: Commercial   FACADE: Brick
   TYPE OF THEATRE: (b)   DEGREE OF RESTORATION: (c)
   CLOSING DATE: 1925   CURRENT USE: Business and apartments
   PERFORMANCE SPACES IN BUILDING: 1
   LOCATION OF AUDITORIUM: Second floor
   SEATING (1 level): 1st level, 500
   MAJOR TYPES OF ENTERTAINMENT: Drama, concerts, movies
   ADDITIONAL INFORMATION: The theatre was built for David
   Caskey. It was the site of Newark's first Nickelodeon.

Smyrna, DE

SMYRNA OPERA HOUSE
  OPENING DATE: December 20, 1869
  STYLE OF ARCHITECTURE: Commercial   TYPE OF BUILDING: Civic
  FACADE: Brick   TYPE OF THEATRE: (b)   DEGREE OF
  RESTORATION: (c)   CLOSING DATE: 1948   CURRENT USE: City
    offices   PERFORMANCE SPACES IN BUILDING: 1
  LOCATION OF AUDITORIUM: Second floor
  STAGE DIMENSIONS AND EQUIPMENT: Height and width of
    proscenium, 12ft x 18ft; Shape of proscenium arch,
    rectangular; Distance from edge of stage to back wall of
    stage, 21ft; Distance from edge of stage to curtain line,
    1ft; Distance between side walls of stage, 42ft; Stage
    floor, flat
  DIMENSIONS OF AUDITORIUM: Distance between side walls
    of auditorium, 42ft; Distance stage to back wall of
    auditorium, 42ft; Orchestra pit, none
  SEATING (1 level)
  SHAPE OF THE AUDITORIUM: Square
  MAJOR TYPES OF ENTERTAINMENT: Drama
  ADDITIONAL INFORMATION: The stage was enlarged in 1886 by
    25 feet. The theatre began showing movies in 1935 and
    continued to serve the town's needs well until 1977 when
    new town hall was built.

Wilmington, DE

DOCKSTADER'S THEATRE, 828 Market Street
  OPENING DATE: November 23, 1903
  OPENING SHOW: Vaudeville bill
  ARCHITECT: George L. Lovett   STYLE OF ARCHITECTURE: French
  TYPE OF BUILDING: Commercial   FACADE: Brick
  TYPE OF THEATRE: (a)   DEGREE OF RESTORATION: (c)
  CLOSING DATE: 1940   CURRENT USE: Commercial
  PERFORMANCE SPACES IN BUILDING: 1
  LOCATION OF AUDITORIUM: First floor
  STAGE DIMENSIONS AND EQUIPMENT: Shape of proscenium arch,
    rectangular
  DIMENSIONS OF AUDITORIUM: Distance between side walls
    of auditorium, 48ft; Distance stage to back wall of
    auditorium, 35ft 6in
  SEATING (2 levels)
  SHAPE OF THE AUDITORIUM: Rectangular
  MAJOR TYPES OF ENTERTAINMENT: Drama, vaudeville
  ADDITIONAL INFORMATION: Only the box office and lobby
    remain from 1941 demolition. The theatre made an attempt
    to make vaudeville acceptable by providing a children's
    nursery and ladies' reception room.

Wilmington, DE

GRAND OPERA HOUSE, INC., 818 Market Street Mall
  OPENING DATE: December 22, 1871

OPENING SHOW: Promenade Concert and Ball featuring McClurg
ARCHITECT: Thomas Dixon   STYLE OF ARCHITECTURE:
  French Second Empire   TYPE OF BUILDING: Masonic Temple
FACADE: Cast-iron, painted white to resemble marble
TYPE OF THEATRE: (a)   DEGREE OF RESTORATION: (a)
CURRENT USE: Community center
PERFORMANCE SPACES IN BUILDING: 1
STAGE DIMENSIONS AND EQUIPMENT: Height and width of
  proscenium, 25ft x 38ft; Shape of proscenium arch,
  rectangular; Distance from edge of stage to back wall of
  stage, 56ft; Distance from edge of stage to curtain line,
  12ft; Distance between side walls of stage, 75ft;
  Distance from stage floor to fly loft. 45ft; Stage floor,
  flat; Trap doors, 1; Dressing rooms, 8 (basement)
DIMENSIONS OF AUDITORIUM: Distance between side walls
  of auditorium, 75ft; Distance stage to back wall of
  auditorium, 133ft; Capacity of orchestra pit, 30
SEATING (3 levels): 1st level, 924; 2nd level, 275;
  3rd level, 500; boxes, 24
SHAPE OF THE AUDITORIUM: Horseshoe-shaped
MAJOR TYPES OF ENTERTAINMENT: Drama, concerts, lectures,
  balls, readings, speeches, opera, minstrel shows
MAJOR STARS WHO APPEARED AT THEATRE: Maggie Mitchell,
  Fanny Janauschek, E. L. Davenport, Junius Brutus Booth,
  Sarah Bernhardt, Buffalo Bill Cody, Groucho Marx

Wilmington, DE

ODD FELLOWS THEATRE, Third and King Streets
  OPENING DATE: May 25, 1849   OPENING SHOW: Formal
    dedication and dance   ARCHITECT: George Read Biddle
  TYPE OF BUILDING: Commercial   FACADE: Brick
  TYPE OF THEATRE: (b)   DEGREE OF RESTORATION: (c)
  CURRENT USE: Vacant   PERFORMANCE SPACES IN BUILDING: 1
  LOCATION OF AUDITORIUM: Second floor
  STAGE DIMENSIONS AND EQUIPMENT: Height and width of
    proscenium, 12ft x 18ft; Shape of proscenium arch,
    square; Distance from edge of stage to back wall of
    stage, 14ft; Distance between side walls of stage, 20ft,
    Dressing rooms, 2 (stage right and left)
  DIMENSIONS OF AUDITORIUM: Distance between side walls
    of auditorium, 30ft; Distance stage to back wall of
    auditorium, 60ft; Orchestra pit, none
  SEATING (1 level): 1st level, 500
  SHAPE OF THE AUDITORIUM: Rectangular
  MAJOR TYPES OF ENTERTAINMENT: Drama, music, lectures,
    vaudeville
  ADDITIONAL INFORMATION: This now-dilapidated theatre was
    the "best house in Wilmington" until the building of the
    Grand Opera House. The stage is gone, but proscenium
    remains. The first play performed was The Lady of Lyons
    on June 23, 1849.

Wilmington, DE

UNION HALL (other names: Strimple Hall, the Old Theatre),
   King Street
  OPENING DATE: October 11, 1878   OPENING SHOW: Variety
    program   TYPE OF BUILDING: Commercial   FACADE: Brick
  TYPE OF THEATRE: (b)   DEGREE OF RESTORATION: (c)
  CURRENT USE: Warehouse   PERFORMANCE SPACES IN BUILDING: 1
  LOCATION OF AUDITORIUM: Second floor
  DIMENSIONS OF AUDITORIUM: Distance between side walls
    of auditorium, 23ft; Distance stage to back wall of
    auditorium, 83ft; Orchestra pit, none
  SEATING (1 level): 1st level, 200
  SHAPE OF THE AUDITORIUM: Rectangular
  MAJOR TYPES OF ENTERTAINMENT: Variety, minstrel shows
  ADDITIONAL INFORMATION: During its history, the hall
    served as a saloon and a temperance hall run by the
    Christian Alliance Church as well as a variety theatre.
    The building is in good condition, but few theatrical
    features remain. The stage was enlarged once in 1859
    and a handsome rural scene was painted on back wall.

District of Columbia (DC)

Washington, DC

FORD'S THEATRE, (other name: Tenth Street Baptist Church,
    Ford's Atheneum), 511 10th Street
  OPENING DATE: 1833 (November 19, 1861 as a theatre)
  OPENING SHOW: Concert, Carlotta Patti Concert Troupe
  ARCHITECT: James B. Gifford   STYLE OF ARCHITECTURE:
    Victorian   TYPE OF BUILDING: Theatre   FACADE: Red brick
  TYPE OF THEATRE: (a)   DEGREE OF RESTORATION: (a)
  CURRENT USE: Theatre   LOCATION OF AUDITORIUM: First floor
  STAGE DIMENSIONS AND EQUIPMENT: Height and width of
  proscenium, 38ft x 36ft; Distance from edge of stage to
  back wall of stage, 45ft; Distance from edge of stage to
  curtain line, 17ft; Distance between side walls of stage,
  62ft 6in; Depth under stage, 14ft; Stage floor, flat
  DIMENSIONS OF AUDITORIUM: Distance between side walls
    of auditorium, 66ft 6in; Distance stage to back
    wall of auditorium, 45ft; Orchestra pit, yes
  SEATING (3 levels): 1st level, 602; 2nd level, 422; 3rd
    level, 676; boxes 48 to 80
  MAJOR STARS WHO APPEARED AT THEATRE: Carlotta Patti, George
    Christy's Minstrels, Edwin Forrest, John Wilkes Booth,
    J. B. Booth, John McCullough, James H. Hackett, Laura
    Keene, Stuart Robson, Commodore Foote, Maggie Mitchell,
    J. S. Clarke, W. J. Florence, Clara Louise Kellogg,
    C. B. Bishop, Brignoli, Colonel Small, and others
  MAJOR TYPES OF ENTERTAINMENT: Drama, minstrel shows,
    concerts
  ADDITIONAL INFORMATION: Ford's Theatre was opened as a
    Baptist Church in 1833. In 1861, it was sold to theatri-
    cal entrepreneur, John T. Ford, who contracted James J.
    Gifford to convert the building into a theatre. The
    theatre became infamous on April 14, 1865 when Abraham
    Lincoln was assassinated while at the theatre. In 1866,
    the government purchased the theatre and converted it
    into an office building. On June 9, 1893, three floors
    of the building collapsed, killing 22 workers. After
    extensive restoration, Ford's reopened as a theatre on
    January 30, 1968.

Florida

De Funiak Springs, FL

CHAUTAUQUA AUDITORIUM, Circle Drive
  OPENING DATE: 1910
  STYLE OF ARCHITECTURE: Classical Revival   TYPE OF
  BUILDING: Theatre   FACADE: Wood   TYPE OF THEATRE: (a)
  DEGREE OF RESTORATION: (c)   CLOSING DATE: 1975
  CURRENT USE: Vacant   PERFORMANCE SPACES IN BUILDING: 1
  MAJOR TYPES OF ENTERTAINMENT: Dance, music, lectures
  ADDITIONAL INFORMATION: The stage and auditorium sections
    of the building were demolished in a 1976 hurricane and
    were never rebuilt. The front of the building, which
    contains the lobby, now houses the Chamber of Commerce.

Monticello, FL

MONTICELLO OPERA HOUSE (other names: Perkins Opera House,
    Perkins Business Block), Intersection of U.S. Routes 19
    and 90
  OPENING DATE: Fall, 1890   OPENING SHOW: The Clipper
    with the Amy Lee Company
  ARCHITECT: W. R. Gunn   TYPE OF BUILDING: Commercial
  FACADE: Red brick   TYPE OF THEATRE: (b)   DEGREE OF
  RESTORATION: (b)   CURRENT USE: Cultural center
  PERFORMANCE SPACES IN BUILDING: 1
  LOCATION OF AUDITORIUM: Second floor
  STAGE DIMENSIONS AND EQUIPMENT: Height and width of
    proscenium, 15ft x 28ft; Shape of proscenium arch,
    rectangular; Distance from edge of stage to back wall of
    stage, 27ft; Distance from edge of stage to curtain line,
    7ft; Distance between side walls of stage, 50ft; Stage
    floor, flat; Scenery storage rooms, 1 (stage right);
    Dressing rooms, 4 (wings)
  DIMENSIONS OF AUDITORIUM: Capacity of orchestra pit, 10
  SEATING (2 levels)
  SHAPE OF THE AUDITORIUM: U-shaped

MAJOR TYPES OF ENTERTAINMENT: Drama, vaudeville, musicals
MAJOR STARS WHO APPEARED AT THEATRE: Mabel Page
ADDITIONAL INFORMATION: Gas lines to footlights are intact.
  Elaborate tin and mirror chandelier has been preserved.
  Some grooves remain.

Quincy, FL

EMPIRE THEATRE (other name: Gardener Opera House until
    early 1900s), 112 East Jefferson Street
  OPENING DATE: 1892
  STYLE OF ARCHITECTURE: Plain Commercial   TYPE OF BUILDING:
    Fire station and movie theatre   FACADE: Brick
  TYPE OF THEATRE: (b)   DEGREE OF RESTORATION: (c)
  CLOSING DATE: 1948   CURRENT USE: Auto service shop
  LOCATION OF AUDITORIUM: Second floor
  ADDITIONAL INFORMATION: All theatrical elements are gone.

Quincy, FL

QUINCY OPERA HOUSE, Washington and Madison
  OPENING DATE: January 1893
  TYPE OF BUILDING: Meeting hall   TYPE OF THEATRE: (c)
  DEGREE OF RESTORATION: (c)   CURRENT USE: Storage
  PERFORMANCE SPACES IN BUILDING: 1
  LOCATION OF AUDITORIUM: Second floor
  STAGE DIMENSIONS AND EQUIPMENT: Width of proscenium, 28ft;
    Shape of proscenium arch, rectangular; Distance between
    side walls of stage, 42ft; Depth under stage, 22ft; Stage
    floor, raked
  DIMENSIONS OF AUDITORIUM: Distance between side walls
    of auditorium, 42ft; Distance stage to back wall of
    auditorium, 40ft
  SEATING (2 levels)
  SHAPE OF THE AUDITORIUM: Rectangular
  MAJOR TYPES OF ENTERTAINMENT: Local and traveling shows,
    minstrel shows
  ADDITIONAL INFORMATION: The theatre was built above a bank.
    The stage and balcony are gone. The theatre is used by
    local dramatic groups and there is occasional interest
    in renovating the building.

St. Petersburg, FL

ARMISTEAD OPERA HOUSE, 26 Central Avenue
  OPENING DATE: 1894
  TYPE OF BUILDING: Commercial   TYPE OF THEATRE: (b)
  DEGREE OF RESTORATION: (c)   CURRENT USE: Hotel
  LOCATION OF AUDITORIUM: Second floor
  ADDITIONAL INFORMATION: First floor was a store and
    third floor was a lodge hall. The building is in poor
    condition now and no theatrical elements have survived.
    The opera house was considered a failure when it opened

and it was offered for sale for $6,000 in 1895, but no buyer appeared. The opera house is registered with the Florida State Archives.

Sanford, FL

SANFORD OPERA HOUSE, South Magnolia Street
OPENING DATE: 1899
TYPE OF BUILDING: Movie theatre   TYPE OF THEATRE: (a)
DEGREE OF RESTORATION: (c)   CURRENT USE: Vacant
PERFORMANCE SPACES IN BUILDING: 1
STAGE DIMENSIONS AND EQUIPMENT: Height and width of
  proscenium, 15ft x 27ft; Distance from edge of stage
  to back wall, 30ft; Depth under stage, 5ft
ADDITIONAL INFORMATION: Theatre is directly across the
  street from the Imperial Opera House and was rediscovered
  by Jack Neeson in February 1979.

Tallahassee, FL

GALLIE'S HALL (other names: Munro's Opera House, Gallie-Munro
  Opera House), Northeast corner of Jefferson and Adam
  Streets
OPENING DATE: January 26, 1874   OPENING SHOW: Alf Burnett
STYLE OF ARCHITECTURE: Commercial   FACADE: Brick
TYPE OF THEATRE: (b)   DEGREE OF RESTORATION: (a)
CLOSING DATE: 1912   CURRENT USE: Offices
PERFORMANCE SPACES IN BUILDING: 1
LOCATION OF AUDITORIUM: Second floor
STAGE DIMENSIONS AND EQUIPMENT: Distance from edge of
  stage to back wall of stage, 30ft; Stage floor, flat
DIMENSIONS OF AUDITORIUM: Distance between side walls
  of auditorium, 50ft; Distance stage to back wall of
  auditorium, 50ft
SEATING (2 levels)
SHAPE OF THE AUDITORIUM: Square
MAJOR TYPES OF ENTERTAINMENT: Drama, opera, musicals,
  minstrel shows
MAJOR STARS WHO APPEARED AT THEATRE: Ada Gray and Company
  (1881), Humpty Dumpty Company (1890), AL G. Fields
  Minstrels (1892)

Tampa, FL

CENTRO ASTURIANO THEATRE, 1913 Nebraska
OPENING DATE: 1914
STYLE OF ARCHITECTURE: Neo-Classical   TYPE OF BUILDING:
  Community center   FACADE: Granite and terra cotta
TYPE OF THEATRE: (b)   DEGREE OF RESTORATION: (d)
CURRENT USE: Theatre and community center
PERFORMANCE SPACES IN BUILDING: 1
LOCATION OF AUDITORIUM: First floor

STAGE DIMENSIONS AND EQUIPMENT: Height and width of
  proscenium, 36ft 6in x 27ft; Shape of proscenium arch,
  rectangular; Distance from edge of stage to back wall of
  stage, 36ft; Distance from stage floor to fly loft, 45ft;
  Depth under stage, 6ft; Stage floor, raked; Trap doors,
  2
DIMENSIONS OF AUDITORIUM: Orchestra pit, yes
SEATING (2 levels)
SHAPE OF THE AUDITORIUM: Square
MAJOR TYPES OF ENTERTAINMENT: Local productions
ADDITIONAL INFORMATION: Theatre was built in and serves
  the Spanish-Italian community. Most plays and operas at
  the theatre are presented in these languages. Asbestos
  curtains with ads still exist.

Tampa, FL

CENTRO ESPANOL, 7th Avenue and 16th Street
  OPENING DATE: 1912
  ARCHITECT: Fred J. James   STYLE OF ARCHITECTURE:
    Classical   TYPE OF BUILDING: Community center
  FACADE: Brick and terra cotta   TYPE OF THEATRE: (a)
  DEGREE OF RESTORATION: (c)   CLOSING DATE: Late 1970s
  CURRENT USE: Closed   PERFORMANCE SPACES IN BUILDING: 1
  LOCATION OF AUDITORIUM: First floor
  ADDITIONAL INFORMATION: Theatre is in Latin section of
    Tampa. The building is in poor condition. It is
    currently closed and may become a disco. The theatre
    was built in 1912 at an original cost of $90,000.

Tampa, FL

CIRCULO CUBANO, Palmetto at Avenida Republica de Cuba
  OPENING DATE: 1907
  FACADE: Yellow brick   TYPE OF THEATRE: (a)   DEGREE OF
  RESTORATION: (d)   CURRENT USE: Theatre
  PERFORMANCE SPACES IN BUILDING: 1
  LOCATION OF AUDITORIUM: First and second floors
  STAGE DIMENSIONS AND EQUIPMENT: Height and width of
    proscenium, 16ft x 24ft; Shape of proscenium arch,
    arched; Distance from edge of stage to back wall of
    stage, 20ft; Distance from edge of stage to curtain line,
    5ft; Distance between side walls of stage, 53ft; Depth
    under stage, 8ft; Stage floor, flat; Trap doors, 2
  DIMENSIONS OF AUDITORIUM: Distance between side walls
    of auditorium, 53ft; Distance stage to back wall of
    auditorium, 50ft; Orchestra pit, yes
  SEATING (2 levels): 1st level, 600
  SHAPE OF THE AUDITORIUM: Rectangular
  MAJOR TYPES OF ENTERTAINMENT: Local productions, both plays
    and operas
  ADDITIONAL INFORMATION: The theatre is in a Latin section
    of Tampa and produces plays in Spanish. The theatre was
    closed between 1959 and 1978. The condition of the

theatre is excellent. The stage has two prosceniums, one
24 feet wide and the other 32 feet wide. The curtain line
is on the inner proscenium. The theatre is a copy of
Teatro Canto in Havana. It was rebuilt after a 1917 fire.

Ybor City, FL

CENTRO ESPANOL, 1526-36 East Seventh Street
  OPENING DATE: 1912
  STYLE OF ARCHITECTURE: Vernacular   TYPE OF BUILDING:
    Community center   FACADE: Brick   TYPE OF THEATRE: (a)
  DEGREE OF RESTORATION: (d)   CURRENT USE: Theatre
  PERFORMANCE SPACES IN BUILDING: 1
  LOCATION OF AUDITORIUM: First floor
  STAGE DIMENSIONS AND EQUIPMENT: Distance from edge of stage
    to back wall of stage, 30ft; Distance between side walls
    of stage, 60ft
  DIMENSIONS OF AUDITORIUM: Distance between side walls
    of auditorium, 75ft; Distance stage to back wall of
    auditorium, 69ft
  SHAPE OF THE AUDITORIUM: Square
  MAJOR TYPES OF ENTERTAINMENT: Community productions
  ADDITIONAL INFORMATION: The theatre is in the Spanish and
    Italian section of Tampa and continues to produce operas
    and plays in those languages. As the first of the Latin
    clubs, it fostered L'Unione Italiano, Circulo Cubano, and
    Centro Asturiano Theatre. It was remodeled in 1932.

Georgia

Albany, GA

RAWLINGS OPERA HOUSE (other names: Liberty, Broad Avenue
    Cinema), Broad and North Jackson Streets
    OPENING DATE: 1900
    TYPE OF BUILDING: Movie theatre   TYPE OF THEATRE: (b)
    DEGREE OF RESTORATION: (c)   CURRENT USE: Movies
    LOCATION OF AUDITORIUM: First floor
    STAGE DIMENSIONS AND EQUIPMENT: Height and width of
        proscenium, 26ft x 30ft; Distance from edge of stage to
        back wall of stage, 32ft; Distance from edge of stage to
        curtain line, 3ft; Distance between side walls of stage,
        65ft; Distance from stage floor to fly loft, 50ft; Depth
        under stage, 7ft; Trap doors, 3
    DIMENSIONS OF AUDITORIUM: Orchestra pit, none
    MAJOR TYPES OF ENTERTAINMENT: Traveling companies;
        primarily movies after 1914
    ADDITIONAL INFORMATION: The theatre was originally on
        the second floor. The building burned in 1900 and
        the theatre was rebuilt on first floor. Remodeling in
        1970s did not change interior significantly. Facade was
        altered to match other buildings in mall. Condition of
        the building is good.

Albany, GA

TIFTS HALL, 112-114 Front Street (Bridge House)
    OPENING DATE: 1857   OPENING SHOW: Our American Cousin
    ARCHITECT: Horace, a freed slave   STYLE OF ARCHITECTURE:
        Classical   TYPE OF BUILDING: Commercial   FACADE: Wood
    TYPE OF THEATRE: (b)   DEGREE OF RESTORATION: (c)
    CURRENT USE: Offices   LOCATION OF AUDITORIUM: Second floor
    DIMENSIONS OF AUDITORIUM: Distance between side walls of
        auditorium, 32ft
    SHAPE OF THE AUDITORIUM: Square
    MAJOR TYPES OF ENTERTAINMENT: Local and traveling plays

MAJOR STARS WHO APPEARED AT THEATRE: Sarah Siddons, Laura
   Keene
ADDITIONAL INFORMATION: Originally the private residence of
   Colonel Tift, the bridge keeper, the building was used as
   a slaughter and packing house during the 1860s. No
   evidence of stage location nor outfitting remains. Our
   American Cousin with Laura Keene played here before going
   to Washington, DC.

Americus, GA

GLOVER OPERA HOUSE, 117 Forsythe
   OPENING DATE: January 1882
   ARCHITECTS: Parkins and Bruce (Atlanta)
   STYLE OF ARCHITECTURE: Commercial   TYPE OF BUILDING:
      Storage   FACADE: Brick   TYPE OF THEATRE: (b)
   DEGREE OF RESTORATION: (c)   CLOSING DATE: 1930s
   CURRENT USE: Vacant   LOCATION OF AUDITORIUM: Second floor
   STAGE DIMENSIONS AND EQUIPMENT: Height and width of
      proscenium, 13ft x 26ft; Distance from edge of stage to
      back wall of stage, 30ft; Distance from edge of stage to
      curtain line, 3ft; Distance between side walls of stage,
      54ft; Stage floor, flat; Trap doors, 2; Dressing rooms,
      4 (upstage right)
   DIMENSIONS OF AUDITORIUM: Distance between side walls
      of auditorium, 54ft; Distance stage to back wall of
      auditorium, 55ft; Orchestra pit, none
   SEATING (3 levels)
   SHAPE OF THE AUDITORIUM: Square
   ADDITIONAL INFORMATION: The balcony and stage still exist,
      but the building is in poor condition. Scenery was
      hoisted through double doors at rear of the building.
      Auditorium had four boxes. Theatre seated between 600
      and 1,000 persons. The entrance was somewhat unusual,
      consisting of a porch and stairs over sidewalk leadint to
      the theatre above. This has now been removed and theatre
      is now almost totally inaccesible.

Athens, GA

LUCY COBB INSTITUTE, Milledgeville Avenue
   OPENING DATE: 1850   STYLE OF ARCHITECTURE: Victorian
   TYPE OF BUILDING: Lecture hall   FACADE: Brick
   TYPE OF THEATRE: (c)   DEGREE OF RESTORATION: (b)
   CURRENT USE: Vacant
   PERFORMANCE SPACES IN BUILDING: 1
   SHAPE OF THE AUDITORIUM: Octagonal
   MAJOR TYPES OF ENTERTAINMENT: Drama, concerts
   ADDITIONAL INFORMATION: The Cobb Institute was absorbed
      by the University of Georgia and the hall is now
      situated on the University of Georgia campus. The
      original balcony and stage are intact.

Athens, GA

MORTON THEATRE, Corner of Washington and Hull Streets
  OPENING DATE: 1910   OPENING SHOW: Classical piano recital
    by Alice Carter Simmons (May 18, 1910)
  ARCHITECT: Frank Cox, Chicago   STYLE OF ARCHITECTURE:
    Beaux Arts   TYPE OF BUILDING: Commercial and offices
  FACADE: Light tan brick   TYPE OF THEATRE: (b)
  DEGREE OF RESTORATION: (c)   CLOSING DATE: 1954
  CURRENT USE: Commercial and office space
  PERFORMANCE SPACES IN BUILDING: 1
  LOCATION OF AUDITORIUM: Second, third and fourth floors
  STAGE DIMENSIONS AND EQUIPMENT: Height and width of
    proscenium, 21ft x 27ft; Shape of proscenium arch,
    square; Stage floor, raked
  DIMENSIONS OF AUDITORIUM: Capacity of orchestra pit, 20
  SEATING (3 levels): 1st level, 320; 2nd level, 160;
    3rd level, 120
  SHAPE OF THE AUDITORIUM: Horseshoe-shaped
  MAJOR TYPES OF ENTERTAINMENT: Drama, movies
  MAJOR STARS WHO APPEARED AT THEATRE: Duke Ellington,
    Bessie Smith, Louis Armstrong, Cab Calloway, Butterbeans
    and Susie, Black Patti, and the Whitman Sisters
  ADDITIONAL INFORMATION: The stage floor is 1,323 feet
    square and has a 10 degree slope. All dressing rooms are
    located on two levels. The original wooden auditorium
    walls remain. The Morton family sold the building in
    1972.

Atlanta, GA

MUNICIPAL AUDITORIUM
  OPENING DATE: 1915
  FACADE: Marble and granite   TYPE OF THEATRE: (a)
  DEGREE OF RESTORATION: (c)   CURRENT USE: City auditorium
  PERFORMANCE SPACES IN BUILDING: 1
  LOCATION OF AUDITORIUM: First floor
  ADDITIONAL INFORMATION: The original stage and auditorium
    were demolished and a completely new building exists
    behind the original granite and marble facade.

Atlanta, GA

ODD FELLOWS HALL, Sweet Auburn District
  OPENING DATE: 1913
  TYPE OF THEATRE: (b)
  DEGREE OF RESTORATION: (b)
  CURRENT USE: Community events
  ADDITIONAL INFORMATION: The theatre is situated in
    historic black community of Atlanta's "Sweet Auburn" and
    was financed by Black businessmen.

Columbus, GA

SPRINGER OPERA HOUSE, 103 10th Street
  OPENING DATE: 1871 OPENING SHOW: Fanchon The Cricket
  ARCHITECT: Daniel Matthew Folley   STYLE OF ARCHITECTURE:
    Classical Federal   TYPE OF BUILDING: Movie theatre
  FACADE: Brick   TYPE OF THEATRE: (b)   DEGREE OF
  RESTORATION: (a)   CURRENT USE: Theatre
  PERFORMANCE SPACES IN BUILDING: 1
  STAGE DIMENSIONS AND EQUIPMENT: Height and width of
    proscenium, 32ft x 32ft 8in; Shape of proscenium arch,
    rectangular; Distance from edge of stage to back wall of
    stage, 40ft; Distance from edge of stage to curtain line,
    4ft; Distance between side walls of stage, 68ft; Distance
    from stage floor to fly loft, 65ft; Depth under stage,
    10ft; Stage floor, flat; Scenery storage rooms, 1;
    Dressing rooms, 4 (upstairs)
  DIMENSIONS OF AUDITORIUM: Distance between side walls
    of auditorium, 60ft; Distance stage to back wall of
    auditorium, 50ft; Capacity of orchestra pit, 15
  SEATING (3 levels): 1st level, 709; 2nd level, 268;
    3rd level, 314; boxes, 72
  SHAPE OF THE AUDITORIUM: Rectangular
  MAJOR TYPES OF ENTERTAINMENT: Local and traveling
    productions
  MAJOR STARS WHO APPEARED AT THEATRE: Franklin D.
    Roosevelt, John L. Sullivan, William Jennings Bryan
  ADDITIONAL INFORMATION: The present theatre occupies the
    entire building after a 1902 renovation of the 1871
    second floor opera house. The previous theatre had its
    stage at the north end of the building, while it is
    presently at the east end. The theatre has been
    designated "The State Theatre of Georgia."

Griffin, GA

NEW OPERA HOUSE (other names: Olympic Theatre, Odd Fellows
    Hall), Northeast Corner of Hill and Solomon Streets
  OPENING DATE: January 10, 1895   OPENING SHOW: Lead for
    Life (January 12, 1895)
  ARCHITECT: Mr. Cowan, Builder   TYPE OF BUILDING:
    Community center   FACADE: Brick   TYPE OF THEATRE: (c)
  DEGREE OF RESTORATION: (c) PERFORMANCE SPACES IN
  BUILDING: 1   LOCATION OF AUDITORIUM: Second floor
  STAGE DIMENSIONS AND EQUIPMENT: Height and width of
    proscenium, 16ft x 32ft; Shape of proscenium arch,
    rectangular; Distance from edge of stage to back wall of
    stage, 26ft; Distance from edge of stage to curtain line,
    1ft 6in; Distance between side walls of stage; 62ft;
    Depth under stage, 3ft; Stage floor, flat; Trap doors, 3;
    Dressing rooms, 4 (two each side)
  DIMENSIONS OF AUDITORIUM: Distance between side walls
    of auditorium, 62ft; Distance stage to back wall of
    auditorium, 40ft
  SEATING (2 levels)

SHAPE OF THE AUDITORIUM: Rectangular with curved balcony
ADDITIONAL INFORMATION: Part of lodge rooms became fly-
space (third floor) and is still visible. Theatre has
been closed for many years, but stage, auditorium, and
some seating are intact. Accessibility to theatre is
difficult because the "grand staircase" has been cut off
at the second floor. Theatre can now be entered by a
concealed ladder,

Griffin, GA

PATTERSON'S (other name: Scheuerman's), Hill Street (above
the Dollar Store)
OPENING DATE: 1870
STYLE OF ARCHITECTURE: Vernacular   TYPE OF BUILDING:
Commercial   FACADE: Brick   TYPE OF THEATRE: (b)
DEGREE OF RESTORATION: (c)   CURRENT USE: Dance studio
PERFORMANCE SPACES IN BUILDING: 1
LOCATION OF AUDITORIUM: Second floor
STAGE DIMENSIONS AND EQUIPMENT: Height and width of
proscenium, 18ft x 22ft; Shape of proscenium arch,
arched; Distance from edge of stage to back wall of
stage, 20ft; Distance from edge of stage to curtain line,
1ft; Distance between side walls of stage, 28ft; Stage
floor, flat
DIMENSIONS OF AUDITORIUM: Distance between side walls
of auditorium, 27ft; Distance stage to back wall of
auditorium, 48ft
SEATING (2 levels)
SHAPE OF THE AUDITORIUM: Rectangular
ADDITIONAL INFORMATION: Theatre is believed to be
Scheuerman's Opera House, known as the "first opera
house in Griffin." Scheuerman's Opera House was over
Scheuerman's Store which later became the Thomas J.
White Store. Most of the theatre's equipment and
trappings were destroyed in a fire and the space now
houses a dance studio.

Hawkinsville, GA

OPERA HOUSE (other name: Hawkinsville City Hall
Auditorium), Lumpkin and Broad Street
OPENING DATE: 1907
ARCHITECT: W. R. Gunn   STYLE OF ARCHITECTURE:
Commercial Victorian   TYPE OF BUILDING: City Hall,
library, church   FACADE: Brick   TYPE OF THEATRE: (a)
DEGREE OF RESTORATION: (a)   CURRENT USE: City Hall,
theatre   PERFORMANCE SPACES IN BUILDING: 1
LOCATION OF AUDITORIUM: Ground floor
STAGE DIMENSIONS AND EQUIPMENT: Height and width of
proscenium, 18ft x 34ft; Shape of proscenium arch,
rectangular; Distance from edge of stage to back wall of
stage, 24ft; Distance from edge of stage to curtain line,
4ft; Distance between side walls of stage, 60ft; Distance

from stage floor to fly loft, 24ft; Stage floor, flat;
Dressing rooms, 9 (3 each on 3 separate levels)
DIMENSIONS OF AUDITORIUM: Distance between side walls
of auditorium, 55ft; Distance stage to back wall of
auditorium, 50ft; Orchestra pit, yes
SEATING (2 levels): 1st level, 575; 2nd level, 200
SHAPE OF THE AUDITORIUM: Rectangular
MAJOR TYPES OF ENTERTAINMENT: Local and touring productions
ADDITIONAL INFORMATION: Wooden sheaves on grid are in
working order. Upstage crossover bridge exists along
back wall. Some scenery remains. Balcony supports are
cast iron with nice capitals. Old knife switchboard
survives.

Macon, GA

DOUGLAS THEATRE, 363 Broadway
OPENING DATE: 1912
ARCHITECT: C. H. Douglas, builder   STYLE OF ARCHITECTURE:
Commercial   TYPE OF BUILDING: Hotel, pool room
FACADE: Brick   TYPE OF THEATRE: (c)   DEGREE OF
RESTORATION: (c)   CLOSING DATE: 1921   CURRENT USE:
Commercial   PERFORMANCE SPACES IN BUILDING: 1
LOCATION OF AUDITORIUM: First floor
DIMENSIONS OF AUDITORIUM: Capacity of orchestra pit, 4
MAJOR TYPES OF ENTERTAINMENT: Vaudeville, films
MAJOR STARS WHO APPEARED AT THEATRE: All major black
entertainers between 1912 and 1921
ADDITIONAL INFORMATION: Douglas, a successful black
entrepreneur, converted part of his Colonial Hotel into
a theatre for vaudeville and movies. An auditorium, fly
house, and stage were built. This particular Douglas
Theatre was closed in 1921 when a larger Douglas Theatre
was opened at 1223 Broadway. Only the domed ceiling and
wall molding remain of the original theatre. The Second
Douglas Theatre operated until 1925 when it became
commercial space.

Macon, GA

GRAND OPERA HOUSE (other names: Academy of Music, The
Grand), 651 Mulberry Street
OPENING DATE: September 22, 1884
OPENING SHOW: Amateur musical entertainment
ARCHITECT: A. Blair (1884); W. R. Gunn (1905)
STYLE OF ARCHITECTURE: Vernacular   TYPE OF BUILDING:
Movie theatre   FACADE: Brick   TYPE OF THEATRE: (a)
DEGREE OF RESTORATION: (a)   CURRENT USE: Theatre, concerts
LOCATION OF AUDITORIUM: First floor
STAGE DIMENSIONS AND EQUIPMENT: Height and width of
proscenium, 34ft x 37ft; Shape of proscenium arch,
rectangular; Distance from edge of stage to back wall of
stage, 58ft; Distance between side walls of stage, 90ft;
Distance from stage floor to fly loft, 26ft; Depth under

stage, 12ft; Stage floor, flat; Trap doors, 4; Dressing
rooms, 20 (sides)
DIMENSIONS OF AUDITORIUM: Distance between side walls
of auditorium, 90ft; Distance stage to back wall of
auditorium, 58ft; Capacity of orchestra pit, 30
SEATING (3 levels): 1st level, 733; 2nd level, 510;
3rd level, 800; boxes, 96
SHAPE OF THE AUDITORIUM: Rectangular
MAJOR TYPES OF ENTERTAINMENT: Drama
MAJOR STARS WHO APPEARED AT THEATRE: Ben Hur production
including large chariot race
ADDITIONAL INFORMATION: The theatre originally occupied the
entire building, but the 1905 renovation added commercial
offices at front of the building. The number of seats
was reduced from 2,139 to the present 1,014. The stage
floor has sloats, troughs, and handles for locking the
sloats. There are twelve boxes in three tiers on each
side. Theatre exterior is unimpressive, but interior
is elegant.

Pelham, GA

THE OPERA HOUSE, West Railroad Street
OPENING DATE: 1900
STYLE OF ARCHITECTURE: Vernacular   TYPE OF BUILDING:
Commercial   FACADE: Brick   TYPE OF THEATRE: (b)
DEGREE OF RESTORATION: (c)   CURRENT USE: Offices
LOCATION OF AUDITORIUM: Second floor
STAGE DIMENSIONS AND EQUIPMENT: Distance from edge of stage
to back wall of stage, 18ft; Distance from edge of stage
to curtain line, 2ft; Distance between side walls of
stage, 22ft; Stage floor, flat; Dressing rooms, 2
(downstage right and left)
DIMENSIONS OF AUDITORIUM: Distance between side walls
of auditorium, 50ft; Distance stage to back wall, 59ft;
Orchestra pit, none
SEATING (1 level)
ADDITIONAL INFORMATION: Georgia Power Company now occupies
former theatre space. City Hall and Opera House were
built as a joint enterprise. The space was converted to
offices around 1935. Trapdoors stage right were for
scenery not actors and a large room stage left which was
marked "actors space" on a 1983 blueprint may have been a
dressing room or the greenroom.

Quitman, GA

QUITMAN THEATRE, Screven Street
OPENING DATE: 1887
STYLE OF ARCHITECTURE: Commercial   TYPE OF BUILDING:
Store   FACADE: Brick   TYPE OF THEATRE: (b)
DEGREE OF RESTORATION: (c)   CURRENT USE: City Hall
LOCATION OF AUDITORIUM: Second floor
STAGE DIMENSIONS AND EQUIPMENT: Height and width of

proscenium, 20ft x 24ft; Distance from edge of stage
to back wall of stage, 24ft; Distance from edge of stage
to curtain line, 4ft 6in; Distance between side walls of
stage, 42ft; Distance from stage floor to fly loft, 26ft;
Depth under stage, 5ft
MAJOR TYPES OF ENTERTAINMENT: Local and touring companies
ADDITIONAL INFORMATION: Most of stage elements were lost
during remodeling. The theatre was built with town funds
for purposes of "cultural enrichment."

Savannah, GA

SAVANNAH THEATRE (other name: Atheneum), Bull Street and
Chippewa Square
OPENING DATE: 1818   OPENING SHOW: The Soldier's Daughter
ARCHITECT: William Jay, English architect
STYLE OF ARCHITECTURE: Federal   TYPE OF BUILDING: Movie
theatre   FACADE: Brick   TYPE OF THEATRE: (a)
DEGREE OF RESTORATION: (a)   CURRENT USE: Theatre
PERFORMANCE SPACES IN BUILDING: 1
LOCATION OF AUDITORIUM: First floor
STAGE DIMENSIONS AND EQUIPMENT: Height and width of
proscenium, 27ft x 32ft; Distance from edge of stage to
back wall of stage, 38ft; Distance from edge of stage to
curtain line, 5ft; Distance between side walls of stage,
60ft; Distance from stage floor to fly loft, 53ft; Depth
under stage, 10ft; Trap doors, 1; Scenery storage
rooms, 1
DIMENSIONS OF AUDITORIUM: Orchestra pit, yes
SHAPE OF THE AUDITORIUM: Rectangular
MAJOR TYPES OF ENTERTAINMENT: Drama, movies
MAJOR STARS WHO APPEARED AT THEATRE: Sarah Bernhardt, Fanny
Davenport, Joseph Jefferson, Charles Coburn, Lillian
Russell, E. H. Sothern, Edwin Forrest, Mary Anderson,
Henry Irving, and Ellen Terry
ADDITIONAL INFORMATION: The theatre was remodeled in
1895. It burned in 1906, 1944, and 1948. In the 1980s,
it was restored to its "original" appearance. The
Drayton Street wall is most likely the only part of
the building which remains from 1818.

Winder, GA

SHARPTON OPERA HOUSE (other name: Barrow County Court House
1914-15), Broad Street
OPENING DATE: 1907
STYLE OF ARCHITECTURE: Commercial   TYPE OF BUILDING:
Business, court house, theatre   FACADE: Red brick
TYPE OF THEATRE: (b)   DEGREE OF RESTORATION: (a)
CLOSING DATE: 1922   CURRENT USE: Furniture store,
restaurant   PERFORMANCE SPACES IN BUILDING: 1
LOCATION OF AUDITORIUM: Second floor
DIMENSIONS OF AUDITORIUM: Orchestra pit, none
SEATING (1 level)

MAJOR TYPES OF ENTERTAINMENT: Drama, vaudeville, burlesque, opera, and chautauqua events

ADDITIONAL INFORMATION: Building has been restored to a restaurant where plays were once performed. In 1914 the stage served as a court setting for newly formed Barrow County.

Hawaii

Honolulu, HI

LIBERTY THEATRE
OPENING DATE: 1912   OPENING SHOW: Vaudeville bill
TYPE OF BUILDING: Movie theatre and meeting hall
TYPE OF THEATRE: (b)   DEGREE OF RESTORATION: (c)
CURRENT USE: Movie theatre
LOCATION OF AUDITORIUM: First floor
MAJOR TYPES OF ENTERTAINMENT: Vaudeville, movies
ADDITIONAL INFORMATION: The theatre is owned by the
  Consolidated Amusement Company, 510 South Street,
  Honolulu, HI.

Idaho

Boise, ID

SONNA'S OPERA HOUSE, 9th and Main Streets
  OPENING DATE: 1886
  TYPE OF BUILDING: Office building   TYPE OF THEATRE: (b)
  CURRENT USE: Office building
  LOCATION OF AUDITORIUM: Second floor
  MAJOR TYPES OF ENTERTAINMENT: Drama, movies
  ADDITIONAL INFORMATION: Sonna's Opera House hosted
    the first movie to be seen in Boise in 1897.

Boise, ID

TURNVEREIN HALL (other names: Jake's Turnverein Hall, Boise
    Turnverein), 6th and Main Streets
  OPENING DATE: August 1, 1906   OPENING SHOW: Band concert
  ARCHITECT: Charles Frederick Hummel   TYPE OF THEATRE: (b)
  CLOSING DATE: 1916   CURRENT USE: Restaurant
  PERFORMANCE SPACES IN BUILDING: 1
  SEATING (2 levels): 1st level, 400; 2nd level, 200
  MAJOR TYPES OF ENTERTAINMENT: Vaudeville, drama, concerts,
    balls, lectures
  ADDITIONAL INFORMATION: The present building replaced
    Slocum's Hall at 6th and Main Streets. It was initially
    planned to include a bowling alley, an exercise area,
    showers, locker rooms, a kitchen, a dining room and a
    "gents parlor."

Oakley, ID

HOWELLS OPERA HOUSE (other name: Oakley Playhouse)
  OPENING DATE: February 16, 1890
  OPENING SHOW: Ingomar, the Barbarian
  FACADE: Rose-colored brick

TYPE OF THEATRE: (a)   DEGREE OF RESTORATION: (a)
CURRENT USE: Movies, plays, concerts
LOCATION OF AUDITORIUM: Ground floor
STAGE DIMENSIONS AND EQUIPMENT: Height and width of
  proscenium, 17ft x 27ft 11in; Shape of proscenium arch,
  arched; Distance from edge of stage to back wall of
  stage, 35ft; Distance from edge of stage to curtain line,
  5ft; Distance between side walls of stage, 45ft 3in;
  Depth under stage, 7ft 2in; Stage floor, raked; Trap
  doors, 1; Scenery storage rooms, 0 (scenery kept
  backstage); Dressing rooms, 4 (under stage)
DIMENSIONS OF AUDITORIUM: Distance between side walls
  of auditorium, 39ft 3in; Distance stage to back wall of
  auditorium, 54ft; Capacity of orchestra pit, 10
SEATING (2 levels): 1st level, 340; 2nd level, 160
SHAPE OF THE AUDITORIUM: Rectangular
MAJOR TYPES OF ENTERTAINMENT: Drama, vaudeville
ADDITIONAL INFORMATION: Newspaper articles comment on how
  the rake of both the stage and the house enhance viewing.

Illinois

Alexis, IL

ALEXIS OPERA HOUSE, 103 North Main
OPENING DATE: 1890   OPENING SHOW: The May Bretonne Company
FACADE: Red brick   TYPE OF THEATRE: (b)   DEGREE OF
RESTORATION: (c)   CLOSING DATE: 1920s   CURRENT USE:
Vacant   LOCATION OF AUDITORIUM: Top floor
STAGE DIMENSIONS AND EQUIPMENT: Height and width of
proscenium, 14ft x 26ft; Shape of proscenium arch,
rectangular; Distance from edge of stage to back wall of
stage, 20ft; Distance between side walls of stage, 41ft;
Depth under stage, 4ft; Stage floor, flat; Trap doors, 1;
Scenery storage rooms, 1; Dressing rooms, 3 (upstairs,
stage right)
DIMENSIONS OF AUDITORIUM: Distance between side walls
of auditorium, 40ft 6in; Distance stage to back wall of
auditorium, 45ft; Orchestra pit, none
SEATING (1 level): 1st level, 500
SHAPE OF THE AUDITORIUM: Square
MAJOR TYPES OF ENTERTAINMENT: Drama, vaudeville, opera
MAJOR STARS WHO APPEARED AT THEATRE: The Crow Sisters,
Blind Boone, John Thomas, C. Tubs (1897), Hayl Adams
(July 14, 1898), Ella Gladman (September 1898), Ed
Landon, Georgia Troubadors (August 1910), Gay's
Entertainers (January 1915)

Bloomington, IL

CHATTERTON OPERA HOUSE (other name: Illini Theatre),
106-114 East Market
OPENING DATE: 1910   OPENING SHOW: Madame Sherry
ARCHITECTS: George Miller   STYLE OF ARCHITECTURE:
Neo-Classical   FACADE: Masonry, white
TYPE OF THEATRE: (a)   DEGREE OF RESTORATION: (c)
CLOSING DATE: 1933   CURRENT USE: Advertising firm
MAJOR TYPES OF ENTERTAINMENT: Drama, vaudeville

MAJOR STARS WHO APPEARED AT THEATRE: Harry Lauder, Lionel
  Barrymore, Ethel Barrymore, Maude Adams, John Phillip
  Sousa

Camp Point, IL

BAILEY OPERA HOUSE (other name: Camp Point Theatre),
  State Street
OPENING DATE: 1893
STYLE OF ARCHITECTURE: Victorian   TYPE OF BUILDING:
  Commercial   FACADE: Brick   TYPE OF THEATRE: (b)
DEGREE OF RESTORATION: (b)   CLOSING DATE: 1930S
CURRENT USE: Business
LOCATION OF AUDITORIUM: Second floor
STAGE DIMENSIONS AND EQUIPMENT: Height amd width of
  proscenium, 11ft 2 in x 20ft 6in; Shape of proscenium
  arch, rectangular; Distance from edge of stage to back
  wall of stage, 21ft 6in; Distance from edge of stage to
  curtain line, 17ft; Distance between side walls of stage,
  29ft 5in; Depth under stage, 4ft; Stage floor, raked;
  Trap doors, 1; Dressing rooms, 2; Scenery storage rooms,
  none
DIMENSIONS OF AUDITORIUM: Distance between side walls
  of auditorium, 45ft 8in; Distance stage to back wall of
  auditorium, 55ft 6in
SEATING (1 level): 1st level, 400
SHAPE OF THE AUDITORIUM: Rectangular
MAJOR TYPES OF ENTERTAINMENT: Drama, concerts, musicals,
  recitals, medicine shows, operettas, movies

Chicago, IL

AUDITORIUM THEATRE, 70 East Congress Parkway
OPENING DATE: December 10, 1899
OPENING SHOW: Concert, Adelina Patti
ARCHITECTS: Dankmar Adler and Louis Sullivan
TYPE OF BUILDING: Hotel (theatre in center)
FACADE: Grey stone   TYPE OF THEATRE: (b)
DEGREE OF RESTORATION: (a)   CURRENT USE: Concert hall
PERFORMANCE SPACES IN BUILDING: 3   NAME OF AUDITORIUM:
  Auditorium   LOCATION OF AUDITORIUM: Ground floor
STAGE DIMENSIONS AND EQUIPMENT: Height and width of
  proscenium, 40ft x 75ft 3in; Shape of proscenium arch,
  arched; Distance from edge of stage to back wall of
  stage, 65ft, Distance from edge of stage to curtain line,
  3ft; Distance between side walls of stage, 97ft 3in;
  Depth under stage, 17ft 6in; Stage floor, flat; Trap
  doors, 1; Dressing rooms, 20 (stage right)
DIMENSIONS OF AUDITORIUM: Distance between side walls
  of auditorium, 99ft; Distance stage to back wall of
  auditorium, 165ft; Capacity of orchestra pit, 110
SEATING (7 levels): 1st level, 1427; 2nd level, 586; 3rd
  level, 486; 4th level, 363; 5th level, 514; boxes, 234

SHAPE OF THE AUDITORIUM: Trapezoid
MAJOR TYPES OF ENTERTAINMENT: Opera, drama, concerts,
   recitals, dance
MAJOR STARS WHO APPEARED AT THEATRE: Patti, Mary Garden,
   Marian Anderson, Sembrich, Caruso, Paderewski, Pavlova,
   Melba, Calbe, Tetrazzini, Toscanini, Prokofiev,
   Rachmaninoff, Rimski-Korsakov, Massine, John Phillip
   Sousa, Heifetz, Otis Skinner, Menuhin, Rubinstein,
   Piatigorsky, Laurence Olivier, Pavarotti, Leontyne
   Price, and others
ADDITIONAL INFORMATION: Internationally acclaimed for
   its acoustics, the theatre was called "the greatest
   room for music and opera in the world bar none..." by
   Frank Lloyd Wright who worked on the construction of
   the theatre as a draftsman. During the depression, the
   theatre, which was without a resident company, fell into
   disrepair and was in danger of being razed. In the 1960s,
   the theatre was "rescued" and a massive restoration
   project was undertaken.

Chicago, IL

BLACKSTONE THEATRE, 60 East Balbo
   OPENING DATE: December 24, 1910
   ARCHITECTS: Marshall and Fox   STYLE OF ARCHITECTURE:
   French Renaissance   FACADE: Gray sandstone
   TYPE OF THEATRE: (a)   DEGREE OF RESTORATION: (d)
   CURRENT USE: Legitimate theatre
   STAGE DIMENSIONS AND EQUIPMENT: Height and width of
   proscenium, 36ft x 37ft; Shape of proscenium arch,
   rectangular; Distance from edge of stage to back wall of
   stage, 34ft; Distance from edge of stage to curtain line,
   3ft 9in; Distance between side walls of stage, 70ft 6in;
   Distance from stage floor to fly loft, 34ft; Stage floor,
   flat; Trap doors, 1; Scenery storage rooms, 1 (basement);
   Dressing rooms, 16 (stage right)
   DIMENSIONS OF AUDITORIUM: Capacity of orchestra pit, 20
   SEATING (3 levels): 1st level, 660; 2nd level, 383; 3rd
   level, 365; boxes, 16
   SHAPE OF THE AUDITORIUM: Rectangular
   MAJOR TYPES OF ENTERTAINMENT: Drama, musical comedy,
   vaudeville
   MAJOR STARS WHO APPEARED AT THEATRE: Hume Cronyn,
   Jessica Tandy, Patricia Collinge, Henry Miller, Blanche
   Bates, Margalo Gilmore, James Earl Jones, Anne Jackson,
   Eli Wallach, Maggie Smith, Lillian Gish, and others

Chicago, IL

FINE ARTS THEATRES, 418 South Michigan Avenue
   OPENING DATE: September 29, 1898   OPENING SHOW: Concert
   by Fannie Bloomfield-Zeisler
   ARCHITECTS: Solon S. Beman   STYLE OF ARCHITECTURE:
   Romanesque   TYPE OF BUILDING: Office building

TYPE OF THEATRE): (a)   DECREE OF RESTORATION: (d)
CURRENT USE: Movie theatre
PERFORMANCE SPACES IN BUILDING: 2 (Studebaker Theatre,
   World Playhouse)

1. Studebaker Theatre, Ground floor
STAGE DIMENSIONS AND EQUIPMENT: * Height and width of
   proscenium, 28ft x 36ft; Shape of proscenium arch,
   rectangular; Distance from edge of stage to back wall
   of stage, 37ft
SEATING (3 levels): 1st level, 712; 2nd level, 406; 3rd
   level, 299; boxes, 132
MAJOR TYPES OF ENTERTAINMENT: Drama, musical comedy, opera,
   vaudeville, movies, concerts, television, revue
MAJOR STARS WHO APPEARED AT THEATRE: Henrietta Crosman,
   Dustin Farnum, Bernhardt, Marjorie Rambeau, Fay Bainter,
   George Arliss, Walker Whiteside, Otis Skinner, De Wolf
   Hopper, Cornelia Otis Skinner, Ethel Barrymore, Fred
   Stone, Tallulah Bankhead, Katherine Dunham, Mae West, and
   others
ADDITIONAL INFORMATION: The Studebaker Building was erected
   in 1886 for use as a carriage showroom and factory. In
   1898, it was converted into the Fine Arts Building and
   was used to house artists, musicians and various artistic
   organizations. The Studebaker theatre opened as the
   Studebaker Music Hall, being converted to dramatic uses
   shortly thereafter. It was in this theatre that Chicago
   playwright George Ade produced plays that helped
   establish his career. The theatre was converted to a
   movie house in 1915, but was reopened as a legitimate
   theatre in November of 1917. During the 1920s, the
   theatre was remodeled again and many of its original
   Victorian features (with the exception of the ceiling)
   were obliterated.

2. World Playhouse, Ground floor
SEATING (2 levels)
MAJOR TYPES OF ENTERTAINMENT: Concerts, movies
ADDITIONAL INFORMATION: In 1980, the long-dark playhouse, which was used for chamber music concerts and
   recitals during the 1930s and 1940s, reopened as a
   concert hall. Today, the hall remains open as a movie
   theatre.

Chicago, IL

ORCHESTRA HALL (other names: Theodore Thomas Orchestra Hall,
   Chicago Symphony Hall), 220 South Michigan Avenue
OPENING DATE: December 14, 1904   OPENING SHOW: Concert
ARCHITECTS: Daniel Burnham   STYLE OF ARCHITECTURE:
   Georgian   TYPE OF BUILDING: Offices   FACADE: Red brick,
   grey limestone, terra cotta   TYPE OF THEATRE: (a)
DEGREE OF RESTORATION: (a)   CURRENT USE: Concert Hall
LOCATION OF AUDITORIUM: Ground floor

STAGE DIMENSIONS AND EQUIPMENT: Height and width of
proscenium, 50ft x 88ft; Shape of proscenium arch,
arched; Distance from edge of stage to back wall of
stage, 40ft; Depth under stage, 14ft; Stage floor, flat;
Trap doors, 1; Scenery storage rooms (under stage and
front of orchestra); Dressing rooms, 7 (basement: 5
private, 2 group)
DIMENSIONS OF AUDITORIUM: Orchestra pit, none
SEATING: 1st level, 1009; 2nd level, 931; 3rd level,
496; boxes, 138
SHAPE OF THE AUDITORIUM: Modified U-shape
MAJOR TYPES OF ENTERTAINMENT: Classical symphony concerts

Chicago, IL

SHUBERT THEATRE (other name: Majestic), 22 West Monroe
OPENING DATE: January 1, 1906
OPENING SHOW: Vaudeville bill
ARCHITECT: E. R. Krause   TYPE OF BUILDING: Office building
TYPE OF THEATRE: (a)   DEGREE OF RESTORATION: (d)
CURRENT USE: Legitimate theatre PERFORMANCE SPACES IN
BUILDING: 1   LOCATION OF AUDITORIUM: Ground floor
STAGE DIMENSIONS AND EQUIPMENT: Height and width of
proscenium, 36ft x 35ft 9in; Shape of proscenium arch,
rectangular; Distance from edge of stage to back wall of
stage, 34ft 2in; Distance from edge of stage to curtain
line, 5ft 4in; Distance between side walls of stage,
76ft; Distance from stage floor to fly loft, 28ft 8in;
Stage floor, flat; Trap doors, 0; Scenery storage rooms,
0; Dressing rooms, 13 (below stage and auditorium)
DIMENSIONS OF AUDITORIUM: Capacity of orchestra pit, 25
SEATING (4 levels): 1st level, 798; 2nd level, 295; 3rd
level, 498; 4th level, 395; boxes, 24
SHAPE OF THE AUDITORIUM: Rectangular
MAJOR TYPES OF ENTERTAINMENT: Drama, musical comedy,
vaudeville, burlesque
MAJOR STARS WHO APPEARED AT THEATRE, Eddie Foy, Houdini,
The Cohans, Lillie Langtry, Mabel McKinley, Rose Coghlan,
and others
ADDITIONAL INFORMATION: When the Majestic opened in 1906,
it was operated as a first-class vaudeville theatre
offering a bill of 12 to 15 acts running continuously
from 1:30 PM to 10:30 PM. The theatre became part of
the Orpheum circuit in the 1920s and quickly became one
of the circuit's most successful theatres. In 1945, the
theatre was purchased by the Shuberts and re-named the
Shubert in memory of Sam Shubert.

Danville, IL

FISCHER THEATER (other name: Grand Opera House), Southeast
corner, Vermilion and Harrison Streets
OPENING DATE: November 1884
OPENING SHOW: The Bohemian Girl

TYPE OF THEATRE: (a)   CURRENT USE: Vacant
LOCATION OF AUDITORIUM: First floor
STAGE DIMENSIONS AND EQUIPMENT: * Height and width of
  proscenium, 32ft x 31ft 6in; Shape of proscenium arch,
  square; Distance from edge of stage to back wall of
  stage, 40ft; Distance from edge of stage to curtain line,
  3ft 6in; Distance between side walls of stage, 62ft;
  Depth under stage, 10ft; Trap doors, 2; Scenery storage
  rooms, 1
SEATING (4 levels)
MAJOR TYPES OF ENTERTAINMENT: Drama, burlesque, opera
MAJOR STARS WHO APPEARED AT THEATRE: Lillian Russell (1885)
ADDITIONAL INFORMATION: The building was extensively
  remodeled in 1929.

Ellisville, IL

ELLISVILLE OLD OPERA HOUSE (other name: I.O.O.F. Lodge),
    Main and Mechanic
  OPENING DATE: 1891
  TYPE OF BUILDING: Commercial
  FACADE: Red brick, white wood trim   TYPE OF THEATRE: (b)
  DEGREE OF RESTORATION: (d)   CURRENT USE: Theatre
  LOCATION OF AUDITORIUM: Second floor
  STAGE DIMENSIONS AND EQUIPMENT: Shape of proscenium arch,
    square; Distance from edge of stage to back wall of
    stage, 13ft 6in; Distance from edge of stage to curtain
    line, 1ft 8in; Distance between side walls of stage, 2ft
    3in; Depth under stage, 12ft; Stage floor, flat; Trap
    doors, 1; Dressing rooms, 2 (side of stage)
  DIMENSIONS OF AUDITORIUM: Distance between side walls,
    of auditorium, 41ft 4in; Orchestra pit, none
  SEATING (1 level): 1st level, 120
  MAJOR TYPES OF ENTERTAINMENT: Drama, vaudeville

Elsah, IL

FARLEY'S MUSIC HALL (other names: Methodist Recreation Hall,
    Elsah Emporium, Knights of Pythias Hall), 41 Mill Street
  OPENING DATE: June 18, 1885
  TYPE OF BUILDING: Meeting hall   FACADE: Painted wood
  TYPE OF THEATRE: (b)   DEGREE OF RESTORATION: (b)
  CURRENT USE: Public meeting hall
  LOCATION OF AUDITORIUM: Second floor
  SEATING (1 level)
  MAJOR TYPES OF ENTERTAINMENT: Drama, poetry readings,
    medicine shows
  ADDITIONAL INFORMATION: The second floor of the building
    was added by the Knights of Pythias who used it as their
    meeting room.

Freeport, IL

GERMANIA (other name: Turner Hall), Main Street
  OPENING DATE: 1869
  TYPE OF BUILDING: Club   TYPE OF THEATRE: (b)
  DEGREE OF RESTORATION: (d)   CURRENT USE: Club
  MAJOR TYPES OF ENTERTAINMENT: Drama, minstrel shows,
    vaudeville

Galena, IL

TURNER HALL, 105 South Bench Street
  OPENING DATE: c. 1857
  STYLE OF ARCHITECTURE: Romanesque Revival
  TYPE OF BUILDING: Public building
  FACADE: Limestone   CURRENT USE: Public building
  STAGE DIMENSIONS AND EQUIPMENT: Height and width of
    proscenium, 22ft x 24ft; Distance from edge of stage to
    back wall of stage, 30ft; Distance from edge of stage to
    curtain line, 2ft 6in: Stage floor, flat; Trap doors, 3;
    Scenery storage rooms (along side of auditorium, behind a
    wall)
  SEATING (2 levels)
  MAJOR TYPES OF ENTERTAINMENT: Drama, lectures
  MAJOR STARS WHO APPEARED AT THEATRE: Tom Thumb
    (1877), U.S. Grant (1880), Theodore Roosevelt (1900)
  ADDITIONAL INFORMATION: According to the Galena Gazette,
    November 23, 1857, "The building was erected to supply a
    want long felt in Galena, and [was] designed for the
    special use of the citizens of this city, without
    regard to politics, religion or nationality, as well
    as for entertainments of a respectable character."The
    interior of the building was totally destroyed by fire
    in 1926 and subsequently rebuilt.

LeRoy, IL

LEROY OPERA HOUSE, Center Street
  OPENING DATE: 1892
  STYLE OF ARCHITECTURE: Victorian   TYPE OF BUILDING:
    Commercial   FACADE: Red brick   TYPE OF THEATRE: (b)
  DEGREE OF RESTORATION: (c)   CURRENT USE: Storage
  LOCATION OF AUDITORIUM: Second floor
  MAJOR TYPES OF ENTERTAINMENT: Drama, vaudeville, concerts,
    lectures, dances

Marengo, IL

OPERA HOUSE (other name: Community Building), State Street
    north of Washington
  OPENING DATE: April 1883
  FACADE: Yellow brick   TYPE OF THEATRE: (b)
  DEGREE OF RESTORATION: (c)   CLOSING DATE: 1916

CURRENT USE: Bank   LOCATION OF AUDITORIUM: 2nd & 3rd
   floors
STAGE DIMENSIONS AND EQUIPMENT: * Height and width of
   proscenium, 20ft x 25ft; Distance from edge of stage
   to back wall of stage, 25ft; Distance from edge of stage
   to curtain line, 5ft; Distance between side walls of
   stage, 50ft; Depth under stage, 5ft; Trap doors, 2
MAJOR TYPES OF ENTERTAINMENT: Drama, concerts, lectures,
   opera

Normal, IL

COPEN AUDITORIUM, Illinois State University Campus
   OPENING DATE: 1909   OPENING SHOW: College debate
   STYLE OF ARCHITECTURE: Neo-Classical
   TYPE OF BUILDING: Classrooms   FACADE: Red brick
   TYPE OF THEATRE: (b)   DEGREE OF RESTORATION: (d)
   CURRENT USE: Lectures and movies
   LOCATION OF AUDITORIUM: Second and third floors
   SHAPE OF THE AUDITORIUM: Elipse
   MAJOR TYPES OF ENTERTAINMENT: Drama, concerts, lectures

Palestine, IL

OPERA HOUSE
   OPENING DATE: September 18, 1901
   OPENING SHOW: They Want Me
   ARCHITECT: John W. Ranson
   TYPE OF BUILDING: Furniture store   FACADE: White brick
   TYPE OF THEATRE: (a)   CLOSING DATE: 1908
   CURRENT USE: Storage   LOCATION OF AUDITORIUM: Second floor
   STAGE DIMENSIONS AND EQUIPMENT: Height and width of
      proscenium, 15ft x 25ft; Stage floor, raked; Scenery
      storage rooms (basement, reached by elevator); Dressing
      rooms, 4 (both sides of stage)
   DIMENSIONS OF AUDITORIUM: Orchestra pit, yes
   SEATING (1 level)
   SHAPE OF THE AUDITORIUM: U-shaped
   MAJOR TYPES OF ENTERTAINMENT: Drama, musical comedy

Princeton, IL

APOLLO TWIN CINEMAS (other name: Apollo Opera House),
   455 South Main Street
   TYPE OF THEATRE: (a)   CURRENT USE: Movie theatre
   LOCATION OF AUDITORIUM: Ground floor
   STAGE DIMENSIONS AND EQUIPMENT: * Height and width of
      proscenium, 26ft x 18ft; Distance from edge of stage to
      back wall of stage, 34ft; Distance from edge of stage to
      curtain line, 2ft 6in; Distance between side walls of
      stage, 60ft
   MAJOR TYPES OF ENTERTAINMENT: Drama, movies

Rochelle, IL

BAIN OPERA HOUSE, 300 Block, Lincoln Highway
OPENING DATE: July 4, 1878
OPENING SHOW: Madrigal Club from Chicago
ARCHITECT: Angus Bain   TYPE OF BUILDING: Commercial
FACADE: Red brick   TYPE OF THEATRE: (b)
DEGREE OF RESTORATION: (c)   CURRENT USE: Vacant
LOCATION OF AUDITORIUM: Second and third floors
STAGE DIMENSIONS AND EQUIPMENT: * Height and width of
  proscenium, 23ft x 23ft; Shape of proscenium
  arch, square; Distance from edge of stage to back wall
  of stage, 26ft; Distance from edge of stage to curtain
  line. 5ft 6in; Distance between side walls of stage,
  30ft; Depth under stage, 3ft; Trap doors, 1
SEATING (2 levels)
SHAPE OF THE AUDITORIUM: Horseshoe-shaped
MAJOR TYPES OF ENTERTAINMENT: Drama, musical comedy
MAJOR STARS WHO APPEARED AT THEATRE: Charley Winninger
ADDITIONAL INFORMATION: The opera house is in danger of
  being demolished.

Rushville, IL

PHOENIX OPERA HOUSE, South Side Square
OPENING DATE: December 3, 1882
OPENING SHOW: "Blind" Boone, pianist
TYPE OF BUILDING: Commercial building   FACADE: Red brick
TYPE OF THEATRE: (b)   DEGREE OF RESTORATION: (b)
CLOSING DATE: 1910   CURRENT USE: Being restored
LOCATION OF AUDITORIUM: Second floor
STAGE DIMENSIONS AND EQUIPMENT: Width of proscenium, 20ft;
  Shape of proscenium arch, arched; Distance from edge of
  stage to back wall of stage, 20ft; Depth under stage,
  3ft; Stage floor, flat
DIMENSIONS OF AUDITORIUM: Distance between side walls
  of auditorium, 45ft; Distance stage to back wall of
  auditorium, 20ft; Orchestra pit, none
SEATING (1 level): 1st level, 500
SHAPE OF THE AUDITORIUM: Rectangular
MAJOR TYPES OF ENTERTAINMENT: Drama, vaudeville, burlesque,
  opera, lectures, dances, debates, and social functions
MAJOR STARS WHO APPEARED AT THEATRE: "Blind" Boone, Belva
  Lockwood (first woman to run for President)

Sesser, IL

SESSER OPERA HOUSE, 206 West Franklin Avenue
OPENING DATE: 1914
ARCHITECTS: James H. Hill, contractor
STYLE OF ARCHITECTURE: Mission Style
FACADE: Stucco and terra cotta   TYPE OF THEATRE: (a)
DEGREE OF RESTORATION: (b)   CURRENT USE: None

STAGE DIMENSIONS AND EQUIPMENT: Height and width of
    proscenium, 15ft 4in x 21ft; Shape of proscenium arch,
    rectangular; Distance from edge of stage to back wall of
    stage,25ft 9in; Distance from edge of stage to curtain
    line, 2ft; Distance between side walls of stage, 37ft;
    Depth under stage, 7ft 6in; Stage floor, flat; Trap
    doors, 2; Scenery storage rooms, 1 (under stage);
    Dressing rooms, 4 (under stage)
DIMENSIONS OF AUDITORIUM: Distance between side walls of
    auditorium, 37ft 11in; Distance stage to back wall, 25ft
    9in; Capacity of orchestra pit, 10
SEATING (1 level): 1st level, 500
SHAPE OF THE AUDITORIUM: Rectangular
MAJOR TYPES OF ENTERTAINMENT: Drama, vaudeville, movies,
    local variety shows, concerts
MAJOR STARS WHO APPEARED AT THEATRE: Various stars from the
    Grand 'ole Opry
ADDITIONAL INFORMATION: According to recent clippings, much
    of the early projection equipment is still in place in
    the projection room.

Watseka, IL

BRADEN BROTHERS' OPERA HOUSE (other names: Stephens Brothers'
    Opera House, Crystal Theatre), Northwest corner, Walnut
    and 3rd Streets
OPENING DATE: December 18, 1884
OPENING SHOW: Variety program
TYPE OF BUILDING: Store   FACADE: Red brick with white
    brick trim   TYPE OF THEATRE: (b)
DEGREE OF RESTORATION: (c)   CURRENT USE: Storage
LOCATION OF AUDITORIUM: Second floor
STAGE DIMENSIONS AND EQUIPMENT: * Height and width of
    proscenium, 40ft x 19ft; Distance from edge of stage to
    back wall of stage, 26ft; Distance from edge of stage to
    curtain line, 3ft; Distance between side walls of stage,
    50ft; Depth under stage, 4ft; Trap doors, 1
DIMENSIONS OF AUDITORIUM: Orchestra pit, none
SEATING (2 levels)
SHAPE OF THE AUDITORIUM: Rectangular
MAJOR TYPES OF ENTERTAINMENT: Drama, minstrel shows,
    dances, lectures, social events
MAJOR STARS WHO APPEARED AT THEATRE: W. C. Handy, Maharas
    Minstrels (1903), William Jennings Bryan (1904), Carrie
    Nation (1905), Samuel S. McClure (1910), Dr. Frederick A.
    Cook, explorer (1911), Opie Reed (1910), "Blind" Boone,
    pianist
ADDITIONAL INFORMATION: When the opera house opened, 700
    people could be seated in temporary seating on the main
    floor and gallery. Later, with the installation of opera
    chairs, the capacity was reduced to 600.

West Chicago, IL

BOLLES OPERA HOUSE, 185 West Washington
  OPENING DATE: November 27, 1894
  OPENING SHOW: Concert by Chicago Rival Company
  ARCHITECTS: Frank Thompson   TYPE OF BUILDING: Commercial
  FACADE: Brick and stone
  TYPE OF THEATRE: (b)   DEGREE OF RESTORATION: (c)

Woodstock, IL

WOODSTOCK OPERA HOUSE (other names: Woodstock City Hall and
      Opera House), 121 Van Buran Street
  OPENING DATE: September 2, 1889
  OPENING SHOW: Patti Rosa Players
  ARCHITECTS: Smith Hoag   STYLE OF ARCHITECTURE: Romanesque
  FACADE: Masonry, terra cotta and sandstone   TYPE OF
  THEATRE: (b)   DEGREE OF RESTORATION: (a)   CURRENT USE:
    Arts center   PERFORMANCE SPACES IN BUILDING: 1
  LOCATION OF AUDITORIUM: Second and third floors
  STAGE DIMENSIONS AND EQUIPMENT: Height and width of
    proscenium, 15ft 2in x 24ft; Shape of proscenium arch,
    rectangular; Distance from edge of stage to back wall of
    stage, 26ft; Distance from edge of stage to curtain line,
    8ft; Distance between side walls of stage, 36ft; Stage
    floor, flat; Trap doors, 2; Scenery storage rooms,
    3 (basement); Dressing rooms, 3 (below stage level)
  DIMENSIONS OF AUDITORIUM: Distance between side walls
    of auditorium, 49ft; Distance stage to back wall, 57ft;
    Orchestra pit, none
  SEATING (2 levels): 1st level, 216; 2nd level, 213
  SHAPE OF THE AUDITORIUM: Horseshoe-shaped
  MAJOR TYPES OF ENTERTAINMENT: Drama, vaudeville, burlesque,
    opera
  MAJOR STARS WHO APPEARED AT THEATRE: Orson Welles (1934-
    35), Paul Newman, Tom Bosley, Shelley Berman, Geraldine
    Page, Betsy Palmer, Lois Nettleton (members of a local
    company between 1949-1951)

Indiana

Bristol, IN

BRISTOL OPERA HOUSE (other name: Mosier Opera House),
   210 East Vistula
   OPENING DATE: 1897   OPENING SHOW: H.M.S. Pinafore
   TYPE OF BUILDING: Post office, barber shop
   FACADE: Clapboard, blue with white trim   TYPE OF THEATRE:
   (a)   DEGREE OF RESTORATION: (a)   CURRENT USE: Theatre
   LOCATION OF AUDITORIUM: Ground floor
   STAGE DIMENSIONS AND EQUIPMENT: Height and width of
   proscenium, 13ft 3in x 17ft 2in; Shape of proscenium
   arch, rectangular; Distance from edge of stage to back
   wall of stage, 28ft; Distance from edge of stage to
   curtain line, 9ft 2in; Distance between side walls of
   stage, 3ft; Depth under stage, 8ft; Stage floor, raked;
   Trap doors, 1; Scenery storage rooms, 1 (rear of Post
   Office area); Dressing rooms, 3 (A2 below stage; 1
   backstage)
   DIMENSIONS OF AUDITORIUM: Distance between side walls
   of auditorium, 30ft; Distance stage to back wall of
   auditorium, 55ft; Orchestra pit, yes
   SEATING (1 level): 1st level, 231
   SHAPE OF THE AUDITORIUM: Rectangular
   MAJOR TYPES OF ENTERTAINMENT: Drama, medicine shows, local
   variety shows
   ADDITIONAL INFORMATION: The theatre was originally equipped
   with a "full set of roll drops and sliding shutter wings"
   This included a formal garden, formal room, rustic
   interior, jail, and wooded scenes.

Columbus, IN

CRUMPS THEATRE
   OPENING DATE: Pre-1910   TYPE OF THEATRE: (a)
   DEGREE OF RESTORATION: (d)   CURRENT USE: Movie theatre
   LOCATION OF AUDITORIUM: Ground floor
   STAGE DIMENSIONS AND EQUIPMENT: Height and width of

proscenium, 28ft x 28ft; Distance from edge of stage to
back wall of stage, 30ft; Distance from edge of stage to
curtain line, 3ft; Distance between side walls of stage,
60ft; Depth under stage, 9ft; Trap doors, 3
MAJOR TYPES OF ENTERTAINMENT: Drama, movies

Goshen, IN

GOSHEN (other name: Jefferson), 216 South Main Street
OPENING DATE: Pre-1910   TYPE OF THEATRE: (a)
DEGREE OF RESTORATION: (d)   CURRENT USE: Movie theatre
LOCATION OF AUDITORIUM: Ground floor
STAGE DIMENSIONS AND EQUIPMENT: Height and width of
proscenium, 37ft x 37ft 6in; Distance from edge of stage
to back wall of stage, 42ft 3in; Distance from edge of
stage to curtain line, 3ft 3in; Distance between side
walls of stage, 64ft; Distance from stage floor to fly
loft, 25ft 6in; Depth under stage, 8ft; Trap doors, 1
SEATING: 1st level, 485; 2nd level, 305; 3rd level, 300;
boxes, 24
MAJOR TYPES OF ENTERTAINMENT: Drama, movies

Greensburg, IN

KNIGHTS OF PYTHIAS THEATRE, 211 North Broadway
OPENING DATE: 1906
FACADE: Red brick   DEGREE OF RESTORATION: (c)
CLOSING DATE: 1954   CURRENT USE: Vacant
STAGE DIMENSIONS AND EQUIPMENT: Height and width of
proscenium, 20ft 4in x 36ft 2in; Shape of proscenium
arch, arched; Distance from edge of stage to back wall of
stage, 21ft 6in; Distance from edge of stage to curtain
line, 5ft; Distance between side walls of stage, 36ft
2in; Depth under stage, 10ft 6in; Stage floor, flat;
Trap doors, 4; Scenery storage rooms, 4 (side of stage);
Dressing rooms, 5
DIMENSIONS OF AUDITORIUM: Distance between side walls
of auditorium, 66ft; Distance stage to back wall of
auditorium, 41ft 5in; Capacity of orchestra pit, 20
SEATING (3 levels): 1st level, 345; 2nd level, 300;
3rd level, 100
SHAPE OF THE AUDITORIUM: U-shaped
MAJOR TYPES OF ENTERTAINMENT: Drama, vaudeville, opera

Huntington, IN

HUNTINGTON, 534 North Jefferson
OPENING DATE: c. 1910
DEGREE OF RESTORATION: (d)   CURRENT USE: Movie theatre
LOCATION OF AUDITORIUM: Ground floor
STAGE DIMENSIONS AND EQUIPMENT: Height and width of
proscenium, 28ft x 36ft 9in; Distance from edge of stage
to back wall of stage, 38ft 6in; Distance from edge of

stage to curtain line, 3ft; Distance between side walls
of stage, 60ft; Distance from stage floor to fly loft,
24ft; Depth under stage, 8ft; Trap doors, 2
ADDITIONAL INFORMATION: The theatre has been remodeled many
times. Seating capacities varied: 1,100 in 1910; 900 in
1921; and 669 from 1974-78.

Indianapolis, IN

MURAT THEATRE (other names: Murat Shrine, Shubert-Murat
Theatre), 502 North Jersey
OPENING DATE: February 28, 1910   OPENING SHOW: Havana
ARCHITECTS: D. A. Bohlen and Son   TYPE OF BUILDING:
Masonic Shriner hall   FACADE: Cream and gray brick
with terracotta   TYPE OF THEATRE: (b)   DEGREE OF
RESTORATION: (c)   CURRENT USE: Theatre
STAGE DIMENSIONS AND EQUIPMENT: Height and width of
proscenium, 30ft x 40ft; Distance from edge of stage
to back wall of stage, 43ft 6in; Distance between side
walls of stage, 92ft
SEATING (2 levels): 1st level, 1180; 2nd level, 676;
boxes, 144
MAJOR TYPES OF ENTERTAINMENT: Drama, musical comedy, opera,
dance, circus, concerts, lectures, civic functions
MAJOR STARS WHO APPEARED AT THEATRE: James T. Powers,
Robert Mantell, William Faversham, John Drew, Marie
Dressler, Ellen Terry, E. H. Sothern, Julia Marlowe, Al
Jolson, Eddie Cantor, Eva Le Gallienne, Lionel Barrymore,
Fanny Brice, Nazimova, the Marx Brothers, Ruth St.Denis,
Eddie Foy, Eva Tanguay, George Arliss, Ed Wynn, Harry
Lauder, Ruth Gordon, Blanche Yurka, Dudley Digges, Peggy
Wood, Will Geer, Fay Bainter, and others
ADDITIONAL INFORMATION: From 1910 to 1930 the theatre was
part of the Shubert chain. The theatre was the home of
the Indianapolis Symphony from 1933 to 1963 and for years
it housed the annual Shrine Circus.

Lebanon, IN

GRAND OPERA HOUSE, 216 1/2 West Main Street
OPENING DATE: Fall 1886
OPENING SHOW: The Burton Stock Company
TYPE OF BUILDING: Commercial   TYPE OF THEATRE: (b)
DEGREE OF RESTORATION: (c)   CLOSING DATE: 1918
CURRENT USE: Furniture store
LOCATION OF AUDITORIUM: Second floor
STAGE DIMENSIONS AND EQUIPMENT: Height and width of
proscenium, 30ft x 28ft; Distance from edge of stage to
back wall of stage, 58ft; Distance from edge of stage to
curtain line, 8ft; Distance between side walls of stage,
60ft; Depth under stage, 8ft
SHAPE OF THE AUDITORIUM: Horseshoe-shaped balcony
MAJOR TYPES OF ENTERTAINMENT: Drama, vaudeville, movies

ADDITIONAL INFORMATION: The balcony, boxes and stage are
   still intact despite a fire in June of 1980. The building
   was opened in 1885 as a skating rink and was converted to
   a theatre the following year.

Lewisville, IN

GUYER OPERA HOUSE, National Road US 40
   OPENING DATE: June 3, 1901
   OPENING SHOW: Holden Comedy Company
   STYLE OF ARCHITECTURE: Edwardian   TYPE OF BUILDING: Bank,
   store   FACADE: Brick and cast iron; aqua, ivory and gray
   TYPE OF THEATRE: (b)   DEGREE OF RESTORATION: (b)
   CLOSING DATE: 1942   CURRENT USE: Recitals, exhibits,
   receptions   LOCATION OF AUDITORIUM: Second floor
   STAGE DIMENSIONS AND EQUIPMENT: Height and width of
   proscenium, 16ft x 20ft; Shape of proscenium arch,
   rectangular; Distance from edge of stage to back wall of
   stage, 23ft; Distance from edge of stage to curtain line,
   3ft 1in; Distance between side walls of stage, 40ft;
   Depth under stage, 8ft; Stage floor, flat; Trap doors, 1;
   Dressing rooms, 5 (under stage)
   DIMENSIONS OF AUDITORIUM: Distance between side walls
   of auditorium, 42ft; Distance stage to back wall of
   auditorium, 54ft; Orchestra pit, none
   SEATING (1 level): 1st level, 150
   SHAPE OF THE AUDITORIUM: Slight U-shape
   MAJOR TYPES OF ENTERTAINMENT: Drama, vaudeville, medicine
   shows, local variety shows
   MAJOR STARS WHO APPEARED AT THEATRE: The Hoosier Sisters

Marion, IN

VETERANS ADMINISTRATION MEDICAL CENTER THEATRE (other name:
   Colonel Daniel Stinson Memorial Theatre), East 38th
   Street
   OPENING DATE: 1891   TYPE OF BUILDING: Clinic
   FACADE: Red brick with white wood trim
   TYPE OF THEATRE: (b)   DEGREE OF RESTORATION: (a)
   CURRENT USE: Theatre   LOCATION OF AUDITORIUM: Ground floor
   DIMENSIONS OF AUDITORIUM: Capacity of orchestra pit, 40
   SEATING (2 levels): 1st level, 110; 2nd level, 30
   SHAPE OF THE AUDITORIUM: U-shaped
   MAJOR TYPES OF ENTERTAINMENT: Drama, musical comedy,
   movies, patient variety shows

Mitchell, IN

OPERA HOUSE (other name: County Hall), 7th and Brook Streets
   OPENING DATE: 1906   OPENING SHOW: Flirtation
   ARCHITECT: Mr. Pritchard, Loogootee, IN   FACADE: Red brick
   TYPE OF THEATRE: (a)   DEGREE OF RESTORATION: (a)
   CURRENT USE: Theatre   LOCATION OF AUDITORIUM: Ground floor

STAGE DIMENSIONS AND EQUIPMENT: Height and width of
   proscenium, 15ft 5in x 25ft; Shape of proscenium arch,
   rectangular; Distance from edge of stage to back wall of
   stage, 25ft; Distance from edge of stage to curtain line,
   10ft; Distance between side walls of stage, 50ft;
   Distance from stage floor to fly loft, 15ft 5in; Stage
   floor, flat; Dressing rooms, 4 (2 each side of stage)
DIMENSIONS OF AUDITORIUM: Distance between side walls of
   auditorium, 50ft; Orchestra pit, none
SEATING (2 levels): 1st level, 301; 2nd level, 89
SHAPE OF THE AUDITORIUM: U-shaped
MAJOR TYPES OF ENTERTAINMENT: Drama, musical comedy,
   vaudeville
MAJOR STARS WHO APPEARED AT THEATRE: Theodore Shaler, The
   Great Blackstone, Norma Talmadge, John Phillip Sousa,
   various stars on the Keith circuit

New Albany, IN

MAENNERCHOR HALLE (other names: Beer Hall, Maennerchor
   Society Hall), 316 East Spring Street
OPENING DATE: September 3, 1891   OPENING SHOW: Concert
STYLE OF ARCHITECTURE: Italianate   TYPE OF BUILDING:
   Club house   FACADE: Brick   TYPE OF THEATRE: (b)
DEGREE OF RESTORATION: (c)   CLOSING DATE: 1919
CURRENT USE: Auto parts dealership
LOCATION OF AUDITORIUM: Second floor
MAJOR TYPES OF ENTERTAINMENT: Drama, concerts, lectures

New Albany, IN

OPERA HOUSE (other names: Music Hall, Lyceum Theater),
   Northeast corner of Pearl and Spring Streets
OPENING DATE: November 26, 1866
OPENING SHOW: A Comedy of Fashion
ARCHITECTS: Stancliffe and Vodges, Louisville, KY
STYLE OF ARCHITECTURE: Italianate   TYPE OF BUILDING:
   Commercial   FACADE: Brick   TYPE OF THEATRE: (b)
DEGREE OF RESTORATION: (c)   CURRENT USE: Stores and
   offices   LOCATION OF AUDITORIUM: Third floor
STAGE DIMENSIONS AND EQUIPMENT: Height and width of
   proscenium, 34ft x 65ft; Dressing rooms, 10 (under
   stage)
DIMENSIONS OF AUDITORIUM: Distance between side walls
   of auditorium, 65ft; Distance stage to back wall of
   auditorium, 116ft
SHAPE OF THE AUDITORIUM: Rectangular
MAJOR TYPES OF ENTERTAINMENT: Drama, concerts, minstrel
   shows, opera, lectures
MAJOR STARS WHO APPEARED AT THEATRE: Fanny Janauschek,
   Alice Oats, Julia Dean, Nat Goodwin, Effie Johns, Tony
   Pastor, Victoria Woodhull, Buffalo Bill, Kate Claxton,
   Mrs. Tom Thumb, Sallie Partington, Georgia Minstrels,
ADDITIONAL INFORMATION: Drop curtain measures 28ft x

30 ft.   Seating was as follows: Parquette, 175; Dress
Circle, 640; Family Circle, 800.   There were also four
private boxes.   There may also have been a gallery.   In
1940, the third floor was removed and the building was
remodeled.

New Albany, IN

WOODWARD HALL, 130 West Main Street
  OPENING DATE: January 17, 1853
  OPENING SHOW: Readings by Professor Kennedy
  STYLE OF ARCHITECTURE: Italianate
  TYPE OF BUILDING: Stores, offices   FACADE: First floor,
    stone; upper floors, brick   TYPE OF THEATRE: (b)
  DEGREE OF RESTORATION: (c)   CLOSING DATE: 1887
  CURRENT USE: Vacant   LOCATION OF AUDITORIUM: Third floor
  DIMENSIONS OF AUDITORIUM: Distance between side walls
    of auditorium, 31ft; Distance stage to back wall of
    auditorium, 75ft
  SEATING (1 level)
  SHAPE OF THE AUDITORIUM: Rectangular
  MAJOR TYPES OF ENTERTAINMENT: Drama, concerts, minstrel
    shows, lectures, exhibits
  MAJOR STARS WHO APPEARED AT THEATRE: Louis M. Gottschalk,
    Madam Rosa DeVries, Riley Family, Oliver Wendell Holmes,
    William G. Dix, Madame Varian, Professor J. Tosso,
    Adelina Patti (at age 12), Blind Tom (pianist)
  ADDITIONAL INFORMATION: Woodward Hall was the first theatre
    in New Albany.   The building is presently being restored,
    but not as a theatre.

New Harmony, IN

THRALL'S OPERA HOUSE (other name: Union Hall), Church Street
  OPENING DATE: 1857   OPENING SHOW: Damon and Pythias
  FACADE: Red brick   TYPE OF THEATRE: (a)
  DEGREE OF RESTORATION: (a)   CURRENT USE: Historic site
  STAGE DIMENSIONS AND EQUIPMENT: Height and width of
    proscenium, 13ft 3in x 22ft; Shape of proscenium arch,
    arched; Distance from edge of stage to back wall of
    stage, 27ft; Distance from edge of stage to curtain line,
    6ft; Distance between side walls of stage, 41ft 10in;
    Distance from stage floor to fly loft, 10ft; Depth under
    stage, 7ft 3in; Stage floor, flat; Trap doors, 2;
    Scenery storage rooms, 1 (rear shop); Dressing rooms, 2
  SEATING (2 levels): 1st level, 200; 2nd level, 50
  SHAPE OF THE AUDITORIUM: Rectangular
  MAJOR TYPES OF ENTERTAINMENT: Drama, vaudeville, burlesque,
    opera
  ADDITIONAL INFORMATION: Thrall's Opera House is now part of
    the New Harmony Historic Site.   The building is used for
    theatrical performances, community events, a film series,
    the Posey County Quilt Show, a Christmas open house and a

Christmas ball. It is open daily as part of the State
Memorial tour.

Remington, IN

FOUNTAIN PARK TABERNACLE
  OPENING DATE: 1898
  FACADE: Wood   TYPE OF THEATRE: (a)
  DEGREE OF RESTORATION: (d)
  STAGE DIMENSIONS AND EQUIPMENT: Height and width of
    proscenium, 10ft x 12ft; Shape of proscenium arch,
    arched; Distance from edge of stage to back wall of
    stage, 20ft; Distance between side walls of stage, 65ft;
    Stage floor, flat; Dressing rooms, 1 (backstage)
  DIMENSIONS OF AUDITORIUM: Distance between side walls
    of auditorium, 55ft; Distance stage to back wall of
    auditorium, 65ft; Orchestra pit, none
  SEATING (1 level): 1st level, 600
  SHAPE OF THE AUDITORIUM: Rectangualr
  MAJOR TYPES OF ENTERTAINMENT: Drama, concerts
  MAJOR STARS WHO APPEARED AT THEATRE: Paul Harvey, William
    Jennings Bryan
  ADDITIONAL INFORMATION: The building is currently used by
    the Fountain Park Chautauqua.

Richmond , IN

MURRAY THEATRE (other names: Indiana Theatre, 1930-1960;
    Norbert Silbiger Theatre, 1960s-1984), 1003 East Main
    Street
  OPENING DATE: October 1909   OPENING SHOW: Vaudeville bill
  FACADE: Tan brick and dark brown wood trim
  TYPE OF THEATRE: (a)   DEGREE OF RESTORATION: (b)
  CURRENT USE: Theatre
  STAGE DIMENSIONS AND EQUIPMENT: Height and width of
    proscenium, 35ft x 29ft 6in; Shape of proscenium arch,
    arched; Distance from edge of stage to back wall of
    stage, 27ft 6in; Distance from edge of stage to curtain
    line, 3ft; Distance between side walls of stage, 57ft;
    Depth under stage, 9ft 6in; Stage floor, flat; Scenery
    storage rooms, 2 (front of basement); Dressing rooms,
    6 (under stage)
  DIMENSIONS OF AUDITORIUM: Capacity of orchestra pit, 20
  SEATING (3 levels): 1st level, 395; 2nd level, 120;
    3rd level, 90
  SHAPE OF THE AUDITORIUM: U-shaped
  MAJOR TYPES OF ENTERTAINMENT: Drama, vaudeville, movies
  MAJOR STARS WHO APPEARED AT THEATRE: Fanny Brice, the Marx
    Brothers, John Phillip Sousa, Bob Hope, Jack Benny
  ADDITIONAL INFORMATION: The theatre now houses the Richmond
    Civic Theatre.

Rockville, IN

RITZ THEATER (other name: Rockville Opera House), 216 West
    Ohio Street
OPENING DATE: October 15, 1912
OPENING SHOW: The Only Son
ARCHITECT: W. H. Ffloyd   STYLE OF ARCHITECTURE: Neo-
    Classic Revival   TYPE OF BUILDING: Retail businesses
FACADE: Buff brick   TYPE OF THEATRE: (a)   DEGREE OF
RESTORATION: (a)   CURRENT USE: Theatre
STAGE DIMENSIONS AND EQUIPMENT: Height of proscenium, 19ft;
    Shape of proscenium arch, rectangular; Distance between
    side walls of stage, 32ft; Stage floor, flat; Scenery
    storage rooms, 2 (both sides of stage); Dressing rooms,
    4 (2 each side of stage)
DIMENSIONS OF AUDITORIUM: Capacity of orchestra pit, 8
SEATING (1 level): 1st level, 456
SHAPE OF THE AUDITORIUM: Fan-shaped
MAJOR TYPES OF ENTERTAINMENT: Drama, vaudeville, movies
MAJOR STARS WHO APPEARED AT THEATRE: Eugenie Blair, Billy
    Clifford, George Sidney

Rockville, IN

ROCKVILLE OPERA HOUSE, Ohio and Jefferson Streets
OPENING DATE: June 9, 1883
OPENING SHOW: The Esmeralda Company
STYLE OF ARCHITECTURE: Gothic   FACADE: Red brick
TYPE OF THEATRE: (a)   DEGREE OF RESTORATION: (c)
CLOSING DATE: 1907   CURRENT USE: Masonic lodge
LOCATION OF AUDITORIUM: Ground floor
STAGE DIMENSIONS AND EQUIPMENT: Distance between side walls
    of stage, 24ft; Dressing rooms, 18
SEATING (2 levels)
MAJOR TYPES OF ENTERTAINMENT: Drama, musical comedy,
    minstrel shows, operetta
MAJOR STARS WHO APPEARED AT THEATRE: C. W. Couldock, Annie
    Russell, De Wolf Hopper, Mrs. Fiske, Anna Dickinson,
    Bella Moore, Madame Rhea, Alexander Salvini, Creston
    Clark, Walker Whiteside, E. H. Sothern, Clara Louise
    Kellogg, Frederick Bryson, Haverly's Mastadon Minstrels,
    E. R. Spencer, Gorman Bros. Minstrels, Gilmore's Band

Rushville, IN

MELODEON HALL, Second and Morgan Streets
OPENING DATE: 1880s
STYLE OF ARCHITECTURE: Victorian   TYPE OF BUILDING:
    Commercial   FACADE: Brick   TYPE OF THEATRE: (b)
DEGREE OF RESTORATION: (c)   CURRENT USE: Photography
    studio   LOCATION OF AUDITORIUM: Second floor
STAGE DIMENSIONS AND EQUIPMENT: Shape of proscenium arch,
    square; Stage floor, flat
DIMENSIONS OF AUDITORIUM: Orchestra pit, none

SEATING (1 level): 1st level, 200
SHAPE OF THE AUDITORIUM: Square
MAJOR TYPES OF ENTERTAINMENT: Drama, vaudeville, musical
  comedy, burlesque, public meetings
MAJOR STARS WHO APPEARED AT THEATRE: James Whitcomb Riley,
  Walker Whiteside

Shelbyville, IN

BLESSING'S OPERA HOUSE, Northeast corner of Public Square
OPENING DATE: December 27, 1869
OPENING SHOW: The Lady of Lyons
TYPE OF BUILDING: Storage, first floor
TYPE OF THEATRE: (b)   DEGREE OF RESTORATION: (c)
CLOSING DATE: 1906   CURRENT USE: Storage
LOCATION OF AUDITORIUM: Second floor
SEATING (1 level)
MAJOR TYPES OF ENTERTAINMENT: Drama
MAJOR STARS WHO APPEARED AT THEATRE: General Tom Thumb,
  Commodore Nutt, Minnie Warren, May Howard, James Whitcomb
  Riley

Sheridan, IN

SHERIDAN OPERA HOUSE, 204 North Main Street
OPENING DATE: 1886
STYLE OF ARCHITECTURE: Italianate   DEGREE OF
RESTORATION: (c)   CURRENT USE: Farm supply and feed store
LOCATION OF AUDITORIUM: Second floor
STAGE DIMENSIONS AND EQUIPMENT: Height and width of
  proscenium, 14ft x 20ft; Distance from edge of stage to
  back wall of stage, 24ft; Distance from edge of stage to
  curtain line, 3ft; Distance between side walls of stage,
  44ft
MAJOR TYPES OF ENTERTAINMENT: Drama, vaudeville, movies

Spencer, IN

SPENCER OPERA HOUSE
OPENING DATE: Pre-1910
TYPE OF BUILDING: Bar and dance hall   DEGREE OF
RESTORATION: (c)   CURRENT USE: VFW Bar and dance hall
LOCATION OF AUDITORIUM: Second floor
STAGE DIMENSIONS AND EQUIPMENT: Height and width of
  proscenium, 12ft x 18ft; Distance from edge of stage to
  back wall of stage, 20ft; Distance from edge of stage to
  curtain line, 4ft; Distance between side walls of stage,
  60ft; Trap doors, 2

Valparaiso, IN

OPERA HOUSE (other name: Memorial Opera House)
  OPENING DATE: 1898   TYPE OF THEATRE: (a)
  DEGREE OF RESTORATION: (d)   CURRENT USE: Theatre
  LOCATION OF AUDITORIUM: Ground floor
  STAGE DIMENSIONS AND EQUIPMENT: Height of proscenium, 20ft;
    Distance from edge of stage to back wall of stage, 45ft;
    Distance between side walls of stage, 48ft; Depth under
    stage, 12ft; Trap doors, 8
  SEATING: 1st level, 500; 2nd level, 200; 3rd level, 285
  MAJOR TYPES OF ENTERTAINMENT: Drama, vaudeville, movies

Wabash, IN

EAGLES THEATRE, West Market Street
  OPENING DATE: 1905
  TYPE OF THEATRE: (b)   DEGREE OF RESTORATION: (c)
  CURRENT USE: Movie theatre
  LOCATION OF AUDITORIUM: Ground floor
  STAGE DIMENSIONS AND EQUIPMENT: Height and width of
    proscenium, 40ft x 45ft; Shape of proscenium arch,
    arched; Distance from edge of stage to back wall of
    stage, 30ft; Distance from edge of stage to curtain
    line, 15ft; Distance between side walls of stage, 70ft;
    Distance from stage floor to fly loft, 24ft; Stage floor,
    flat; Trap doors, 1
  DIMENSIONS OF AUDITORIUM: Orchestra pit, yes
  SEATING (3 levels): 1st level, 335; 2nd level, 189;
    3rd level, 240
  MAJOR TYPES OF ENTERTAINMENT: Drama, vaudeville, movies

Winamac, IN

VURPILLAT'S OPERA HOUSE, Corner of Main and Market Streets
  OPENING DATE: Spring 1883
  OPENING SHOW: Unnamed opera, Bijou Opera Company
  TYPE OF BUILDING: Storage and offices   FACADE: Brick
    with stone trim   TYPE OF THEATRE: (b)   DEGREE OF
  RESTORATION: (c)   CLOSING DATE: c. 1910   CURRENT USE:
    Vacant   LOCATION OF AUDITORIUM: Third floor
  MAJOR TYPES OF ENTERTAINMENT: Drama, local variety shows
  ADDITIONAL INFORMATION: A clipping published shortly before
    the opening of the opera house in 1883 describes the
    stage as "large" and sets the seating capacity at nearly
    600 with the last few rows being slightly elevated.

Iowa

Akron, IA

AKRON OPERA HOUSE
  TYPE OF BUILDING: Offices   CURRENT USE: Theatre
  STAGE DIMENSIONS AND EQUIPMENT: Height and width of
    proscenium, 16ft x 22ft; Shape of proscenium arch,
    rectangular; Distance from edge of stage to back wall
    of stage, 24ft; distance between side walls of stage,
    44ft
  SEATING (2 levels): 1st level, 260; 2nd level, 230

Cedar Falls, IA

REGENT THEATRE (other names: Cotton Theatre, Isis Theatre)
    103 Main Street
  OPENING DATE: June 23, 1910
  OPENING SHOW: The Rejuvenation of Aunt Mary
  ARCHITECTS: Albans and Fisher   FACADE: Red brick
  TYPE OF THEATRE: (a)   DEGREE OF RESTORATION: (d)
  CURRENT USE: Movie theatre   LOCATION OF AUDITORIUM:
    Ground floor
  STAGE DIMENSIONS AND EQUIPMENT: Height of proscenium, 22ft
    6in; Shape of proscenium arch, arched; Distance from edge
    of stage to back wall of stage, 36ft 2in; Distance from
    edge of stage to curtain line, 3ft; Distance between side
    walls of stage, 66ft 2in; Distance from stage floor to
    fly loft, 20ft; Depth under stage, 7ft 6in; Stage floor,
    flat; Trap doors, 1; Dressing rooms, 14 (4 offstage, 10
    in basement)
  DIMENSIONS OF AUDITORIUM: Distance between side walls
    of auditorium, 66ft 6in; Distance stage to back wall of
    auditorium, 53ft; Orchestra pit, yes
  SEATING (2 levels): 1st level, 334; 2nd level, 174
  SHAPE OF THE AUDITORIUM: Horseshoe-shaped
  MAJOR TYPES OF ENTERTAINMENT: Drama, musical comedy,
    vaudeville, concerts, minstrel shows, lectures, movies,

local variety shows
MAJOR STARS WHO APPEARED AT THEATRE: May Robson, Jack
    Storey, Henry Woodruff, and others
ADDITIONAL INFORMATION: When the theatre opened in 1910,
    seating capacity was 1,034 and was divided as follows:
    permanent chairs, 886; box seats, 48; temporary seats,
    100. Seating was later reduced to 785 (two levels) and
    is now 508. At the time of its opening, the theatre was
    regarded as one of the largest in Iowa.

Clermont, IA

CLERMONT OPERA HOUSE, Mill and Clay Streets
OPENING DATE: 1912
ARCHITECT: Harry E. Netcott   TYPE OF BUILDING: Municipal
    building   FACADE: White brick   TYPE OF THEATRE: (b)
DEGREE OF RESTORATION: (a)   CURRENT USE: Little theatre
STAGE DIMENSIONS AND EQUIPMENT: Height and width of
    proscenium, 16ft x 24ft; Shape of proscenium arch,
    arched; Distance from edge of stage to back wall of
    stage, 21ft; Distance from edge of stage to curtain line,
    4ft; Distance between side walls of stage, 44ft; Stage
    floor, flat
DIMENSIONS OF AUDITORIUM: Distance between side walls
    of auditorium, 44ft; Distance stage to back wall of
    auditorium, 60ft; Orchestra pit, none
SEATING (2 levels): 1st level, 200; 2nd level, 100
SHAPE OF THE AUDITORIUM: Rectangular
MAJOR TYPES OF ENTERTAINMENT: Drama, lectures, movies

Cresco, IA

THE CRESCO (other names: Cresco Opera House), 115 2nd
    Avenue West
OPENING DATE: February 18, 1915
OPENING SHOW: High Jinks
FACADE: Brick   TYPE OF THEATRE: (a)
DEGREE OF RESTORATION: (a)   CURRENT USE: Theatre
PERFORMANCE SPACES IN BUILDING: 2
LOCATION OF AUDITORIUM: Ground floor
STAGE DIMENSIONS AND EQUIPMENT: Height and width of
    proscenium, 20ft x 28ft; Shape of proscenium arch,
    rectangular; Distance from edge of stage to back wall of
    stage, 20ft; Distance between side walls of stage, 47ft;
    Stage floor, flat; Trap doors, 2; Scenery storage rooms,
    2; Dressing rooms, 2 (under stage)
DIMENSIONS OF AUDITORIUM: Distance between side walls
    of auditorium, 47ft; Distance stage to back wall of
    auditorium, 80ft; Capacity of orchestra pit, 10
SEATING (3 levels): 1st level, 228; 2nd level, 140;
    3rd level, 120
SHAPE OF THE AUDITORIUM: U-shaped
MAJOR TYPES OF ENTERTAINMENT: Drama, musical comedy,
    vaudeville, burlesque, concerts, lectures, movies

MAJOR STARS WHO APPEARED AT THEATRE: Fiske O'Hara, Victor
    Jory, Madge Evans
ADDITIONAL INFORMATION: As originally constructed, the
    theatre had a seating capacity of 725 "with every seat
    commanding a good view of the stage." There was also an
    assembly room in the basement of the building.

Dubuque, IA

FIVE FLAGS THEATRE (other names: Majestic, Orpheum,
    Spensley), 4th and Main Streets
OPENING DATE: November 16, 1910
OPENING SHOW: Vaudeville bill
ARCHITECTS: Rapp and Rapp   STYLE OF ARCHITECTURE:
    Renaissance Revival   FACADE: Bedford stone and pressed
    brick TYPE OF THEATRE: (a)   DEGREE OF RESTORATION: (a)
CURRENT USE: Theatre   LOCATION OF AUDITORIUM: Ground
    floor
STAGE DIMENSIONS AND EQUIPMENT: Height and width of
    proscenium, 26ft x 31ft 10in; Shape of proscenium arch,
    arched; Distance from edge of stage to back wall of
    stage, 34ft 6in; Distance between side walls of stage,
    49ft 11in; Depth under stage, 10ft 2in; Stage floor,
    flat; Trap doors, 5; Scenery storage rooms, 1 (backstage
    shop area); Dressing rooms, 5 (below stage)
DIMENSIONS OF AUDITORIUM: Capacity of orchestra pit, 20
SEATING (3 levels): 1st level, 327; 2nd level, 38; 3rd
    level, 352
SHAPE OF THE AUDITORIUM: Horseshoe-shaped
MAJOR TYPES OF ENTERTAINMENT: Vaudeville, drama, concerts,
    movies
MAJOR STARS WHO APPEARED AT THEATRE: Bernhardt, George
    Burns, Edwin Booth, Ethel Barrymore, Al Jolson, Eddie
    Cantor, Buffalo Bill
ADDITIONAL INFORMATION: By 1970, the theatre was scheduled
    for demolition as part of an urban renewal project, but
    was saved by a civic group. It was renamed Five Flags
    after the five different flags that have flown over the
    region. The theatre is considered one of the earliest
    extant examples of a Rapp and Rapp designed theatre

Elkader, IA

ELKADER OPERA HOUSE (other name: Elkader Municipal Building),
    207 North Main Street
OPENING DATE: November 1903   OPENING SHOW: The Governor's
    Son   ARCHITECTS: Schick and Roth   STYLE OF
ARCHITECTURE: Victorian   FACADE: Pressed brick
TYPE OF THEATRE: (a) DEGREE OF RESTORATION: (a)
CURRENT USE: Community functions
LOCATION OF AUDITORIUM: Ground floor
STAGE DIMENSIONS AND EQUIPMENT: Height and width of
    proscenium, 15ft x 27ft; Shape of proscenium arch,

rectangular; Distance from edge of stage to back wall of
stage, 31ft; Distance from edge of stage to curtain line,
9ft; Distance between side walls of stage, 48ft; Distance
from stage floor to fly loft, 20ft; Depth under stage,
6ft; Dressing rooms, 2 (rear of stage)
DIMENSIONS OF AUDITORIUM: Distance between side walls
of auditorium, 47ft; Distance stage to back wall of
auditorium, 66ft; Capacity of orchestra pit, 20
SEATING (2 levels): 1st level, 301; 2nd level, 250
SHAPE OF THE AUDITORIUM: Rectangular with horseshoe balcony
MAJOR TYPES OF ENTERTAINMENT: Drama, vaudeville, movies,
chautauquas, dances
MAJOR STARS WHO APPEARED AT THEATRE: Ed Wynn, George M.
Cohan
ADDITIONAL INFORMATION: Theatre building included a dance
hall, and wardrobe and "retiring" rooms in the basement.

Harlan, IA

HARLAN THEATRE (other name: Long's Opera House), 621 Court
OPENING DATE: 1882   TYPE OF BUILDING: Commercial
FACADE: Sandstone brick   TYPE OF THEATRE: (b)
DEGREE OF RESTORATION: (d)   CURRENT USE: Theatre
LOCATION OF AUDITORIUM: Second floor
STAGE DIMENSIONS AND EQUIPMENT: Height and width of
proscenium, 12ft x 21ft; Distance from edge of stage to
back wall of stage, 26ft; Distance between side walls of
stage, 42ft
DIMENSIONS OF AUDITORIUM: Distance between side walls
of auditorium, 44ft; Distance stage to back wall of
auditorium, 66ft
SEATING (2 levels)
SHAPE OF THE AUDITORIUM: Rectangular
MAJOR TYPES OF ENTERTAINMENT: Drama, musical comedy,
vaudeville
ADDITIONAL INFORMATION: Original equipment included a 12
x 21 foot drop curtain representing a Scottish scene with
"an elaborate castlery, with moat, drawbridge, tower
standing beside a beautiful lake in Scotland." There
were also backdrops representing parlor scenes, a prison,
woods, a garden, city street scenes, a rocky pass and a
full set of wings, grand drapery and three sky borders.

Jefferson, IA

SIERRA THEATRE (other names: Head's Opera House, Jefferson
Opera House), 212 East State Street
OPENING DATE: 1884   TYPE OF BUILDING: Masonic lodge
FACADE: Red brick   TYPE OF THEATRE: (b)   DEGREE OF
RESTORATION: (d)   CURRENT USE: Movie theatre
LOCATION OF AUDITORIUM: Ground floor
STAGE DIMENSIONS AND EQUIPMENT: * Height and width of

proscenium, 30ft x 20ft; Shape of proscenium arch,
rectangular; Distance from edge of stage to back wall
of stage, 25ft; Distance from edge of stage to curtain
line, 10ft; Distance between side walls of stage, 40ft;
Distance from stage floor to fly loft, 18ft 6in; Depth
under stage, 4ft; Stage floor, flat
DIMENSIONS OF AUDITORIUM: Distance between side walls of
auditorium, 60ft
SEATING (2 levels): 1st level, 70; 2nd level, 30
SHAPE OF THE AUDITORIUM: Rectangular
MAJOR TYPES OF ENTERTAINMENT: Drama, vaudeville, opera,
movies

Lamoni, IA

COLISEUM THEATRE, Corner of Main and Maple Streets
OPENING DATE: 1911
TYPE OF THEATRE: (a)   DEGREE OF RESTORATION: (d)
CURRENT USE: Movie theatre
LOCATION OF AUDITORIUM: Ground floor
STAGE DIMENSIONS AND EQUIPMENT: Height and width of
proscenium, 25ft x 30ft; Shape of proscenium arch,
rectangular; Distance from edge of stage to back wall of
stage, 25ft; Distance from edge of stage to curtain line,
3ft 6in; Distance between side walls of stage, 48ft;
Depth under stage, 12ft; Stage floor, flat; Trap doors,
1; Scenery storage rooms, 1 (basement); Dressing rooms, 2
(basement)
DIMENSIONS OF AUDITORIUM: Distance between side walls
of auditorium, 48ft; Distance stage to back wall of
auditorium, 46ft 3in; Capacity of orchestra pit, 25
SEATING (2 levels): 1st level, 271; 2nd level, 75
SHAPE OF THE AUDITORIUM: Rectangular

West Union, IA

AVALON THEATRE (other name: Princess), 129 North Vine Street
OPENING DATE: c. 1913
FACADE: Red and black brick   TYPE OF THEATRE: (a)
DEGREE OF RESTORATION: (a)   CURRENT USE: Commercial
LOCATION OF AUDITORIUM: Ground floor
SEATING (1 level): 1st level, 250
SHAPE OF THE AUDITORIUM: Oblong
MAJOR TYPES OF ENTERTAINMENT: Drama, musical comedy,
operettas, lectures, wild west shows, movies
ADDITIONAL INFORMATION: The building was erected in 1860 to
house various businesses and was later converted into a
theatre.

What Cheer, IA

WHAT CHEER OPERA HOUSE (other name: Masonic Lodge Hall),
Corner of Briney and Barns Streets

OPENING DATE: c. 1893   OPENING SHOW: Pete Peterson and
   a repertory company
ARCHITECT: J. J. Gordineer   STYLE OF ARCHITECTURE:
   Romanesque   TYPE OF BUILDING: Masonic hall
FACADE: Red brick   TYPE OF THEATRE: (a)   DEGREE
OF RESTORATION: (d) CURRENT USE: Community center
LOCATION OF AUDITORIUM: Ground floor
STAGE DIMENSIONS AND EQUIPMENT: Height and width of
   proscenium, 19ft x 21ft; Shape of proscenium arch,
   square; Distance from edge of stage to back wall of
   stage, 21ft; Distance from edge of stage to curtain line,
   3ft 10in; Distance between side walls of stage, 42ft;
   Depth under stage, 6ft; Stage floor, raked; Scenery
   storage rooms (in wings); Dressing rooms, 4
DIMENSIONS OF AUDITORIUM: Capacity of orchestra pit, 9
SEATING (2 levels): 1st level, 380; 2nd level, 217
SHAPE OF THE AUDITORIUM: U-shaped
MAJOR TYPES OF ENTERTAINMENT: Drama, musical comedy,
   concerts, lectures, minstrel shows
MAJOR STARS WHO APPEARED AT THEATRE: Weber and Fields,
   Walker Whiteside, Skinner Harris Minstrels, John Phillip
   Sousa, Wayne King, Harry James, Stan Kenton, Fred Waring,
   Vaughn Monroe, Sammy Kay, Porter Wagoner, Ernest Tubb,
   George Hamilton IV, Hank Williams Jr., Bob Crosby, Russ
   Morgan, Clyde McCoy

Kansas

Abiline, KS

PLAZA THEATRE (other names: J. E. Bonebrake Opera House,
   1879-1900; Seelye Theatre, 1900-1935)
   OPENING DATE: 1879
   ARCHITECT: J. E. Bonebrake, builder   STYLE OF
   ARCHITECTURE: Renaissance   TYPE OF BUILDING: Movie
   theatre   FACADE: Red brick   TYPE OF THEATRE: (b)
   DEGREE OF RESTORATION: (c)   CURRENT USE: Movie theatre
   LOCATION OF AUDITORIUM: First floor
   STAGE DIMENSIONS AND EQUIPMENT: * Height and width of
   proscenium, 21ft x 32ft; Distance from edge of stage to
   back wall of stage, 32ft; Distance from edge of stage to
   curtain line, 3ft; Distance between side walls of stage,
   65ft; Distance from stage floor to fly loft, 21ft; Depth
   under stage, 4ft; Trap doors, 1
   SEATING: 1st level, 475; 2nd level, 296
   MAJOR TYPES OF ENTERTAINMENT: Professional road shows,
   movies
   ADDITIONAL INFORMATION: The theatre has had various
   stage locations. The building was bought in 1900 by Dr.
   Seeyle. An arched pedimented facade reads "A.= B. Seeyle
   Medical, Co. Laboratory". The theatre has been remodeled
   several times.

Axtell, KS

OPERA HOUSE, 103 5th Street
   OPENING DATE: 1893
   STYLE OF ARCHITECTURE: Eclectic   TYPE OF BUILDING:
   Commercial   FACADE: Red brick   DEGREE OF
   RESTORATION: (c)   CURRENT USE: Appliance store
   PERFORMANCE SPACES IN BUILDING: 1
   LOCATION OF AUDITORIUM: Second floor
   STAGE DIMENSIONS AND EQUIPMENT: Height and width of
   proscenium, 16ft x 20ft; Distance from edge of stage to

back wall of stage, 21ft; Distance between side walls of
  stage, 21ft
SEATING (2 levels): 1st level, 350; 2nd level, 150
ADDITIONAL INFORMATION: Building condition is good.
  Evidence of roll drop mechnanism in ceiling and
  three sets of wings remain.

Blue Rapids, KS

LADIES OPERA HOUSE (other names: Opera House, Regent Opera
  House), 6th Street and Genesee
OPENING DATE: 1895
FACADE: Brick and stone   TYPE OF THEATRE: (a)
DEGREE OF RESTORATION: (d)   CURRENT USE: Movie theatre
PERFORMANCE SPACES IN BUILDING: 1
LOCATION OF AUDITORIUM: First floor
STAGE DIMENSIONS AND EQUIPMENT: Height and width of
  proscenium, 14ft x 22ft; Distance from edge of stage to
  back wall of stage, 24ft 10in; Distance from edge of
  stage to curtain line, 4ft; Distance between side walls
  of stage, 48ft; Distance from stage floor to fly loft,
  16ft; Trap doors, 1
ADDITIONAL INFORMATION: Building is only one story high.
  Condition is fair.

Carbondale, KS

CARBONDALE OPERA HOUSE (other name: Opera House), Main and
  Third Streets
OPENING DATE: 1913
TYPE OF BUILDING: City hall   FACADE: Red brick
TYPE OF THEATRE: (a)   DEGREE OF RESTORATION: (c)
CURRENT USE: City hall
PERFORMANCE SPACES IN BUILDING: 1
ADDITIONAL INFORMATION: This is a large, rectangular
  building in good condition.

Chanute, KS

ROOF GARDEN THEATRE, 112 East Main Street
  OPENING DATE: Pre-1884   TYPE OF BUILDING: Commercial
  TYPE OF THEATRE: (b)   CURRENT USE: Commercial
  PERFORMANCE SPACES IN BUILDING: 1
  LOCATION OF AUDITORIUM: Roof of building
  ADDITIONAL INFORMATION: Building condition is good.

Chanute, KS

WILLIAMS THEATRE (other names: George Williams Theatre,
  Hetrick), 23 West Main Street
  OPENING DATE: 1880
  TYPE OF BUILDING: Commercial   CURRENT USE: Store

PERFORMANCE SPACES IN BUILDING: 1
LOCATION OF AUDITORIUM: Second floor
STAGE DIMENSIONS AND EQUIPMENT: Height and width of
    proscenium, 36ft x 37ft; Distance from edge of stage to
    back wall of stage, 40ft; Distance from edge of stage to
    curtain line, 2ft; Distance between side walls of stage,
    60ft; Distance from stage floor to fly loft, 26ft; Depth
    under stage, 7ft; Trap doors, 1
ADDITIONAL INFORMATION: Building condition is excellent
    The seating capacity in 1915 was 1,050.

Concordia, KS

BROWN GRAND THEATRE (other name: Brown Grand Opera House),
    West 6th Street
OPENING DATE: September 17, 1907
OPENING SHOW: Vanderbilt Cup
ARCHITECT: Carl Boller   STYLE OF ARCHITECTURE: Renaissance
FACADE: Red brick; limestone foundation   TYPE OF
THEATRE:, (a)   DEGREE OF RESTORATION: (a)
CURRENT USE: Community center   PERFORMANCE SPACES IN
BUILDING: 1   LOCATION OF AUDITORIUM: Ground floor
STAGE DIMENSIONS AND EQUIPMENT: Height and width of
    proscenium, 34ft x 26ft; Shape of proscenium arch,
    rectangular; Distance from edge of stage to back wall of
    stage, 50ft; Distance from edge of stage to curtain line,
    3ft; Distance between side walls of stage, 60ft; Distance
    from stage floor to fly loft, 45ft; Depth under stage,
    9ft; Stage floor, flat; Scenery storage rooms, 1 (rear
    west); Dressing rooms, 5 (behind and above stage)
DIMENSIONS OF AUDITORIUM: Distance between side walls
    of auditorium, 60ft; Distance stage to back wall of
    auditorium, 50ft; Capacity of orchestra pit, 12
SEATING (3 levels): 1st level, 301; 2nd level, 202;
    3rd level, 117
SHAPE OF THE AUDITORIUM: U-shaped
MAJOR TYPES OF ENTERTAINMENT: Drama, musical comedy, movies
MAJOR STARS WHO APPEARED AT THEATRE: Ruth St. Denis, Ted
    Shawn, Laurette Taylor, Ernestine Schumann-Heink, Sarah
    Padden
ADDITIONAL INFORMATION: Some original scenery and a copy of
    the original house curtain remain.

Concordia, KS

LA ROCQUE OPERA HOUSE (other name: Old Opera House Mall),
    105 East 6th Street
OPENING DATE: January 31, 1884
OPENING SHOW: New Year's Eve Dance
ARCHITECT: La Rocque Brothers   TYPE OF BUILDING:
    Commercial   TYPE OF THEATRE: (b)   DEGREE OF
RESTORATION: (c)   CURRENT USE: Vacant
LOCATION OF AUDITORIUM: Second floor
SHAPE OF THE AUDITORIUM: U-shaped

MAJOR TYPES OF ENTERTAINMENT: Vaudeville
MAJOR STARS WHO APPEARED AT THEATRE: Tom Thumb

Coolidge, KS

OLD OPERA HOUSE
  OPENING DATE: 1887
  STYLE OF ARCHITECTURE: Vernacular
  TYPE OF BUILDING: Masonic lodge   FACADE: Yellow limestone
  TYPE OF THEATRE: (a)   DEGREE OF RESTORATION: (c)
  CURRENT USE: Masonic lodge
  ADDITIONAL INFORMATION: Building condition is good.

Downs, KS

OPERA HOUSE, Margan and Delay Streets
  OPENING DATE: 1890
  TYPE OF BUILDING: Apartments   FACADE: Red brick
  DEGREE OF RESTORATION: (c)   CURRENT USE: Apartments
  PERFORMANCE SPACES IN BUILDING: 1

Eureka, KS

EUREKA OPERA HOUSE, 2nd and Main Streets
  OPENING DATE: 1880
  STYLE OF ARCHITECTURE: Italianate   TYPE OF BUILDING:
    Commercial   FACADE: Brick and stone
  TYPE OF THEATRE: (b)   DEGREE OF RESTORATION: (c)
  CURRENT USE: Store and apartments
  PERFORMANCE SPACES IN BUILDING: 1
  LOCATION OF AUDITORIUM: Second floor
  STAGE DIMENSIONS AND EQUIPMENT: Height and width of
    proscenium, 14ft x 25ft; Distance from edge of stage
    to back wall of stage, 22ft; Distance from edge of
    stage to curtain line, 3ft; Dressing rooms, 4
  ADDITIONAL INFORMATION: Apartments occupy former theatre
    space. The building is in fair condition.

Florence, KS

FLORENCE OPERA HOUSE, 5th and Main Streets
  OPENING DATE: January 24, 1884
  OPENING SHOW: The Linwood Case
  STYLE OF ARCHITECTURE: Renaissance   TYPE OF BUILDING:
    Business   FACADE: Natural stone   TYPE OF THEATRE: (b)
  DEGREE OF RESTORATION: (c)   CLOSING DATE: 1917
  CURRENT USE: Vacant   PERFORMANCE SPACES IN BUILDING: 1
  LOCATION OF AUDITORIUM: Second floor

Fort Smith, KS

RICHARD'S THEATRE, 108 South Main Street
  OPENING DATE: 1887
  STYLE OF ARCHITECTURE: Italianate   TYPE OF BUILDING:
    Commercial   FACADE: Red brick   TYPE OF THEATRE: (b)
  DEGREE OF RESTORATION: (c)   CURRENT USE: Store
  ADDITIONAL INFORMATION: The building is in fair condition.

Frankfort, KS

WEIS OPERA HOUSE, 106 North Kansas
  OPENING DATE: 1900
  TYPE OF BUILDING: Firehouse   FACADE: Stone
  TYPE OF THEATRE: (a)   DEGREE OF RESTORATION: (c)
  CURRENT USE: Firehouse   PERFORMANCE SPACES IN BUILDING: 1
  LOCATION OF AUDITORIUM: First floor
  STAGE DIMENSIONS AND EQUIPMENT: Height and width of
    proscenium, 14ft x 22ft 4in
  ADDITIONAL INFORMATION: The building now houses
    fire department on first floor. The stage is now
    completely gone and the facade has been altered
    beyond recognition.

Fredonia, KS

HUDSON OPERA HOUSE (other name: The Opera House),
    514 Madison Street
  OPENING DATE: 1888
  STYLE OF ARCHITECTURE: Victorian   TYPE OF BUILDING:
    Commercial   FACADE: Red brick with stone
  TYPE OF THEATRE: (b)   DEGREE OF RESTORATION: (c)
  CLOSING DATE: 1915   CURRENT USE: Apartments
  PERFORMANCE SPACES IN BUILDING: 1
  LOCATION OF AUDITORIUM: Second and third floors
  STAGE DIMENSIONS AND EQUIPMENT: Height of proscenium,
    18ft; Distance from edge of stage to back wall of stage,
    30ft; Distance between side walls of stage, 60ft;
    Distance from stage floor to fly loft, 20ft; Depth under
    stage, 5ft; Trap doors, 3
  MAJOR TYPES OF ENTERTAINMENT: Drama, musical comedy, local
    talent shows

Grainfield, KS

GRAINFIELD OPERA HOUSE, Main and Third Streets
  OPENING DATE: 1886
  FACADE: Brick and cast iron   TYPE OF THEATRE: (b)
  DEGREE OF RESTORATION: (c)   CURRENT USE: Lodge and storage
  ADDITIONAL INFORMATION: Building is in fair condition.

Hartford, KS

OPERA HOUSE BLOCK, 469 Commercial Street
    OPENING DATE: 1880
    STYLE OF ARCHITECTURE: Commercial   FACADE: Red brick
    DEGREE OF RESTORATION: (c)   CURRENT USE: Store
    PERFORMANCE SPACES IN BUILDING: 1

Junction City, KS

COLONIAL THEATRE (other name: Opera House), Jefferson and 7th
    OPENING DATE: 1898
    STYLE OF ARCHITECTURE: Romanesque   FACADE: Native stone
    TYPE OF THEATRE: (a)   DEGREE OF RESTORATION: (d)
    CURRENT USE: Movies   PERFORMANCE SPACES IN BUILDING: 1
    LOCATION OF AUDITORIUM: First floor
    STAGE DIMENSIONS AND EQUIPMENT: Width of proscenium, 30ft;
        Distance from edge of stage to back wall of stage, 34ft;
        Distance from edge of stage to curtain line, 3ft;
        Distance between side walls of stage, 62ft; Distance from
        stage floor to fly loft, 50ft; Depth under stage, 8ft;
        Trap doors, 1
    ADDITIONAL INFORMATION: Building is adjacent to the
        former City Hall Theatre (1900) and the two have been
        combined to created a motion picture theatre. All side
        windows have been sealed with stone. Building is in good
        condition.

Kincaid, KS

KINCAID MUNICIPAL THEATRE, Second and Commercial Streets
    OPENING DATE: 1908
    FACADE: Red brick   TYPE OF THEATRE: (a)
    DEGREE OF RESTORATION: (c)   CURRENT USE: Municipal theatre
    PERFORMANCE SPACES IN BUILDING: 1
    ADDITIONAL INFORMATION: Building is in fair condition.

La Crosse, KS

LA CROSSE OPERA HOUSE, 120 West 8th Street
    OPENING DATE: 1910
    STYLE OF ARCHITECTURE: Eclectic   FACADE: Red brick
    DEGREE OF RESTORATION: (c)   CURRENT USE: Vacant
    PERFORMANCE SPACES IN BUILDING: 1
    ADDITIONAL INFORMATION: Building condition is good.

Lawrence, KS

BOWERSOCK OPERA HOUSE (other name: Lawrence Opera House),
    Massachusetts and 7th Streets
    OPENING DATE: 1912

ARCHITECT: Samuel B. Tarbet and Company   STYLE OF
ARCHITECTURE: Neo-Classical   FACADE: Brick and
   terra cotta   TYPE OF THEATRE: (a)
LOCATION OF AUDITORIUM: First floor
STAGE DIMENSIONS AND EQUIPMENT: Distance from edge of stage
   to back wall of stage, 35ft; Distance between side walls
   of stage, 60ft
ADDITIONAL INFORMATION: Building condition is fair.

Lenora, KS

NEAL THEATRE
   OPENING DATE: 1906
   STYLE OF ARCHITECTURE: Vernacular   TYPE OF BUILDING:
   Commercial   FACADE: Stone-textured block
   DEGREE OF RESTORATION: (c)   CURRENT USE: Vacant
   PERFORMANCE SPACES IN BUILDING: 1
   ADDITIONAL INFORMATION: Building condition has
   deteriorated.

Manhattan, KS

MARSHALL THEATRE (other names: Dickinson Theatre, State
   Theatre), 326 Houston Street
   OPENING DATE: 1909
   TYPE OF BUILDING: Commercial   FACADE: Red brick
   TYPE OF THEATRE: (b)   DEGREE OF RESTORATION: (c)
   CLOSING DATE: 1957   CURRENT USE: Store
   PERFORMANCE SPACES IN BUILDING: 1
   MAJOR TYPES OF ENTERTAINMENT: Stage shows
   ADDITIONAL INFORMATION: The 1913 Mercury Industrial Edition
   notes ample stage room, a scenery dome, daylight and
   moonlight effects. The theatre was originally built for
   stage shows, but was quickly converted to movies.

Manhattan, KS

WAREHAM THEATRE (other names: Moore's Opera House, Wareham
   Opera House, Wareham Theatre), 410 Poynts
   OPENING DATE: 1884
   FACADE: Limestone   TYPE OF THEATRE: (a)
   DEGREE OF RESTORATION: (d)   CURRENT USE: Theatre
   PERFORMANCE SPACES IN BUILDING: 1
   LOCATION OF AUDITORIUM: Ground floor
   STAGE DIMENSIONS AND EQUIPMENT: Height and width of
   proscenium, 18ft x 28ft; Distance from edge of stage
   to back wall of stage, 30ft; Distance from edge of
   stage to curtain line, 3ft; Distance between side walls
   of stage, 47ft; Distance from stage floor to fly loft,
   45ft; Depth under stage, 8ft

McCune, KS

MCCUNE OPERA HOUSE, 505 Main Street
    OPENING DATE: c. 1890
    TYPE OF BUILDING: Lodge hall   FACADE: Brick front,
        stone sides   TYPE OF THEATRE: (b)   DEGREE OF
    RESTORATION: (c)   CURRENT USE: Vacant
    PERFORMANCE SPACES IN BUILDING: 1
    LOCATION OF AUDITORIUM: Ground floor
    ADDITIONAL INFORMATION: Respondent recalled when
        movies were shown here in the 1940s. The building
        has been vacant since January 1985 when the lodge
        moved. The condition of the building is good.

McPherson, KS

MCPHERSON OPERA HOUSE (other name: Empire Theatre),
        Northeast corner of Main and Sutherland Streets
    OPENING DATE: January 28, 1889
    OPENING SHOW: Chimes of Normandy
    ARCHITECT: George Shaffer   FACADE: Red brick and stone
    TYPE OF THEATRE: (b)   DEGREE OF RESTORATION: (c)
    CLOSING DATE: 1960   CURRENT USE: Vacant
    STAGE DIMENSIONS AND EQUIPMENT: Height and width of
        proscenium, 20ft x 24ft 8in; Distance from edge of stage
        to back wall of stage, 35ft; Distance from edge of stage
        to curtain line, 2ft; Distance between side walls of
        stage, 54ft; Distance from stage floor to fly loft, 54ft
    SEATING (3 levels, 2 boxes)
    MAJOR STARS WHO APPEARED AT THEATRE: William Jennings Bryan
    ADDITIONAL INFORMATION: There have been a number of
        attempts to finance the restoration of the theatre,
        but they have been unsuccessful. The building has
        been deteriorating for 15 years.

McPherson, KS

OPERA HOUSE, Main Street
    OPENING DATE: 1880
    STYLE OF ARCHITECTURE: Eclectic   TYPE OF BUILDING: Bank
    FACADE: Red brick   TYPE OF THEATRE: (b)
    DEGREE OF RESTORATION: (c)   CURRENT USE: Storage
    PERFORMANCE SPACES IN BUILDING: 1
    ADDITIONAL INFORMATION: This was the first opera house in
        town and was housed above the Bank of McPherson. A poor
        photo exists in the Chesley Collection clipping file.

Mound City, KS

MOUND CITY OPERA HOUSE, 6th and Main Streets
    STYLE OF ARCHITECTURE: Renaissance
    TYPE OF BUILDING: Commercial   FACADE: Red brick
    DEGREE OF RESTORATION: (c)   CURRENT USE: Store

PERFORMANCE SPACES IN BUILDING: 1
ADDITIONAL INFORMATION: The building is in fair
    condition.

Moundridge, KS

JOSEPH SCHRAG OPERA HOUSE (other names: Schrag Hall, Schwan
    Hall), Southwest corner of Cole and Christian Streets
OPENING DATE: 1888
STYLE OF ARCHITECTURE: Renaissance   TYPE OF BUILDING:
    Offices, store   FACADE: Red brick with stone trim
TYPE OF THEATRE: (b)   DEGREE OF RESTORATION: (c)
CURRENT USE: Apartments and commercial
DIMENSIONS OF AUDITORIUM: Distance between side walls
    of auditorium, 25ft; Distance stage to back wall of
    auditorium, 50ft
SHAPE OF THE AUDITORIUM: Rectangular
MAJOR TYPES OF ENTERTAINMENT: Local balls, meetings,
    and social events

Oberlin, KS

OBERLIN OPERA HOUSE (other name: Chief Theatre)
OPENING DATE: December 31, 1906
OPENING SHOW: The Mikado
STYLE OF ARCHITECTURE: Romanesque   FACADE: Red brick
TYPE OF THEATRE: (a)   DEGREE OF RESTORATION: (c)
CLOSING DATE: 1973   CURRENT USE: Vacant
LOCATION OF AUDITORIUM: First floor
STAGE DIMENSIONS AND EQUIPMENT: Height and width of
    proscenium, 22ft x 28ft; Distance from edge of stage to
    back wall of stage, 29ft; Distance from edge of stage to
    curtain line, 19ft; Distance between side walls of stage,
    54ft; Distance from stage floor to fly loft, 21ft; Depth
    under stage, 9ft; Trap doors, 1
DIMENSIONS OF AUDITORIUM: Capacity of orchestra pit, 8
SEATING (4 levels): 1st level, 352; 2nd level, 244; 3rd
    level, 275; boxes, 4
MAJOR TYPES OF ENTERTAINMENT: Drama, operas, graduations
ADDITIONAL INFORMATION: The theatre was badly damaged in
    1973 and has not been repaired.

Osage City, KS

GRAND OPERA HOUSE, 126 South 6th Street
OPENING DATE: 1886
STYLE OF ARCHITECTURE: Vernacular   TYPE OF BUILDING:
    Commercial   FACADE: Red brick   TYPE OF THEATRE: (b)
DEGREE OF RESTORATION: (c)   CURRENT USE: Community
    playhouse   PERFORMANCE SPACES IN BUILDING: 1
LOCATION OF AUDITORIUM: Second floor
STAGE DIMENSIONS AND EQUIPMENT: Stage floor, flat; Scenery
    storage rooms, 1 (rear of stage)

SHAPE OF THE AUDITORIUM: Rectangular
MAJOR TYPES OF ENTERTAINMENT: Drama
ADDITIONAL INFORMATION: The theatre is located above a
  bowling alley and is presently used by Vassar Players.
  A semi-enclosed balcony existed for the "elite" and
  allowed them to eat and drink during the performance.
  The building is 50ft x 100ft.

Osage City, KS

HOWE'S OPERA HOUSE (other name: Osage City Opera house),
  526-528 Market Street
OPENING DATE: November 20, 1879
STYLE OF ARCHITECTURE: Vernacular   TYPE OF BUILDING:
  Commercial   FACADE: Red brick   TYPE OF THEATRE: (b)
DEGREE OF RESTORATION: (c)   CLOSING DATE: c. 1900
CURRENT USE: Storage   PERFORMANCE SPACES IN BUILDING: 1
LOCATION OF AUDITORIUM: Second floor
ADDITIONAL INFORMATION: Building condition is fair.

Oskaloosa, KS

CRITCHFIELD OPERA HOUSE, Liberty Street
OPENING DATE: 1887
FACADE: Red brick   TYPE OF THEATRE: (b)
DEGREE OF RESTORATION: (c) CURRENT USE: Government offices
LOCATION OF AUDITORIUM: Second floor
STAGE DIMENSIONS AND EQUIPMENT: Distance from edge of stage
  to back wall of stage. 16ft; Distance between side walls
  of stage, 24ft
MAJOR TYPES OF ENTERTAINMENT: Drama, vaudeville
ADDITIONAL INFORMATION: The building is in good
  condition.

Oswego, KS

COMMERCIAL THEATRE, 5th and Commercial Streets
OPENING DATE: 1880s
TYPE OF BUILDING: Commercial   FACADE: Brick
TYPE OF THEATRE: (b)   DEGREE OF RESTORATION: (c)
CURRENT USE: Grocery store
PERFORMANCE SPACES IN BUILDING: 1
LOCATION OF AUDITORIUM: Second floor
ADDITIONAL INFORMATION: Building condition is fair.

Perry, KS

OPERA HOUSE, Front Street
OPENING DATE: c. 1913   FACADE: Red brick
TYPE OF THEATRE: (b)   DEGREE OF RESTORATION: (c)
CURRENT USE: Storage   PERFORMANCE SPACES IN BUILDING: 1

Phillipsburg, KS

MAJESTIC THEATRE (other name: Winship Opera House), 4th and
    State Streets
    OPENING SHOW: 1905
    STYLE OF ARCHITECTURE: Renaissance   FACADE: Brick
    TYPE OF THEATRE: (a)   DEGREE OF RESTORATION: (c)
    CURRENT USE: Movies   LOCATION OF AUDITORIUM: Third floor
    STAGE DIMENSIONS AND EQUIPMENT: Distance from edge of stage
        to back wall of stage, 26ft; Distance between side walls
        of stage, 36ft; Distance from stage floor to fly loft,
        23ft
    MAJOR TYPES OF ENTERTAINMENT: Drama, vaudeville,
        burlesque
    ADDITIONAL INFORMATION: Condition of building is fair.

Pittsburg, KS

HARTEEL AND SHOUT BUILDING (other name: La Belle Theatre),
    110-118 West Third Street
    OPENING DATE: 1902
    STYLE OF ARCHITECTURE: Eclectic   TYPE OF BUILDING:
        Commercial   FACADE: Metal, brick and concrete
    CURRENT USE: Commercial and apartments   PERFORMANCE SPACES
    IN BUILDING: 1   LOCATION OF AUDITORIUM: First floor
    STAGE DIMENSIONS AND EQUIPMENT: Height and width of
        proscenium, 28ft 6in x 32ft; Distance from edge of stage
        to back wall of stage, 32ft; Distance between side walls
        of stage, 63ft; Distance from stage floor to fly loft,
        46ft; Depth under stage, 8ft; Stage floor, flat; Trap
        doors, 3
    MAJOR TYPES OF ENTERTAINMENT: Drama, vaudeville, musicals
    ADDITIONAL INFORMATION: Building condition is good.

Pleasanton, KS

KINCAID CROCKERS OPERA HOUSE, 8th and Main Streets
    OPENING DATE: 1870
    STYLE OF ARCHITECTURE: Renaissance   TYPE OF BUILDING:
        Commercial   FACADE: Red brick   DEGREE OF
    RESTORATION: (c)   CURRENT USE: Garment factory
    PERFORMANCE SPACES IN BUILDING: 1
    ADDITIONAL INFORMATION: Building condition is fair.

St. John, KS

CONVENTION HALL OR OPERA HOUSE, 4th and Broadway
    OPENING DATE: February 24, 1904
    OPENING SHOW: Paying the Penalty
    TYPE OF BUILDING: City offices   FACADE: Brick
    TYPE OF THEATRE: (a)   DEGREE OF RESTORATION: (c)
    CLOSING DATE: 1933   CURRENT USE: City offices
    PERFORMANCE SPACES IN BUILDING: 1

LOCATION OF AUDITORIUM: Ground floor
STAGE DIMENSIONS AND EQUIPMENT: Height and width of
   proscenium, 42ft x 34ft; Shape of proscenium arch,
   square; Depth under stage, 42ft; Stage floor, flat;
   Scenery storage rooms, 1 (basement); Dressing rooms,
   4 (under stage)
DIMENSIONS OF AUDITORIUM: Distance between side walls
   of auditorium, 62ft; Distance stage to back wall of
   auditorium, 68ft; Capacity of orchestra pit, 12
SEATING (2 levels): 1st level, 320; 2nd level, 120
SHAPE OF THE AUDITORIUM: Rectangular
MAJOR TYPES OF ENTERTAINMENT: Drama, musicals, lectures,
   graduation excercises, conventions

Smith Center, KS

SMITH CENTER OPERA HOUSE, East Main Street
OPENING DATE: 1888
TYPE OF BUILDING: Commercial   FACADE: Cut stone and
   brick   TYPE OF THEATRE: (b)
DEGREE OF RESTORATION: (c)   CURRENT USE: Apartments
LOCATION OF AUDITORIUM: Second floor
STAGE DIMENSIONS AND EQUIPMENT: Shape of proscenium
   arch, rectangular
SEATING: 1st level, 300; 2nd level, 350
SHAPE OF THE AUDITORIUM: Rectangular
MAJOR TYPES OF ENTERTAINMENT: Drama, vaudeville

Strong City, KS

AUDITORIUM, Highway 177
OPENING DATE: 1900
STYLE OF ARCHITECTURE: Vernacular   FACADE: Native stone
DEGREE OF RESTORATION: (a)   CURRENT USE: Government
   theatre   PERFORMANCE SPACES IN BUILDING: 1
ADDITIONAL INFORMATION: The building is now a government
   theatre.

Topeka, KS

NOVELTY THEATRE (other names: State, 1931-1958; Dickinson,
   1944-present), 120 East Eighth Street
OPENING DATE: January 5, 1908
OPENING SHOW: Vaudeville bill
ARCHITECT: Kansas Amusement Company, builder
STYLE OF ARCHITECTURE: Spanish   FACADE: Brick
TYPE OF THEATRE: (a)   DEGREE OF RESTORATION: (d)
CURRENT USE: Private society   PERFORMANCE SPACES IN
BUILDING: 1   LOCATION OF AUDITORIUM: First floor
MAJOR TYPES OF ENTERTAINMENT: Vaudeville, drama, movies
ADDITIONAL INFORMATION: A stone building directly to the
   west was incorporated into the theatre during a 1926

remodeling which saw the addition of a Spanish interior
and a Spanish exterior. A 1926 photo shows a marquee
containing the announcement "novelty vaudeville."
Present condition of the building is fair.

Wamego, KS

LEACH OPERA HOUSE, Elm and 5th Streets
    OPENING DATE: 1885
    ARCHITECT: Lew Leach, Builder   STYLE OF ARCHITECTURE:
       Renaissance   TYPE OF BUILDING: Funeral home
    FACADE: Brick   TYPE OF THEATRE: (b)   DEGREE OF
    RESTORATION: (c)   CLOSING DATE: 1897   CURRENT USE:
       Funeral home   PERFORMANCE SPACES IN BUILDING: 1
    LOCATION OF AUDITORIUM: First floor
    STAGE DIMENSIONS AND EQUIPMENT: Distance from edge of stage
       to back wall of stage, 26ft; Distance between side walls
       of stage, 46ft
    SHAPE OF THE AUDITORIUM: Rectangular
    MAJOR TYPES OF ENTERTAINMENT: Local and touring productions
    ADDITIONAL INFORMATION: The theatre was built with basement
       rooms for manufacturing gas for lighting. On the first
       floor were also fourteen rooms comprising a large Turkish
       bath.

Wamego, KS

THE ROGERS BROTHERS COLUMBIAN THEATRE (other name: Rogers
    Building), Lincoln, between 5th and 6th Streets
    OPENING DATE: 1895
    TYPE OF BUILDING: Commercial   CURRENT USE: Store
    PERFORMANCE SPACES IN BUILDING: 1
    LOCATION OF AUDITORIUM: Second floor
    STAGE DIMENSIONS AND EQUIPMENT: Height and width of
       proscenium, 16ft x 30ft; Distance from edge of stage
       to back wall of stage, 40ft; Distance between side
       walls of stage, 50ft
    ADDITIONAL INFORMATION: The proscenium arch columns and
       six large paintings in auditorium were taken from the
       Columbian Exposition (1893). An old drop exists. The
       stage house has been removed.

Waterville, KS

WATERVILLE OPERA HOUSE (other name: Waterville City Hall),
    204 East Front Street
    OPENING DATE: 1903
    ARCHITECT: Mr. Snodgrass (Frankfort)   STYLE OF
    ARCHITECTURE: Elizabethan   FACADE: Natural cut stone
    TYPE OF THEATRE: (b)   DEGREE OF RESTORATION: (c)
    CURRENT USE: Summer theatre   PERFORMANCE SPACES IN
    BUILDING: 1   LOCATION OF AUDITORIUM: First floor

STAGE DIMENSIONS AND EQUIPMENT: Height and width of
    proscenium, 16ft x 22ft; Shape of proscenium arch,
    square; Distance from edge of stage to back wall of
    stage, 22ft; Distance from edge of stage to curtain
    line, 19ft; Distance between side walls of stage, 41ft;
    Distance from stage floor to fly loft, 20ft; Depth under
    stage, 4ft; Stage floor, flat; Scenery storage rooms,
    2 (beneath stage); Dressing rooms, 2 (beneath stage)
DIMENSIONS OF AUDITORIUM: Distance between side walls
    of auditorium, 41ft; Distance stage to back wall of
    auditorium, 60ft; Capacity of orchestra pit, 20
SEATING (1 level): 1st level, 340
SHAPE OF THE AUDITORIUM: Rectangular
MAJOR TYPES OF ENTERTAINMENT: Drama, vaudeville and
    traveling shows
MAJOR STARS WHO APPEARED AT THEATRE: Hillman Stock Company,
    North Players, McOwens Players, Ted North (early 1900s)
ADDITIONAL INFORMATION: The building currently houses the
    Waterville Summer Theatre. The city owns and maintains
    the building.

West Phalia, KS

J. C. MERRILL'S OPERA HOUSE, Main Street between Second
    and Third streets
OPENING DATE: 1886
STYLE OF ARCHITECTURE: Renaissance   TYPE OF BUILDING:
    Commercial   FACADE: Cut stone   TYPE OF THEATRE: (a)
DEGREE OF RESTORATION: (c)   CURRENT USE: Warehouse
ADDITIONAL INFORMATION: Building is in fair condition.

Wilson, KS

WILSON OPERA HOUSE, Old Highway 540
OPENING DATE: 1903
STYLE OF ARCHITECTURE: Romanesque   TYPE OF BUILDING:
    Czech lodge hall   FACADE: Native stone block
CURRENT USE: Commercial opera house
PERFORMANCE SPACES IN BUILDING: 1
ADDITIONAL INFORMATION: Building is in good condition.

Kentucky

Elizabethtown, KY

STEWART OPERA HOUSE, 12 Public Square
OPENING DATE: 1907   TYPE OF THEATRE: (b)   DEGREE OF
RESTORATION: (c)   CLOSING DATE: 1920s   CURRENT USE:
Offices   LOCATION OF AUDITORIUM: Second floor
STAGE DIMENSIONS AND EQUIPMENT: Height and width of
proscenium, 15ft x 26ft; Distance from edge of stage to
back wall of stage, 21ft
ADDITIONAL INFORMATION: The Stewart Opera House has not
been used as a theatre since the 1920s. It was used for
storage by Hub Department Store until about 1980 when it
was converted into insurance offices. Dimensions are
from Julius Cahn's 1910 Guidebook. All theatrical
elements have been removed.

Lawrenceburg, KY

LAWRENCEBURG THEATRE (other name: New Opera House), 201 East
Court Street
OPENING DATE: 1907
STYLE OF ARCHITECTURE: Vernacular   TYPE OF BUILDING:
Commercial   FACADE: Brick   TYPE OF THEATRE: (a)
DEGREE OF RESTORATION: (c)   CLOSING DATE: 1915
CURRENT USE: Warehouse
LOCATION OF AUDITORIUM: First floor
ADDITIONAL INFORMATION: The theatre is mentioned in Julius
Cahn's guidebook (1910) with no dimensions, but is not
listed in Gus Hall's guidebook (1915).

Lexington, KY

MELODIAN HALL (other name: Theatre in McAdams Building),
200 West Main Street
OPENING DATE: 1849
STYLE OF ARCHITECTURE: Greek   TYPE OF BUILDING: Movie

theatre   FACADE: Cast iron facade   TYPE OF
THEATRE: (b)   DEGREE OF RESTORATION: (c)   CURRENT USE:
   Movie theatre   LOCATION OF AUDITORIUM: Second floor
MAJOR TYPES OF ENTERTAINMENT: Drama, movies
MAJOR STARS WHO APPEARED AT THEATRE: Jenny Lind, Adelina
   Patti, General Tom Thumb
ADDITIONAL INFORMATION: This second floor auditorium
   hosted performances by Jenny Lind, Adelina Patti,
   and General Tom Thumb. It is now a 300-seat movie
   house in the McAdams Building and no trace of earlier
   theatre remains.

Lexington, KY

OPERA HOUSE, 401 West Short Street (at Broadway)
   OPENING DATE: August 19, 1887
   STYLE OF ARCHITECTURE: Romanesque Victorian   FACADE: Brick
   TYPE OF THEATRE: (a)   DEGREE OF RESTORATION: (d)
   CURRENT USE: Theatre
   STAGE DIMENSIONS AND EQUIPMENT: Height and width of
   proscenium, 34ft x 35ft 6in; Distance from edge of stage
   to back wall of stage, 42ft; Distance from edge of stage
   to curtain line, 4ft; Distance between side walls of
   stage, 65ft; Distance from stage floor to fly loft, 60ft;
   Depth under stage, 10ft; Stage floor, flat; Trap doors, 4

Louisville, KY

BELNAP PLAYHOUSE (other name: House of Refuge), Between 2nd
   and 3rd Streets, Avery and Bradey
   ARCHITECT: C. J. Clark   STYLE OF ARCHITECTURE: Carpenter
   Gothic   TYPE OF BUILDING: Church   FACADE: White board
   TYPE OF THEATRE: (a)   DEGREE OF RESTORATION: (d)
   CURRENT USE: Theatre   LOCATION OF AUDITORIUM: First floor
   ADDITIONAL INFORMATION: This beautiful Carpenter Gothic
   church was converted into a University Theatre in 1925.
   To avoid demolition, the theatre was moved and re-
   constructed board by board in 1977.

Louisville, KY

HIGHLAND THEATER (other name: Highland Hall), 919 Barter
   Avenue
   OPENING DATE: 1909
   STYLE OF ARCHITECTURE: Classical Revival   TYPE OF
   BUILDING: Commercial   TYPE OF THEATRE: (a)
   DEGREE OF RESTORATION: (c)   CLOSING DATE: 1924
   CURRENT USE: Commercial
   ADDITIONAL INFORMATION: This two-story Classical Revival
   building now houses a sewing company. Long rows of
   highback, leather benches and a small stage remain.
   The building is in poor condition.

Louisville, KY

SAVOY THEATRE (other names: Grand Opera House, Wonderland
    Museum), 209-13 West Jefferson
    OPENING DATE: 1894
    ARCHITECT: D. X. Murphy   STYLE OF ARCHITECTURE:
    Commercial Eclectic   FACADE: Brick
    TYPE OF THEATRE: (a)   DEGREE OF RESTORATION: (c)
    CURRENT USE: X-rated movie house
    ADDITIONAL INFORMATION: In 1894, the reconstructed
    Wonderland Museum opened as the 2,000-seat Grand Opera
    House built in the Victorian style of architecture.
    The exterior is plain, but the interior is quite ornate.

Louisville, KY

WALNUT STREET THEATRE (other names: The Ritz, Drury Lane,
    The Schoop Theatre), 530 West Walnut Street
    OPENING DATE: 1910
    ARCHITECT: John Eberson   STYLE OF ARCHITECTURE:
    Italian Renaissance Revival   TYPE OF BUILDING:
    Convention center   FACADE: Unpainted brick and terra
    cotta   TYPE OF THEATRE: (b)   DEGREE OF RESTORATION: (c)
    CLOSING DATE: 1952   CURRENT USE: Apartments, stores
    STAGE DIMENSIONS AND EQUIPMENT: Distance from edge of stage
    to back wall of stage, 30ft; Distance between side walls
    of stage, 80ft; Distance from stage floor to fly loft,
    52ft
    ADDITIONAL INFORMATION: Early vaudeville house designed by
    John Eberson, McDonald and Dodd. Now vacant and stripped
    of all interior details. Exterior is covered in aluminum
    and wood.

Russellville, KY

OLD OPERA HOUSE, Main and Fifth Streets
    OPENING DATE: 1903   OPENING SHOW: Human Hearts
    ARCHITECT: Barclay Caldwell, builder   TYPE OF BUILDING:
    Commercial   TYPE OF THEATRE: (b)   DEGREE OF
    RESTORATION: (c)   LOCATION OF AUDITORIUM: Second floor
    DIMENSIONS OF AUDITORIUM: Orchestra pit, yes
    MAJOR TYPES OF ENTERTAINMENT: Local and traveling plays and
    minstrel shows
    ADDITIONAL INFORMATION: The building now houses the Chamber
    of Commerce and the firehouse.

Springfield, KY

OPERA HOUSE (other name: Washington Opera House), 124 West
    Main Street
    OPENING DATE: 1900
    STYLE OF ARCHITECTURE: Vernacular   TYPE OF THEATRE: (b)
    DEGREE OF RESTORATION: (c)   CURRENT USE: Storage

ADDITIONAL INFORMATION: This two-story brick building
features a pyramidal tower in its front. The theatre
is situated above small retail businesses. It was
converted to movies in 1926.

1. FORT PAYNE OPERA HOUSE. Fort Payne, Alabama. Opened in 1889. Photographer: James Kuykendall.

2. BIRD CAGE THEATRE. Tombstone, Arizona. Used by permission of the Chesley Collection.

3. NEVADA THEATRE. Nevada, California. Used by permission of the Chesley Collection.

4. OPERA HALL GARAGE. Sonora, California. Used by permission of the Chesley Collection.

5. WHEELER OPERA HOUSE. Aspen, Colorado. Used by permission of the Chesley Collection.

6. CHAUTAUQUA AUDITORIUM. Boulder, Colorado. Used by permission of the Chesley Collection.

7. TABOR OPERA HOUSE. Leadville, Colorado. Opened in 1879. Denver Post photo, 1965. Exterior view.

8. GOODSPEED OPERA HOUSE. East Haddam, Connecticut. Wilson H. Brownell, photographer.

9. CAPITOL. Dover, Delaware. Credit: Jack Neeson.

10. GRAND OPERA HOUSE. Wilmington, Delaware. Used by permission of the Chesley Collection.

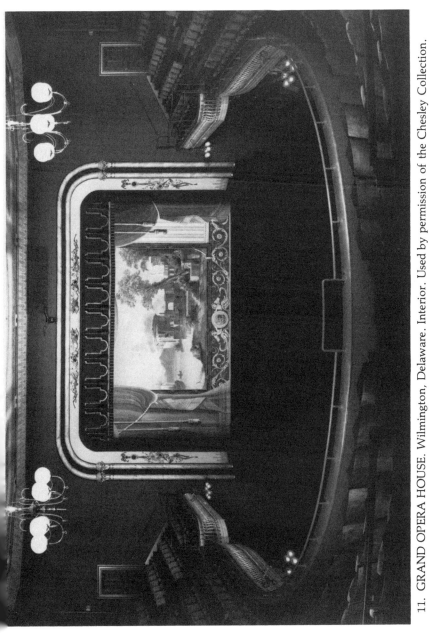

11. GRAND OPERA HOUSE. Wilmington, Delaware. Interior. Used by permission of the Chesley Collection.

12. FORD'S THEATRE. Washington, DC. Constructed: 1863. Restored: 1968.
Photo by Andrew Lautman, Copyright, 1984.

13. FORD'S THEATRE. Washington, DC. Constructed: 1863. Restored: 1968.
Photo by Andrew Lautman, Copyright, 1984.

14. GALLIE'S HALL. Tallahassee, Florida. Credit: Jack Neeson.

15. CENTRO ASTURIANO. Tampa, Florida. Credit: Jack Neeson.

16. CENTRO ASTURIANO. Tampa, Florida. Credit: Jack Neeson.

17. SPRINGER OPERA HOUSE. Columbus, Georgia. Credit: Jack Neeson.

8. FISHER OPERA HOUSE. Hawkinsville, Gerorgia. Used by permission of the
:sley Collection.

19. OPERA HOUSE. Hawkinsville, Georgia. Credit: Jack Neeson.

20. GRAND OPERA HOUSE. Macon, Georgia. Credit: Jack Neeson.

21. AUDITORIUM. Chicago, Illinois. Used by permission of the Chesley Collection.

22. BLACKSTONE THEATRE. Chicago, Illinois. Used by permission of the Chesley Collection.

23. ORCHESTRA HALL. Chicago, Illinois. Used by permission of the Chesley Collection.

24. SHUBERT THEATRE. Chicago, Illinois. Used by permission of the Chesley Collection.

25. BRADEN BROTHERS' OPERA HOUSE. Watseka, Illinois. Used by permission of the Chesley Collection.

26. BRISTOL OPERA HOUSE. Bristol, Indiana. Used by permission of the Chesley Collection.

27. THRALL'S OPERA HOUSE. New Harmony, Indiana. Used by permission of the Chesley Collection.

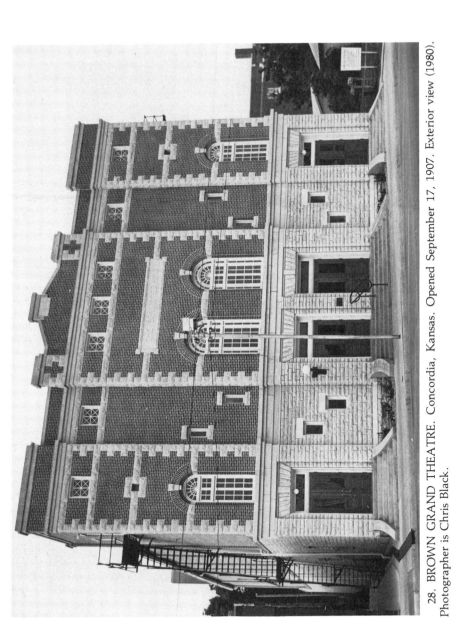

28. BROWN GRAND THEATRE. Concordia, Kansas. Opened September 17, 1907. Exterior view (1980). Photographer is Chris Black.

29. BROWN GRAND THEATRE. Concordia, Kansas. Opened September 17, 1907. View of stage from balcony. Drop is entitled "Napolean at Austerlitz." Unknown photographer.

30. LA ROQUE OPERA HOUSE. Concordia, Kansas. Used by permission of the Chesley Collection.

31. MCPHERSON OPERA HOUSE. McPherson, Kansas. Used by permission of the Chesley Collection.

32. CUSTOM HALL. Monmouth, Maine. Used by permission of the Chesley Collection.

33. ACADEMY OF MUSIC. Northampton, Massachusetts. Used by permission of the Chesley Collection.

34. COLONIAL. Pittsfield, Massachusetts. Used by permission of the Chesley Collection.

35. BERKSHIRE THEATRE FESTIVAL. Stockbridge, Massachusetts. Used by permission of the Chesley Collection.

36. WINCHENDON TOWN HALL. Winchendon, Massachusetts. Used by permission of the Chesley Collection.

37. GRAND OPERA HOUSE. Meridian, Mississippi. Used by permission of the Chesley Collection.

38. VERMONTVILLE OPERA HOUSE. Vermontville, Michigan. Used by permission of the Chesley Collection.

40. FOLLY THEATRE. Kansas City, Missouri. Used by permission of the Chesley Collection.

39. CONCERT HALL. Hermann, Missouri. Used by permission of the Chesley Collection.

Louisiana

Crowley, LA

GRAND OPERA HOUSE, Corner of North Parkerson and 5th Streets
  OPENING DATE: 1901
  TYPE OF BUILDING: Drugstore   FACADE: Brick
  TYPE OF THEATRE: (a)   DEGREE OF RESTORATION: (c)
  CLOSING DATE: 1941   CURRENT USE: Dixie Hardware Store
  LOCATION OF AUDITORIUM: Second floor
  STAGE DIMENSIONS AND EQUIPMENT: Height and width of
    proscenium, 45ft x 45ft; Distance from edge of stage
    to back wall of stage, 45ft 2in; Distance between side
    walls of stage, 60ft
  DIMENSIONS OF AUDITORIUM: Orchestra pit, yes
  SHAPE OF THE AUDITORIUM: Horseshoe-shaped balcony
  MAJOR TYPES OF ENTERTAINMENT: Drama, vaudeville, movies,
    graduations
  MAJOR STARS WHO APPEARED AT THEATRE: Babe Ruth, William
    Jennings Bryan, Irene Dunn, Busby Berkleley
  ADDITIONAL INFORMATION: The theatre is located in an
    historic district.

Fisher, LA

FISHER OPERA HOUSE,
  OPENING DATE: c. 1900
  STYLE OF ARCHITECTURE: Colonial Revival   FACADE: White
    wood   TYPE OF THEATRE: (a)   DEGREE OF RESTORATION: (a)
  LOCATION OF AUDITORIUM: Ground floor
  ADDITIONAL INFORMATION: This is a well-preserved theatre
    located in a mill town.

Lake Charles, LA

ARCADE THEATRE, 822 Ryan Street
  OPENING DATE: September 26, 1910
  OPENING SHOW: Billy starring Sidney Drew

ARCHITECT: I. C. Carter   FACADE: Grey stucco
TYPE OF THEATRE: (a)   CLOSING DATE: 1973
CURRENT USE: Vacant   PERFORMANCE SPACES IN BUILDING: 1
LOCATION OF AUDITORIUM: Ground floor
STAGE DIMENSIONS AND EQUIPMENT: Height and width of
  proscenium, 25ft x 32ft; Distance from edge of stage to
  back wall of stage, 40ft; Distance from edge of stage to
  curtain line, 50ft; Distance between side walls of stage,
  60ft; Distance from stage floor to fly loft, 55ft;
  Dressing rooms, 10 (backstage)
SEATING (3 levels): 1st level, 700; 2nd level, 350;
  3rd level, 250
MAJOR TYPES OF ENTERTAINMENT: Drama, vaudeville, burlesque,
  opera
MAJOR STARS WHO APPEARED AT THEATRE: Ethel Barrymore,
  Sousa, Houdini

Ville Platte, LA

DARDEAU BUILDING, 224 West Main Street
  OPENING DATE: 1912
  STYLE OF ARCHITECTURE: Italianate   TYPE OF BUILDING:
    Commercial   FACADE: White pressed tin
  TYPE OF THEATRE: (b)   DEGREE OF RESTORATION: (c)
  CURRENT USE: Storage
  LOCATION OF AUDITORIUM: Second and third levels
  ADDITIONAL INFORMATION: A beautifully painted auditorium
    ceiling remains.

Maine

Bethel, ME

IDEAL HALL (other name: Opera House), Main Street
OPENING DATE: 1884
STYLE OF ARCHITECTURE: Victorian   TYPE OF BUILDING:
   Commercial   FACADE: Gray clapboard   TYPE OF
THEATRE: (b)   DEGREE OF RESTORATION: (c)   CURRENT USE:
   Condominiums   LOCATION OF AUDITORIUM: Second floor
MAJOR TYPES OF ENTERTAINMENT: Drama

Bethel, ME

ODEON HALL, Main Street
OPENING DATE: 1891
ARCHITECT: George M. Coombs   STYLE OF ARCHITECTURE:
   Queen Anne   TYPE OF BUILDING: Commercial
FACADE: Clapboard, tan with dark brown trim
TYPE OF THEATRE: (b)   DEGREE OF RESTORATION: (c)
CURRENT USE: Vacant   LOCATION OF AUDITORIUM: Second floor
DIMENSIONS OF AUDITORIUM: Orchestra pit, none
SHAPE OF THE AUDITORIUM: U-shaped
MAJOR TYPES OF ENTERTAINMENT: Drama, minstrel shows,
   dances, concerts, lectures, chautauqua meetings, movies
MAJOR STARS WHO APPEARED AT THEATRE: Geraldine Farrar, Jane
   Addams

Biddeford, ME

CITY THEATRE (other name: Opera House), 205 Main Street
OPENING DATE: January 1896   OPENING SHOW: The Octoroon
ARCHITECT: John Calvin Stevens   STYLE OF ARCHITECTURE:
   Italianate   TYPE OF BUILDING: City Hall   FACADE: Red
   brick   TYPE OF THEATRE: (b)   DEGREE OF RESTORATION: (b)
CURRENT USE: Theatre   LOCATION OF AUDITORIUM: Second floor
STAGE DIMENSIONS AND EQUIPMENT: Height and width of
   proscenium, 24ft 6in x 23ft; Shape of proscenium arch,

arched; Distance from edge of stage to back wall of
stage, 35ft; Distance from edge of stage to curtain line,
5ft; Distance between side walls of stage, 42ft; Distance
from stage floor to fly loft, 40ft; Depth under stage,
8ft; Stage floor, raked; Trap doors, 0; Scenery storage
rooms, 0; Dressing rooms, 8 (2 each level)
DIMENSIONS OF AUDITORIUM: Distance between side walls
of auditorium, 40ft; Distance stage to back wall of
auditorium, 50ft; Orchestra pit, none
SEATING (3 levels): 1st level, 374; 2nd level, 220; 3rd
level, 66
SHAPE OF THE AUDITORIUM: Square with horseshoe balcony
MAJOR TYPES OF ENTERTAINMENT: Drama, vaudeville, opera
MAJOR STARS WHO APPEARED AT THEATRE: Edwin Booth, Joseph
Jefferson, W .C. Fields, Will Rogers, Gene Autry, Roy
Rogers, Abbott and Costello

Damariscotta, ME

LINCOLN THEATRE, Main Street
OPENING DATE: 1860s
TYPE OF BUILDING: Commercial   FACADE: Brick
TYPE OF THEATRE: (b)   DEGREE OF RESTORATION: (a)
CURRENT USE: Theatre LOCATION OF AUDITORIUM: Second floor
DIMENSIONS OF AUDITORIUM: Capacity of orchestra pit, 36
SEATING (2 levels): 1st level, 330; 2nd level, 30
SHAPE OF THE AUDITORIUM: Square
MAJOR TYPES OF ENTERTAINMENT: Drama, vaudeville

Lewiston, ME

EMPIRE THEATRE, 144 Main Street
OPENING DATE: November 23, 1903
OPENING SHOW: Yankee Consul
STYLE OF ARCHITECTURE: Victorian   TYPE OF BUILDING: Church
FACADE: Brick; light brown   TYPE OF THEATRE: (a)   DEGREE
OF RESTORATION: (a)   CLOSING DATE: 1982
CURRENT USE: Church and church school
LOCATION OF AUDITORIUM: Ground floor
STAGE DIMENSIONS AND EQUIPMENT: Height and width of
proscenium, 20ft x 40ft; Shape of proscenium arch,
arched; Distance from edge of stage to back wall of
stage, 16ft; Distance from edge of stage to curtain line,
2ft; Distance between side walls of stage, 60ft; Depth
under stage, 6ft; Stage floor, flat; Trap doors, 1 (above
stage); Dressing rooms, 2 (stage left and right)
DIMENSIONS OF AUDITORIUM: Distance between side walls of
auditorium, 60ft; Orchestra pit, none
SEATING (3 levels): 1st level, 594; 2nd level, 348;
3rd level, 509; boxes, 48
SHAPE OF THE AUDITORIUM: Predominantly rectangular
MAJOR TYPES OF ENTERTAINMENT: Drama, vaudeville, movies
ADDITIONAL INFORMATION: Until June of 1984, when it was

purchased for conversion to church activitites, the
Empire Theatre was scheduled for demolition to make room
for a parking lot. A 1940 conversion to a movie theatre
had resulted in the removal of the stage, orchestra pit
and boxes and the installation of new interior walls.

Madison, ME

LAKEWOOD THEATRE (other name: State of Maine Theatre),
    Lakewood Avenue
    OPENING DATE: June 1901
    OPENING SHOW: The Private Secretary
    FACADE: White wood   TYPE OF THEATRE: (a)
    DEGREE OF RESTORATION: (b)   CURRENT USE: Theatre
    LOCATION OF AUDITORIUM: Ground floor
    STAGE DIMENSIONS AND EQUIPMENT: Width of proscenium,
        60ft.; Shape of proscenium arch, square; Distance
        from edge of stage to back wall of stage, 100ft;
        Distance from edge of stage to curtain line, 5ft;
        Distance between side walls of stage, 150ft; Depth
        under stage, 5ft; Stage floor, flat; Trap doors, 1;
        Scenery storage rooms, 2 (separate building);
        Dressing rooms, 7 (backstage)
    DIMENSIONS OF AUDITORIUM: Orchestra pit, none
    SEATING (2 levels): 1st level, 600; 2nd level, 400
    SHAPE OF THE AUDITORIUM: U-shaped
    MAJOR TYPES OF ENTERTAINMENT: Drama, musical comedy,
        vaudeville, burlesque
    MAJOR STARS WHO APPEARED AT THEATRE: Edward Everett
        Horton, Fay Bainter, Lillian Gish, Hume Cronyn,
        Jessica Tandy, Victor Jory, Blanche Yurka, Florence
        Reed, Ethel Barrymore, Billie Burke, Humphrey Bogart,
        Keenan Wynn, Ed Wynn, Cornelia Otis Skinner, Mary Astor,
        Gloria Swanson, Myrna Loy, Cyril Richard, Ginger Rogers,
        Walter Pidgeon, Tallulah Bankhead, and others
    ADDITIONAL INFORMATION: In 1967, The Maine State
        Legislature passed a resolution designating the
        Lakewood the Official Theatre of the State of Maine.

Monmouth, ME

    CUMSTON HALL (other names: Monmouth Town Hall, The Theatre
        at Monmouth), North Main Street
    OPENING DATE: June 28, 1900
    ARCHITECT: Harry H. Cochrane   STYLE OF ARCHITECTURE:
        Victorian   TYPE OF BUILDING: Town hall and library
    FACADE: Buff colored wood   TYPE OF THEATRE: (a)
    DEGREE OF RESTORATION: (d)   CURRENT USE: Theatre
    LOCATION OF AUDITORIUM: Second floor
    STAGE DIMENSIONS AND EQUIPMENT: Height and width of
        proscenium, 12ft x 20ft 6in; Shape of proscenium arch,
        arched; Distance from edge of stage to back wall of
        stage, 16ft 4in; Distance from edge of stage to curtain

line, 5ft; Depth under stage, 5ft; Stage floor, raked;
Trap doors, 1; Dressing rooms, 1 (caucus hall)
DIMENSIONS OF AUDITORIUM: Distance between side walls
of auditorium, 52ft; Distance stage to back wall of
auditorium, 35ft; Orchestra pit, none
SEATING (2 levels): 1st level, 242; 2nd level, 22
SHAPE OF THE AUDITORIUM: Horseshoe-shaped
MAJOR TYPES OF ENTERTAINMENT: Drama, operettas
MAJOR STARS WHO APPEARED AT THEATRE: Joan Crawford
ADDITIONAL INFORMATION: Architect Cochrane, a well-known
artist, not only designed the theatre, but also created
the stained glass windows, the interior plaster carving,
and frescoes, as well as writing the music and poetry for
opening night. Local selectmen refer to the theatre as
"our lovely white elephant."

Norway, ME

OPERA HOUSE BLOCK (other name: Norway Opera House),
Main Street
OPENING DATE: January 29, 1895
OPENING SHOW: Readings and musical selections
TYPE OF BUILDING: Commercial   FACADE: Red brick
TYPE OF THEATRE: (b)   DEGREE OF RESTORATION: (c)
CURRENT USE: Vacant   LOCATION OF AUDITORIUM: Second floor
STAGE DIMENSIONS AND EQUIPMENT: * Height and width of
proscenium, 18ft x 24ft; Distance from edge of stage to
back wall of stage, 24ft; Distance from edge of stage to
curtain line, 4ft 6in; Depth under stage, 3ft 6in; Trap
doors, 2
DIMENSIONS OF AUDITORIUM: Distance between side walls
of auditorium, 53ft; Distance stage to back wall of
auditorium, 62ft; Orchestra pit, none
SEATING (2 levels)
SHAPE OF THE AUDITORIUM: Oblong with a U-shaped balcony
ADDITIONAL INFORMATION: The theatre was erected to
replace an earlier opera house which had burned in
May of 1894. The stage right apron was extended 8
feet to accommodate a piano.

Ocean Park, ME

THE TEMPLE, Temple Avenue
OPENING DATE: August 2, 1881
OPENING SHOW: Religious service
ARCHITECTS: Dow & Wheeler   STYLE OF ARCHITECTURE:
Victorian, post and beam   TYPE OF BUILDING:
Multi-purpose amphitheatre   FACADE: White with green
trim   TYPE OF THEATRE: (c)   DEGREE OF RESTORATION: (d)
CURRENT USE: Amphitheatre
STAGE DIMENSIONS AND EQUIPMENT: Distance from edge of stage
to back wall of stage, 32ft; Distance from edge of stage
to curtain line, 6ft; Distance between side walls of
stage, 34ft; Depth under stage, 3ft; Stage floor, flat;

Trap doors, 0; Scenery storage rooms, 0; Dressing rooms,
  2 (sides of stage)
DIMENSIONS OF AUDITORIUM: Distance between side walls
  of auditorium, 80ft; Distance stage to back wall of
  auditorium, 80ft; Orchestra pit, none
SEATING (1 level): 1st level, 925
SHAPE OF THE AUDITORIUM: Octagonal
MAJOR TYPES OF ENTERTAINMENT: Drama, chautauquas, musical
  performances, movies
MAJOR STARS WHO APPEARED AT THEATRE: Booker T. Washington
ADDITIONAL INFORMATION: In 1927, The Temple was expanded
  and the stage was built into a rear extension. A Mason
  and Hamlin grand piano manufactured in 1893 had already
  been added in 1920 and a center post had been removed in
  1926 so that movies could be shown.

Portland, ME

PORTLAND THEATRE (other names: Portland Playhouse, Preble
  Street Playhouse), 11 Preble Street
OPENING DATE: February 14, 1910
OPENING SHOW: Vaudeville bill
ARCHITECT: G. Henri Desmond   TYPE OF BUILDING: Commercial
FACADE: Cast stone   TYPE OF THEATRE: (b)
DEGREE OF RESTORATION: (c)   CLOSING DATE: 1960s
CURRENT USE: Vacant; in danger of demolition
LOCATION OF AUDITORIUM: Second and third floors
STAGE DIMENSIONS AND EQUIPMENT: Distance from edge of stage
  to back wall of stage, 25ft; Distance between side walls
  of stage, 60ft; Stage floor, flat
DIMENSIONS OF AUDITORIUM: Distance between side walls
  of auditorium, 75ft; Distance stage to back wall of
  auditorium, 80ft; Orchestra pit, yes
SEATING (2 levels)
SHAPE OF THE AUDITORIUM: Square
MAJOR TYPES OF ENTERTAINMENT: Drama, vaudeville, movies

Saco, ME

CITY HALL (other name: Saco Opera House), 300 Main Street
OPENING DATE: October 1888
ARCHITECT: Thomas Hill   STYLE OF ARCHITECTURE:
  Transitional Greek Revival   TYPE OF BUILDING: Municipal
FACADE: Red brick   TYPE OF THEATRE: (b)   DEGREE OF
RESTORATION: (b)   CURRENT USE: City Hall
LOCATION OF AUDITORIUM: Second floor
STAGE DIMENSIONS AND EQUIPMENT: Height and width of
  proscenium, 18ft x 25ft; Shape of proscenium arch,
  rectangular; Distance from edge of stage to back wall of
  stage, 28ft; Distance from edge of stage to curtain line,
  9ft; Distance between side walls of stage, 33ft
DIMENSIONS OF AUDITORIUM: Distance between side walls
  of auditorium, 48ft; Distance stage to back wall of
  auditorium, 75ft; Orchestra pit, none

SEATING (2 levels)
SHAPE OF THE AUDITORIUM: Rectangular
MAJOR TYPES OF ENTERTAINMENT: Drama, operettas, local
   variety shows, civic functions
ADDITIONAL INFORMATION: The building was erected in 1856
   and a portion was converted into a theatre in 1887 at a
   cost of $7,000.

Searsport, ME

UNION HALL (other name: Searsport Opera House), 3 Reservoir
   Street
OPENING DATE: 1863
ARCHITECT: John Lane   STYLE OF ARCHITECTURE: Italianate
TYPE OF BUILDING: Municipal offices   FACADE: White
   clapboard   TYPE OF THEATRE: (b)   DEGREE OF
RESTORATION: (b)   CLOSING DATE: November 1985   CURRENT
USE: Vacant   LOCATION OF AUDITORIUM: Second floor
STAGE DIMENSIONS AND EQUIPMENT: Height and width of
   proscenium, 20ft x 33ft; Shape of proscenium arch,
   arched; Distance from edge of stage to back wall of
   stage, 15ft; Distance from edge of stage to curtain line,
   2ft; Depth under stage, 3ft; Stage floor, flat; Scenery
   storage rooms, 2 (rear of theatre)
DIMENSIONS OF AUDITORIUM: Distance between side walls
   of auditorium, 45ft; Distance stage to back wall of
   auditorium, 60ft;   Orchestra pit, none
SEATING (2 levels): 1st level, 250; 2nd level, 90
SHAPE OF THE AUDITORIUM: Square
ADDITIONAL INFORMATION: The theatre is not in use currently
   due to the lack of access for the handicapped.

Skowhegan, ME

SKOWHEGAN OPERA HOUSE, 90 Water Street
OPENING DATE: 1907
ARCHITECT: John Calvin Stevens   TYPE OF BUILDING:
   Municipal   FACADE: Red brick   TYPE OF THEATRE: (b)
DEGREE OF RESTORATION: (a)   CURRENT USE: Theatre/meeting
   hall   LOCATION OF AUDITORIUM: Second floor
STAGE DIMENSIONS AND EQUIPMENT: Height and width of
   proscenium, 24ft x 30ft 6in; Shape of proscenium arch,
   square; Distance from edge of stage to back wall of
   stage, 31ft; Distance from edge of stage to curtain line,
   4ft; Distance between side walls of stage, 65ft 6in;
   Depth under stage, 5ft; Stage floor, flat; Trap doors, 1;
   Scenery storage rooms, 2; Dressing rooms, 3 (side of
   stage)
DIMENSIONS OF AUDITORIUM: Distance between side walls of
   auditorium, 65ft 6in; Distance stage to back wall of
   auditorium, 63ft; Capacity of orchestra pit, 12
SEATING (2 levels): 1st level, 546; 2nd level, 352
SHAPE OF THE AUDITORIUM: U-shaped

MAJOR TYPES OF ENTERTAINMENT: Drama, musical comedy,
  vaudeville, concerts, movies

Thomaston, ME

WATTS HALL, Main and Knox Streets
  OPENING DATE: January 1, 1891
  OPENING SHOW: Black Diamond Minstrels
  TYPE OF BUILDING: Municipal building
  FACADE: Brick and granite   TYPE OF THEATRE: (b)
  DEGREE OF RESTORATION: (c)   CURRENT USE: Theatre
  LOCATION OF AUDITORIUM: Second floor
  STAGE DIMENSIONS AND EQUIPMENT: Height and width of
    proscenium, 15ft x 20ft; Shape of proscenium arch,
    square; Distance between side walls of stage, 42ft;
    Stage floor, flat
  DIMENSIONS OF AUDITORIUM: Distance between side walls
    of auditorium, 55ft; Distance stage to back wall of
    auditorium, 35ft; Orchestra pit, none
  MAJOR TYPES OF ENTERTAINMENT: Drama, local variety shows,
    civic functions
  ADDITIONAL INFORMATION: Old Watts Hall burned in 1915, but
    Samuel Watts' will provided insurance and the hall was
    rebuilt. All dimensions and seating capacity provided
    are for the hall which reopened in 1916, although
    descriptions indicate that the interior was little
    changed from the first hall.

Waterville, ME

WATERVILLE OPERA HOUSE (other name: City Hall), Castonguay
    Square
  OPENING DATE: June 22, 1902   OPENING SHOW: Dedication
  STYLE OF ARCHITECTURE: Victorian   TYPE OF BUILDING: City
    Hall   FACADE: Red brick   TYPE OF THEATRE: (b)
  DEGREE OF RESTORATION: (a)   CURRENT USE: Theatre
  LOCATION OF AUDITORIUM: Second floor
  STAGE DIMENSIONS AND EQUIPMENT: Height and width of
    proscenium, 21ft x 32ft; Shape of proscenium arch,
    arched; Distance from edge of stage to back wall of
    stage, 34ft; Distance from edge of stage to curtain line,
    3ft; Distance between side walls of stage, 64ft; Depth
    under stage, 3ft 6in; Stage floor, flat; Dressing rooms,
    9 (3 levels, stage left and right)
  DIMENSIONS OF AUDITORIUM: Distance between side walls of
    auditorium, 60ft; Distance stage to back wall of
    auditorium, 72ft; Capacity of orchestra pit, 68
  SEATING (2 levels): 1st level, 500; 2nd level, 500
  SHAPE OF THE AUDITORIUM: Horseshoe-shaped
  MAJOR TYPES OF ENTERTAINMENT: Drama, musical comedy, dance
  MAJOR STARS WHO APPEARED AT THEATRE: Tom Mix
  ADDITIONAL INFORMATION: According to local legend, when Tom
    Mix appeared at the theatre, his horse was hoisted up two
    stories to the stage right loading door.

Maryland

Annapolis, MD

OPERA HOUSE (other names: Masonic, Weems Preparatory School), 44-46 Maryland Avenue
OPENING DATE: 1872   OPENING SHOW: Laura Dean and Company
STYLE OF ARCHITECTURE: High Victorian   TYPE OF BUILDING: Post office, commercial   FACADE: Brick
TYPE OF THEATRE: (b)   DEGREE OF RESTORATION: (c)
CURRENT USE: Commercial, art gallery   PERFORMANCE SPACES IN BUILDING: 1   LOCATION OF AUDITORIUM: Second floor
MAJOR TYPES OF ENTERTAINMENT: Opera, other "varied performances"
MAJOR STARS WHO APPEARED AT THEATRE: Lillian Russell
ADDITIONAL INFORMATION: All theatrical elements have been removed.

Baltimore, MD

LYRIC OPERA HOUSE (other names: Lyric Theatre, Music Hall), 1404 Maryland Avenue
OPENING DATE: October 30, 1894
OPENING SHOW: Concert, Boston Symphony Orchestra
ARCHITECTS: Righter, Cornbrooks, Gribble
FACADE: Red and brown brick   TYPE OF THEATRE: (a)
DEGREE OF RESTORATION: (a)   CURRENT USE: Theatre
PERFORMANCE SPACES IN BUILDING: 1
LOCATION OF AUDITORIUM: First floor
STAGE DIMENSIONS AND EQUIPMENT: Height and width of proscenium, 24ft x 64ft 5in; Shape of proscenium arch, arched; Distance from edge of stage to back wall of stage, 40ft 10in; Distance from edge of stage to curtain line, 3ft 8in; Distance between side walls of stage, 92ft 8in; Distance from stage floor to fly loft, 62ft 8in; Stage floor, flat; Scenery storage rooms, 1 (basement, below stage); Dressing rooms, 7 (stage right and below stage)

DIMENSIONS OF AUDITORIUM: Distance between side walls of
   auditorium, 110ft; Distance stage to back wall of
   auditorium, 160ft; Capacity of orchestra pit, 90
SEATING (4 levels): 1st level, 1000; 2nd level, 208; 3rd
   level, 540; 4th level, 816
SHAPE OF THE AUDITORIUM: Rectangular
MAJOR TYPES OF ENTERTAINMENT: Concerts, opera, ballet
ADDITIONAL INFORMATION: A modern (1974) front and lobby
   replace the previous ones. The original front (1894) was
   never completed.

Hagerstown, MD

MARYLAND THEATRE, 21 South Potomac Street
   OPENING DATE: May 10, 1915
   OPENING SHOW: Concert, The Maryland Theatre Orchestra
   ARCHITECT: Thomas W. Lamb   FACADE: Brick
   TYPE OF THEATRE: (a)   DEGREE OF RESTORATION: (a)
   CURRENT USE: Theatre   PERFORMANCE SPACES IN BUILDING: 1
   LOCATION OF AUDITORIUM: First floor
   STAGE DIMENSIONS AND EQUIPMENT: Height and width of
     proscenium, 25ft x 33ft 9in; Shape of proscenium arch,
     arched; Distance from edge of stage to back wall of
     stage, 39ft; Distance from edge of stage to curtain line,
     34ft; Distance between side walls of stage, 62ft 3in;
     Distance from stage floor to fly loft, 52ft; Depth under
     stage, 10ft; Stage floor, flat; Dressing rooms, 5 (base-
     ment and stage)
   DIMENSIONS OF AUDITORIUM: Distance between side walls of
     auditorium, 62ft 3in; Distance stage to back wall of
     auditorium, 39ft; Orchestra pit, yes
   SEATING (2 levels): 1st level, 729; 2nd level, 674
   SHAPE OF THE AUDITORIUM: Square
   MAJOR TYPES OF ENTERTAINMENT: Vaudeville, movies
   MAJOR STARS WHO APPEARED AT THEATRE: Sousa, Will Rogers,
     Pavlova
   ADDITIONAL INFORMATION: The front of the theatre was
     destroyed by fire in 1974.

Massachusetts

Beverly, MA

LARCOM THEATRE (other name: Fine Arts), 13 Wallis Street
  OPENING DATE: October 28, 1912
  OPENING SHOW: Ware Glee Club and two films
  ARCHITECT: George Swan   FACADE: Brick and wood
  TYPE OF THEATRE: (a)   DEGREE OF RESTORATION: (a)
  CURRENT USE: Theatre   LOCATION OF AUDITORIUM: Ground floor
  STAGE DIMENSIONS AND EQUIPMENT: Height and width of
    proscenium, 22ft x 30ft; Shape of proscenium arch,
    arched; Distance from edge of stage to back wall of
    stage, 30ft; Distance from edge of stage to curtain
    line, 12ft; Distance between side walls of stage, 50ft;
    Distance from stage floor to fly loft, 25ft; Depth under
    stage, 9ft; Stage floor, flat; Trap doors, 2; Dressing
    rooms, 4 (under stage)
  DIMENSIONS OF AUDITORIUM: Distance between side walls
    of auditorium, 40ft; Distance stage to back wall of
    auditorium, 50ft; Orchestra pit, yes
  SEATING (3 levels): 1st level, 293; 2nd level, 135; 3rd
    level, 158; boxes, 45
  SHAPE OF THE AUDITORIUM: Horseshoe-shaped
  MAJOR TYPES OF ENTERTAINMENT: Vaudeville, movies, magic
    shows

Boston, MA

COLONIAL THEATRE, 100 Boylston Street
  OPENING DATE: December 20, 1900   OPENING SHOW: Ben Hur
  ARCHITECT: Clarence H. Blackall   TYPE OF BUILDING: Ten-
    story office building   TYPE OF THEATRE: (a)
  DEGREE OF RESTORATION: (d)   CURRENT USE: Legitimate
    theatre   LOCATION OF AUDITORIUM: Ground floor
  STAGE DIMENSIONS AND EQUIPMENT: * Height and width of
    proscenium, 38ft x 38ft; Shape of proscenium arch,
    square; Distance from edge of stage to back wall of
    stage, 45ft; Distance from edge of stage to curtain line,

4ft; Distance between side walls of stage, 80ft;
Depth under stage, 25ft; Dressing rooms, 36
SEATING: * 1st level, 618; 2nd level, 552; 3rd level,
368; boxes, 60
SHAPE OF THE AUDITORIUM: U-shaped
MAJOR TYPES OF ENTERTAINMENT: Drama, musical comedy,
variety
MAJOR STARS WHO APPEARED AT THEATRE: George M. Cohan (1908-
09), Ziegfeld Follies (1907), Fritzi Scheff, Gertrude
Lawrence, William Farnum, Ralph Richardson, Elsie Janis,
Ethel Barrymore, Richard Mansfield, Will Rogers, Anna
Held, Olga Nethersole, Noel Coward, Katherine Hepburn,
Douglas Fairbanks Sr., Helen Hayes, and others

Boston, MA

NATIONAL THEATRE, 533 Tremont Street
OPENING DATE: September 18, 1911   OPENING SHOW:
Consolidated Modern Minstrels and The Wound Up
ARCHITECT: Clarence H. Blackall   FACADE: Stucco and wood,
ochre with rose   TYPE OF THEATRE: (a)   DEGREE OF
RESTORATION: (b)   CLOSING DATE: April 1976   CURRENT
USE: Vacant   LOCATION OF AUDITORIUM: Ground floor
STAGE DIMENSIONS AND EQUIPMENT: Height and width of
proscenium, 20ft x 25ft; Shape of proscenium arch,
square; Distance from edge of stage to back wall of
stage, 30ft; Distance from edge of stage to curtain line,
8ft; Distance between side walls of stage, 35ft; Depth
under stage, 16ft; Stage floor, flat; Trap doors, 0;
Scenery storage rooms, 1 (basement); Dressing rooms,
4 (rear of stage)
DIMENSIONS OF AUDITORIUM: Orchestra pit, yes
SEATING (3 levels): 1st level, 1,500; 2nd level, 1,000;
3rd level, 500
SHAPE OF THE AUDITORIUM: U-shaped
MAJOR TYPES OF ENTERTAINMENT: Drama, musical comedy,
vaudeville, concerts
MAJOR STARS WHO APPEARED AT THEATRE: Fred Allen, Ray
Bolger, Jack Donahue, Ray Fontaine, Frank Fontaine, The
Will Mastin Trio with Sammy Davis Jr., Eva Tanguay, Irene
Franklin, Cissie Loftus, Eddie Cantor, Duke Ellington,
Jimmy Lunceford, Fletcher Henderson and May Hallatt

Boston, MA

PAGODA THEATRE (other names: Center Cinema, Globe Theatre),
686 Washington Street
OPENING DATE: September 14, 1903
OPENING SHOW: John Ermine of the Yellowstone
ARCHITECT: Arthur H. Vinal
STYLE OF ARCHITECTURE: Beaux Arts   FACADE: Light-colored
brick   TYPE OF THEATRE: (a) DEGREE OF RESTORATION: (c)
CURRENT USE: Chinese movie theatre
STAGE DIMENSIONS AND EQUIPMENT: * Height and width of

proscenium, 34ft x 34ft; Shape of proscenium arch,
square; Distance from edge of stage to back wall of
stage, 55ft; Distance between side walls of stage,
106ft; Dressing rooms, 21 (see ADDITIONAL INFORMATION)
DIMENSIONS OF AUDITORIUM: Distance between side walls
of auditorium, 74ft; Distance stage to back wall of
auditorium, 175ft
SEATING: 1st level, 637; 2nd level, 383; 3rd level, 404;
boxes, 112
SHAPE OF THE AUDITORIUM: U-shaped
MAJOR TYPES OF ENTERTAINMENT: Drama, musical comedy,
vaudeville, burlesque, movies
MAJOR STARS WHO APPEARED AT THEATRE: James K. Hackett
(1903), Weber and Fields (1903), Lillian Russell (1903),
Al Jolson, W. C. Fields, Abbott and Costello, Gypsy Rose
Lee, the Kiralfy Brothers
ADDITIONAL INFORMATION: The theatre has 21 dressing rooms -
3 in the basement and 6 each on the next three levels
above. It is also equipped with a 22'x 66' chorus room
in the basement, a 20'x 55' costume room above the
dressing rooms, two 15'x 32' carpenter shops off the fly
gallery, and a musicians' room under the stage.

Boston, MA

PILGRIM THEATRE (other names: Olympia, Gordon's Olympia),
658 Washington Street
OPENING DATE: May 5, 1912
ARCHITECT: C. H. Blackall   TYPE OF BUILDING:
Office building   TYPE OF THEATRE: (a)
DEGREE OF RESTORATION: (c)   CURRENT USE: Vacant
MAJOR TYPES OF ENTERTAINMENT: Vaudeville, movies
ADDITIONAL INFORMATION: When the Olympia opened, the
Gordon vaudeville circuit had two Olympias open in
Boston. The other was in Scollay Square which is
now Government Center. The Scollay Square theatre
was larger, but in most respects the theatres were
identical. The Washington Street Olympia cost over a
million dollars to construct and was called "the house
with the moving stairs" due to the escalator in its
lobby. The theatre had two balconies which were pitched
so steeply that they were compared to the Matterhorn.

Boston, MA

PUBLIX (other names: Gaiety, Lyceum), 663 Washington Street
OPENING DATE: November 23, 1908
OPENING SHOW: The Trocadero Burlesquers
ARCHITECT: Clarence H. Blackall   FACADE: Brick with
inlaid marble   TYPE OF THEATRE: (a)   DEGREE OF
RESTORATION: (c)   CURRENT USE: Movie theatre
STAGE DIMENSIONS AND EQUIPMENT: * Distance from edge of
stage to back wall of stage, 36ft; Distance between side
walls of stage, 67ft

DIMENSIONS OF AUDITORIUM: Distance between side walls
   of auditorium, 66ft; Distance stage to back wall of
   auditorium, 130ft
SEATING (3 levels)
MAJOR TYPES OF ENTERTAINMENT: Vaudeville, burlesque, movies
ADDITIONAL INFORMATION: At the time of its construction,
   the theatre was noted for the absence of support columns.

Boston, MA

SAXON THEATRE (other name: Majestic), 219 Tremont Street
   OPENING DATE: February 16, 1903
   OPENING SHOW: The Storks
   ARCHITECT: John Galen Howard   FACADE: Buff-colored brick
   TYPE OF THEATRE: (a)   CURRENT USE: See ADDITIONAL
   INFORMATION   LOCATION OF AUDITORIUM: Ground floor
   STAGE DIMENSIONS AND EQUIPMENT: * Height and width of
      proscenium, 38ft x 36ft; Shape of proscenium arch,
      square; Distance from edge of stage to back wall of
      stage, 40ft; Distance between side walls of stage, 78ft;
      Scenery storage rooms (below and above stage)
   DIMENSIONS OF AUDITORIUM: Distance between side walls
      of auditorium, 78ft; Distance stage to back wall of
      auditorium, 134ft
   SEATING: * 1st level, 597; 2nd level, 502; 3rd
      level, 600; boxes, 112
   MAJOR TYPES OF ENTERTAINMENT: Drama, musical comedy, light
      opera, movies
   MAJOR STARS WHO APPEARED AT THEATRE: Blanche Bates, James
      T. Powers, Mrs. Fiske, De Wolf Hopper, Lew Fields
   ADDITIONAL INFORMATION: The building is now owned by
      Emerson College which plans to use it for a lecture
      hall and theatre.

Boston, MA

SHUBERT THEATRE, 265 Tremont Street
   OPENING DATE: January 24, 1910
   OPENING SHOW: Taming of the Shrew,   Sothern and Marlowe
   ARCHITECT: Thomas M. James   FACADE: Grey/white stone
   TYPE OF THEATRE: (a)   DEGREE OF RESTORATION: (d)
   CURRENT USE: Legitimate theatre
   LOCATION OF AUDITORIUM: Ground floor
   STAGE DIMENSIONS AND EQUIPMENT: * Height and width of
      proscenium, 33ft x 40ft; Shape of proscenium arch,
      rectangular; Distance from edge of stage to back wall of
      stage, 45ft; Distance from edge of stage to curtain line,
      2ft; Distance between side walls of stage, 80ft; Depth
      under stage, 15ft; Dressing rooms, 18 (see ADDITIONAL
      INFORMATION)
   DIMENSIONS OF AUDITORIUM: Distance between side walls
      of auditorium, 80ft; Distance stage to back wall of
      auditorium, 80ft
   SEATING: * 1st level, 618; 2nd level, 474; 3rd

level, 401; boxes, 72
SHAPE OF THE AUDITORIUM: U-shaped
MAJOR TYPES OF ENTERTAINMENT: Drama, musical comedy
MAJOR STARS WHO APPEARED AT THEATRE: Katherine Cornell,
    Noel Coward, Gertrude Lawrence, Maurice Evans (1960), Al
    Jolson (1912), John Gielgud, Laurence Olivier, and others
ADDITIONAL INFORMATION: 12 dressing rooms are located at
    balcony level; 3 are below the stage; 3 are on stage.

Boston, MA

STATE THEATRE (other names: Park, Music Hall, Minsky's Park
    Burlesque, Trans Lux, Hub), 617 Washington Street
OPENING DATE: April 14, 1879   OPENING SHOW: La Cigale
ARCHITECT: C. H. Blackall (1903 renovation)
TYPE OF BUILDING: Office building   TYPE OF THEATRE: (a)
DEGREE OF RESTORATION: (c)   CURRENT USE: Porno films
LOCATION OF AUDITORIUM: Ground floor
STAGE DIMENSIONS AND EQUIPMENT: * Height and width of
    proscenium, 35ft x 30ft; Shape of proscenium arch,
    rectangular; Distance from edge of stage to back wall of
    stage, 39ft; Distance between side walls of stage, 50ft
DIMENSIONS OF AUDITORIUM: Distance between side walls
    of auditorium, 60ft; Distance stage to back wall of
    auditorium, 65ft
SEATING (3 levels): 1st level, 492; 2nd level, 250;
    3rd level, 381; boxes, 24
MAJOR TYPES OF ENTERTAINMENT: Drama, vaudeville, burlesque,
    opera, movies
MAJOR STARS WHO APPEARED AT THEATRE: Lotta Crabtree,
    Gypsy Rose Lee, Edwin Booth (1881), Richard Mansfield,
    Lawrence Barrett, William Florence, Joseph Jefferson,
    Clara Morris, Fanny Davenport, Fanny Janauschek, Nat
    Goodwin, Otis Skinner, Henry Miller, James T. Powers
ADDITIONAL INFORMATION: The theatre is considered the old-
    est surviving playhouse in Boston. When Lotta Crabtree
    owned the theatre, she lived next door in the Hotel
    Brewster which was connected to the theatre by a tunnel.

Boston, MA

STEINERT HALL, 162 Boylston Street
OPENING DATE: 1896   OPENING SHOW: Kneissel String Quartet
ARCHITECTS: Winslow and Wetherell   STYLE OF ARCHITECTURE:
    Italian Renaissance   TYPE OF BUILDING: Commercial and
    offices   FACADE: Off-white stone and brick
TYPE OF THEATRE: (b)   DEGREE OF RESTORATION: (c)
CURRENT USE: Vacant and decaying
LOCATION OF AUDITORIUM: Basement
STAGE DIMENSIONS AND EQUIPMENT: Distance from edge of stage
    to back wall of stage, 10ft; Distance between side walls
    of stage, 18ft; Stage floor, flat
DIMENSIONS OF AUDITORIUM: Distance between side walls
    of auditorium, 35ft; Distance stage to back wall of

auditorium, 60ft; Orchestra pit, none
SEATING (2 levels)
SHAPE OF THE AUDITORIUM: Elliptical
MAJOR TYPES OF ENTERTAINMENT: Concerts, poetry readings
MAJOR STARS WHO APPEARED AT THEATRE: Paderewski
ADDITIONAL INFORMATION: The theatre is an elliptical space
  35 feet below street level. The stage is a platform
  raised approximately 18 inches from the orchestra floor.

Boston, MA

WILBUR THEATRE, 252 Tremont Street
  OPENING DATE: April 19, 1914   OPENING SHOW: Romance
  ARCHITECT: Clarence H. Blackall   STYLE OF ARCHITECTURE:
    Colonial   FACADE: Dark, Harvard brick with white trim
  TYPE OF THEATRE: (a)   DEGREE OF RESTORATION: (d)
  CURRENT USE: Legitimate theatre
  LOCATION OF AUDITORIUM: Ground floor
  STAGE DIMENSIONS AND EQUIPMENT: Distance between side walls
    of stage, 67ft
  SEATING: 1st level, 600; 2nd level, 300; 3rd level, 300
  MAJOR TYPES OF ENTERTAINMENT: Drama, musical comedy
  MAJOR STARS WHO APPEARED AT THEATRE: Ruth Gordon, Zazu
    Pitts, Marlon Brando, the Barrymores, Eva Le Gallienne,
    Joseph Schildkraut, Helen Hayes, Katherine Cornell,
    Lillian Gish, Fritzi Scheff, Julia Sanderson, and others

Dighton, MA

SMITH MEMORIAL HALL (other name: Parish Hall), 207 Main
    Street
  OPENING DATE: November 1889   STYLE OF ARCHITECTURE:
    Victorian   FACADE: Painted shingles
  TYPE OF THEATRE: (c)   DEGREE OF RESTORATION: (a)
  CURRENT USE: Church activities
  STAGE DIMENSIONS AND EQUIPMENT: Shape of proscenium arch,
    rectangular; Distance from edge of stage to back wall of
    stage, 25ft; Distance from edge of stage to curtain line,
    10ft; Depth under stage, 20ft; Stage floor, flat;
    Dressing rooms, 2 (backstage)
  DIMENSIONS OF AUDITORIUM: Orchestra pit, none
  SHAPE OF THE AUDITORIUM: Rectangular
  MAJOR TYPES OF ENTERTAINMENT: Drama, vaudeville

Fall River, MA

ACADEMY OF MUSIC (other name: Academy Theatre),
    Borden Block, Main and Central
  OPENING DATE: January 6, 1876
  OPENING SHOW: Concert by Theodore Thomas
  ARCHITECTS: Hartwell and Swazey   STYLE OF ARCHITECTURE:
    Gothic   TYPE OF BUILDING: Shops, offices, apartments
  FACADE: Brick, tile, granite and sandstone

TYPE OF THEATRE: (a)   DEGREE OF RESTORATION: (a)
CURRENT USE: Apartments
STAGE DIMENSIONS AND EQUIPMENT: * Height and width of
  proscenium, 35ft x 36ft; Shape of proscenium arch,
  square; Distance from edge of stage to back wall of
  stage, 45ft; Distance from edge of stage to curtain line,
  3ft; Distance between side walls of stage, 69ft; Depth
  under stage, 9ft; Trap doors, 6
SEATING (3 levels)
MAJOR TYPES OF ENTERTAINMENT: Drama, musical comedy,
  concerts, opera, operetta, dance, balls, movies
MAJOR STARS WHO APPEARED AT THEATRE: Bernhardt, Edwin
  Booth, Buffalo Bill, Lillian Russell, The Barrymores,
  John L. Sullivan, Dan Dailey, Fritz Kreisler, Joseph
  Jefferson, Ruth Chatterton, Mary Anderson, Maude Adams,
  John Drew, the Rhinehart Sisters, Henry Miller, Thomas
  W. Keene, Lotta Crabtree, and others

Fitchburg, MA

WHITNEY OPERA HOUSE (other name: Bijou), Main Street
  OPENING DATE: October 20, 1880   OPENING SHOW: The Mascot
  TYPE OF BUILDING: Offices   TYPE OF THEATRE: (b)
  DEGREE OF RESTORATION: (c)   CLOSING DATE: 1924
  CURRENT USE: Offices   LOCATION OF AUDITORIUM: Second floor
  MAJOR TYPES OF ENTERTAINMENT: Drama, musical comedy,
    vaudeville, local variety shows
  MAJOR STARS WHO APPEARED AT THEATRE: Joseph Jefferson,
    Maurice Barrymore, John L. Sullivan, Lillian Russell

Hyde Park, MA

FRENCH'S OPERA HOUSE (other name: French's Hall),
    Fairmont Avenue
  OPENING DATE: 1890s   TYPE OF BUILDING: Commercial
  FACADE: Yellow brick   TYPE OF THEATRE: (b)
  DEGREE OF RESTORATION: (a)   CURRENT USE: Theatre
  LOCATION OF AUDITORIUM: Second floor
  STAGE DIMENSIONS AND EQUIPMENT: Width of proscenium, 40ft;
    Distance from edge of stage to back wall of stage, 20ft
  SEATING (2 levels)
  SHAPE OF THE AUDITORIUM: Rectangular
  MAJOR TYPES OF ENTERTAINMENT: Drama, musical comedy, opera

Northampton, MA

  ACADEMY OF MUSIC, 274 Main Street
  OPENING DATE: 1890
  OPENING SHOW: Concert, Beethoven Orchestral Club
  ARCHITECTS: W. C. Brocklesby   STYLE OF ARCHITECTURE:
    Italianate   FACADE: Brown stone
  TYPE OF THEATRE: (a)   DEGREE OF RESTORATION: (a)
  CURRENT USE: Theatre   LOCATION OF AUDITORIUM: Ground floor

STAGE DIMENSIONS AND EQUIPMENT: Height and width of
    proscenium, 30ft x 36ft; Shape of proscenium arch,
    arched; Distance from edge of stage to back wall of
    stage, 32ft; Distance from edge of stage to curtain line,
    4ft; Distance between side walls of stage, 63ft 6in;
    Distance from stage floor to fly loft, 30ft; Depth under
    stage, 8ft; Stage floor, flat; Trap doors, 1; Scenery
    storage rooms, 1 (rear of stage); Dressing rooms, 11
DIMENSIONS OF AUDITORIUM: Distance between side walls
    of auditorium, 45ft; Distance stage to back wall of
    auditorium, 100ft; Capacity of orchestra pit, 30
SEATING (3 levels): 1st level, 400; 2nd level, 200; 3rd
    level, 200; Boxes, 12
SHAPE OF THE AUDITORIUM: Horseshoe-shaped
MAJOR TYPES OF ENTERTAINMENT: Drama, musical comedy,
    vaudeville, burlesque, opera, movies
MAJOR STARS WHO APPEARED AT THEATRE: Bernhardt, Ethel
    Barrymore, George M. Cohan, Dorothy and Lillian Gish,
    Victor Herbert, Maude Adams, Mrs. Fiske, William Powell,
    Helena Modjeska, Nazimova, Rudolph Valentino, Pavlova,
    Otis Skinner, Frank Morgan, George Nolan
ADDITIONAL INFORMATION: In 1970 the stage and rigging of
    this city-owned theatre were declared unsafe and live
    performance was prohibited after a production of Man of
    La Mancha closed. Restored, the theatre, which was once
    home to the Northampton Players, as well as being a road
    house and movie theatre, now presents opera, ballet, and
    live theatre again.

Pittsfield, MA

BERKSHIRE PUBLIC THEATRE (other name: Union Square Theatre),
    30 Union Street
OPENING DATE: September 16, 1912
ARCHITECT: Edward S. Ostevee   STYLE OF ARCHITECTURE:
    Utilitarian Western Commercial   FACADE: Red brick
    painted tan and white   TYPE OF THEATRE: (a)
DEGREE OF RESTORATION: (a)   CURRENT USE: Performing arts
    center   LOCATION OF AUDITORIUM: Ground floor
STAGE DIMENSIONS AND EQUIPMENT: Height and width of
    proscenium, 21ft x 35ft; Shape of proscenium arch,
    rectangular; Distance from edge of stage to back wall of
    stage, 49ft; Distance from edge of stage to curtain line,
    14ft; Distance between side walls of stage, 65ft; Depth
    under stage, 12ft; Stage floor, raked; Trap doors, 2;
    Scenery storage rooms, 1 (basement); Dressing rooms, 1
    (basement)
DIMENSIONS OF AUDITORIUM: Distance between side walls
    of auditorium, 82ft; Distance stage to back wall of
    auditorium, 65ft; Capacity of orchestra pit, 18
SEATING (2 levels): 1st level, 600; 2nd level, 400
SHAPE OF THE AUDITORIUM: Rectangular
MAJOR TYPES OF ENTERTAINMENT: Vaudeville, drama, musical
    comedy, movies
MAJOR STARS WHO APPEARED AT THEATRE: Mae and Hill, Olga

and Nichols, Grant Gardener, Newport and Parker, the Four
Nightons
ADDITIONAL INFORMATION: Originally, there were six dressing
rooms located under the stage.

Pittsfield, MA

COLONIAL, 113 South Street
OPENING DATE: September 28, 1903
OPENING SHOW: Robin Hood
ARCHITECT: Joseph McA. Vance   FACADE: Yellow brick
TYPE OF THEATRE: (a)   DEGREE OF RESTORATION: (d)
CURRENT USE: Paint store
LOCATION OF AUDITORIUM: Ground floor
STAGE DIMENSIONS AND EQUIPMENT: Height and width of
  proscenium, 30ft x 30ft; Shape of proscenium arch,
  square; Distance from edge of stage to back wall of
  stage, 40ft; Distance between side walls of stage,
  60ft; Depth under stage, 7ft 6in; Stage floor, flat;
  Trap doors, 4; Scenery storage rooms, 1 (shed at rear
  of building reached via tunnel); Dressing rooms, 8
  (rear of stage and basement)
DIMENSIONS OF AUDITORIUM: Distance between side walls
  of auditorium, 60ft; Distance stage to back wall of
  auditorium, 120ft; Orchestra pit, yes
SEATING (3 levels): 1st level, 1,295: 2nd level, 291;
  3rd level, 275
SHAPE OF THE AUDITORIUM: U-shaped
MAJOR TYPES OF ENTERTAINMENT: Drama, musical comedy,
  minstrel shows, movies
MAJOR STARS WHO APPEARED AT THEATRE: George Arliss
  (1916), Dudley Digges, Blackstone the Magician (1926),
  Ethel Barrymore (1906), Grace George (1907), Sothern
  and Marlowe (1905), William Gillette (1905 and 1916),
  Walter Hampden (1919), Bernhardt (1917), Maude Adams
  (1913), Billie Burke (1913), May Robson (1919), Mrs.
  Fiske, Harry Lauder, Fritz Kreisler, Rachmaninoff,
  Pavlova, Dockstader's Minstrels, Ruth St. Denis

Pittsfield, MA

PALACE THEATRE (other name: Majestic), 140 North Street
OPENING DATE: November 23, 1910
OPENING SHOW: The Deserters
ARCHITECT: Joseph McA. Vance   TYPE OF BUILDING: Office
  building   TYPE OF THEATRE: (a)
DEGREE OF RESTORATION: (d)
CURRENT USE: Movie theatre
LOCATION OF AUDITORIUM: Ground floor
STAGE DIMENSIONS AND EQUIPMENT: Height and width of
  proscenium, 30ft x 32ft; Shape of proscenium arch,
  square; Distance from edge of stage to back wall of

stage, 35ft; Distance from edge of stage to curtain
line, 5ft; Distance between side walls of stage, 63ft
SEATING (2 levels): 1st level, 750; 2nd level, 450;
 boxes, 48
MAJOR TYPES OF ENTERTAINMENT: Drama, vaudeville, local
 variety shows, movies
MAJOR STARS WHO APPEARED AT THEATRE: Evelyn Nesbit

Sherborn, MA

SHERBORN OLD TOWN HALL, 1 Sanger Street
 OPENING DATE: c. 1858
 ARCHITECT: Edbridge Boyden   STYLE OF ARCHITECTURE:
  Italian Revival   TYPE OF BUILDING: School, library,
  town hall   FACADE: Wood; buff-colored clapboard
 TYPE OF THEATRE: (b)   DEGREE OF RESTORATION: (b)
 CURRENT USE: Vacant   LOCATION OF AUDITORIUM: Second floor
 STAGE DIMENSIONS AND EQUIPMENT: Height and width of
  proscenium, 8ft 4in x 23ft; Shape of proscenium arch,
  arched; Distance from edge of stage to back wall of
  stage, 11ft; Distance from edge of stage to curtain
  line, 2ft 6in; Distance between side walls of stage,
  27ft; Depth under stage, 2ft 10in; Stage floor, flat;
  Trap doors, 2
 DIMENSIONS OF AUDITORIUM: Distance between side walls
  of auditorium, 34ft; Distance stage to back wall of
  auditorium, 43ft; Orchestra pit, none
 SEATING (1 level): 1st level, 200
 SHAPE OF THE AUDITORIUM: Rectangle
 MAJOR TYPES OF ENTERTAINMENT: Drama

South Weymouth, MA

FOGG OPERA HOUSE, Columbian Square, 100-110 Pleasant Street
 OPENING DATE: c. December 1888
 ARCHITECT: J. W. Beals   STYLE OF ARCHITECTURE: Romanesque
 TYPE OF BUILDING: Commercial   FACADE: Granite, brick and
  brown stone   TYPE OF THEATRE: (b)   DEGREE OF
 RESTORATION: (d)   CURRENT USE: Apartments
 LOCATION OF AUDITORIUM: Top floor
 STAGE DIMENSIONS AND EQUIPMENT: Width of proscenium, 35ft
 DIMENSIONS OF AUDITORIUM: Distance between side walls
  of auditorium, 75ft; Distance stage to back wall of
  auditorium, 65ft
 SEATING (2 levels)
 MAJOR TYPES OF ENTERTAINMENT: Drama, minstrel shows,
  lectures, opera, vaudeville
 MAJOR STARS WHO APPEARED AT THEATRE: Booker T. Washington

Springfield, MA

SYMPHONY HALL (other name: Municipal Auditorium),
 Court Street

OPENING DATE: 1913   OPENING SHOW: Leopold Stokowski and
the Philadelphia Orchestra
ARCHITECTS: Pell and Corbett   STYLE OF ARCHITECTURE:
Neo-Classical Revival   FACADE: Indiana limestone
TYPE OF THEATRE: (b)   DEGREE OF RESTORATION: (a)   CURRENT
USE: Concert hall   LOCATION OF AUDITORIUM: Ground floor
STAGE DIMENSIONS AND EQUIPMENT: Width of proscenium, 60ft;
Distance from edge of stage to back wall of stage, 24ft;
MAJOR TYPES OF ENTERTAINMENT: Concerts, lectures
MAJOR STARS WHO APPEARED AT THEATRE: Boston Pops, Arthur
Fiedler, Chubby Checker, James Brown, Janis Joplin,
Caruso, Benny Goodman, Ella Fitzgerald, Van Cliburn,
Eamon De Valera, Helen Keller, Paul Robeson

Stockbridge, MA

BERKSHIRE THEATRE FESTIVAL (other names: Berkshire Playhouse,
Stockbridge Casino), East Main Street
OPENING DATE: 1886 as casino
OPENING SHOW: The Cradle Song, June 4, 1928
ARCHITECTS: McKim, Mead and White   FACADE: White wood
TYPE OF THEATRE: (a)   DEGREE OF RESTORATION: (d)
CURRENT USE: Summer theatre
LOCATION OF AUDITORIUM: Ground floor
STAGE DIMENSIONS AND EQUIPMENT: Height and width of
proscenium, 14ft 6in x 44ft 10in; Shape of proscenium
arch, rectangular; Distance from edge of stage to back
wall of stage, 26ft 11in; Distance from edge of stage to
curtain line, 8in; Distance between side walls of stage,
41ft 10in; Stage floor, flat; Dressing rooms, 9
(basement)
DIMENSIONS OF AUDITORIUM: Distance between side walls of
auditorium, 41ft 10in; Distance stage to back wall of
auditorium, 49ft 6in; Orchestra pit, none
SEATING (2 levels): 1st level, 333; 2nd level, 96
SHAPE OF THE AUDITORIUM: Rectangular
MAJOR TYPES OF ENTERTAINMENT: As casino - vaudeville,
minstrel shows, musical recitals, drama; as a summer
theatre - drama, musical comedy
MAJOR STARS WHO APPEARED AT THEATRE: Eva Le Gallienne,
James Cagney, Leo G. Carroll, Laurette Taylor, Katherine
Hepburn, Ina Claire, Tallulah Bankhead, Buster Keaton,
Lillian Gish, Thornton Wilder, Ruth Gordon, Anne Jackson,
Eli Wallach, Joanne Woodward, Maureen Stapleton, others
ADDITIONAL INFORMATION: The building was moved the entire
length of the main street of Stockbridge to its present
site to make room for another historic building.

Winchendon, MA

WINCHENDON TOWN HALL, Front Street
OPENING DATE: 1952
OPENING SHOW: Lecture, Oliver Wendell Holmes
STYLE OF ARCHITECTURE: Colonial   TYPE OF BUILDING:

Municipal building   FACADE: Brick with white wood trim
TYPE OF THEATRE: (b)   DEGREE OF RESTORATION: (d)
  CURRENT USE: Town hall and theatre
  LOCATION OF AUDITORIUM: Second floor
  DIMENSIONS OF AUDITORIUM: Orchestra pit, none
  MAJOR TYPES OF ENTERTAINMENT: Drama, lectures, balls,
    concerts
  MAJOR STARS WHO APPEARED AT THEATRE: Oliver Wendell Holmes,
    Henry Ward Beecher, Ralph Waldo Emerson, Horace Mann

Worcester, MA

LOTHROP'S OPERA HOUSE (other names: Fine Arts Theatre,
    Pleasant Street Theatre, Olympia), 17-27 Pleasant
    Street
  OPENING DATE: August 17, 1891
  OPENING SHOW: The Specter Bridegroom and Queena
  ARCHITECTS: Cutting and Forbush   FACADE: Yellow/Brown
    Roman brick   TYPE OF THEATRE: (a)   DEGREE OF
  RESTORATION: (c)   CURRENT USE: Movie theatre
  MAJOR TYPES OF ENTERTAINMENT: Drama, vaudeville, movies
  MAJOR STARS WHO APPEARED AT THEATRE: Al Jolson, Charlie
    Murray

Michigan

Adrian, MI

CROSWELL OPERA HOUSE (other name: Adrian Union Hall),
129 East Maumee Street
OPENING DATE: 1866   STYLE OF ARCHITECTURE: Romanesque
FACADE: Brick   TYPE OF THEATRE: (a)   DEGREE OF
RESTORATION: (d)   CURRENT USE: Theatre
STAGE DIMENSIONS AND EQUIPMENT: Height and width of
proscenium, 24ft x 30ft; Shape of proscenium arch,
rectangular; Distance from edge of stage to back wall of
stage, 39ft; Distance from edge of stage to curtain line,
5ft; Distance between side walls of stage, 60ft; Depth
under stage, 9ft 11in; Stage floor, flat; Trap doors, 0;
Scenery storage rooms, 1 (rear, stage level); Dressing
rooms, 6 (under stage)
DIMENSIONS OF AUDITORIUM: Distance between side walls
of auditorium, 60ft; Distance stage to back wall of
auditorium, 77ft; Capacity of orchestra pit, 24
SEATING (2 levels): 1st level, 482; 2nd level, 252
MAJOR TYPES OF ENTERTAINMENT: Drama, musical comedy,
vaudeville, minstrel shows, operettas, concerts, lectures
MAJOR STARS WHO APPEARED AT THEATRE: Laura Keene,
Edwin Forrest, Edwin Booth, Lawrence Barrett, Maggie
Mitchell, McKee Rankin, John Drew, Ada Rehan, Frank Mayo,
De Wolf Hopper, Bartley Campbell, Ada Gray, Annie Pixley,
The Vokes Family, Kate Claxton, Fanny Janauschek, Frank
Chanfrau, Viola Allen, Mrs. Fiske, Annie Yeamans, Effie
Shannon, Otis Skinner, Maude Adams, Joseph Jefferson,
Haverly's Minstrels, Georgia Minstrels, Gilmore's Band,
John Phillip Sousa, Pat Rooney; John L. Sullivan, and
others

Bay City, MI

BAY THEATER (other name: West Bay City Opera House), 204
North Walnut Street
OPENING DATE: 1892

TYPE OF BUILDING: Commercial   TYPE OF THEATRE: (b)
DEGREE OF RESTORATION: (c)
LOCATION OF AUDITORIUM: Upper floors
MAJOR TYPES OF ENTERTAINMENT: Drama, musical comedy,
   operettas, minstrel shows, local variety shows, lectures,
   movies
ADDITIONAL INFORMATION: The 500-seat theatre had a gallery
   that could be cleared for dances or roller skating. The
   West Bay City Town Hall was also in the building from
   1900 to 1905.

Calumet, MI

CALUMET THEATRE (other names: Calumet Opera House, Red Jacket
   Opera House), 340 Sixth Street
   OPENING DATE: March 20, 1900
   OPENING SHOW: The Highwayman
   ARCHITECT: Charles K. Shand   STYLE OF ARCHITECTURE:
   Italian Renaissance   TYPE OF BUILDING: Town hall,
   ballroom   FACADE: Buff brick and red sandstone
   TYPE OF THEATRE: (a)   DEGREE OF RESTORATION: (a)
   CURRENT USE: Theatre, arts center
   STAGE DIMENSIONS AND EQUIPMENT: Height and width of
   proscenium, 26ft x 32ft; Shape of proscenium arch,
   arched; Distance from edge of stage to back wall, 30ft
   6in; Distance from edge of stage to curtain line, 4ft
   6in; Distance between side walls of stage, 60ft; Distance
   from stage floor to fly loft, 30ft; Depth under stage,
   8ft; Stage floor, flat; Trap doors, 1; Scenery storage
   rooms, 3 (across the street); Dressing rooms, 6 (under
   the stage)
   DIMENSIONS OF AUDITORIUM: Distance between side walls of
   auditorium, 60ft; Distance stage to back wall, 54ft;
   Capacity of orchestra pit, 15
   SEATING (3 levels): 1st level, 395; 2nd level, 316; 3rd
   level, 250
   SHAPE OF THE AUDITORIUM: Fan-shaped
   MAJOR TYPES OF ENTERTAINMENT: Drama, musical comedy,
   opera, concerts, lectures, movies, civic functions
   MAJOR STARS WHO APPEARED AT THEATRE: Bernhardt, Maude
   Adams, Lillian Russell, John Philip Sousa, Douglas
   Fairbanks Sr., Lon Chaney Sr., Jason Robards, James
   O'Neill, Helena Modjeska, Wallace Beery, Raymond
   Hitchcock, John L. Sullivan, Donald Crisp, William S.
   Hart, Frank Morgan, Clara Blanding

Cheboygan, MI

CHEBOYGAN OPERA HOUSE, 403 North Huron Street
   OPENING DATE: July 30, 1888   OPENING SHOW: Fogg's Ferry
   STYLE OF ARCHITECTURE: Victorian   TYPE OF BUILDING:
   Municipal   FACADE: Brick, black and brown blend
   TYPE OF THEATRE: (b)   DEGREE OF RESTORATION: (a)
   CURRENT USE: Theatre

STAGE DIMENSIONS AND EQUIPMENT: Height and width of
  proscenium, 23ft x 34ft; Shape of proscenium arch,
  arched; Distance from edge of stage to back wall of
  stage, 27ft 3in; Distance from edge of stage to curtain
  line, 6ft 6in; Distance between side walls of stage, 49ft
  8in; Depth under stage, 7ft; Stage floor, raked; Trap
  doors, 1; Scenery storage rooms, 3 (back stage and below
  stage); Dressing rooms, 4 (below stage)
DIMENSIONS OF AUDITORIUM: Distance between side walls of
  auditorium, 38ft 8in; Distance stage to back wall of
  auditorium, 57ft 9in; Capacity of orchestra pit, 24
SEATING (3 levels): 1st level, 322; 2nd level, 152; 3rd
  level, 100; boxes, 8
SHAPE OF THE AUDITORIUM: Rectangular
MAJOR TYPES OF ENTERTAINMENT: Drama, musical comedy,
  vaudeville, burlesque, minstrel shows, opera, boxing,
  bear wrestling, civic functions
MAJOR STARS WHO APPEARED AT THEATRE: Marie Dressler, Ned
  Wayburn, Charles Winninger, Lewis Stone, Willard Mack,
  Annie Oakley, Frank Butler, Mary Pickford, Tell Taylor,
  Thurston, the Magician, William S. Hart, Hi Henry, Donnie
  and Marie Osmond, Maxene Andrews, "Whip" Wilson, and
  others
ADDITIONAL INFORMATION: The first opera house in Cheboygan
  was erected in 1877. It was totally destroyed by fire in
  1886 and the current building was constructed on the same
  site. It, in turn, was damaged by fire in 1903, reopening on December 19, 1904 with a production of Othello by
  the Sellman, Paige and Foley Lyceum Company. The advent
  of movies caused a decline in live entertainment at the
  opera house and in 1960 it was condemned and closed.
  During the 1970s, it was saved and renovated by several
  local groups and reopened on April 3, 1984 with a PBS
  video special featuring Skitch Henderson and Suzanne
  McCormick.

Coldwater, MI

TIBBITS OPERA HOUSE, 14 South Hanchett Street
  OPENING DATE: September 21, 1882
  OPENING SHOW: Maid of Arran
  ARCHITECT: Mortimer L. Smith   STYLE OF ARCHITECTURE:
    French Empire   FACADE: Red brick   TYPE OF THEATRE: (a)
  DEGREE OF RESTORATION: (c)   CURRENT USE: Arts center
  STAGE DIMENSIONS AND EQUIPMENT: Height and width of
    proscenium, 22ft x 26ft; Shape of proscenium arch,
    arched; Distance from edge of stage to back wall of
    stage, 28ft; Distance between side walls of stage, 52ft;
    Stage floor, flat; Scenery storage rooms, 1 (upstage
    left); Dressing rooms, 7 (upstage)
  DIMENSIONS OF AUDITORIUM: Distance between side walls of
    auditorium, 52ft; Distance stage to back wall, 54ft 8in;
    Capacity of orchestra pit, 12
  SEATING: 1st level, 350 ; 2nd level, 130; 3rd level, 87

SHAPE OF THE AUDITORIUM: Horseshoe-shaped
MAJOR TYPES OF ENTERTAINMENT: Drama, vaudeville, minstrel
   shows, opera, concerts, lectures, dances, wrestling,
   civic functions
MAJOR STARS WHO APPEARED AT THEATRE: De Wolf Hopper, Otis
   Skinner, Ethel Barrymore, Joseph Jefferson, Eddie Foy
   Jr., Maude Adams, Viola Allen, Fanny Davenport, Louis
   James, Fanny Janauschek, Maggie Mitchell, Chauncey
   Olcott, Roland Reed, Sol Smith Russell, Denman Thompson

Colon, MI

HILL OPERA HOUSE, 123 East State Street
   OPENING DATE: 1898   TYPE OF BUILDING: Bank
   TYPE OF THEATRE: (b)   DEGREE OF RESTORATION: (c)
   LOCATION OF AUDITORIUM: Second floor
   STAGE DIMENSIONS AND EQUIPMENT: * Height and width of
      proscenium, 17ft x 21ft; Distance from edge of stage to
      back wall of stage, 28ft; Distance from edge of stage to
      curtain line, 4ft; Distance between side walls of stage,
      47ft; Trap doors, 1
   SEATING (2 levels)
   SHAPE OF THE AUDITORIUM: U-shaped
   MAJOR TYPES OF ENTERTAINMENT: Vaudeville, magic shows
   MAJOR STARS WHO APPEARED AT THEATRE: Blackstone
   ADDITIONAL INFORMATION: The opera house has been closed for
      over 35 years. There is no access from the outside (the
      stairs have been removed) nor is there electricity or
      plumbing.

Detroit, MI

HARMONIE CLUB, 267 East Grand River
   OPENING DATE: December 26, 1895
   ARCHITECT: Richard Raseman   STYLE OF ARCHITECTURE:
      Beaux Arts/Renaissance   TYPE OF BUILDING: Clubhouse
   FACADE: Buff-colored pressed brick   TYPE OF THEATRE: (b)
   DEGREE OF RESTORATION: (c)   CLOSING DATE: 1978
   CURRENT USE: Vacant
   MAJOR TYPES OF ENTERTAINMENT: Concerts

Detroit, MI

NATIONAL THEATRE (other names: Palace, National Burlesk
   Theatre), Monroe Street
   OPENING DATE: 1910
   ARCHITECT: Albert Kahn
   MAJOR TYPES OF ENTERTAINMENT: Burlesque, movies

Frankenmuth, MI

FISCHER OPERA HAUS, 713 South Main Street

OPENING DATE: 1894   FACADE: Wood shingles
TYPE OF THEATRE: (a)   DEGREE OF RESTORATION: (a)
CURRENT USE: Theatre   LOCATION OF AUDITORIUM: Ground floor
STAGE DIMENSIONS AND EQUIPMENT: Height and width of
  proscenium, 10ft 2in x 16ft 3in; Shape of proscenium
  arch, arched; Distance from edge of stage to back wall of
  stage, 18ft 6in; Distance from edge of stage to curtain
  line, 7ft 2in; Distance between side walls of stage,
  30ft 10in; Depth under stage, 7ft; Stage floor, flat;
  Trap doors, 0; Scenery storage rooms, 0; Dressing rooms,
  1 (behind stage)
DIMENSIONS OF AUDITORIUM: Distance between side walls
  of auditorium, 31ft; Distance stage to back wall of
  auditorium, 38ft; Orchestra pit, none
SEATING (1 level): 1st level, 160
SHAPE OF THE AUDITORIUM: Rectangular
MAJOR TYPES OF ENTERTAINMENT: Drama, musical comedy,
  medicine shows, revues, recitals, movies, puppet shows
ADDITIONAL INFORMATION: The theatre still retains wooden
  seats and a stage curtain with 1932 advertisements. In
  1973, the opera house reopened as a summer theatre which
  presents gay-90s entertainments or other nostalgic productions during an 8-9 week season.

Grand Ledge, MI

ACME OPERA HOUSE, 219-221 North Bridge Street
  OPENING DATE: Pre-1894
  FACADE: "Rustic" cement block   TYPE OF THEATRE: (b)
  DEGREE OF RESTORATION: (c)   CURRENT USE: Bar and Grill

Grand Ledge, MI

BLAKE'S OPERA HOUSE (other names: Sackett's Opera House,
  Island City Opera House), 121 South Bridge Street
  OPENING DATE: 1886
  OPENING SHOW: Mackley-Salisbury Comedy Company
  FACADE: Originally clapboard; currently brick
  TYPE OF THEATRE: (a)   DEGREE OF RESTORATION: (b)
  CURRENT USE: Store   LOCATION OF AUDITORIUM: Ground floor
  STAGE DIMENSIONS AND EQUIPMENT: * Height and width of
    proscenium, 16ft x 23ft; Distance from edge of stage to
    back wall of stage, 30ft; Distance from edge of stage to
    curtain line, 4ft 6in; Distance between side walls of
    stage, 36ft; Depth under stage, 4ft
  DIMENSIONS OF AUDITORIUM: Distance between side walls
    of auditorium, 38ft; Capacity of orchestra pit, 4
  SEATING (2 levels)
  SHAPE OF THE AUDITORIUM: Rectangular with U-shaped balcony
  MAJOR TYPES OF ENTERTAINMENT: Drama, musical comedy,
    vaudeville, opera, local variety shows, dances,
    concerts, medicine shows, social events
  MAJOR STARS WHO APPEARED AT THEATRE: Al Jolson, Marie
    Dressler

ADDITIONAL INFORMATION: The stage has been removed,
but the balcony still remains.

Holland, MI

HOLLAND THEATRE (other name: The Knickerbocker),
    86 East 8th Street
OPENING DATE: February 1911
FACADE: Brick and Chicago sandstone   TYPE OF THEATRE: (a)
DEGREE OF RESTORATION: (a)   CURRENT USE: Theatre
LOCATION OF AUDITORIUM: Ground floor
STAGE DIMENSIONS AND EQUIPMENT: Height and width of
    proscenium, 19ft x 36ft; Shape of proscenium arch,
    rectangular; Distance from edge of stage to back wall of
    stage, 24ft; Distance from edge of stage to curtain line,
    5ft; Distance between side walls of stage, 47ft; Depth
    under stage, 8ft; Trap doors, 1; Dressing rooms, 2
    (in basement)
DIMENSIONS OF AUDITORIUM: Distance between side walls of
    auditorium, 40ft 6in; Distance stage to back wall of
    auditorium, 67ft; Orchestra pit, none
SEATING (3 levels): 1st level, 350; 2nd level, 106;
    3rd level, 173
SHAPE OF THE AUDITORIUM: Rectangular
MAJOR TYPES OF ENTERTAINMENT: Drama, musical comedy,
    vaudeville, concerts, lectures, movies
MAJOR STARS WHO APPEARED AT THEATRE: Franklin Delano
    Roosevelt (lecture), Sally Rand, Blackstone, the Magician
ADDITIONAL INFORMATION: The theatre originally had box
    seats along the walls, but these were removed sometime
    after live performances at the theatre declined.

Howell, MI

THE OPERA HOUSE, Southeast corner of Grand River and Walnut
OPENING DATE: December 30, 1881
OPENING SHOW: Galley Slave
ARCHITECT: A. C. Varney   STYLE OF ARCHITECTURE: Italianate
TYPE OF BUILDING: Commercial   FACADE: Red brick
TYPE OF THEATRE: (b)   DEGREE OF RESTORATION: (c)
CLOSING DATE: 1930s   CURRENT USE: Storage
LOCATION OF AUDITORIUM: Second and third floors
STAGE DIMENSIONS AND EQUIPMENT: Width of proscenium, 26ft;
    Shape of proscenium arch, arched; Distance from edge of
    stage to back wall of stage, 22ft; Depth under stage,
    4ft; Dressing rooms, 2 (under stage)
DIMENSIONS OF AUDITORIUM: Orchestra pit, yes
SEATING (2 levels)
SHAPE OF THE AUDITORIUM: Square with horseshoe-shaped
    balcony
MAJOR TYPES OF ENTERTAINMENT: Drama, vaudeville
MAJOR STARS WHO APPEARED AT THEATRE: Jessie Bonstelle,
    Emily Mutter, violinist

Manistee, MI

RAMSDELL THEATRE (other name: Ramsdell Opera House),
191 Maple Street
OPENING DATE: September 4, 1903
OPENING SHOW: A Chinese Honeymoon
ARCHITECT: Mr. Beman   STYLE OF ARCHITECTURE: Colonial
FACADE: Red brick   TYPE OF THEATRE: (a)
DEGREE OF RESTORATION: (b)   CURRENT USE: Theatre
LOCATION OF AUDITORIUM: Ground floor
STAGE DIMENSIONS AND EQUIPMENT: Height and width of
proscenium, 26ft x 26ft; Shape of proscenium arch,
square; Distance from edge of stage to back wall of
stage, 34ft; Distance from edge of stage to curtain
line, 6ft 10in; Distance between side walls of stage,
60ft; Distance from stage floor to fly loft, 30ft;
Depth under stage, 9ft; Stage floor, flat; Trap doors,
9; Scenery storage rooms, 1 (above stage); Dressing
rooms, 8 (in basement)
DIMENSIONS OF AUDITORIUM: Distance between side walls
of auditorium, 60ft; Distance stage to back wall of
auditorium, 57ft; Orchestra pit, yes
SEATING (4 levels): 1st level, 328; 2nd level, 235;
3rd level, 30; boxes, 16
SHAPE OF THE AUDITORIUM: Horseshoe-shaped
MAJOR TYPES OF ENTERTAINMENT: Drama, musical comedy,
vaudeville, burlesque, opera
MAJOR STARS WHO APPEARED AT THEATRE: James Earl Jones,
Madge Skelly
ADDITIONAL INFORMATION: The theatre was erected to
replace an earlier opera house which had burned.

Marcellus, MI

CENTENNIAL HALL, Main and Center Streets
OPENING DATE: 1876
TYPE OF BUILDING: Commercial   FACADE: Brick   TYPE OF
THEATRE: (b)   DEGREE OF RESTORATION: (d)   CURRENT USE:
Meeting hall   LOCATION OF AUDITORIUM: Second floor
STAGE DIMENSIONS AND EQUIPMENT: Height and width of
proscenium, 18ft x 24ft; Shape of proscenium arch,
arched; Distance from edge of stage to back wall of
stage, 20ft; Distance from edge of stage to curtain
line, 4ft; Distance between side walls of stage, 43ft;
Depth under stage, 3ft; Stage floor, flat; Trap doors,
1; Scenery storage rooms, 1 (west wing); Dressing rooms,
2 (upstairs in east and west wings)
DIMENSIONS OF AUDITORIUM: Distance between side walls
of auditorium, 43ft; Distance stage to back wall of
auditorium, 67ft; Orchestra pit, none
SEATING (1 level): 1st level, 200
SHAPE OF THE AUDITORIUM: Rectangular
MAJOR TYPES OF ENTERTAINMENT: Drama, vaudeville, balls,
Ku Klux Klan meetings

Milan, MI

GAY OPERA HOUSE, 28 East Main Street
    OPENING DATE: 1892
    TYPE OF BUILDING: Commercial   FACADE: Natural brick
    TYPE OF THEATRE: (a)   DEGREE OF RESTORATION: (c)
    CLOSING DATE: 1920s   CURRENT USE: Apartments and storage

Suttons Bay, MI

SUTTONS BAY OPERA HOUSE, Broadway
    OPENING DATE: c. 1900
    TYPE OF BUILDING: Commercial   TYPE OF THEATRE: (a)
    DEGREE OF RESTORATION: (c)   CURRENT USE: Antique store
    ADDITIONAL INFORMATION: The proscenium of the opera house
        has been donated to the Leelanau Historical Society of
        Leland, Michigan.

Traverse City, MI

CITY OPERA HOUSE, 118 East Front Street
    OPENING DATE: February 8, 1892
    OPENING SHOW: Play with Orson Clifford and Madeline Merli
    ARCHITECT: E.R. Prall   STYLE OF ARCHITECTURE: Victorian
    TYPE OF BUILDING: Commercial   FACADE: Red brick; beige
        stone trim; iron panels   TYPE OF THEATRE: (b)
    DEGREE OF RESTORATION: (b)   CLOSING DATE: 1945
    CURRENT USE: Civic functions   LOCATION OF AUDITORIUM:
        Second and third floors
    STAGE DIMENSIONS AND EQUIPMENT: * Height and width of
        proscenium, 20ft x 36ft; Distance from edge of stage to
        back wall of stage, 45ft; Distance from edge of stage to
        curtain line, 3ft 6in; Distance between side walls of
        stage, 60ft; Depth under stage, 4ft; Stage floor, raked;
        Trap doors, 1
    SEATING (2 levels)
    MAJOR TYPES OF ENTERTAINMENT: Drama, vaudeville, opera,
        movies
    MAJOR STARS WHO APPEARED AT THEATRE: William Jennings Bryan
    ADDITIONAL INFORMATION: Unlike many opera houses of the
        same era, the City Opera House was not demolished when
        it closed. The theatre remains as it was earlier in
        the century, according to an article in SUMMER MAGAZINE.
        In 1979, action was taken to begin the process of
        restoration. The building is open for regularly
        scheduled tours and a 10-minute sound-slide show is
        presented.

Vermontville, MI

VERMONTVILLE OPERA HOUSE, South Main Street
    OPENING DATE: 1898

OPENING SHOW: L. Vern Slout and company
TYPE OF BUILDING: Meeting hall   FACADE: Gray and red
  brick; foundation of cut stone
TYPE OF THEATRE: (b)   DEGREE OF RESTORATION: (d)
CURRENT USE: Theatre and library
LOCATION OF AUDITORIUM: Second floor
STAGE DIMENSIONS AND EQUIPMENT: Height and width of
  proscenium, 11ft 6in x 17ft 6in; Shape of proscenium
  arch, rectangular; Distance from edge of stage to back
  wall of stage, 20ft; Distance from edge of stage to
  curtain line, 3ft; Distance between side walls of stage,
  34ft; Depth under stage, 2ft 7in; Stage floor, flat;
  Trap doors, 1; Scenery storage rooms, 1 (rear of stage);
  Dressing rooms, none
DIMENSIONS OF AUDITORIUM: Distance between side walls of
  auditorium, 33ft 10in; Distance stage to back wall of
  auditorium, 49ft 4in; Orchestra pit, none
SEATING (2 levels): 1st level, 350; 2nd level, 50
SHAPE OF THE AUDITORIUM: Rectangular
MAJOR TYPES OF ENTERTAINMENT: Drama, movies, variety shows,
  dances, movies
MAJOR STARS WHO APPEARED AT THEATRE: L. Vern Slout and
  company
ADDITIONAL INFORMATION: L. Vern Slout and his players, one
  of Michigan's oldest tent companies, gave their first and
  last performances at the opera house. The building is
  being restored.

Minnesota

Belview, MN

ODEON
  OPENING DATE: 1902
  ARCHITECT: August F. Pattratz   STYLE OF ARCHITECTURE:
    Queen Anne   TYPE OF BUILDING: Municipal building
  TYPE OF THEATRE: (a)   DEGREE OF RESTORATION: (a)
  CURRENT USE: Civic center
  STAGE DIMENSIONS AND EQUIPMENT: Width of proscenium, 22ft;
    Distance from edge of stage to back wall of stage, 12ft
  DIMENSIONS OF AUDITORIUM: Distance between side walls
    of auditorium, 40ft; Distance stage to back wall of
    auditorium, 90ft; Orchestra pit, none
  SEATING (2 levels)
  SHAPE OF THE AUDITORIUM: Rectangular
  MAJOR TYPES OF ENTERTAINMENT: Drama, musical comedy,
    vaudeville
  ADDITIONAL INFORMATION: A special act of the Minnesota
    State Legislature allowed Belview to erect the theatre.
    During its history, overflow audiences were common and
    were accommodated in a nearby garage, with shows moving
    from one audience to the other. The building now serves
    as a community center. Permanent seats were removed in
    the 1920s to accomodate basketball and a balcony has been
    removed, but the stage curtain with advertising, interior
    tin walls and barrel-vault ceiling remain intact.

Clearwater, MN

CLEARWATER MASONIC HALL (other name: G.A.R. Hall),
    205 Oak Street
  OPENING DATE: 1888
  TYPE OF BUILDING: Masonic hall   FACADE: Yellow brick
  TYPE OF THEATRE: (b)   DEGREE OF RESTORATION: (c)
  CLOSING DATE: 1940   CURRENT USE: Recreation programs
  STAGE DIMENSIONS AND EQUIPMENT: Height and width of
    proscenium, 14ft x 24ft; Shape of proscenium arch,

rectangular; Distance from edge of stage to back wall of
stage, 20ft; Distance from edge of stage to curtain line,
1ft 6in; Distance between side walls of stage, 24ft;
Stage floor, flat; Trap doors, 0; Scenery storage rooms,
0; Dressing rooms, 1 (rear of auditorium)
DIMENSIONS OF AUDITORIUM: Distance between side walls
of auditorium, 24ft; Distance stage to back wall of
auditorium, 40ft; Orchestra pit, none
SEATING (1 level): 1st level, 120
SHAPE OF THE AUDITORIUM: Rectangular
MAJOR TYPES OF ENTERTAINMENT: Drama, medicine shows, local
variety shows

Fairmont, MN

FAIRMONT OPERA HOUSE (other names: Haynic Theater, Nicholas
Theater), 45 Downtown Plaza
OPENING DATE: February 11, 1902
OPENING SHOW: The Chaperones
ARCHITECTS: Kees and Bowman (1921 remodeling)
FACADE: Red brick   TYPE OF THEATRE: (a)   DEGREE OF
RESTORATION: (b)   CURRENT USE: Theatre and exhibition hall
LOCATION OF AUDITORIUM: Ground floor
STAGE DIMENSIONS AND EQUIPMENT: Height and width of
proscenium, 18ft x 39ft 6in; Shape of proscenium arch,
rectangular; Distance from edge of stage to back wall of
stage, 35ft; Distance from edge of stage to curtain line,
2ft; Distance between side walls of stage, 60ft; Depth
under stage, 12ft; Stage floor, flat; Trap doors, 0;
Scenery storage rooms, 1 (lower level); Dressing rooms,
2 (under stage)
DIMENSIONS OF AUDITORIUM: Distance between side walls
of auditorium, 57ft; Distance stage to back wall of
auditorium, 136ft; Capacity of orchestra pit, 20
SEATING (2 levels): 1st level, 297; 2nd level, 192
SHAPE OF THE AUDITORIUM: U-shaped
MAJOR TYPES OF ENTERTAINMENT: Drama, vaudeville, opera,
movies, civic functions
ADDITIONAL INFORMATION: In 1926 a marquee was added as
was a $12,000 Marr and Coltoon organ with nearly 1,000
pipes. Presently, the organ rests in the same spot in
the orchestra pit that it occupied in the 1920s. The
theatre is currently undergoing renovation and is
scheduled for reopening in February 1988.

Glencoe, MN

CRYSTAL THEATRE (other names: Glencoe Theatre, Buffalo Creek
Players Theatre), 1118 Hennepin Avenue
OPENING DATE: 1913
FACADE: Red brick   TYPE OF THEATRE: (a)
DEGREE OF RESTORATION: (c)   CURRENT USE: Theatre
LOCATION OF AUDITORIUM: Ground floor
STAGE DIMENSIONS AND EQUIPMENT: Height and width of

proscenium, 16ft x 26ft; Shape of proscenium arch,
rectangular; Distance from edge of stage to back wall of
stage, 20ft; Distance from edge of stage to curtain line,
4ft; Distance between side walls of stage, 27ft; Depth
under stage, 3ft 6in; Stage floor, flat; Trap doors, 0;
Scenery storage rooms, 0; Dressing rooms, 2 (in basement)
DIMENSIONS OF AUDITORIUM: Distance between side walls
of auditorium, 27ft; Distance stage to back wall of
auditorium, 34ft; Capacity of orchestra pit, 20
SEATING (2 levels): 1st level, 102; 2nd level, 84
SHAPE OF THE AUDITORIUM: Rectangular
MAJOR TYPES OF ENTERTAINMENT: Drama, musical comedy,
vaudeville, minstrel shows, movies
MAJOR STARS WHO APPEARED AT THEATRE: William Jennings
Bryan, Hubert Humphrey
ADDITIONAL INFORMATION: The building was designed to be
a replica of the Minneapolis Bijou Theatre and was
reputedly the "first concrete steel reinforced completely
fire-proof building built west of Minneapolis" when it
was erected.

Litchfield, MN

LITCHFIELD OPERA HOUSE, 126 North Marshall
OPENING DATE: November 8, 1900
OPENING SHOW: The Marble Heart
ARCHITECT: W. H. Towner   TYPE OF THEATRE: (a)
CLOSING DATE: c. 1930   CURRENT USE: Town offices
LOCATION OF AUDITORIUM: Ground floor
STAGE DIMENSIONS AND EQUIPMENT: Height and width of
proscenium, 18ft x 24ft; Distance from edge of stage
to back wall of stage, 36ft; Distance between side walls
of stage, 50ft
DIMENSIONS OF AUDITORIUM: Distance between side walls
of auditorium, 50ft; Distance stage to back wall of
auditorium, 60ft
SEATING (2 levels): 1st level, 400; 2nd level, 200
SHAPE OF THE AUDITORIUM: U-shaped
MAJOR TYPES OF ENTERTAINMENT: Drama

Luverne, MN

PALACE THEATRE (other name: New Opera House), Corner of Main
and Freeman
OPENING DATE: September 29, 1915
OPENING SHOW: The Prince of Tonight
ARCHITECT: W. E. E. Greene   FACADE: Pressed brick
with Kasota stone trim   TYPE OF THEATRE: (a)
DEGREE OF RESTORATION: (d)   CURRENT USE: Movie theatre
LOCATION OF AUDITORIUM: Ground floor
STAGE DIMENSIONS AND EQUIPMENT: Height and width of
proscenium, 18ft x 38ft; Shape of proscenium arch,
arched; Distance from edge of stage to back wall of
stage, 26ft; Distance from edge of stage to curtain line,

4ft; Distance between side walls of stage, 54ft; Depth
under stage, 8ft; Stage floor, flat; Trap doors, 1;
Scenery storage rooms, 1 (basement); Dressing rooms, 8
(in basement)
DIMENSIONS OF AUDITORIUM: Distance between side walls
of auditorium, 63ft; Distance stage to back wall of
auditorium, 52ft; Capacity of orchestra pit, 12
SEATING (2 levels): 1st level, 550; 2nd level, 144
SHAPE OF THE AUDITORIUM: Semi-circular
MAJOR TYPES OF ENTERTAINMENT: Drama, vaudeville, movies
MAJOR STARS WHO APPEARED AT THEATRE: Lyle Talbet, the
Albright Sisters, Clint and Bessie Robbins
ADDITIONAL INFORMATION: Restoration of the theatre
continues. Seats in the orchestra have been re-
upholstered and there are plans to reupholster
seats in the balcony in the near future.

Minneapolis, MN

ACADEMY THEATRE (other names: Shubert, 1909-1935;
Alvin, 1935-1957), 22 North 7th Street
OPENING DATE: 1909
ARCHITECT: Albert Swasey   STYLE OF ARCHITECTURE:
Neo-Classical   FACADE: Gray stone   TYPE OF THEATRE: (a)
DEGREE OF RESTORATION: (c)   CLOSING DATE: September 1983
CURRENT USE: Vacant   LOCATION OF AUDITORIUM: Ground floor
STAGE DIMENSIONS AND EQUIPMENT: Width of proscenium, 32ft;
Distance from edge of stage to back wall of stage, 26ft;
Dressing rooms (on the 3 floors above stage level)
MAJOR TYPES OF ENTERTAINMENT: Drama, musical comedy,
burlesque, movies
MAJOR STARS WHO APPEARED AT THEATRE: Victor Jory, Gladys
George, Marie Gale, Blanche Yurka, Florence Reed
ADDITIONAL INFORMATION: Original seating capacity was
1,218. Seating capacity was reduced to 850 during a
1957 renovation and 3 levels of box seats were removed.
As a film house, only the orchestra and one balcony
were used. The theatre, originally owned and run by the
Shubert organization, was later run by A. G. "Buzz" Bainbridge until he became Mayor of Minneapolis in 1933. From
1935 to 1941, when the theatre was nearly destroyed by
fire, it was run by Harry Hirsch as a burlesque house.
For a short period in the 1950s, the building was used as
a church, returned briefly to burlesque, and in 1957 was
remodeled to accomodate Mike Todd's Around the World in
Eighty Days.

Minneapolis, MN

DANIA HALL, 427-29 Cedar Avenue
OPENING DATE: November 11, 1886
OPENING SHOW: Dedication with a banquet and dance
ARCHITECT: Carl F. Struck   STYLE OF ARCHITECTURE:
"Restrained Eclectic/Victorian"   TYPE OF BUILDING:

Library and benevolent socety   FACADE: White brick and
gray Ohio stone   TYPE OF THEATRE: (b)   DEGREE OF
RESTORATION: (d)   CURRENT USE: Occasional meetings
LOCATION OF AUDITORIUM: Third floor
DIMENSIONS OF AUDITORIUM: Distance between side walls
of auditorium, 44ft; Distance stage to back wall of
auditorium, 65ft
SEATING (2 levels): 1st level, 600; 2nd level, 200
SHAPE OF THE AUDITORIUM: Horseshoe-shaped balcony
MAJOR TYPES OF ENTERTAINMENT: Drama, ballet, vaudeville in
Scandinavian language
ADDITIONAL INFORMATION: The theatre has been described as
a 19th-century "gem" with a hand-carved railing around
the balcony, a painted stage drop and a domed ceiling.
During its heyday, the theatre hosted troupes like the
Budapest Gypsies and the "Spirited" Edgewater Eight
Singing and Dancing Troupe. Vaudeville continued in
the theatre until the 1930s.

Minneota, MN

MINNEOTA OPERA HOUSE (other name: Anderson Opera House),
Jefferson and 2nd Streets
OPENING DATE: 1898
TYPE OF BUILDING: Commercial   FACADE: Red sand; brick
TYPE OF THEATRE: (b)   DEGREE OF RESTORATION: (c)
CLOSING DATE: c. 1940   CURRENT USE: Display; occasional
plays   LOCATION OF AUDITORIUM: Second floor
STAGE DIMENSIONS AND EQUIPMENT: * Height and width of
proscenium, 10ft x 24ft; Shape of proscenium arch,
rectangular; Distance from edge of stage to back wall of
stage, 22ft; Distance from edge of stage to curtain line,
3ft; Distance between side walls of stage, 48ft; Depth
under stage, 3ft 6in; Stage floor, flat; Trap doors, 1
DIMENSIONS OF AUDITORIUM: Orchestra pit, none
SEATING (1 level): 1st level, 200
SHAPE OF THE AUDITORIUM: U-shaped
MAJOR TYPES OF ENTERTAINMENT: Drama, dances
ADDITIONAL INFORMATION: The building is now owned by The
Society for the Preservation of Minneota's Heritage.

Red Wing, MN

THEODORE B. SHELDON MEMORIAL AUDITORIUM, East Avenue and
Third Street
OPENING DATE: October 10, 1904
OPENING SHOW: The Royal Chef
ARCHITECT: Lowell Lamoreaux   STYLE OF ARCHITECTURE:
Renaissance Revival   FACADE: Buff brick and terra cotta
TYPE OF THEATRE: (a)   DEGREE OF RESTORATION: (b)
CURRENT USE: Movie theatre
LOCATION OF AUDITORIUM: Ground floor

STAGE DIMENSIONS AND EQUIPMENT: Height and width of
   proscenium, 23ft x 32ft; Shape of proscenium arch,
   rectangular; Distance from edge of stage to back wall of
   stage, 35ft; Distance from edge of stage to curtain line,
   4ft; Distance between side walls of stage, 60ft; Distance
   from stage floor to fly loft, 25ft; Depth under stage,
   10ft; Stage floor,flat; Dressing rooms, 10 (wing on side
   of building at the rear)
DIMENSIONS OF AUDITORIUM: Distance between side walls
   of auditorium, 60ft; Distance stage to back wall of
   auditorium, 54ft; Capacity of orchestra pit, 12
SEATING: 1st level, 363; 2nd level, 241; 3rd level,
   108; 4th level, 120; boxes, 32
SHAPE OF THE AUDITORIUM: Horseshoe-shaped
MAJOR TYPES OF ENTERTAINMENT: Drama, vaudeville, concerts,
   movies
MAJOR STARS WHO APPEARED AT THEATRE: William Gillette,
   Marie Doro, May Robson, James K. Hackett, Margaret
   Anglin, John Phillip Sousa, May Irwin, Nat Goodwin,
   Eva Tanguay, Joseph Jefferson, Walker Whiteside, Dustin
   Farnum, Chauncey Olcott, Fiske O'Hara, Billie Burke, Otis
   Skinner, James J. Corbett, Mrs. Leslie Carter, Blanche
   Bates, William Jennings Bryan, and others
ADDITIONAL INFORMATION: In 1918, the theatre burned.
   It was later restored to its original apprearance by
   the original contractor. In 1936, it was remodeled
   and seating was expanded. Figures provided are c.
   1904. The theatre was closed in 1986 for restoration
   and reopening was scheduled for May 1987.

St. Cloud, MN

DAVIDSON OPERA HOUSE (other names: Miner Theatre, Roxy
   Theatre), 115 5th Avenue South
   OPENING DATE: December 17, 1897   OPENING SHOW: Iskander
   ARCHITECT: Harry G. Carter   STYLE OF ARCHITECTURE:
   Byzantine/Romanesque   FACADE: Gray granite
   TYPE OF THEATRE: (a)   DEGREE OF RESTORATION: (c)
   CLOSING DATE: May 10, 1937   CURRENT USE: Offices
   LOCATION OF AUDITORIUM: Ground floor
   STAGE DIMENSIONS AND EQUIPMENT: * Height and width
   of proscenium, 30ft x 30ft; Shape of proscenium arch,
   square; Distance from edge of stage to back wall of
   stage, 30ft; Distance from edge of stage to curtain
   line, 6ft; Distance between side walls of stage, 54ft;
   Depth under stage, 10ft; Trap doors, 4
   MAJOR STARS WHO APPEARED AT THEATRE: Ethel Barrymore,
   Chauncey Olcott, Billie Burke, John Phillip Sousa

St. Paul, MN

CSPS HALL (other name: Czech Hall), 383 Michigan Avenue
   OPENING DATE: 1887
   ARCHITECT: Emil W. Ulrici   TYPE OF BUILDING: Lodge and

gymnasium   FACADE: Red brick   TYPE OF THEATRE: (b)
DEGREE OF RESTORATION: (b)   CURRENT USE: Lodge, gymnasium
  LOCATION OF AUDITORIUM: Second floor
  STAGE DIMENSIONS AND EQUIPMENT: Height and width of
    proscenium, 13ft x 20ft; Shape of proscenium arch,
    rectangular; Distance from edge of stage to back wall of
    stage, 15ft; Distance from edge of stage to curtain line,
    12ft 6in; Distance between side walls of stage, 34ft;
    Depth under stage, 3ft 11in; Stage floor, flat; Trap
    doors, 2; Scenery storage rooms, 1 (stage right);
    Dressing rooms, 1
  DIMENSIONS OF AUDITORIUM: Distance between side walls of
    auditorium, 46ft 8in; Distance stage to back wall of
    auditorium, 46ft 8in; Orchestra pit, none
  SHAPE OF THE AUDITORIUM: Square
  MAJOR TYPES OF ENTERTAINMENT: Drama, music recitals,
    concerts, dances, social functions
  MAJOR STARS WHO APPEARED AT THEATRE: Antonin Dvorak
  ADDITIONAL INFORMATION: CSPS Hall was a center of culture
    for a small group of Czechs in St. Paul until World War
    II. In addition to providing theatre and music, the hall
    also offered Czech language classes and served as home to
    a well-known gymnastic team and a folkdance group.

St. Paul, MN

WORLD THEATRE (other name: Sam S. Shubert Theatre),
    10 East Exchange Street
  OPENING DATE: August 1910
  OPENING SHOW: The Fourth Estate
  ARCHITECTS: Marshall and Fox   STYLE OF ARCHITECTURE:
  Neo-Classical   FACADE: Light tan sandstone   TYPE OF
  THEATRE: (a)   DEGREE OF RESTORATION: (a)   CURRENT USE:
    Theatre   LOCATION OF AUDITORIUM: Ground floor
  STAGE DIMENSIONS AND EQUIPMENT: Height and width of
    proscenium, 30ft x 36ft; Shape of proscenium arch,
    rectangular; Distance from edge of stage to back wall of
    stage, 37ft; Distance from edge of stage to curtain line,
    1ft; Distance between side walls of stage, 54ft; Depth
    under stage, 10ft; Stage floor, flat; Trap doors, 1;
    Scenery storage rooms, 1 (under stage); Dressing rooms,
    7 (4 floors, stage right)
  DIMENSIONS OF AUDITORIUM: Distance between side walls
    of auditorium, 65ft; Distance stage to back wall of
    auditorium, 85ft; Capacity of orchestra pit, 15
  SEATING (3 levels): 1st level, 370; 2nd level, 314;
    3rd level, 236; boxes, 24
  SHAPE OF THE AUDITORIUM: U-shaped
  MAJOR TYPES OF ENTERTAINMENT: Drama, movies, radio
  MAJOR STARS WHO APPEARED AT THEATRE: Stars of Shubert shows
    and A Prairie Home Companion
  ADDITIONAL INFORMATION: When the Shuberts opened the
    theatre, original features included 16 dressing rooms,
    a stage that could be raised and lowered two feet, a
    built-in vacuum cleaning system and nearly 2,000 electric

lights. In making the theatre safe from fire, the
architects exhibited a "near hysterical devotion" to
the latest safety features and installed two dozen exits.
In 1933, the theatre was converted to movies, remodeled
in the Art Deco style, and renamed The World. In 1980,
Minnesota Public Radio purchased the theatre which became
home to A Prairie Home Companion. In 1984, the theatre
was declared unsafe and the show moved to the Orpheum
Theatre while The World was being restored, a process
that has since been completed.

Springfield, MN

OPERA HOUSE, East Central
  OPENING DATE: 1893
  TYPE OF BUILDING: Commercial   FACADE: Red brick
  TYPE OF THEATRE: (b)   DEGREE OF RESTORATION: (c)
  CURRENT USE: 1st floor, shops; 2nd floor, vacant
  LOCATION OF AUDITORIUM: Second floor
  DIMENSIONS OF AUDITORIUM: Distance between side walls
    of auditorium, 50ft; Distance stage to back wall of
    auditorium, 75ft
  SEATING: (2 levels)
  SHAPE OF THE AUDITORIUM: U-shaped
  MAJOR TYPES OF ENTERTAINMENT: Drama, vaudeville, medicine
    shows, local variety shows, musical comedy, boxing,
    movies, civic functions
  ADDITIONAL INFORMATION: The balcony remains.

Virginia, MN

KALEVA HALL, (other name: Finnish Temperance Hall),
    Third Road and Second Avenue North
  OPENING DATE: c. 1906   TYPE OF BUILDING: Lodge
  FACADE: Brown brick   TYPE OF THEATRE: (b)
  DEGREE OF RESTORATION: (a)   CURRENT USE: Lodge
  LOCATION OF AUDITORIUM: Second floor
  STAGE DIMENSIONS AND EQUIPMENT: Height and width of
    proscenium, 13ft 6in x 20ft; Shape of proscenium arch,
    arched; Distance from edge of stage to back wall of
    stage, 25ft; Distance from edge of stage to curtain line,
    6ft 6in; Depth under stage, 3ft; Stage floor, flat; Trap
    doors, 1; Scenery storage rooms, 0; Dressing rooms, 0
  DIMENSIONS OF AUDITORIUM: Distance between side walls of
    auditorium, 37ft 6in; Distance stage to back wall of
    auditorium, 65ft; Orchestra pit, none
  SEATING (1 level) 1st level, 250
  SHAPE OF THE AUDITORIUM: Rectangular
  MAJOR TYPES OF ENTERTAINMENT: Drama (both Finnish and
    English), local variety shows

Winona, MN

WINONA OPERA HOUSE (other name: Winona Theatre)
   OPENING DATE: December 1892
   LOCATION OF AUDITORIUM: Ground floor
   STAGE DIMENSIONS AND EQUIPMENT: * Height and width of
      proscenium, 34ft x 32ft; Distance from edge of stage to
      back wall of stage, 37ft; Distance from edge of stage to
      curtain line, 2ft; Distance between side walls of stage,
      64ft; Depth under stage, 10ft; Trap doors, 5
   MAJOR TYPES OF ENTERTAINMENT: Opera, concerts

Mississippi

Meridian, MS

GRAND OPERA HOUSE, 2208 5th Street
  OPENING DATE: December 19, 1890
  OPENING SHOW: The Gypsy Baron, opera by Johann Strauss
  ARCHITECT: G. M. Tergenson   TYPE OF BUILDING: Storage
  FACADE: Brick   TYPE OF THEATRE: (b)   DEGREE OF
  RESTORATION: (c)   CLOSING DATE: 1926   CURRENT USE:
    Storage   LOCATION OF AUDITORIUM: Second floor
  STAGE DIMENSIONS AND EQUIPMENT: Height and width of
    proscenium, 35ft x 29ft; Distance from edge of stage to
    back wall of stage, 41ft; Distance from edge of stage to
    curtain line, 6ft; Distance between side walls of stage,
    55ft; Distance from stage floor to fly loft, 47ft; Depth
    under stage, 8ft; Trap doors, 1; Dressing rooms, 2
    (behind stage)
  DIMENSIONS OF AUDITORIUM: Distance between side walls
    of auditorium, 55ft; Distance stage to back wall of
    auditorium, 64ft; Capacity of orchestra pit, 25
  SEATING: (3 levels)
  SHAPE OF THE AUDITORIUM: Horseshoe-shaped balcony
  MAJOR TYPES OF ENTERTAINMENT: Local and touring
    productions, movies
  MAJOR STARS WHO APPEARED AT THEATRE: John Gilbert, Lon
    Chaney, Helen Hayes, Sarah Bernhardt, Otis Skinner,
    Marion Davies, Norma Shearer
  ADDITIONAL INFORMATION: The theatre is in poor condition
    and efforts to restore it have been unsuccessful to date.

Missouri

Boonville, MO

THESPIAN HALL (other names: Stephens Opera House, Lyric
   Theatre), Main and Vine Streets
   OPENING DATE: July 4, 1857
   STYLE OF ARCHITECTURE: Greek Revival   FACADE: Red brick
   TYPE OF THEATRE: (b)   DEGREE OF RESTORATION: (a)
   CURRENT USE: Community events
   LOCATION OF AUDITORIUM: Ground floor
   STAGE DIMENSIONS AND EQUIPMENT: Height and width of
      proscenium, 18ft 6in x 30ft 6in; Shape of proscenium
      arch, rectangular; Distance from edge of stage to back
      wall of stage, 29ft 4in; Distance from edge of stage to
      curtain line, 2ft 6in; Distance between side walls of
      stage, 47ft; Distance from stage floor to fly loft, 50ft;
      Depth under stage, 8ft 8in; Stage floor, raked; Scenery
      storage rooms, 1 (off-stage); Dressing rooms, 4 (in an
      additon to the stage on first and second floors)
   DIMENSIONS OF AUDITORIUM: Distance between side walls of
      auditorium, 43ft 2in; Distance stage to back wall of
      auditorium, 65ft 6in; Capacity of orchestra pit, 20
   SEATING (2 levels): 1st level, 453; 2nd level, 113
   SHAPE OF THE AUDITORIUM: Rectangular
   MAJOR TYPES OF ENTERTAINMENT: Drama, vaudeville, burlesque,
      opera, movies
   MAJOR STARS WHO APPEARED AT THEATRE: Carlos Montoya, The
      Barrymores, Eddie Foy, "Blind" Boone, Dee Witt Harper,
      Kevin McCarthy

Hermann, MO

CONCERT HALL (other name: Concert Hall Bar and Grill),
   206 East 1st
   OPENING DATE: 1878
   ARCHITECTS: John Peautsch and Phillip Kuhn, builders
   STYLE OF ARCHITECTURE: Spanish   TYPE OF BUILDING: Bowling
      alley and movie theatre   FACADE: Brick

TYPE OF THEATRE: (b)   DEGREE OF RESTORATION: (a)
CURRENT USE: Parties and dances
LOCATION OF AUDITORIUM: Second floor
SHAPE OF THE AUDITORIUM: Rectangular
MAJOR TYPES OF ENTERTAINMENT: Drama, concerts, movies
ADDITIONAL INFORMATION: The building is now used for
  community functions, including plays.

Hermann, MO

ERHOLUNG
  OPENING DATE: 1841
  STYLE OF ARCHITECTURE: Spanish   TYPE OF BUILDING:
    Residence, stores   FACADE: Brick   TYPE OF THEATRE: (a)
  DEGREE OF RESTORATION: (c)   CLOSING DATE: 1860
  CURRENT USE: Printing business   PERFORMANCE SPACES IN
  BUILDING: 1   LOCATION OF AUDITORIUM: First floor
  SEATING (1 level): 1st level, 200
  SHAPE OF THE AUDITORIUM: Rectangular
  MAJOR TYPES OF ENTERTAINMENT: Plays produced by local
    German population
  ADDITIONAL INFORMATION: The local Theatre Society ceased to
    exist in 1866 and the building was then converted into
    storage space for the store located next door. Later, it
    was converted into living quarters.

Kansas City, MO

FOLLY THEATRE   (other names: Standard, Century, Shubert's
    Missouri), 20 West Ninth
  OPENING DATE: September 23, 1900
  OPENING SHOW: Burlesque show
  ARCHITECT: Louis Curtiss   STYLE OF ARCHITECTURE:
    Neo-Classical Palladian   TYPE OF BUILDING: Movie
    theatre   FACADE: Limestone block   TYPE OF THEATRE: (a)
  DEGREE OF RESTORATION: (a)   CURRENT USE: Theatre
  LOCATION OF AUDITORIUM: First floor
  STAGE DIMENSIONS AND EQUIPMENT: Height and width of
    proscenium, 33ft x 33ft; Shape of proscenium arch,
    square; Distance from edge of stage to back wall of
    stage, 35ft; Distance from edge of stage to curtain line,
    5ft; Distance between side walls of stage, 45ft; Distance
    from stage floor to fly loft, 35ft; Depth under stage,
    10ft; Trap doors, 1; Scenery storage rooms, 1
  SEATING (2 levels): 1st level, 1,000; 2nd level, 1,000
  MAJOR TYPES OF ENTERTAINMENT: Burlesque, drama, vaudeville,
  MAJOR STARS WHO APPEARED AT THEATRE: Al Jolson, Fanny
    Brice, Eddie Foy, Jack Johnson, Jack Dempsey, Gypsy Rose
    Lee
  ADDITIONAL INFORMATION: Theatre's name "Folly" was
    added during striptease era in the theatre's history.
    The theatre was kept alive by X-rated films until 1973.
    It was purchased in 1974 by the Performing Arts

Foundation which has instituted a four-phase restoration
plan.

Shelbina, MO

SHELBINA OPERA HOUSE (other name: Miller Opera House),
   202A South Center
OPENING DATE: 1888
ARCHITECT: Mr. Brown   STYLE OF ARCHITECTURE: Commercial
TYPE OF BUILDING: Retail store   FACADE: Red brick
TYPE OF THEATRE: (b)   DEGREE OF RESTORATION: (c)
CLOSING DATE: 1903   CURRENT USE: Furniture warehouse
LOCATION OF AUDITORIUM: Second floor
STAGE DIMENSIONS AND EQUIPMENT: Height and width of
   proscenium, 14ft x 19ft; Shape of proscenium arch,
   arched; Distance from edge of stage to back wall of
   stage, 25ft; Distance from edge of stage to curtain line,
   3ft; Distance between side walls of stage, 43ft; Distance
   from stage floor to fly loft, 18ft; Depth under stage,
   3ft 6in; Stage floor, flat; Trap doors, 1; Scenery
   storage rooms, 2 (stage right and left); Dressing rooms,
   3 (2 upstairs and 1 stage level)
DIMENSIONS OF AUDITORIUM: Distance between side walls
   of auditorium, 43ft; Distance stage to back wall of
   auditorium, 25ft; Orchestra pit, none
SEATING (2 levels): 1st level, 300; 2nd level, 100
SHAPE OF THE AUDITORIUM: U-shaped
MAJOR TYPES OF ENTERTAINMENT: Drama, vaudeville, lectures,
   high school commencement exercises

Montana

Butte, MT

MONTANA THEATRE (other names: Broadway Theatre, Sutton's
    Theatre), 204 West Broadway
    OPENING DATE: September 29, 1901
    OPENING SHOW: The Belle of New York
    ARCHITECT: H. M. Patterson   STYLE OF ARCHITECTURE:
    Renaissance Revival   FACADE: Unpainted brick with
    terra cotta trim   TYPE OF THEATRE: (a)
    DEGREE OF RESTORATION: (c)   CURRENT USE: Vacant
    LOCATION OF AUDITORIUM: Ground floor
    STAGE DIMENSIONS & EQUIPMENT: Distance from edge of stage
    to back wall of stage, 45ft; Distance between side walls
    of stage, 72ft; Dressing rooms, 10 (beneath stage)
    SEATING: 1st level, 730
    MAJOR TYPES OF ENTERTAINMENT: Drama, vaudeville, opera
    MAJOR STARS WHO APPEARED AT THEATRE: Clark Gable, Charlie
    Chaplin, Al Jolson, Vivian Vance
    ADDITIONAL INFORMATION: Once billed as "the Largest and
    Finest Theatre in the West," the 100ft by 129ft theatre
    has been boarded up and "mothballed" since 1983-4.

Elkhorn, MT

FRATERNITY HALL, Main Street
    OPENING DATE: c. 1893
    STYLE OF ARCHITECTURE: Neo-Classical
    TYPE OF BUILDING: Meeting hall   TYPE OF THEATRE: (a)
    DEGREE OF RESTORATION: (c)   CURRENT USE: Vacant
    LOCATION OF AUDITORIUM: Ground floor
    SEATING (2 levels)
    MAJOR TYPES OF ENTERTAINMENT: Drama, boxing matches,
    meetings, dances
    ADDITIONAL INFORMATION: The building, located in a
    ghost town, is owned by the Western Montana Ghost Town
    Preservation Society. It has two floors and interior
    walls made of wood planks. The main hall is situated

on the first floor with a small landing, reception room
with balcony access, and a lodge room on the second
floor. In addition to entertainment and community
events, the hall has been the site of two funerals and
one murder.

Nebraska

AURORA OPERA HOUSE, 1121 M Street
  OPENING DATE: May 25, 1891
  OPENING SHOW: Wanted, the Earth
  ARCHITECT: James Tyler   STYLE OF ARCHITECTURE: Gothic
    Revival   TYPE OF BUILDING: Commercial   FACADE: Brick
    and stone   TYPE OF THEATRE: (b)   DEGREE OF
  RESTORATION: (c)   CLOSING DATE: 1923   CURRENT USE: Store
  LOCATION OF AUDITORIUM: Second and third floors
  STAGE DIMENSIONS AND EQUIPMENT: * Height and width of
    proscenium, 16ft x 21ft; Shape of proscenium arch,
    rectangular; Distance from edge of stage to back wall
    of stage, 24ft; Distance from edge of stage to curtain
    line, 3ft; Distance between side walls of stage, 26ft;
    Depth under stage, 6ft 6in; Trap doors, 1
  DIMENSIONS OF AUDITORIUM: Distance between side walls
    of auditorium, 40ft; Distance stage to back wall of
    auditorium, 40ft
  SEATING (2 levels): 1st level, 300; 2nd level, 300
  SHAPE OF THE AUDITORIUM: Horseshoe-shaped balcony
  MAJOR TYPES OF ENTERTAINMENT: Drama, vaudeville, opera,
    concerts, lectures, dances
  MAJOR STARS WHO APPEARED AT THEATRE: John Dillon, Abbie
    Carrington, Ethel Chandler, Mabel Owen, Hugo Koch, Fred
    Byers
  ADDITIONAL INFORMATION: The upper floor of the building was
    removed in 1940.

Fort Robinson, NE

FORT ROBINSON GYMNASIUM/THEATER (other name: Army Theater),
    U.S. Highway 20
  OPENING DATE: 1904
  TYPE OF BUILDING: Gymnasium   FACADE: White wood frame
    with green trim   TYPE OF THEATRE: (a)   DEGREE OF
  RESTORATION: (a)   CLOSING DATE: 1948

CURRENT USE: Natural History Museum
LOCATION OF AUDITORIUM: Ground floor
DIMENSIONS OF AUDITORIUM: Distance between side walls
  of auditorium, 45ft; Distance stage to back wall of
  auditorium, 99ft; Orchestra pit, none
SEATING (1 level)
SHAPE OF THE AUDITORIUM: Rectangular
MAJOR TYPES OF ENTERTAINMENT: Drama, minstrel shows
MAJOR STARS WHO APPEARED AT THEATRE: Sally Rand, Victor
  Borge
ADDITIONAL INFORMATION: When constructed, the building
  also contained a bowling alley, shooting galleries and
  the most up-to-date gymnastic equipment. The stage was
  moveable, as were the seats. There is a second theatre
  at Fort Robinson. In the late 1960s, since the original
  1904 gym/theatre had been adapted to other uses, a frame
  Quartermaster storehouse [c. 1892] was converted into the
  Post Playhouse.

Fremont, NE

LOVE-LARSON OPERA HOUSE, 541 North Broad
  OPENING DATE: December 14, 1888
  OPENING SHOW: Minnie Maddern in Caprice
  ARCHITECT: Francis Ellis   STYLE OF ARCHITECTURE:
    Richardsonian Romanesque   FACADE: Red brick and
    limestone facing   TYPE OF THEATRE: (b)   DEGREE OF
  RESTORATION: (c)   CURRENT USE: Occasional use for social
    events   LOCATION OF AUDITORIUM: Second, third, and
    fourth floors
  STAGE DIMENSIONS AND EQUIPMENT: * Height and width of
    proscenium, 22ft x 28ft; Distance from edge of stage to
    back wall of stage, 38ft; Distance from edge of stage to
    curtain line, 3ft; Distance between side walls of stage,
    55ft; Depth under stage, 12ft; Trap doors, 4
  DIMENSIONS OF AUDITORIUM: Capacity of orchestra pit, 6
  MAJOR TYPES OF ENTERTAINMENT: Drama, vaudeville
  MAJOR STARS WHO APPEARED AT THEATRE: Will Geer

Hampton, NE

HAMPTON OPERA HOUSE (other name: I.O.O.F. Hall), Main Street
  OPENING DATE: December 22, 1893
  OPENING SHOW: The Holden Comedy Company
  ARCHITECT: James M. Cox   TYPE OF BUILDING: Commercial
  FACADE: Red brick   TYPE OF THEATRE: (b)
  DEGREE OF RESTORATION: (c)   CLOSING DATE: 1928
  CURRENT USE: Vacant
  MAJOR TYPES OF ENTERTAINMENT: Drama, vaudeville, concerts,
    musical comedy, dances, lectures
  MAJOR STARS WHO APPEARED AT THEATRE: Brose and Clemens,
    Canadian Colored Jubilee Singers, Georgia Troubadors,
    Hugo and Applegate Co., Lacey Comedy Co., Knowlton and
    Dixon Comedy Co., Holden Comedy Company, "Blind" Boone

Indianola, NE

INDIANOLA OPERA HOUSE (other names: Beardslee's Opera
    House, Uerling's Opera House), Southeast corner of
    4th and D Streets
    OPENING DATE: 1883
    ARCHITECT: William H. McCartney   TYPE OF BUILDING:
    Commercial   TYPE OF THEATRE: (b)   DEGREE OF
    RESTORATION: (a)   CLOSING DATE: c. 1940   CURRENT USE:
    Food lockers   LOCATION OF AUDITORIUM: Second floor
    STAGE DIMENSIONS AND EQUIPMENT: Width of proscenium, 23ft;
    Distance from edge of stage to back wall of stage, 20ft;
    Depth under stage, 3ft; Dressing rooms, 2 (behind stage)
    DIMENSIONS OF AUDITORIUM: Distance between side walls
    of auditorium, 23ft; Distance stage to back wall of
    auditorium, 70ft
    SEATING (1 level)
    MAJOR TYPES OF ENTERTAINMENT: Drama, vaudeville, minstrel
    shows, medicine shows
    MAJOR STARS WHO APPEARED AT THEATRE: The Helman Brothers,
    L. J. Story
    ADDITIONAL INFORMATION: The auditorium floor was flat and
    seating was on benches which lined both side walls and on
    folding chairs. When cleared, the theatre also served as
    a dance hall.

Red Cloud, NE

RED CLOUD OPERA HOUSE, Webster Street
    OPENING DATE: April 26, 1885   TYPE OF BUILDING: Commercial
    FACADE: Originally brick, now stucco   TYPE OF THEATRE: (b)
    DEGREE OF RESTORATION: (c)   CLOSING DATE: 1917   CURRENT
    USE: Storage   LOCATION OF AUDITORIUM: Second floor
    STAGE DIMENSIONS AND EQUIPMENT: * Height and width of
    proscenium, 15ft x 26ft; Distance from edge of stage to
    back wall, 18ft; Depth under stage, 4ft; Stage floor,
    flat; Trap doors, 1
    MAJOR TYPES OF ENTERTAINMENT: Drama, musical comedy,
    concerts
    ADDITIONAL INFORMATION: The opera house is notable as the
    site of Willa Cather's graduation from high school.

Table Rock, NE

TABLE ROCK OPERA HOUSE
    OPENING DATE: 1893
    TYPE OF THEATRE: (b)   CURRENT USE: Historical museum
    LOCATION OF AUDITORIUM: Upper floor
    STAGE DIMENSIONS AND EQUIPMENT: Height and width of
    proscenium, 13ft 6in x 20ft 4in; Distance between side
    walls of stage, 44ft; Stage floor, raked; Trap doors,
    1; Dressing rooms, 2

Wood River, NE

MOORE OPERA HOUSE, Ninth and Main
OPENING DATE: c. 1893   STYLE OF ARCHITECTURE: Victorian
TYPE OF BUILDING: Commercial   FACADE: Red brick
TYPE OF THEATRE: (b)   DEGREE OF RESTORATION: (c)
CLOSING DATE: Mid-1940s   CURRENT USE: Vacant
LOCATION OF AUDITORIUM: Second floor
STAGE DIMENSIONS AND EQUIPMENT: Height and width of
  proscenium, 12ft x 33ft; Shape of proscenium arch,
  arched; Distance from edge of stage to back wall of
  stage, 20ft; Distance from edge of stage to curtain
  line, 3ft; Depth under stage, 2ft 6in; Stage floor,
  flat; Trap doors, 1; Dressing rooms, 2 (sides of stage)
DIMENSIONS OF AUDITORIUM: Distance between side walls
  of auditorium, 63ft; Distance stage to back wall of
  auditorium, 63ft; Orchestra pit, none
SEATING (1 level): 1st level, 200
SHAPE OF THE AUDITORIUM: Square
MAJOR TYPES OF ENTERTAINMENT: Drama, lectures, dances,
  civic functions
ADDITIONAL INFORMATION: Dubbed the "Grand Dame," the opera
  house was the hub of the community and was managed by a
  citizens' association. Closed since the mid-1940s, the
  stage has since rotted and a previous owner sold anything
  of value as an antique.

Nevada

Virginia City, NV

PIPER'S OPERA HOUSE, B and Union Streets
OPENING DATE: 1885
STYLE OF ARCHITECTURE: Spanish Western   TYPE OF BUILDING:
   Roller skating rink, basketball court   FACADE: Wood
TYPE OF THEATRE: (a)   DEGREE OF RESTORATION: (b)
CLOSING DATE: 1920   CURRENT USE: Concerts, touring shows
LOCATION OF AUDITORIUM: First floor
STAGE DIMENSIONS AND EQUIPMENT: Height and width of
   proscenium, 20ft x 30ft; Shape of proscenium arch,
   arched; Distance from edge of stage to back wall of
   stage, 32ft; Distance from edge of stage to curtain line,
   4ft 6in; Distance between side walls of stage, 50ft;
   Distance from stage floor to fly loft, 26ft; Depth under
   stage, 6ft; Stage floor, raked; Trap doors, 1
DIMENSIONS OF AUDITORIUM: Distance between side walls of
   auditorium, 50ft
SEATING (3 levels)
MAJOR TYPES OF ENTERTAINMENT: Local and touring companies
MAJOR STARS WHO APPEARED AT THEATRE: Maude Adams, Lillian
   Russell, Lillie Langtry, Julia Marlowe, Enrico Caruso
ADDITIONAL INFORMATION: This is the third Piper's Opera
   House to be built on this site. The previous two were
   destroyed by fire. Tours are conducted and recitals are
   presented at the theatre. The building was offered for
   sale in August 1986. The raked stage, original scenery,
   and a sun-lamp chandelier remain.

Winnemucca, NV

NIXON OPERA HOUSE (other name: Nixon), 48 West Winnemucca
   Boulevard
OPENING DATE: 1907
OPENING SHOW: Willard the Mystery Man (hypnotist)
ARCHITECT: Dave LaPoint   STYLE OF ARCHITECTURE: Art Deco
   and Modern   TYPE OF THEATRE: (b)   DEGREE OF

RESTORATION: (b)   CURRENT USE: Meetings, arts and
  crafts shows   LOCATION OF AUDITORIUM: First floor
STAGE DIMENSIONS AND EQUIPMENT: Distance from edge of stage
  to back wall of stage, 40ft; Distance between side walls
  of stage, 80ft; Distance from stage floor to fly loft,
  35ft
MAJOR TYPES OF ENTERTAINMENT: Drama, vaudeville, opera
ADDITIONAL INFORMATION: The upstairs of the building has
  been closed by the fire marshall.

New Hampshire

Franklin, NH

OPERA HOUSE (other names: City Hall Theatre, Soldiers'
    Memorial Hall), Central Street
OPENING DATE: 1892
ARCHITECT: H. H. Richardson   STYLE OF ARCHITECTURE:
    Richardsonian Romanesque   TYPE OF BUILDING: Municipal
    building   FACADE: Stone, brick with rough-face stone
    trim   TYPE OF THEATRE: (b)   DEGREE OF RESTORATION: (c)
CLOSING DATE: 1970   CURRENT USE: Vacant
LOCATION OF AUDITORIUM: Ground floor
STAGE DIMENSIONS AND EQUIPMENT: Width of proscenium,
    28ft; Distance from edge of stage to back wall of stage,
    18ft; Distance from edge of stage to curtain line, 4ft;
    Distance between side walls of stage, 54ft; Dressing
    rooms, 3 (under stage)
DIMENSIONS OF AUDITORIUM: Distance between side walls
    of auditorium, 54ft; Distance stage to back wall of
    auditorium, 58ft; Orchestra pit, yes
SEATING (2 levels)
SHAPE OF THE AUDITORIUM: Rectangular
MAJOR TYPES OF ENTERTAINMENT: Drama, musical comedy,
    vaudeville, movies

Littleton, NH

LITTLETON OPERA HOUSE (other names: Grand Opera House, Town
    Hall), Corner of Main and Union
OPENING DATE: 1895   OPENING SHOW: Beresford concert
ARCHITECT: Fred T. Austin   STYLE OF ARCHITECTURE: Queen
    Anne   TYPE OF BUILDING: Town offices   FACADE: Grey wood
TYPE OF THEATRE: (b)   DEGREE OF RESTORATION: (a)   CURRENT
USE: Civic functions   LOCATION OF AUDITORIUM: Ground floor
STAGE DIMENSIONS AND EQUIPMENT: Height and width of
    proscenium, 19ft 2in x 21ft 11in; Shape of proscenium
    arch, arched; Distance from edge of stage to back wall of
    stage, 18ft 5in; Distance from edge of stage to curtain

line, 4ft 10in; Distance between side walls of stage,
31ft 10in; Stage floor, flat; Trap doors, 1; Scenery
storage rooms, 1 (stage left); Dressing rooms, 1 (stage
left)
DIMENSIONS OF AUDITORIUM: Distance between side walls
of auditorium, 52ft 8in; Distance stage to back wall
of auditorium, 46ft 5in; Orchestra pit, none
SEATING (2 levels): 1st level, 198; 2nd level, 265
SHAPE OF THE AUDITORIUM: Horseshoe-shaped balcony
MAJOR TYPES OF ENTERTAINMENT: Drama, musical comedy,
vaudeville, opera, minstrel shows, wrestling
ADDITIONAL INFORMATION: When the opera house opened, a
painting of The Old Man of the Mountains appeared above
the proscenium. Original equipment included 4 sets of
scenery in 18' grooves, a front drop and roll curtains.

Manchester, NH

MANCHESTER OPERA HOUSE (other names: Strand, the Nickel, the
Auditorium), Hanover Street near Elm
OPENING DATE: January 24, 1881   OPENING SHOW: Richelieu
ARCHITECT: J. T. Fanning   TYPE OF BUILDING: In block with
stores   FACADE: Brick   TYPE OF THEATRE: (b)
CLOSING DATE: March 1985   CURRENT USE: Stores
LOCATION OF AUDITORIUM: Ground floor
STAGE DIMENSIONS AND EQUIPMENT: Height and width of
proscenium, 30ft x 34ft; Distance between side walls of
stage, 70ft; Distance from stage floor to fly loft, 60ft;
Trap doors, 8; Dressing rooms, 11
SEATING (3 levels): 1st level, 550; 2nd level, 580;
3rd level, 336; boxes, 30
MAJOR TYPES OF ENTERTAINMENT: Drama, vaudeville, opera,
movies
MAJOR STARS WHO APPEARED AT THEATRE: The Barrymores,
Bernhardt, Edwin Booth
ADDITIONAL INFORMATION: The auditorium has been gutted.

Manchester, NH

PALACE THEATRE, 80 Hanover Street
OPENING DATE: April 9, 1915   OPENING SHOW: Modern Eve
ARCHITECTS: Leon Lempart and Harry Macropol
FACADE: White brick   TYPE OF THEATRE: (a)
DEGREE OF RESTORATION: (a)   CURRENT USE: Performing arts
center   LOCATION OF AUDITORIUM: Ground floor
STAGE DIMENSIONS AND EQUIPMENT: Height and width of
proscenium, 26ft x 40ft; Shape of proscenium arch,
rectangular; Distance from edge of stage to back wall of
stage, 32ft; Distance from edge of stage to curtain line,
4ft; Distance between side walls of stage, 69ft 3in;
Depth under stage, 10ft; Stage floor, flat; Trap doors,
1; Scenery storage rooms, 0; Dressing rooms, 8 (basement)
DIMENSIONS OF AUDITORIUM: Orchestra pit, yes

SEATING (2 levels): 1st level, 483; 2nd level, 414
SHAPE OF THE AUDITORIUM: U-shaped
MAJOR TYPES OF ENTERTAINMENT: Drama, musical comedy,
   opera, concerts, vaudeville, movies, dance
MAJOR STARS WHO APPEARED AT THEATRE: Mickey Rooney,
   Jimmy Durante, Ray Charles, Marcel Marceau, Carole
   King, Mark Russell, Helen Reddy
ADDITIONAL INFORMATION: The theatre, billed as "the
   only fireproof first class theatre in the state of New
   Hampshire" when it opened, was converted to movies
   during the 1940s. It was restored in 1974 and reopened
   as a performing arts center with a performance titled
   The Palace Theatre Follies.

Plainfield, NH

PLAINFIELD TOWN HALL (other name: Howard Hart Stage)
   OPENING DATE: 1846
   ARCHITECTS: Bradbury Dyer and Charles Eggleston, Builders
   STYLE OF ARCHITECTURE: Greek Revival   TYPE OF BUILDING:
      Town Hall   FACADE: White wood   TYPE OF THEATRE: (b)
   DEGREE OF RESTORATION: (c)   CURRENT USE: Town hall,
      theatre   LOCATION OF AUDITORIUM: Ground floor
   STAGE DIMENSIONS AND EQUIPMENT: Distance from edge of
      stage to back wall of stage, 25ft 7in; Distance from
      edge of stage to curtain line, 3ft; Distance between
      side walls of stage, 24ft; Stage floor, flat; Trap
      doors, 0; Dressing rooms, 2 (rear of stage); Scenery
      storage rooms (in wings)
   DIMENSIONS OF AUDITORIUM: Distance between side walls
      of auditorium, 46ft; Distance stage to back wall of
      auditorium, 37ft 8in
   SEATING (1 level): 1st level, 200
   SHAPE OF THE AUDITORIUM: Rectangular
   MAJOR TYPES OF ENTERTAINMENT: Vaudeville, drama, local
      variety shows
   ADDITIONAL INFORMATION: The building is used by theatre
      groups from throughout the area. The stage was installed
      in 1917.

Portsmouth, NH

ARCADIA, Congress near Vaugh Street
   OPENING DATE: Late 1800s   TYPE OF BUILDING: Commercial
   FACADE: Red brick   TYPE OF THEATRE: (b)   DEGREE OF
   RESTORATION: (c)   CLOSING DATE: 1960s
   CURRENT USE: Office building
   LOCATION OF AUDITORIUM: Second and third floors
   SHAPE OF THE AUDITORIUM: U-shaped
   MAJOR TYPES OF ENTERTAINMENT: Drama, vaudeville, movies

Rochester, NH

ROCHESTER OPERA HOUSE, 31 Wakefield Street
  OPENING DATE: May 30, 1908
  ARCHITECT: George Gilman Adams   TYPE OF BUILDING:
    Municipal   FACADE: Red brick with cement trim
  TYPE OF THEATRE: (b)   DEGREE OF RESTORATION: (b)
  CLOSING DATE: c. 1975   CURRENT USE: Vacant
  LOCATION OF AUDITORIUM: Second and third floors
  STAGE DIMENSIONS AND EQUIPMENT: Height and width of
    proscenium, 18ft x 29ft; Shape of proscenium arch,
    rectangular; Distance from edge of stage to back wall
    of stage, 33ft; Distance from edge of stage to curtain
    line, 5ft; Distance between side walls of stage, 55ft;
    Depth under stage, 5ft; Trap doors, 0; Dressing rooms,
    4 (sides of stage)
  DIMENSIONS OF AUDITORIUM: Distance between side walls
    of auditorium, 65ft; Distance stage to back wall of
    auditorium, 50ft; Capacity of orchestra pit, 5
  SEATING (2 levels): 1st level, 270; 2nd level, 264
  SHAPE OF THE AUDITORIUM: U-shaped
  MAJOR TYPES OF ENTERTAINMENT: Drama, vaudeville, musical
    comedy, operettas, ballroom dancing
  ADDITIONAL INFORMATION: The opera house is equipped with
    a moveable floor which could be raised for viewing live
    performances or lowered for dancing. The sloping is
    achieved by a mechanical system of gears, belts and
    drums.

New Jersey

Atlantic City, NJ

APOLLO (other names: Nixon's Apollo, Apollo Burlesk),
   1509-11 Boardwalk
   OPENING DATE: April 1907   OPENING SHOW: Mary's Lamb
   TYPE OF THEATRE: (a)   DEGREE OF RESTORATION: (c)
   MAJOR TYPES OF ENTERTAINMENT: Drama, musical comedy,
      operettas, minstrel shows, movies; revue
   MAJOR STARS WHO APPEARED AT THEATRE: Maude Adams, George
      Arliss, David Warfield, Frances Starr, Lew Dockstader,
      Billie Burke, Al Jolson, Marilyn Miller, James K.
      Hackett, Mrs. Leslie Carter, George M. Cohan, Victor
      Moore, Nance O'Neil, Lillian Russell, Maxine Elliot, and
      others
   ADDITIONAL INFORMATION: The Apollo was erected by Joseph
      F. Fralinger to replace the Academy of Music which had
      burned in 1902. In its day, the Apollo was one of the
      most celebrated tryout houses in the country, attracting
      showmen of the magnitude of Florenz Ziegfeld, George
      White, Earl Carroll, George M. Cohan, Sam H. Harris,
      and David Belasco as well as the Shubert brothers and
      A.L. Erlanger. By the early 1930s, the theatre had
      lost its status as a booking house and in 1934 it was
      converted to movies.

Clinton, NJ

CLINTON MUSIC HALL, 23 West Main Street
   OPENING DATE: 1890   OPENING SHOW: Uncle Tom's Cabin
   ARCHITECTS: James and Herman Altemus   TYPE OF BUILDING:
      Commercial   FACADE: Brick and pine   TYPE OF THEATRE: (b)
   DEGREE OF RESTORATION: (a)   CLOSING DATE: 1976
   CURRENT USE: Offices
   STAGE DIMENSIONS AND EQUIPMENT: Height and width of
      proscenium, 14ft x 22ft; Shape of proscenium arch,
      rectangular; Distance from edge of stage to back wall of
      stage, 28ft; Distance from edge of stage to curtain line,

2ft; Distance between side walls of stage, 38ft; Depth
under stage, 10ft; Stage floor, raked; Trap doors, 1;
Scenery storage rooms, 1 (backstage); Dressing rooms,
1 (backstage)
DIMENSIONS OF AUDITORIUM: Distance between side walls
of auditorium, 38ft; Distance stage to back wall of
auditorium, 40ft; Capacity of orchestra pit, 12
SEATING (2 levels): 1st level, 250; 2nd level, 75
SHAPE OF THE AUDITORIUM: Square
MAJOR TYPES OF ENTERTAINMENT: Drama, vaudeville, minstrel
shows, "Tom" shows, medicine shows, variety, chautauquas,
movies

Jersey City, NJ

MAJESTIC THEATRE, 275 Grove Street
OPENING DATE: September 17, 1907
OPENING SHOW: The Mazuma Man
ARCHITECTS: William B. McElfatrick   STYLE OF ARCHITECTURE:
Neo-Classical   TYPE OF BUILDING: Offices   FACADE: Red
brick, white brick, pressed tin   TYPE OF THEATRE: (a)
DEGREE OF RESTORATION: (b)   CLOSING DATE: 1938
CURRENT USE: See ADDITIONAL INFORMATION
LOCATION OF AUDITORIUM: Ground floor
STAGE DIMENSIONS AND EQUIPMENT: Height and width of
proscenium, 35ft x 36ft; Distance from edge of stage
to back wall of stage, 41ft; Distance from edge of stage
to curtain line, 3ft; Distance between side walls of
stage, 77ft; Depth under stage, 10ft; Scenery storage
rooms, 1 (under stage); Dressing rooms, 8 (stage left)
DIMENSIONS OF AUDITORIUM: Orchestra pit, yes
SEATING (3 levels): 1st level, 726; 2nd level, 478;
3rd level, 342
MAJOR TYPES OF ENTERTAINMENT: Drama, musical comedy,
vaudeville, burlesque, movies
MAJOR STARS WHO APPEARED AT THEATRE: Mae West, Fanny Brice,
George M. Cohan, Chauncey Olcott, the Marx Brothers,
Jason Robards Sr.
ADDITIONAL INFORMATION: The stage is presently being used
as a performance space while the main house is being
restored to its 1907 condition for use as The Liberty
Center for the Performing Arts. The center will offer
performances, workshops and seminars in theatre, dance,
opera, and music.

Keyport, NJ

STRAND THEATRE (other name: Surf Theatre), West Front Street
OPENING DATE: c. 1900
FACADE: Tan cement   TYPE OF THEATRE: (a)   DEGREE OF
RESTORATION: (c)   CLOSING DATE: 1983
CURRENT USE: Being converted to apartments
LOCATION OF AUDITORIUM: Ground floor
STAGE DIMENSIONS AND EQUIPMENT: Distance from edge of stage

to back wall of stage, 15ft; Distance between side
    walls of stage, 30ft
DIMENSIONS OF AUDITORIUM: Distance between side walls of
    auditorium, 40ft; Distance stage to back wall, 60ft;
    Orchestra pit, yes
SEATING (2 levels)
MAJOR TYPES OF ENTERTAINMENT: Drama, vaudeville

Keyport, NJ

WALLING HALL, West Front and Broad Streets
    OPENING DATE: c. 1878
    STYLE OF ARCHITECTURE: Victorian   TYPE OF BUILDING:
      Commercial   FACADE: Red brick with gray stone cornices
    TYPE OF THEATRE: (b)   DEGREE OF RESTORATION: (b)
    CURRENT USE: In process of being renovated
    LOCATION OF AUDITORIUM: Second floor
    STAGE DIMENSIONS AND EQUIPMENT: Distance from edge of stage
      to back wall of stage, 16ft; Distance between side walls
      of stage, 50ft
    DIMENSIONS OF AUDITORIUM: Distance between side walls
      of auditorium, 50ft; Distance stage to back wall of
      auditorium, 60ft
    SEATING (2 levels)
    SHAPE OF THE AUDITORIUM: Rectangular

Somerville, NJ

SOMERSET HALL, Corner of West Main and Union Streets
    OPENING DATE: 1901
    TYPE OF BUILDING: Commercial   TYPE OF THEATRE: (b)
    DEGREE OF RESTORATION: (c)   CURRENT USE: Furniture store
    LOCATION OF AUDITORIUM: Fourth floor
    MAJOR TYPES OF ENTERTAINMENT: Drama, opera, dance, concerts
    MAJOR STARS WHO APPEARED AT THEATRE: Ruth St. Denis, Anna
      Case

Tenafly, NJ

TENAFLY HALL, Jay Street and Highwood Avenue
    OPENING DATE: June 9, 1893
    OPENING SHOW: Concert and reception
    ARCHITECT: W. L. Stoddart   STYLE OF ARCHITECTURE: Queen
      Anne   TYPE OF BUILDING: Meeting hall   TYPE OF
    THEATRE: (b)   DEGREE OF RESTORATION: (c)   CURRENT USE:
      Offices   LOCATION OF AUDITORIUM: Second floor
    DIMENSIONS OF AUDITORIUM: Distance between side walls
      of auditorium, 50ft; Distance stage to back wall of
      auditorium, 60ft
    SEATING (1 level)
    SHAPE OF THE AUDITORIUM: Rectangular
    MAJOR TYPES OF ENTERTAINMENT: Drama, musical comedy,
      minstrel shows, vaudeville

New Mexico

Albuquerque, NM

ORPHEUM THEATRE (other name: Orpheum Amusement, 1916;
    Orpheum Dance Hall, 1917)
    OPENING DATE: 1911   TYPE OF BUILDING: Furniture
    store, garage   TYPE OF THEATRE: (c)
    DEGREE OF RESTORATION: (c)   CLOSING DATE: c. 1922
    CURRENT USE: Vacant   PERFORMANCE SPACES IN BUILDING: 1
    LOCATION OF AUDITORIUM: First floor
    MAJOR TYPES OF ENTERTAINMENT: Vaudeville, movies
    ADDITIONAL INFORMATION: The building which houses the
    theatre was built in 1901 as a furniture store and
    converted to vaudeville and films in 1911. A news-
    paper account states that the scenery and decorations
    are the work of John Heboth, a German scenic artist.
    There is occasional interest in restoring the theatre.

Mesilla, NM

FOUNTAIN THEATRE
    OPENING DATE: 1905
    STYLE OF ARCHITECTURE: Spanish   TYPE OF BUILDING:
    Community usage   FACADE: Adobe   TYPE OF THEATRE: (a)
    DEGREE OF RESTORATION: (a)   CURRENT USE: Theatre
    PERFORMANCE SPACES IN BUILDING: 1
    LOCATION OF AUDITORIUM: First floor
    MAJOR TYPES OF ENTERTAINMENT: Drama, movies, zarzuelas,
    concerts
    ADDITIONAL INFORMATION: This one-story adobe structure
    was built by Albert Fountain. Murals depicting valley
    scenes were painted by Fountain in 1914 and still exist
    on interior walls. The building is now owned and operated
    by his great grandson, Albert Fountain, Jr., who hosts
    occasional performing groups.

Raton, NM

SHULER AUDITORIUM (other name: Shuler Theatre), 1312 North
    Second Street
OPENING DATE: April 27, 1915
OPENING SHOW: The Red Rose
ARCHITECT: W. M. Rapp   STYLE OF ARCHITECTURE: Victorian
    Vernacular   TYPE OF BUILDING: Municipal building
FACADE: Rust, ivory brick with iron fittings
TYPE OF THEATRE: (a)   DEGREE OF RESTORATION: (a)
CURRENT USE: Theatre and offices   PERFORMANCE SPACES IN
BUILDING: 1   LOCATION OF AUDITORIUM: Second floor
STAGE DIMENSIONS AND EQUIPMENT: Height and width of
    proscenium, 21ft 8in x 30ft; Shape of proscenium
    arch, arched; Distance from edge of stage to back
    wall of stage, 33ft 6in; Distance from edge of stage
    to curtain line, 3ft 6in; Distance between side walls
    of stage, 55ft; Distance from stage floor to fly loft,
    45ft; Depth under stage, 9ft 2in; Stage floor, flat;
    Trap doors, 1; Scenery storage rooms, 1 (upstage left);
    Dressing rooms, 3 (under stage)
DIMENSIONS OF AUDITORIUM: Distance between side walls of
    auditorium, 55ft 2in; Distance stage to back wall of
    auditorium, 54ft 2in; Capacity of orchestra pit, 25
SEATING (2 levels): 1st level, 289; 2nd level, 170
SHAPE OF THE AUDITORIUM: U-shaped
MAJOR TYPES OF ENTERTAINMENT: Drama, vaudeville, movies,
    concerts
MAJOR STARS WHO APPEARED AT THEATRE: George M. Cohan,
    Paul Robeson, Sousa, Madam Schumann-Heink, Phil Silvers,
    Steve Simpson

Santa Fe, NM

SCOTTISH RITE TEMPLE (other name: Scottish Rite Cathedral),
    463 Paso De Peralta
OPENING DATE: 1912   STYLE OF ARCHITECTURE: Moorish
TYPE OF BUILDING: Lodge   FACADE: Stucco
TYPE OF THEATRE: (c)   DEGREE OF RESTORATION: (a)
CURRENT USE: Lodge   PERFORMANCE SPACES IN BUILDING: 1
LOCATION OF AUDITORIUM: First floor
STAGE DIMENSIONS AND EQUIPMENT: Height and width of
    proscenium, 20ft x 26ft; Shape of proscenium arch,
    rectangular; Distance from edge of stage to back wall
    of stage, 40ft; Distance from edge of stage to curtain
    line, 20ft; Distance from stage floor to fly loft, 55ft
SEATING (2 levels)
SHAPE OF THE AUDITORIUM: Rectangular
ADDITIONAL INFORMATION: Stage has 97 drops comprising
    37 separate complete scenes. The front curtain depicts
    a view of Granada and the Alhambra Palace. The stage
    has a very pronounced forestage of roughly 20 feet.
    Dimensions are approximate, but are corroborated by
    a photograph. Clouds painted on the ceiling and a

beautiful mural above the proscenium arch make this
an unusually beautiful theatre.

Socorro, NM

GARCIA OPERA HOUSE (other name: Abeyta Opera House, 1895),
     100 Abeyta Street
   OPENING DATE: December 1, 1886
   OPENING SHOW: Socorro Musical Festival (100 Musicians)
   FACADE: Adobe   TYPE OF THEATRE: (a)   DEGREE OF
   RESTORATION: (a)   CURRENT USE: Theatre, meetings
   PERFORMANCE SPACES IN BUILDING: 1
   LOCATION OF AUDITORIUM: Ground floor
   STAGE DIMENSIONS AND EQUIPMENT: Height and width of
     proscenium, 10ft 4in x 19ft; Shape of proscenium arch,
     arched; Distance from edge of stage to back wall of
     stage, 34ft 2in; Distance between side walls of stage,
     37ft 6in; Distance from stage floor to fly loft, 18ft;
     Depth under stage, 3ft; Stage floor, raked; Trap doors,
     1; Scenery storage rooms, 0; Dressing rooms, 0
   DIMENSIONS OF AUDITORIUM: Distance between side walls of
     auditorium, 38ft 2in; Distance stage to back wall of
     auditorium, 95ft 7in; Orchestra pit, none
   SEATING (1 level)
   SHAPE OF THE AUDITORIUM: Rectangular
   MAJOR TYPES OF ENTERTAINMENT: Vaudeville, drama, opera

New York

TOWN HALL THEATRE (other names: Town Hall Opry, Bainbridge
   Opera House, Avon Theatre), 15 North Main Street
   OPENING DATE: 1910   OPENING SHOW: H. M. S. Pinafore
   TYPE OF BUILDING: Municipal   FACADE: Off-white granite
   TYPE OF THEATRE: (b)   DEGREE OF RESTORATION: (a)
   CURRENT USE: Theatre   LOCATION OF AUDITORIUM: Second floor
   STAGE DIMENSIONS AND EQUIPMENT: Height and width of
   proscenium, 16ft 8in x 20ft; Depth under stage, 4ft 6in;
   Stage floor, flat; Trap doors, 1; Scenery storage rooms,
   2 (above stage); Dressing rooms, 3 (2 off-stage; 1 above
   stage)
   DIMENSIONS OF AUDITORIUM: Orchestra pit, none
   SEATING (2 levels): 1st level, 260; 2nd level, 150
   SHAPE OF THE AUDITORIUM: Rectangular
   MAJOR TYPES OF ENTERTAINMENT: Drama, musical comedy,
   light opera, movies, concerts
   ADDITIONAL INFORMATION: The theatre was used for live
   entertainment until 1938, when it was converted to a
   movie theatre. The theatre was abandoned in the 1950s
   and was not used again until 1974. Today, a variety
   of entertainments, including bluegrass shows, opera,
   and puppet theatre, are presented under the auspices of
   the Jerico Arts Council, Inc. which administers the
   theatre.

Binghamton, NY

STONE OPERA HOUSE (other name: The Riviera), 31-33 Chenango
   Street
   OPENING DATE: October 11, 1892   OPENING SHOW: Fadette
   ARCHITECTS: S. O. Lacey and E. H. Bartoo   STYLE OF
   ARCHITECTURE: Richardsonian Romanesque   TYPE OF BUILDING:
   Commercial   TYPE OF THEATRE: (b)   DEGREE OF
   RESTORATION: (b)   CLOSING DATE: 1973   CURRENT USE:
   Being rebuilt   LOCATION OF AUDITORIUM: Ground floor

STAGE DIMENSIONS AND EQUIPMENT: * Height and width of
  proscenium, 34ft x 35ft; Distance from edge of stage to
  back wall of stage, 45ft; Distance from edge of stage to
  curtain line, 4ft; Distance between side walls of stage,
  66ft; Depth under stage, 15ft; Trap doors, 3; Scenery
  storage rooms, 1
DIMENSIONS OF AUDITORIUM: Orchestra pit, yes
SEATING (3 levels)
SHAPE OF THE AUDITORIUM: Horseshoe-shaped balcony
MAJOR TYPES OF ENTERTAINMENT: Drama, musical comedy,
  opera, vaudeville, burlesque, minstrel shows
MAJOR STARS WHO APPEARED AT THEATRE: Neil O'Brien, Rose
  Coghlan, Richard Mansfield, John Drew, E. H. Sothern,
  Julia Marlowe, Mrs. Fiske, Bernhardt, Henry Irving,
  Maude Adams, Henrietta Crosman, Joseph Jefferson,
  Helena Modjeska, Lew Dockstader's Minstrels, Ethel
  and John Barrymore, Eddie Foy, George M. Cohan,
  Edward G. Robinson
ADDITIONAL INFORMATION: The marquee (the theatre was used
  for movies beginning in 1930) has been removed and the
  first floor store-fronts have been restored to resemble
  the originals. There are plans for constructing two 300-
  seat theatres in the building.

Bronx, NY

BRONX OPERA HOUSE (other name: Bronx Theatre), 436 East
  149th Street
OPENING DATE: 1913
STYLE OF ARCHITECTURE: Originally Beaux Arts
TYPE OF THEATRE: (a)   DEGREE OF RESTORATION: (c)
CLOSING DATE: 1978   LOCATION OF AUDITORIUM: Ground floor
STAGE DIMENSIONS AND EQUIPMENT: * Height and width of
  proscenium, 28ft x 34ft; Distance from edge of stage to
  back wall of stage, 40ft; Distance from edge of stage to
  curtain line, 4ft; Distance between side walls of stage,
  72ft 4in; Distance from stage floor to fly loft, 29ft;
  Depth under stage, 8ft 8in; Trap doors, 4; Dressing
  rooms, 12
SEATING: * 1st level, 799; 2nd level, 537; 3rd
  level, 478; boxes, 78
MAJOR TYPES OF ENTERTAINMENT: Drama, musical comedy,
  vaudeville, movies
MAJOR STARS WHO APPEARED AT THEATRE: Barney Barnard,
  Alexander Carr, John, Ethel and Lionel Barrymore,
  E. H. Sothern, Julia Marlowe, Mrs. Leslie Carter,
  Mrs. Fiske, Fay Bainter, David Warfield, the Marx
  Brothers, George Burns and Gracie Allen, Benny Leonard
ADDITIONAL INFORMATION: In its heyday, the Bronx Opera
  House was an integral part of "The Hub," the area around
  149th Street and 3rd Avenue. The area, which was dotted
  with excellent theatres, restaurants and stores, was a
  center of activity in the Bronx.

Brooklyn, NY

BROADWAY THEATRE (other name: Teller's Broadway Theatre),
    Broadway and Stockton Streets
OPENING DATE: March 21, 1904
OPENING SHOW: Babes in Toyland
ARCHITECT: J. B. McElfatrick   FACADE: White stone and
    brick   TYPE OF THEATRE: (a)   DEGREE OF RESTORATION: (c)
LOCATION OF AUDITORIUM: Ground floor
STAGE DIMENSIONS AND EQUIPMENT: Width of proscenium, 86ft;
    Distance from edge of stage to back wall of stage, 40ft
SEATING: 1st level, 720; 2nd level, 485; 3rd level,
    600; boxes, 90
MAJOR TYPES OF ENTERTAINMENT: Drama, musical comedy, movies
MAJOR STARS WHO APPEARED AT THEATRE: Weber and Fields,
    Lillian Russell

Brooklyn, NY

BROOKLYN ACADEMY OF MUSIC (other name: BAM), 30 Lafayette
    Avenue
OPENING DATE: October 1, 1908
OPENING SHOW: Concert, Ernestine Schumann-Heink
ARCHITECTS: Herts and Tallant (current building)
STYLE OF ARCHITECTURE: Neo-Renaissance
FACADE: Terra cotta and brick; tan
TYPE OF THEATRE: (a)   DEGREE OF RESTORATION: (a)
CURRENT USE: Performing arts center
PERFORMANCE SPACES IN BUILDING: 4 (Opera House, BAM
    Carey Playhouse, Lepercq Space, BAM Attic)

1. Opera House, Main floor
STAGE DIMENSIONS AND EQUIPMENT: Height and width of
    proscenium, 27ft x 45ft 10in; Shape of proscenium arch,
    arched; Distance from edge of stage to back wall of
    stage, 78ft; Distance from edge of stage to curtain line,
    18ft; Distance between side walls of stage, 90ft 8in;
    Depth under stage, 14ft; Stage floor, flat; Trap doors,
    100; Scenery storage rooms, 1 (trap room); Dressing
    rooms, 22 (stage level, 1st through 4th floors)
DIMENSIONS OF AUDITORIUM: Distance between side walls
    of auditorium, 100ft; Distance stage to back wall of
    auditorium, 75ft; Capacity of orchestra pit, 60
SEATING (3 levels): 1st level, 968; 2nd level, 590; 3rd
    level, 530
SHAPE OF THE AUDITORIUM: Rectangular house; fan-shaped
    seating

2. BAM Carey Playhouse, Main Floor
STAGE DIMENSIONS AND EQUIPMENT: Height and width of
    proscenium, 21ft 10in x 39ft; Shape of proscenium arch,
    arched; Distance from edge of stage to back wall of
    stage, 42ft; Distance from edge of stage to curtain line,
    18ft; Distance between side walls of stage, 43ft; Depth
    under stage, none; Stage floor, flat; Trap doors, 0;

Scenery storage rooms, 0; Dressing rooms, same as Opera
House
DIMENSIONS OF AUDITORIUM: Distance between side walls
   of auditorium, 88ft; Distance stage to back wall of
   auditorium, 66ft; Orchestra pit, none
SEATING (2 levels): 1st level, 688; 2nd level, 390
SHAPE OF THE AUDITORIUM: Rectangular

3. Lepercq Space, Second level, front
STAGE DIMENSIONS AND EQUIPMENT: Stage floor, flat; Trap
   doors, 0; Scenery storage rooms, 0; Dressing rooms, 1
   (mezzanine level)
DIMENSIONS OF AUDITORIUM: Distance between side walls of
   auditorium, 125ft 6in; Distance stage to back wall of
   auditorium, 43ft 1in
SEATING (2 levels): 1st level, 400; 2nd level, 100
SHAPE OF THE AUDITORIUM: Rectangular
ADDITIONAL INFORMATION: The Lepercq Space was formerly a
   Ballroom.

4. BAM Attic Theatre, Top floor, front
STAGE DIMENSIONS AND EQUIPMENT: Stage floor, flat; Trap
   doors, 0; Scenery storage rooms, 0; Dressing rooms, 0
DIMENSIONS OF AUDITORIUM: Distance between side walls
   of auditorium, 38ft; Distance stage to back wall of
   auditorium, 54ft; Orchestra pit, none
SEATING (1 level): 1st level, 199
SHAPE OF THE AUDITORIUM: Rectangular
MAJOR TYPES OF ENTERTAINMENT (All performance spaces):
   Drama, musical comedy, opera, concerts, dance, lectures,
   movies
MAJOR STARS WHO APPEARED AT THEATRE: (Present building)
   Ernestine Schumann-Heink, Geraldine Farrar, Caruso,
   Louise Homer, Alma Gluck, Mary Garden, Leo Slezak,
   Mabel Garrison, Toscanini, John McCormack, Nellie Melba,
   Rosa Ponselle, Feodor Chaliapin, John Charles Thomas,
   Lauritz Melchior, Kirsten Flagstad, Richard Crooks, Lotte
   Lehman, Marian Anderson, Serge Koussevitsky, Walter
   Damrosch, Fritz Kreisler, Jan Kubelick, Paderewski, Percy
   Grainger, Rachmaninoff, Artur Rubinstein, Pablo Casals,
   Jascha Heifetz, Efrem Zimbalist, Mischa Elman, Jose
   Iturbi, Andres Segovia, Yehudi Menuhin, Stravinsky,
   Samuel Dushkin, Pavlova, Ruth St. Denis, Ted Shawn,
   Martha Graham, Doris Humphrey, Charles Weidman, Jose
   Limon, Hanya Holm, Anna Sokolow, Helen Tamiris, Ruth
   Draper, Bernhardt, Cornelia Otis Skinner, H.G. Wells,
   Carl Sandburg, Theodore Dreiser, Pearl Buck, Dorothy
   Thompson, Edna St. Vincent Millay, Amelia Earhart,
   Walter Gropius, Rudolf Nureyev, Paul Robeson, Rise
   Stevens, Jan Peerce, Ezio Pinza, Sinclair Lewis, others
ADDITIONAL INFORMATION: "The Brooklyn Academy of Music is a
   traditional Performing Arts Center with a sense of
   continuity and history dating back to its incorporation
   in 1859." (Martha McGowan, Growing up in Brooklyn. The
   Brooklyn Academy of Music: Mirror of a Changing Borough).
   The current building, which contains four performance

spaces, replaced the original Academy of Music on
Montague Street which was destroyed by fire in 1903.
The original house, which was designed by Leopold
Eidlitz, had opened on January 22, 1861 with a pro-
duction of Mercandante's Giuramento.

Brooklyn, NY

BUSHWICK (other name: B. F. Keith's Bushwick Theatre),
   Broadway at Howard Avenue
   OPENING DATE: September 11, 1911
   OPENING SHOW: Vaudeville bill
   ARCHITECT: W. H. McElfatrick   STYLE OF ARCHITECTURE:
   Modernized Renaissance   FACADE: Brick, limestone and
   terra cotta   TYPE OF THEATRE: (a) DEGREE OF
   RESTORATION: (c)   LOCATION OF AUDITORIUM: Ground floor
   STAGE DIMENSIONS AND EQUIPMENT: * Height and width of
   proscenium, 35ft 6in x 38ft; Distance from edge of stage
   to back wall of stage, 35ft; Distance from edge of stage
   to curtain line, 6ft; Distance between side walls of
   stage, 76ft; Distance from stage floor to fly loft, 30ft;
   Dressing rooms, 16 (stage level and 3 stories above)
   SEATING: 1st level, 864; 2nd level, 500; 3rd
   level, 600; 4th level, 600
   MAJOR TYPES OF ENTERTAINMENT: Vaudeville, movies
   MAJOR STARS WHO APPEARED AT THEATRE: Ethel Barrymore, Eddie
   Foy, Weber and Fields, Lillie Langtry, Virginia Harned
   ADDITIONAL INFORMATION: The Bushwick was built and operated
   by Percy Williams and was acquired by B. F. Keith in
   1912. A unique feature of the theatre was its "animal
   room," an apartment under the stage for any animals
   appearing at the Bushwick.

Brooklyn, NY

GRAND PROSPECT HALL (other name: Prospect Hall), 263
   Prospect Avenue
   OPENING DATE: 1892; rebuilt 1902
   ARCHITECT: Ulrich J. Huberty   STYLE OF ARCHITECTURE:
   Modern French Renaissance   TYPE OF BUILDING:
   Entertainment center   FACADE: White brick, Indiana
   limestone   TYPE OF THEATRE: (b)   DEGREE OF
   RESTORATION: (a)   CURRENT USE: Entertainment complex
   LOCATION OF AUDITORIUM: Second and third floors
   STAGE DIMENSIONS AND EQUIPMENT: Height and width of
   proscenium, 30ft x 30ft; Shape of proscenium arch,
   square; Distance from edge of stage to back wall of
   stage, 34ft; Distance from edge of stage to curtain
   line, 30ft; Distance between side walls of stage, 50ft;
   Distance from stage floor to fly loft 30ft; Depth
   under stage, 4ft; Stage floor, flat; Trap doors, 1;
   Dressing rooms, 5 (behind stage)
   DIMENSIONS OF AUDITORIUM: Distance between side walls
   of auditorium, 80ft; Distance stage to back wall of

auditorium, 120ft; Orchestra pit, none
SEATING: 1st level, 900; 2nd level, 400; 3rd
    level, 400
SHAPE OF THE AUDITORIUM: Horseshoe-shaped
MAJOR TYPES OF ENTERTAINMENT: Vaudeville; opera
ADDITIONAL INFORMATION: Before Prospect Hall's reopening
    in 1902, the BROOKLYN EAGLE described the Hall as "an
    architectural addition to South Brooklyn that will rival
    amusement halls in the City." The hall was featured in
    the recent film, Prizzi's Honor.

Brooklyn, NY

MAJESTIC (other name: Stair and Havlin's Majestic Theatre),
    651 Fulton Street
OPENING DATE: August 30, 1904
OPENING SHOW: The Wizard of Oz
ARCHITECT: J. B. McElfatrick   TYPE OF BUILDING:
    Commercial   FACADE: Brick   TYPE OF THEATRE: (a)
DEGREE OF RESTORATION: (b)   CLOSING DATE: 1952
LOCATION OF AUDITORIUM: Ground floor
STAGE DIMENSIONS AND EQUIPMENT: * Height and width of
    proscenium, 34ft x 38ft; Distance from edge of stage to
    back wall of stage, 42ft; Distance from edge of stage to
    curtain line, 4ft; Distance between side walls of stage,
    80ft; Distance from stage floor to fly loft, 28ft; Depth
    under stage, 11ft
MAJOR TYPES OF ENTERTAINMENT: Drama, vaudeville, movies
MAJOR STARS WHO APPEARED AT THEATRE: Florence Reed, Alice
    Brady, Jane Cowl, Montgomery and Stone, Olga Petrova,
    Margaret Anglin, Ina Claire, Eva Le Gallienne, Joseph
    Schildkraut, Al Jolson, William Faversham, Evelyn Nesbit
    Thaw, Nazimova, John Drew, John and Lionel Barrymore,
    Katherine Cornell, Glenn Miller

Cambridge, NY

HUBBARD HALL (other name: Cambridge Opera House),
    25 East Main Street
OPENING DATE: November 1878
OPENING SHOW: Entertainment by Ladies' Aid Society
STYLE OF ARCHITECTURE: Late Gothic Victorian
TYPE OF BUILDING: Commercial   FACADE: Cream wood
    clapboard with brown trim   TYPE OF THEATRE: (a)
DEGREE OF RESTORATION: (b)   CURRENT USE: Community arts
    center   LOCATION OF AUDITORIUM: Second floor
STAGE DIMENSIONS AND EQUIPMENT: Height and width of
    proscenium, 14ft x 23ft; Shape of proscenium arch,
    arched; Distance from edge of stage to back wall of
    stage, 20ft; Distance from edge of stage to curtain
    line, 6ft; Distance between side walls of stage, 43ft;
    Depth under stage, 4ft; Stage floor, raked; Trap doors,
    1; Scenery storage rooms, 1; Dressing rooms, 2
DIMENSIONS OF AUDITORIUM: Distance between side walls of

auditorium, 43ft; Distance stage to back wall of
auditorium, 60ft; Orchestra pit, none
SEATING (2 levels): 1st level, 500; 2nd level, 200
SHAPE OF THE AUDITORIUM: Rectangular
MAJOR TYPES OF ENTERTAINMENT: Drama, musical comedy,
  vaudeville, lectures, concerts, local variety shows,
  chautauquas, movies, balls, civic functions
MAJOR STARS WHO APPEARED AT THEATRE: Buffalo Bill, Mark
  Twain
ADDITIONAL INFORMATION: Reputedly, the "last remaining
  Opera House in Washington County, NY" the hall now hosts
  a variety of programs in both the second floor theatre
  and a basement cafe. Entertainments offered include
  fiddle weekends, new vaudeville performances, contra
  dances, mime, modern dance, folk concerts and a
  children's film series.

Chatham, NY

CADY HALL (other name: Orpheum), Main Street
  OPENING DATE: Late 19th century
  TYPE OF BUILDING: Commercial   FACADE: Red brick
  TYPE OF THEATRE: (b)   DEGREE OF RESTORATION: (d)
  CURRENT USE: Aerobic dance studio
  LOCATION OF AUDITORIUM: Second floor
  STAGE DIMENSIONS AND EQUIPMENT: Shape of proscenium arch,
    rectangular; Trap doors, 1; Dressing rooms, 2 (in wings)
  SEATING (1 level)
  SHAPE OF THE AUDITORIUM: Rectangular
  MAJOR TYPES OF ENTERTAINMENT: Drama, vaudeville, minstrel
    shows, movies

Chautauqua, NY

CHAUTAUQUA AMPHITHEATRE, Clark Avenue
  OPENING DATE: July 1, 1893   OPENING SHOW: Opening
    ceremony   ARCHITECT: Ellis G. Hall   TYPE OF BUILDING:
    Program center FACADE: Wood   TYPE OF THEATRE: (a)
  DEGREE OF RESTORATION: (a)   CURRENT USE: Chautauquas
  LOCATION OF AUDITORIUM: Ground floor
  STAGE DIMENSIONS AND EQUIPMENT: Distance from edge of stage
    to back wall of stage, 50ft; Distance between side walls
    of stage, 52ft 2in; Stage floor, flat; Dressing rooms,
    6 (1st and 2nd levels)
  DIMENSIONS OF AUDITORIUM: Distance between side walls
    of auditorium, 145ft; Distance stage to back wall of
    auditorium, 180ft
  MAJOR TYPES OF ENTERTAINMENT: Drama, opera, concerts,
    lectures, dance, religious services
  MAJOR STARS WHO APPEARED AT THEATRE: Norman Vincent
    Peale, Marian Anderson, Chet Atkins, Jose Iturbi,
    Yehudi Menuhin, the Kingston Trio, Roberta Peters,
    Robert Merrill, Walter Damrosch, Sheena Easton, Bobby
    Kennedy, nine Presidents of the United States, others

ADDITIONAL INFORMATION: The Chautauqua building is a
  natural, open-air, all wood amphitheatre which takes the
  shape of the ravine in which it was erected. It features
  an open stage or platform for multiple uses and seats
  approximately 5,600 on wooden benches in tiers that
  conform to the natural rise of the ravine. The orchestra
  is seated on the stage except for dance programs when
  they occupy a flat area below the stage. The amphitheatre is used during a nine-week Chautauqua summer
  season.

Cherry Valley, NY

CHERRY VALLEY THEATRE, Main Street
  OPENING DATE: Late 1800s
  TYPE OF BUILDING: Municipal building
  FACADE: Grey stone   TYPE OF THEATRE: (b)   DEGREE OF
  RESTORATION: (c)   CURRENT USE: Village offices, garage
  LOCATION OF AUDITORIUM: Second floor
  STAGE DIMENSIONS AND EQUIPMENT: Height and width of
    proscenium, 11ft 10in x 21ft 4in; Shape of proscenium
    arch, rectangular; Distance from edge of stage to back
    wall of stage, 26ft 8in; Distance from edge of stage to
    curtain line, 3ft 8in; Depth under stage, 4ft 9in; Stage
    floor, flat; Trap doors, 1; Dressing rooms, 2 (stage
    right)
  DIMENSIONS OF AUDITORIUM: Distance between side walls of
    auditorium, 39ft 10in; Distance stage to back wall of
    auditorium, 55ft 8in; Orchestra pit, none
  SEATING (2 levels): 1st level, 200; 2nd level, 40
  SHAPE OF THE AUDITORIUM: Rectangular
  MAJOR TYPES OF ENTERTAINMENT: Drama, minstrel shows
  ADDITIONAL INFORMATION: The building was originally erected
    as a foundry for the Judd Iron Works and later converted
    into a theatre and municipal offices.

Cohoes, NY

COHOES MUSIC HALL (other name: Cohoes Opera House),
    58 Remsen Street
  OPENING DATE: November 3, 1874
  OPENING SHOW: London Assurance
  STYLE OF ARCHITECTURE: Italian Renaissance   TYPE OF
  BUILDING: Bank   FACADE: Red brick, black marble
  TYPE OF THEATRE: (b)   DEGREE OF RESTORATION: (a)
  CURRENT USE: Theatre   LOCATION OF AUDITORIUM: Third floor
  STAGE DIMENSIONS AND EQUIPMENT: Height and width of
    proscenium, 15ft x 25ft; Shape of proscenium arch,
    rectangular; Distance from edge of stage to back wall of
    stage, 16ft; Distance from edge of stage to curtain line,
    1ft 1in; Distance between side walls of stage, 34ft 4in;
    Depth under stage, 3ft 1in; Trap doors, 0; Dressing
    rooms, 3 (behind & below stage)
  DIMENSIONS OF AUDITORIUM: Distance between side walls of

auditorium, 59ft 7in; Distance stage to back wall
of auditorium, 56ft 9in; Orchestra pit, none
SEATING (3 levels): 1st level, 90; 2nd level, 140;
3rd level, 200
SHAPE OF THE AUDITORIUM: U-shaped
MAJOR TYPES OF ENTERTAINMENT: Drama, musical comedy,
opera, vaudeville, boxing exhibitions
MAJOR STARS WHO APPEARED AT THEATRE: Eva Tanguay, Elsie
Janis, the Marx Brothers, Buffalo Bill, Frank Fay, Pat
Rooney, John L. Sullivan, Lillian Russell, the Four
Cohans, Eddie Foy, Jimmy Durante, Houdini
ADDITIONAL INFORMATION: The theatre is now home to Heritage
Artists Ltd., which is offering its fourth season of
musicals.

Coxsackie, NY

DOLAN OPERA HOUSE, South River Street
OPENING DATE: c. 1886
TYPE OF BUILDING: Commercial   FACADE: Red brick
TYPE OF THEATRE: (b)   DEGREE OF RESTORATION: (c)
CURRENT USE: Stores
LOCATION OF AUDITORIUM: Second floor
STAGE DIMENSIONS AND EQUIPMENT: Distance from edge of stage
to back wall of stage, 20ft; Distance from edge of stage
to curtain line, 4ft; Distance between side walls of
stage, 40ft; Depth under stage, 3ft 6in; Trap doors, 1
MAJOR TYPES OF ENTERTAINMENT: Drama, vaudeville, movies

Delhi, NY

SMALLEY'S DELHI THEATRE (other name: Delhi Opera House)
OPENING DATE: September 30, 1884
OPENING SHOW: Ticket of Leave Man
ARCHITECT): G. Anson Sturges   FACADE: Wood with yellow
and green trim   TYPE OF THEATRE: (b)   DEGREE OF
RESTORATION: (c)   CURRENT USE: Vacant
LOCATION OF AUDITORIUM: Ground floor
STAGE DIMENSIONS AND EQUIPMENT: Height and width of
proscenium, 19ft x 28ft; Shape of proscenium arch,
rectangular; Distance from edge of stage to back wall of
stage, 28ft; Distance from edge of stage to curtain line,
3ft; Distance between side walls of stage, 48ft; Depth
under stage, 10ft; Stage floor, flat; Trap doors, 1;
Dressing rooms, 2 (rear of stage)
DIMENSIONS OF AUDITORIUM: Distance between side walls
of auditorium, 48ft; Distance stage to back wall of
auditorium, 66ft
SHAPE OF THE AUDITORIUM: Rectangular
MAJOR TYPES OF ENTERTAINMENT: Drama, vaudeville, minstrel
shows
MAJOR STARS WHO APPEARED AT THEATRE: Tom Mix, Ken Maynard,
the Landt Trio

Earlville, NY

EARLVILLE OPERA HOUSE, East Main Street
  OPENING DATE: Summer 1892
  STYLE OF ARCHITECTURE: Victorian   TYPE OF BUILDING:
    Commercial   FACADE: Brick with white wood trim
  TYPE OF THEATRE: (b)   DEGREE OF RESTORATION: (a)
  CURRENT USE: Summer theatre
  DIMENSIONS OF AUDITORIUM: Distance between side walls
    of auditorium, 40ft; Distance stage to back wall of
    auditorium, 58ft; Orchestra pit, none
  SEATING (2 levels): 1st level, 258; 2nd level, 54
  SHAPE OF THE AUDITORIUM: U-shaped
  MAJOR TYPES OF ENTERTAINMENT: Drama, vaudeville, movies,
    concerts

Fishkill, NY

VAN WYCK HALL, Main Street
  OPENING DATE: 1899
  STYLE OF ARCHITECTURE: Victorian   FACADE: White wood
  TYPE OF THEATRE: (a)   DEGREE OF RESTORATION: (d)
  CLOSING DATE: 1946   CURRENT USE: Municipal offices
  STAGE DIMENSIONS AND EQUIPMENT: Shape of proscenium arch,
    arched; Stage floor, flat; Scenery storage rooms, 1
    (rear of stage); Dressing rooms, 3 (in back of stage)
  SEATING (2 levels)
  SHAPE OF THE AUDITORIUM: Square
  MAJOR TYPES OF ENTERTAINMENT: Drama, civic functions
  ADDITIONAL INFORMATION: According to tradition which dates
    to 1902, the Declaration of Independence is read in the
    auditorium each Fourth of July.

Greenport, NY

GREENPORT AUDITORIUM (other name: The Opera House),
    434 Main Street
  OPENING DATE: 1894   OPENING SHOW: A Dress Rehearsal
  ARCHITECT: Mr. Flack   FACADE: White wood
  TYPE OF THEATRE: (a)   DEGREE OF RESTORATION: (a)
  CLOSING DATE: 1939   CURRENT USE: Furniture store
  LOCATION OF AUDITORIUM: Ground floor
  STAGE DIMENSIONS AND EQUIPMENT: Stage floor, flat; Scenery
    storage rooms, 3 (upstage left, under stage); Dressing
    rooms, 4 (Stars' dressing room, upstairs left)
  DIMENSIONS OF AUDITORIUM: Distance between side walls
    of auditorium, 100ft; Distance stage to back wall of
    auditorium, 200ft; Orchestra pit, none
  SEATING (2 levels): 1st level, 300; 2nd level, 100
  SHAPE OF THE AUDITORIUM: Rectangular
  MAJOR TYPES OF ENTERTAINMENT: Drama, vaudeville, opera,
    civic functions

Hammondsport, NY

GOTTLEIB FREY OPERA HOUSE (other name: Frey's Opera House),
    59-67 Sheather Street
  OPENING DATE: February 15, 1902
  OPENING SHOW: The Little Minister
  ARCHITECT: Philip Wheeler   STYLE OF ARCHITECTURE:
    Romanesque   TYPE OF BUILDING: Commercial
  FACADE: Red brick   TYPE OF THEATRE: (b)
  DEGREE OF RESTORATION: (c)   CLOSING DATE: 1912
  CURRENT USE: Storage   LOCATION OF AUDITORIUM: Third
    and fourth floors
  STAGE DIMENSIONS AND EQUIPMENT: * Height and width of
    proscenium, 15ft x 28ft; Distance from edge of stage to
    back wall of stage, 20ft; Distance from edge of stage to
    curtain line, 3ft; Distance between side walls of stage,
    65ft; Depth under stage, 4ft; Scenery storage rooms, 1
    (second floor)
  DIMENSIONS OF AUDITORIUM: Distance between side walls
    of auditorium, 65ft; Distance stage to back wall of
    auditorium, 40ft; Capacity of orchestra pit, 7
  SEATING (2 levels)
  MAJOR TYPES OF ENTERTAINMENT: Drama, musical comedy,
    concerts, circus, movies
  ADDITIONAL INFORMATION: The opera house space still exists,
    but in a damaged state. The building was damaged by a
    fire in 1914 which started on the stage. Consequently,
    the stage no longer exists, but the balcony and many
    other of the original appointments are extant. The hall
    once hosted a travelling circus which was forced to play
    inside due to inclement weather. The star of the circus,
    a young elephant, was lifted to the third-floor theatre
    by means of a block and tackle. The "I" beam for the
    block and tackle and the door through which he passed
    still exist.

Irvington, NY

IRVINGTON TOWN HALL THEATRE, 85 Main Street
  OPENING DATE: May 19, 1902   OPENING SHOW: Concert
  ARCHITECT: A. J. Manning   STYLE OF ARCHITECTURE: Colonial
    Revival   TYPE OF BUILDING: Town hall   FACADE:
    Red brick   TYPE OF THEATRE: (b)   DEGREE OF
  RESTORATION: (a)   CURRENT USE: Performing arts center
  LOCATION OF AUDITORIUM: Second and third floors
  STAGE DIMENSIONS AND EQUIPMENT: Height and width of
    proscenium, 18ft 6in x 20ft 8in; Shape of proscenium
    arch, arched; Distance from edge of stage to back wall
    of stage, 18ft; Distance from edge of stage to curtain
    line, 4ft; Distance between side walls of stage, 48ft;
    Depth under stage, 3ft 6in; Stage floor, flat; Trap
    doors, 0; Scenery storage rooms, 1 (southeast corner);
    Dressing rooms, 3 (stage left and right)
  DIMENSIONS OF AUDITORIUM: Distance between side walls
    of auditorium, 45ft; Distance stage to back wall of

auditorium, 55ft; Orchestra pit, none
SEATING (2 levels): 1st level, 266; 2nd level, 154;
   boxes, 24
SHAPE OF THE AUDITORIUM: U-shaped
MAJOR TYPES OF ENTERTAINMENT: Drama, concerts, minstrel
   shows, local variety shows, civic functions
MAJOR STARS WHO APPEARED AT THEATRE: Lillian Nordica,
   Eleanor Roosevelt
ADDITIONAL INFORMATION: Originally erected by the Mental
   and Moral Improvement Society of Irvington for $80,000,
   the 5,000-square-foot building has been renovated by the
   Irvington Town Hall Theatre Group.

Lancaster, NY

LANCASTER OPERA HOUSE (other name: Town Hall Auditorium),
   OPENING DATE: February 19, 1897
   OPENING SHOW: Rip Van Winkle with Joseph Jefferson
   ARCHITECT: George J. Metzger   STYLE OF ARCHITECTURE:
   Romanesque with Colonial Revival details
   TYPE OF BUILDING: Town hall   FACADE: Red brick
   TYPE OF THEATRE: (b)   DEGREE OF RESTORATION: (a)
   CURRENT USE: Performing arts center
   LOCATION OF AUDITORIUM: Second and third floors
   STAGE DIMENSIONS AND EQUIPMENT: Height and width of
      proscenium, 15ft x 25ft 4in; Shape of proscenium
      arch, arched; Distance from edge of stage to back
      wall of stage, 18ft; Distance from edge of stage to
      curtain line, 3ft; Distance between side walls of stage,
      42ft; Depth under stage, 6ft; Stage floor, raked; Trap
      doors, 0; Dressing rooms, 1 (under stage, 43 x 17 feet)
   DIMENSIONS OF AUDITORIUM: Distance between side walls
      of auditorium, 52ft; Distance stage to back wall of
      auditorium, 57ft; Orchestra pit, none
   SEATING (2 levels): 1st level, 295; 2nd level, 152
   SHAPE OF THE AUDITORIUM: Rectangular
   MAJOR TYPES OF ENTERTAINMENT: Drama, musical comedy,
      minstrel shows, concerts
   ADDITIONAL INFORMATION: Plans to restore the opera
      house were begun as the town planned for the National
      Bicentennial celebration. The restoration plans were
      realized when the opera house reopened on September
      17, 1981 displaying a "turn-of-the-century elegance
      that would be virtually impossible to duplicate in
      the 20th century."

New York, NY

ALHAMBRA (other name: Alhambra Hall), 7th Avenue and
   126th Street
   OPENING DATE: May 15, 1905   OPENING SHOW: Vaudeville bill
   FACADE: Brick and stone   TYPE OF THEATRE: (a)
   DEGREE OF RESTORATION: (c)   CURRENT USE: Vacant
   LOCATION OF AUDITORIUM: Ground floor

STAGE DIMENSIONS AND EQUIPMENT: * Height and width of
   proscenium, 33ft x 40ft; Distance from edge of stage to
   back wall of stage, 32ft; Distance from edge of stage to
   curtain line, 3ft; Distance between side walls of stage,
   68ft; Depth under stage, 9ft
SEATING: * 1st level, 572; 2nd level, 277; 3rd level,
   320
MAJOR TYPES OF ENTERTAINMENT: Vaudeville
MAJOR STARS WHO APPEARED AT THEATRE: Henry Miller, Laura
   Hope Crews, Albert Chevalier, The Millman Trio
ADDITIONAL INFORMATION: The Alhambra was opened by Percy
   Williams as a home of "high class vaudeville" and was
   perhaps the only vaudeville theatre in the city to cater
   to a subscription audience.

New York, NY

ANCO (other names: Wallack's, Lew M. Fields, Hackett,
   Harris, Frazee), 254 West 42nd Street
   OPENING DATE: December 5, 1904
   OPENING SHOW: It Happened at Nordland
   ARCHITECTS: J. B. McElfatrick and Co. TYPE OF THEATRE: (a)
   DEGREE OF RESTORATION: (d)   CURRENT USE: Film house
   PERFORMANCE SPACES IN BUILDING: 1
   STAGE DIMENSIONS AND EQUIPMENT: * Height and width of
   proscenium, 34ft 6in x 34ft; Shape of proscenium arch,
   square; Distance from edge of stage to back wall of
   stage, 36ft; Distance from edge of stage to curtain line,
   3ft; Distance between side walls of stage, 64ft; Depth
   under stage, 20ft 6in
   SEATING (3 levels): 1st level, 594; 2nd level, 274;
   3rd level, 350
   MAJOR TYPES OF ENTERTAINMENT: Drama, movies
   MAJOR STARS WHO APPEARED AT THEATRE: Lew Fields, Marie
   Cahill, May Robson, Harry Davenport, Bessie Clayton,
   Margaret Anglin, Pauline Frederick, Holbrook Blinn, Mrs.
   Fiske, Elsie Ferguson, Margaret Illington, Stuart Robson,
   Edward G. Robinson, Blanche Yurka, Lynn Fontanne,
   Cornelia Otis Skinner, Ruth Gordon, Shirley Booth,
   Humphrey Bogart, Jane Cowl

New York, NY

APOLLO (other names: Bryant, 42nd Street Apollo Burlesque),
   219 West 42nd Street
   OPENING DATE: 1910 (see ADDITIONAL INFORMATION)
   OPENING SHOW: As a legitimate theatre, Jimmie
   ARCHITECT: Eugene DeRosa   TYPE OF THEATRE: (a)
   DEGREE OF RESTORATION: (d)   CURRENT USE: Film house
   PERFORMANCE SPACES IN BUILDING: 1
   LOCATION OF AUDITORIUM: Ground Floor
   STAGE DIMENSIONS AND EQUIPMENT: * Width of proscenium,
   41ft; Distance from edge of stage to back wall of stage,
   28ft 4in; Distance between side walls of stage, 70ft;

distance from stage floor to fly loft, 30ft
SEATING (2 levels)
MAJOR TYPES OF ENTERTAINMENT: Drama, vaudeville, burlesque,
   movies
MAJOR STARS WHO APPEARED AT THEATRE: Lionel Barrymore, Pat
   Rooney, Jacob Ben-Ami, Ann Pennington, Ed Wynn, Bert
   Lahr, Ethel Merman, W. C. Fields, Kate Smith, Ray Bolger
ADDITIONAL INFORMATION: The Apollo opened as a vaudeville
   house in 1910. It was converted to a legitimate theatre
   in 1920.

New York, NY

BELASCO (other name: Stuyvesant), 111 West 44th Street
   OPENING DATE: October 16, 1907
   OPENING SHOW: A Grand Army Man
   ARCHITECT: George Keister   STYLE OF ARCHITECTURE:
      Federal Revival FACADE: Grey and red brick and stone
   TYPE OF THEATRE: (a)   DEGREE OF RESTORATION: (d)
   CURRENT USE: Legitimate theatre
   PERFORMANCE SPACES IN BUILDING: 1
   LOCATION OF AUDITORIUM: Ground floor
   STAGE DIMENSIONS AND EQUIPMENT: Height and width of
      proscenium, 26ft x 32ft; Shape of proscenium arch,
      arched; Distance from edge of stage to back wall of
      stage, 28ft; Distance between side walls of stage, 78ft;
      Distance from stage floor to fly loft, 27ft 3in; Stage
      floor, flat; Dressing rooms, 14 (stage right)
   SEATING (3 levels): 1st level, 415; 2nd level, 285; 3rd
      level, 223
   SHAPE OF THE AUDITORIUM: Rectangular
   MAJOR TYPES OF ENTERTAINMENT: Drama, radio, revues, film
   MAJOR STARS WHO APPEARED AT THEATRE: Melvyn Douglas, John
      Barrymore (1940), Noel Coward, Nicol Williamson, Eileen
      Atkins (1966), Herschel Bernardi (1979), Charles
      Nelson Reilly, Alexander Woollcott (1931), Katherine
      Cornell, Hal Holbrook (1969), Colleen Dewhurst (1977),
      Uta Hagen, Elizabeth Ashley, Ina Claire (1917), George
      Abbott, Lenore Ulric, Luther and Stella Adler, Elia
      Kazan, Lee J. Cobb, Sam Levene, Franchot Tone, Sam Jaffe
   ADDITIONAL INFORMATION: The theatre was opened in 1907 to
      serve the theatrical needs of David Belasco and continued
      to serve "The Bishop of Broadway" until his death in
      1931. Workers in the theatre claim that Belasco's ghost
      still haunts the theatre. When it opened, the theatre
      was equipped with an elevator stage, a 65-dimmer lighting
      board and a private elevator to Mr. Belasco's private
      suite.

New York, NY

BOOTH, 222 West 45th Street
   OPENING DATE: October 16, 1913
   OPENING SHOW: The Great Adventure

ARCHITECT: Henry B. Herts   STYLE OF ARCHITECTURE:
  Beaux Arts   FACADE: Tan brick, stone and terra cotta
TYPE OF THEATRE: (a)   DEGREE OF RESTORATION: (d)
CURRENT USE: Legitimate theatre   PERFORMANCE SPACES
IN BUILDING: 1   LOCATION OF AUDITORIUM: Ground floor
STAGE DIMENSIONS AND EQUIPMENT: Height and width of
  proscenium, 20ft 2in x 36ft 1in; Shape of proscenium
  arch, arched; Distance from edge of stage to back wall
  of stage, 29ft 10in; Distance from edge of stage to
  curtain line, 1ft; Distance between side walls of stage,
  80ft 7in; Distance from stage floor to fly loft, 30ft
  5in; Stage floor, flat; Dressing rooms, 9 (stage right)
DIMENSIONS OF AUDITORIUM: Distance between side walls
  of auditorium, 80ft 2in; Distance stage to back wall
  of auditorium, 55ft; Orchestra pit, yes
SEATING (2 levels): 1st level, 515; 2nd level, 252;
  Boxes, 16
SHAPE OF THE AUDITORIUM: Rectangular
MAJOR TYPES OF ENTERTAINMENT: Drama
MAJOR STARS WHO APPEARED AT THEATRE: William Faversham,
  George Arliss, Jane Cowl, Walter Hampden, Henrietta
  Crosman,   Ruth Gordon,   Leslie Howard,   Helen Hayes,
  Beatrice Lillie, Shirley Booth (1950), Cornelia Otis
  Skinner (1952), Margaret Sullivan (1931), Julie Harris
  (1961), Estelle Winwood (1935), Melvyn Douglas (1935),
  Keenan Wynn, Rex Harrison, Tammy Grimes, Eli Wallach,
  William Gillette, Roland Young, Alfred Lunt, Lynn
  Fontanne, James Cagney, and others

New York, NY

CARNEGIE HALL, 57th Street and 7th Avenue
  OPENING DATE: May 5, 1891   OPENING SHOW: New York
    Symphony Society, Tchaikovsky conducting
  ARCHITECT: William Burnet Tuthill
  STYLE OF ARCHITECTURE: Italianate Romanesque
  FACADE: Iron flecked yellow/brown brick   TYPE OF
  THEATRE: (a)   DEGREE OF RESTORATION: (b)   CURRENT USE:
    Concert hall   PERFORMANCE SPACES IN BUILDING: 3 (Main
    Hall, Recital Hall, Carnegie Cinema)

  1. Main Hall, Ground floor
  STAGE DIMENSIONS AND EQUIPMENT: Height and width of
    proscenium, 44ft x 64ft; Shape of proscenium arch,
    arched; Distance from edge of stage to back wall of
    stage, 43ft; Distance from edge of stage to curtain
    line, 17ft; Distance between side walls of stage, 70ft;
    Distance from stage floor to fly loft, 44ft; Depth under
    stage. 8ft; Stage floor, flat; Trap doors, 1; Scenery
    storage rooms, 0; Dressing rooms, 6 (Second floor)
  DIMENSIONS OF AUDITORIUM: Distance between side walls
    of auditorium, 90ft; Distance stage to back wall of
    auditorium, 100ft; Orchestra pit, none
  SEATING (5 levels): 1st level, 1020; 2nd level, 264;
    3rd level, 248; 4th level, 430; 5th level, 838

SHAPE OF THE AUDITORIUM: U-shaped
MAJOR TYPES OF ENTERTAINMENT: Concerts (classical, jazz,
  folk), dance, lectures
MAJOR STARS WHO APPEARED AT THEATRE: Tchaikovsky, Heifetz,
  Rachmaninoff, Rubinstein, Fritz Kreisler, Paderewski,
  Caruso, Toscanini, Booker T. Washington, Winston
  Churchill, Mark Twain, Tolstoy, Maeterlink, Picasso,
  Isadora Duncan, Vladimir Horowitz, Benny Goodman, W. C.
  Handy, Bernhardt, Bessie Smith, Fats Waller, Mahler,
  Serge Koussevitsky, Yehudi Menuhin, Isaac Stern, Pablo
  Casals, Maria Callas, Paul Robeson, Leopold Godowsky,
  Count Basie, Duke Ellington, Louis Armstrong, Woody
  Guthrie, Pete Seeger, Judy Garland, the Beatles, others
ADDITIONAL INFORMATION: Carnegie Hall is world-famous for
  its acoustical excellence. Architect Tuthill, assisted
  by associates, Dankmar Adler and Louis Sullivan, conducted a worldwide study of the science of acoustics
  before designing the hall. In 1959, the hall escaped
  demolition through the efforts of a group of concerned
  citizens led by violinist Isaac Stern. Recently, the
  hall was renovated and it reopened in the fall of 1986.

2. Recital Hall, Third floor
STAGE DIMENSIONS AND EQUIPMENT: Height and width of
  proscenium, 20ft 5in x 22ft 4in; Shape of proscenium
  arch, rectangular; Distance from edge of stage to curtain
  line, 3ft; Distance between side walls of stage, 33ft
  2in; Distance from stage floor to fly loft, 20ft 5in;
  Stage floor, flat; Trap doors, 0; Dressing rooms, 0
DIMENSIONS OF AUDITORIUM: Distance between side walls
  of auditorium, 22ft; Distance stage to back wall of
  auditorium, 33ft; Orchestra pit, none
SEATING (2 levels): 1st level, 210; 2nd level, 73
SHAPE OF THE AUDITORIUM: Rectangular
MAJOR TYPES OF ENTERTAINMENT: Concerts, recitals
ADDITIONAL INFORMATION: The smallest of the three halls
  in the building, the Recital Hall was originally called
  the Chamber Music Hall. It was frequently used by solo
  recitalists whose teachers occupied studios in Carnegie
  Hall. The Recital Hall retains the Italian Renaissance
  flavor of the Main Hall and has remained virtually intact
  throughout the years.

3. Carnegie Cinema, Basement
STAGE DIMENSIONS AND EQUIPMENT: * Height and width of
  proscenium, 24ft x 28ft; Distance from edge of stage
  to back wall of stage, 27ft; Distance from edge of
  stage to curtain line, 3ft; Distance between side
  walls of stage, 50ft
MAJOR TYPES OF ENTERTAINMENT: Concerts, recitals,
  lectures, movies
ADDITIONAL INFORMATION: Originally called The Lyceum,
  the hall was first used as a recital hall and the first
  public event, a piano recital by Franz Rummel, was held
  there on April 1, 1891, several weeks before Carnegie
  Hall's official opening held in the Main Hall on May 5.

New York, NY

CASTLE GARDEN, Battery Park
  OPENING DATE: See ADDITIONAL INFORMATION
  TYPE OF THEATRE: (c)   DEGREE OF RESTORATION: (c)
  CLOSING DATE: c. 1855   CURRENT USE: Vacant
  MAJOR TYPES OF ENTERTAINMENT: Drama, opera, concerts,
    lectures, minstrel shows
  MAJOR STARS WHO APPEARED AT THEATRE: Jenny Lind (1850),
    George Holland, Mario and Grisi, Henry Clay, Charlotte
    Cushman
  ADDITIONAL INFORMATION: Castle Garden was built in 1808
    as a fort. It was converted into an indoor tropical
    garden in 1824, opening on July 3 of that year, and in
    1839 it became a theatre. In 1847, it became an opera
    house.

New York, NY

COLUMBIA (other names: DeMille, Mayfair, RKO Mayfair, Loew's
    Mayfair, Columbia Burlesque, Mark), Northeast corner,
    7th Avenue and 47th Street
  OPENING DATE: January 3, 1910
  OPENING SHOW: Follies of New York and Paris
  ARCHITECTS: J. B. McElfatrick and Co.   TYPE OF
  BUILDING: Office building   FACADE: White stone
  TYPE OF THEATRE: (a)   DEGREE OF RESTORATION: (d)
  CURRENT USE: Movie theatres
  STAGE DIMENSIONS AND EQUIPMENT: * Height and width of
    proscenium, 31ft x 34ft; Shape of proscenium arch,
    square; Distance from edge of stage to back wall of
    stage, 33ft; Distance from edge of stage to curtain
    line, 3ft 6in; Distance between side walls of stage,
    70ft; Depth under stage, 10ft
  SEATING (3 levels): 1st level, 550; 2nd level, 350;
    3rd level, 350; boxes, 96
  MAJOR TYPES OF ENTERTAINMENT: Drama, burlesque, movies
  MAJOR STARS WHO APPEARED AT THEATRE: Bobby Clark, Fred
    Stone, Sophie Tucker, Eddie Cantor, Fanny Brice, Will
    Rogers, Weber and Fields, Leon Errol, Al Jolson,
    Gallagher and Shean
  ADDITIONAL INFORMATION: When the theatre was operated
    as a burlesque house, the ushers were dressed in
    Japanese costumes.

New York, NY

COLUMBUS (other names: Proctor's 125th Street),
    112 East 125th Street
  STAGE DIMENSIONS AND EQUIPMENT: * Height and width of
    proscenium, 40ft x 32ft; Shape of proscenium arch,
    rectangular; Distance from edge of stage to back wall
    of stage, 43ft, Distance from edge of stage to curtain

line, 3ft; Distance between side walls of stage, 71ft;
Depth under stage, 15ft; Trap doors, 3
SEATING (3 levels)
MAJOR TYPES OF ENTERTAINMENT: Drama, vaudeville, movies

New York, NY

CORT THEATRE, 138 West 48th Street
OPENING DATE: December 20, 1912
OPENING SHOW: Peg O' My Heart
ARCHITECT: Edward B. Corey   STYLE OF ARCHITECTURE:
  Beaux Arts   FACADE: White stone and terra cotta
TYPE OF THEATRE: (a)   DEGREE OF RESTORATION: (d)
CURRENT USE: Legitimate theatre
PERFORMANCE SPACES IN BUILDING: 1
STAGE DIMENSIONS AND EQUIPMENT: Height and width of
  proscenium, 27ft 8in x 37ft 4in; Shape of proscenium
  arch, arched; Distance from edge of stage to back wall
  of stage, 28ft 11in; Distance between side walls of
  stage, 76ft 8in; Distance from stage floor to fly loft,
  24ft 5in; Stage floor, flat
DIMENSIONS OF AUDITORIUM: Orchestra pit, yes
SEATING (3 levels): 1st level, 506; 2nd level, 264; 3rd
  level, 283; boxes, 36
SHAPE OF THE AUDITORIUM: Rectangular
MAJOR TYPES OF ENTERTAINMENT: Drama, vaudeville, television
MAJOR STARS WHO APPEARED AT THEATRE: Laurette Taylor
  (1912), Eva Le Gallienne, Basil Rathbone, Jose Ferrer,
  Frederic March, Katherine Cornell (1946), Cornelia Otis
  Skinner (1946), Estelle Winwood (1946), Cecil Beaton
  (1946), Katherine Hepburn (1950), Judith Anderson,
  Alice Brady, James Cagney, Lillian Gish, Laurence
  Olivier, Sam Levene, Jessica Tandy, Morris Carnovsky,
  Ossie Davis, Ruby Dee, Cedric Hardwicke, and others

New York, NY

EMPIRE THEATRE, (other names: Eltinge, Laff Movie), 236
  West 42nd Street
OPENING DATE: September 11, 1912
OPENING SHOW: Within the Law
ARCHITECT: Thomas A. Lamb   TYPE OF THEATRE: (a)
DEGREE OF RESTORATION: (d)   CURRENT USE: Movie theatre
LOCATION OF AUDITORIUM: Ground floor
STAGE DIMENSIONS AND EQUIPMENT: * Height and width of
  proscenium, 31ft 6in x 31ft 6in; Shape of proscenium
  arch, square; Distance from edge of stage to back wall
  of stage, 21ft; Distance between side walls of stage,
  59ft; Dressing rooms, 10
SEATING: * 1st level, 420; 2nd level, 218; 3rd level, 212;
  boxes, 48
MAJOR TYPES OF ENTERTAINMENT: Drama, vaudeville, burlesque,
  movies
MAJOR STARS WHO APPEARED AT THEATRE: Jane Cowl, Pauline

Frederick, Florence Reed, Estelle Winwood, Lionel
Barrymore, Claudette Colbert, Laurence Olivier,
Cecilia Loftus, Alice Brady, Clark Gable

New York, NY

HARRIS THEATRE (other names: Candler, Cohan and Harris, Sam
    H. Harris), 226 West 42nd Street
    OPENING DATE: August 19, 1914
    OPENING SHOW: On Trial
    ARCHITECT: Thomas W. Lamb   STYLE OF ARCHITECTURE: Italian
    Renaissance   TYPE OF THEATRE: (a)
    DEGREE OF RESTORATION: (d)   CURRENT USE: Movie theatre
    STAGE DIMENSIONS AND EQUIPMENT: * Height and width of
    proscenium, 21ft x 39ft; Distance from edge of stage to
    back wall of stage, 31ft; Distance between side walls of
    stage, 74ft; Distance from stage floor to fly loft, 26ft
    SEATING (2 levels): 1st level, 625; 2nd level, 500
    MAJOR TYPES OF ENTERTAINMENT: Drama, movies, revues

New York, NY

HARRY DE JUR PLAYHOUSE (other name: Henry Street Playhouse),
    466 Grand Street
    OPENING DATE: 1915
    STYLE OF ARCHITECTURE: Georgian/Federal   FACADE: Red
    brick and white wood   TYPE OF THEATRE: (a) DEGREE OF
    RESTORATION: (c)   CURRENT USE: Theatre
    LOCATION OF AUDITORIUM: Ground floor
    STAGE DIMENSIONS AND& EQUIPMENT: Height and width of
    proscenium, 16ft x 25ft; Shape of proscenium arch,
    rectangular; Distance from edge of stage to back wall
    of stage, 36ft; Distance from edge of stage to curtain
    line, 7ft; Distance between side walls of stage, 58ft;
    Distance from stage floor to fly loft, 22ft; Depth under
    stage, 8ft 6in; Scenery storage rooms, 2 (lower level);
    Dressing rooms, 2 (lower level)
    DIMENSIONS OF AUDITORIUM: Distance between side walls
    of auditorium, 41ft; Distance stage to back wall of
    auditorium, 45ft; Capacity of orchestra pit, 22
    SEATING (2 levels): 1st level, 269; 2nd level, 78
    SHAPE OF THE AUDITORIUM: U-shaped
    MAJOR TYPES OF ENTERTAINMENT: Drama, vaudeville, dance,
    opera, concerts, movies
    MAJOR STARS WHO APPEARED AT THEATRE: Isadora Duncan, Jimmy
    Durante, Eddie Cantor, Paul Muni, Edward G. Robinson,
    Alwin Nikolais, Murray Louis, Count Basie, Dizzy
    Gillespie, Ossie Davis, Esther Rolle, Ruby Dee, Debbie
    Allen, Melvin Van Peebles, Ruth Brown, Chita Rivera,
    Harold Nicholas, Cleavon Little, Denise Nicholas
    ADDITIONAL INFORMATION: The theatre is a part of the Henry
    Street Settlement.

New York, NY

HELEN HAYES THEATRE (other names: Little, Winthrop Ames, Anne
    Nichols' Theatre, Times Hall), 240 West 44th Street
    OPENING DATE: March 12, 1912   OPENING SHOW: The Pigeon
    ARCHITECTS: H. C. Ingalls and F. B. Hoffman Jr.
    FACADE: Red brick with white masonry   TYPE OF THEATRE: (a)
    DEGREE OF RESTORATION: (d)   CURRENT USE: Legitimate
    theatre   PERFORMANCE SPACES IN BUILDING: 1
    LOCATION OF AUDITORIUM: Ground floor
    STAGE DIMENSIONS AND EQUIPMENT: Height and width of
    proscenium, 17ft 10in x 28ft; Shape of proscenium arch,
    rectangular; Distance from edge of stage to back wall
    of stage, 29ft 9in; Distance from edge of stage to
    curtain line, 2ft 3in; Distance between side walls of
    stage, 72ft; Distance from stage floor to fly loft, 62ft;
    Stage floor, flat; Trap doors, 0; Scenery storage rooms,
    0; Dressing rooms, 9 (basement)
    DIMENSIONS OF AUDITORIUM: Orchestra pit, yes
    SEATING (2 levels): 1st level, 365; 2nd level, 134
    MAJOR TYPES OF ENTERTAINMENT: Drama, television
    MAJOR STARS WHO APPEARED AT THEATRE: John Barrymore,
    Cedric Hardwicke, Cornelia Otis Skinner, Blanche Yurka,
    Ruth Draper, Edward G. Robinson, Paul Newman, Joanne
    Woodward
    ADDITIONAL INFORMATION: The theatre was used from 1965 to
    1974 as a TV studio.   During those years, the Merv
    Griffin and the David Frost shows were broadcast from
    the Helen Hayes Theatre.

New York, NY

HUDSON THEATRE (other name: Savoy), 139 West 44th Street
    OPENING DATE: October 19, 1903
    OPENING SHOW: Cousin Kate
    ARCHITECTS: J. B. McElfatrick and Co.   TYPE OF THEATRE: (a)
    DEGREE OF RESTORATION: (c)   CURRENT USE: Vacant
    PERFORMANCE SPACES IN BUILDING: 1
    LOCATION OF AUDITORIUM: Ground Floor
    STAGE DIMENSIONS AND EQUIPMENT: * Height and width of
    proscenium, 30ft x 32ft; Shape of proscenium arch,
    square; Distance from edge of stage to back wall of
    stage, 37ft; Distance from edge of stage to curtain
    line, 3ft; Distance between side walls of stage, 67ft

New York, NY

JEFFERSON THEATRE (other names: B. F. Keith's Jefferson,
    RKO Jefferson), 214 East 14th Street
    OPENING DATE: 1913
    TYPE OF THEATRE: (a)   DEGREE OF RESTORATION: (c)
    CLOSING DATE: 1960s
    MAJOR TYPES OF ENTERTAINMENT: Vaudeville, burlesque, movies
    ADDITIONAL INFORMATION: The Jefferson was opened as a

vaudeville house by B. S. Moss. In 1920, it became part of B. F. Keith's chain of theatres. Twelve years later, it became a movie house.

New York, NY

LIBERTY THEATRE, 234 West 42nd Street
  OPENING DATE: October 10, 1904
  OPENING SHOW: The Rogers Brothers in Paris
  ARCHITECTS: Herts and Tallant   TYPE OF THEATRE: (a)
  DEGREE OF RESTORATION: (d)   CURRENT USE: Movie theatre
  STAGE DIMENSIONS AND EQUIPMENT: * Height and width of
    proscenium, 36ft x 36ft; Shape of proscenium arch,
    square; Distance from edge of stage to back wall of
    stage, 37ft 6in; Distance from edge of stage to curtain
    line, 1ft 4in; Distance between side walls of stage,
    70ft; Distance from stage floor to fly loft, 33ft
  MAJOR TYPES OF ENTERTAINMENT: Drama, vaudeville, movies,
    revue

New York, NY

LONGACRE, 220 West 48th Street
  OPENING DATE: May 1, 1913
  OPENING SHOW: Are You a Crook?
  ARCHITECT: Henry B. Herts   STYLE OF ARCHITECTURE: Beaux
    Arts   FACADE: Grey stone and terra cotta   TYPE OF
  THEATRE: (a)   DEGREE OF RESTORATION: (d)   CURRENT USE:
    Legitimate theatre   LOCATION OF AUDITORIUM: Ground floor
  STAGE DIMENSIONS AND EQUIPMENT: Height and width of
    proscenium, 25ft 4in x 35ft 2in; Shape of proscenium
    arch, square; Distance from edge of stage to back wall of
    stage, 29ft; Distance from edge of stage to curtain line,
    2ft 4in; Distance between side walls of stage, 62ft;
    Distance from stage floor to fly loft, 30ft 1in; Stage
    floor, flat
  DIMENSIONS OF AUDITORIUM: Orchestra pit, yes
  SEATING (3 levels): 1st level, 523; 2nd level, 314; 3rd
    level, 243; Boxes, 16
  SHAPE OF THE AUDITORIUM: Rectangular
  MAJOR TYPES OF ENTERTAINMENT: Drama, musical comedy, radio
  MAJOR STARS WHO APPEARED AT THEATRE: Dudley Digges, John
    Barrymore, Ethel Barrymore, Jane Cowl, Alice Brady,
    Nazimova, Constance Collier, Jessica Tandy, Lillian Gish
    (1968), Miriam Hopkins (1923), Judith Anderson (1924),
    Elia Kazan, Lee J. Cobb (1935), Basil Rathbone, Clifford
    Odets, Julie Harris, Cornelia Otis Skinner (1958), Cyril
    Richard (1958), Clark Gable, Zero Mostel (1961), others

New York, NY

LUNT-FONTANNE THEATRE   (other name: Globe),   205 West
  46th Street

OPENING DATE: January 10, 1910
OPENING SHOW: The Old Town
ARCHITECTS: Carrere and Hastings   TYPE OF THEATRE: (a)
DEGREE OF RESTORATION: (d)   CURRENT USE: Legitimate
  theatre
STAGE DIMENSIONS AND EQUIPMENT: Height and width of
  proscenium, 34ft 6in x 41ft 2in; Shape of proscenium
  arch, rectangular; Distance from edge of stage to back
  wall, 34ft; Distance from edge of stage to curtain line,
  2ft; Distance between side walls of stage, 69ft 2in;
  Depth under stage, 11ft; Scenery storage rooms, 1 (above
  orchestra); Dressing rooms, 12 (backstage)
SEATING: 1st level, 888; 2nd level, 168; 3rd level, 436
MAJOR TYPES OF ENTERTAINMENT: Drama, musical comedy,
  revues, film
MAJOR STARS WHO APPEARED AT THEATRE: Alfred Lunt, Lynn
  Fontanne, Laurette Taylor, Sarah Bernhardt, Will Rogers,
  Fanny Brice, Elsie Janis, Eddie Foy, Fred and Adele
  Astaire, John Gielgud, Leon Errol, Helen Hayes, W. C.
  Fields, Bea Lillie, Clifton Webb, Peggy Wood, Fred Stone
ADDITIONAL INFORMATION: As the Globe, the theatre hosted
  George White's Scandals in 1920 and 1922, Ziegfeld
  Follies of 1921, and Ziegfeld's American Revue of
  1926.

New York, NY

LYCEUM THEATRE (other name: New Lyceum), 149 West 45th Street
OPENING DATE: November 2, 1903
OPENING SHOW: The Proud Prince
ARCHITECTS: Herts and Tallent   STYLE OF ARCHITECTURE:
  Beaux Arts   FACADE: Grey stone and terra cotta
TYPE OF THEATRE: (a)   DEGREE OF RESTORATION: (d)
CURRENT USE: Legitimate theatre   PERFORMANCE SPACES
IN BUILDING: 1   LOCATION OF AUDITORIUM: Ground floor
STAGE DIMENSIONS AND EQUIPMENT: Height and width of
  proscenium, 32ft 10in x 32ft 10in; Shape of proscenium
  arch, arched; Distance from edge of stage to back wall
  of stage, 31ft 2in; Distance from edge of stage to
  curtain line, 18ft; Distance between side walls of stage,
  81ft; Distance from stage floor to grid, 55ft; Stage
  floor, flat; Dressing rooms, 14 (behind stage)
DIMENSIONS OF AUDITORIUM: Capacity of orchestra pit, 12
SEATING (3 levels): 1st level, 411; 2nd level, 287; 3rd
  level, 210; boxes, 20
SHAPE OF AUDITORIUM: Rectangular
MAJOR TYPES OF ENTERTAINMENT: Drama
MAJOR STAGE WHO APPEARED AT THEATRE: Billie Burke,
  E. H. Southern, Ethel Barrymore, Mrs. Fiske, Margaret
  Illington, Grace George, Elsie Ferguson, Margaret Anglin,
  Lenore Ulric, Jeanne Eagels, Frances Starr, Otis Skinner,
  David Warfield, Walter Huston, John Garfield, Leslie
  Howard, Ina Claire, Walter Slezak, Judy Holliday, Paul
  Douglas, Maurice Chevalier, Alan Bates, John Gielgud,
  Sam Levene, Robert Preston, Robert Shaw, Burgess

Meredith, Jack Guilford
ADDITIONAL INFORMATION: The Lyceum was opened in 1903 by
impresario Daniel Frohman. Frohman's former office high
above the theatre (now used as the headquarters of the
Shubert Archives) still retains a "peep hole" which
allowed Frohman to watch the action on the stage from
his office.

New York, NY

LYRIC THEATRE, 213 West 42nd Street
  OPENING DATE: October 12, 1903
  OPENING SHOW: Old Heidelberg
  ARCHITECT: V. Hugo Koehler   STYLE OF ARCHITECTURE:
    Italian Renaissance   TYPE OF THEATRE: (a)
  DEGREE OF RESTORATION: (d)   CURRENT USE: Movie theatre
  PERFORMANCE SPACES IN BUILDING: 1
  STAGE DIMENSIONS AND EQUIPMENT: * Height and width of
    proscenium, 38ft x 38ft; Shape of proscenium arch,
    square; Distance from edge of stage to back wall of
    stage, 43ft 6in; Distance from edge of stage to curtain
    line, 4ft; Distance between side walls of stage, 76ft;
    Depth under stage, 12ft 4in
  DIMENSIONS OF AUDITORIUM: Capacity of orchestra pit, 15
  SEATING: 1st level, 563; 2nd level, 399; 3rd level, 443
  MAJOR TYPES OF ENTERTAINMENT: Drama; movies
  MAJOR STARS WHO APPEARED AT THEATRE: Gabrielle Rejane,
    Douglas Fairbanks Sr., Fred and Adele Astaire, the Marx
    Brothers, Otis Skinner, James O'Neill, William Faversham,
    Cecilia Loftus, Nora Bayes, Richard Mansfield

New York, NY

MANHATTAN CENTER (other name: Manhattan Opera House), 315
    West 34th Street
  OPENING DATE: December 3, 1906   OPENING SHOW: I Puritani
  ARCHITECT: Designed by Oscar Hammerstein   TYPE OF
  THEATRE: (a)   DEGREE OF RESTORATION: (d)   CURRENT USE:
    Meetings, concerts   LOCATION OF AUDITORIUM: Ground floor
  STAGE DIMENSIONS AND EQUIPMENT: Height and width of
    proscenium, 53ft x 47ft; Distance from edge of stage to
    back wall of stage, 70ft; Distance from edge of stage to
    curtain line, 5ft; Distance between side walls of stage,
    125ft; Depth under stage, 20ft
  DIMENSIONS OF AUDITORIUM: Distance between side walls
    of auditorium, 100ft; Distance stage to back wall of
    auditorium, 105ft; Capacity of orchestra pit, 110
  SEATING (4 levels): 1st level, 1,230; 2nd level, 565;
    3rd level, 590; 4th level, 645
  MAJOR TYPES OF ENTERTAINMENT: Drama, opera, dance
  MAJOR STARS WHO APPEARED AT THEATRE: Mme. Melba, Mme.
    Trentini, Mme. Calve, Mary Garden, James O'Neill, Nance
    O'Neil, Florence Reed
  ADDITIONAL INFORMATION: Stage and house dimensions are from
    The Architectural Record; seating capacity is from a

1975 brochure. The Manhattan Opera House was Oscar
Hammerstein's personal creation. He not only financed
it, but also worked in close collaboration with the
architect, supervising every aspect of the design.
He lost control of the theatre in March 1910.

New York, NY

NEW AMSTERDAM, 214 West 42nd Street
    OPENING DATE: November 2, 1903
    OPENING SHOW: A Midsummer Night's Dream
    ARCHITECTS: Herts and Tallant   STYLE OF ARCHITECTURE:
    Art Nouveau   TYPE OF BUILDING: Office building
    TYPE OF THEATRE: (a)   DEGREE OF RESTORATION: (c)
    PERFORMANCE SPACES IN BUILDING: 2 (New Amsterdam Theatre,
    Aerial Garden)

    1. New Amsterdam Theatre, Ground floor
    STAGE DIMENSIONS AND EQUIPMENT: Height and width of pro-
    scenium, 31ft x 40ft; Shape of proscenium arch, arched;
    Distance from edge of stage to back wall of stage, 50ft;
    Distance from edge of stage to curtain line, 2ft; Dis-
    tance between side walls of stage, 80ft; Distance from
    stage floor to fly loft, 33ft; Depth under stage, 22ft
    DIMENSIONS OF AUDITORIUM: Distance between side walls
    of auditorium, 86ft; Distance stage to back wall of
    auditorium, 90ft
    SEATING: 1st level, 675; 2nd level, 500; 3rd level, 500
    MAJOR TYPES OF ENTERTAINMENT: Drama, musical comedy,
    burlesque, movies
    MAJOR STARS WHO APPEARED AT THEATRE: Nat Goodwin,
    Ruby Keeler, Fred and Adele Astaire, Al Jolson, Elsie
    Ferguson, William Gillette, John Drew, Pauline Lord,
    Walter Hampden, Fay Bainter, Mary Boland, Eva Le
    Gallienne, Nazimova, Bert Lahr, Rudy Vallee, Libby
    Holman, Fanny Brice, Ann Pennington, W. C. Fields,
    Will Rogers, Gilda Gray, Marilyn Miller, Mary Eaton,
    Eddie Dowling, Mae Murray, Eddie Cantor, Bessie McCoy,
    the Dolly Sisters, Nora Bayes, Ray Dooley, Leon Errol,
    Ina Claire, Helen Morgan, Ed Wynn, Lillian Lorraine
    ADDITIONAL INFORMATION: The New Amsterdam was renowned
    as a showplace for musical comedy. Between 1913 and
    1927 (with the exception of 1921), it was the home of
    the Ziegfeld Follies.

    2. Aerial Garden (see ADDITIONAL INFORMATION), Roof
    DIMENSIONS OF AUDITORIUM: Distance between side walls
    of auditorium, 100ft; Distance stage to back wall of
    auditorium, 100ft
    SEATING (2 levels): 1st level, 480; 2nd level, 200
    SHAPE OF THE AUDITORIUM: U-shaped balcony
    MAJOR TYPES OF ENTERTAINMENT: Vaudeville, musical comedy,
    operetta, drama, television, radio
    MAJOR STARS WHO APPEARED AT THEATRE: Fanny Brice, Will

Rogers, Fred Astaire, Eddie Cantor, Marie Dressler,
George M. Cohan, Fay Templeton, Eddie Leonard, Truly
Shattuck
ADDITIONAL INFORMATION: The roof garden was situated on
top of the eight-story 41st Street tower of the New
Amsterdam Theatre Building. It was reached via two
elevators, each with a capacity of 50 persons, in the
42nd Street segment of the building. The roof garden
was described as a full theatre, not just "a mere roof
garden."   Recent plans to reopen the roof garden have
been stalled because of weaknesses in the building's
structure. The roof garden has been known by various
names throughout its history. These include Dresden,
New Amsterdam Roof, Frolic, NBC Times Square Studio,
WOR Mutual Radio Playhouse, New Amsterdam Roof Theatre.
The New Amsterdam Roof Garden is fully described in
Stephen Burge Johnson's book, The Roof Gardens of
Broadway Theatres, 1883-1942 (UMI Research Press, 1985).

New York, NY

PALACE THEATRE (other name: RKO Palace), 1564 Broadway
OPENING DATE: March 24, 1913
OPENING SHOW: Vaudeville bill
ARCHITECTS: Kirchoff and Rose   TYPE OF THEATRE: (a)
DEGREE OF RESTORATION: (d)   CURRENT USE: Legitimate
theatre   LOCATION OF AUDITORIUM: Ground floor
STAGE DIMENSIONS AND EQUIPMENT: * Height and width of
proscenium, 39ft 6in x 41ft; Distance from edge of
stage to back wall of stage, 32ft; Distance from edge
of stage to curtain line, 1ft; Distance between side
walls of stage, 72ft; Dressing rooms, 12
SEATING: * 1st level, 650; 2nd level, 486; 3rd level, 326;
boxes, 274
MAJOR TYPES OF ENTERTAINMENT: Vaudeville, drama, musical
comedy, movies
MAJOR STARS WHO APPEARED AT THEATRE: Ethel Barrymore,
Sarah Bernhardt, Ed Wynn, Lillian Russell, Fred and
Adele Astaire, Will Rogers, Houdini, Crystal Hearne,
Laurette Taylor, Weber and Fields, Eva Tanguay, Fanny
Brice, Moran and Mack, Sophie Tucker, W. C. Fields,
Eddie Cantor, Nora Bayes, Nazimova, the Marx Brothers,
Jimmy Durante, Jack Benny, Bert Williams, George Jessel,
Julian Eltinge, Bob Hope, MacIntyre and Heath, Elsie
Janis, Mae West, Judy Garland, Danny Kaye, Lionel Atwill,
Fritzi Scheff, Holbrook Blinn, Ina Claire, Otis Skinner,
Burns and Allen, and others. George M. Cohan, Harry
Lauder and Al Jolson, however, never "played the Palace"
although it was the dream of every vaudeville performer
and "the mecca of migrating minstrels."

New York, NY

RIALTO (other name: Victoria), Northwest corner of 7th
    Avenue and 42nd Street
  OPENING DATE: March 2, 1899
  OPENING SHOW: The Reign of Terror
  ARCHITECTS: J. B. McElfatrick and Co. TYPE OF THEATRE: (a)
  DEGREE OF RESTORATION: (d)   PERFORMANCE SPACES IN
  BUILDING: 2 (Rialto, Victoria Roof Garden)

  1. Rialto, Ground floor
  STAGE DIMENSIONS AND EQUIPMENT: * Height and width of
    proscenium, 40ft x 38ft; Shape of proscenium arch,
    square; Distance from edge of stage to back wall of
    stage, 42ft; Distance from edge of stage to curtain
    line, 6ft; Distance between side walls of stage, 100ft;
    Depth under stage, 30ft
  SEATING: 1st level, 700; 2nd level, 650
  MAJOR TYPES OF ENTERTAINMENT: Drama, musical comedy,
    minstrel shows, vaudeville, movies
  MAJOR STARS WHO APPEARED AT THEATRE: Eddie Foy, Lottie
    Gilson, The Rogers Brothers, Will Rogers, Irene and
    Vernon Castle, Lew Dockstader, Nat Wills, John Bunny
  ADDITIONAL INFORMATION: In building the Victoria, Oscar
    Hammerstein reputedly cut costs by using second hand
    materials.

  2. Victoria Roof Garden, Roof of Rialto Theatre
  OPENING DATE: June 26, 1899
  MAJOR TYPES OF ENTERTAINMENT: Variety, topical burlesques,
    vaudeville
  MAJOR STARS WHO APPEARED AT THEATRE: Maggie Cline, Sophie
    Tucker, Ernest Hogan, Abbie Mitchell, Will Rogers, the
    Three Keatons
  ADDITIONAL INFORMATION: The Victoria Roof Garden, also
    called Hammerstein's Venetian Terrace, evolved from a
    rustic, open-air promenade into a roofed theatre with a
    stage and capacity of 1,000 persons. When Hammerstein
    acquired the Republic Theatre next door to the Victoria,
    he linked the roofs of the two theatres and expanded the
    Victoria Roof Garden. The Victoria Roof Garden is fully
    described in Stephen Burge Johnson's book, The Roof
    Gardens of Broadway Theatres, 1883-1942 (UMI Research
    Press, 1985).

New York, NY

SHUBERT (other name: Sam S. Shubert), 225 West 44th Street
  OPENING DATE: September 29, 1913   OPENING SHOW: Hamlet
  ARCHITECT: Henry B. Herts   STYLE OF ARCHITECTURE: Beaux
    Arts   FACADE: Grey brick; stone and terra cotta
  TYPE OF THEATRE: (a)   DEGREE OF RESTORATION: (d)
  CURRENT USE: Legitimate theatre
  PERFORMANCE SPACES IN BUILDING: 1
  LOCATION OF AUDITORIUM: Ground floor

STAGE DIMENSIONS AND EQUIPMENT: Height and width of
proscenium, 25ft 3in x 39ft 8in; Shape of proscenium
arch, arched; Distance from edge of stage to back wall
of stage, 32ft 10in; Distance between side walls of
stage, 77ft 8in; Distance from stage floor to fly loft,
29ft 4in; Depth under stage, 10ft 5in; Stage floor, flat;
Dressing rooms, 13 (stage left)
DIMENSIONS OF AUDITORIUM: Orchestra pit, yes
SEATING (3 levels): 1st level, 732; 2nd level, 410; 3rd
level, 352; boxes, 24
SHAPE OF THE AUDITORIUM: Rectangular
MAJOR TYPES OF ENTERTAINMENT: Drama, musical comedy,
operetta, revue
MAJOR STARS WHO APPEARED AT THEATRE: The Dolly sisters
(1924), Chic Sale (1924), Texas Guinan (1927), Walter
Slezak (1930), Alfred Lunt (1936), Lynne Fontanne (1936),
Walter Huston, Joseph Cotten (1939), Katherine Hepburn,
Katherine Cornell, Shirley Booth, Mae West (1944), Al
Jolson (1940), Ray Bolger (1942), Paul Robeson (1943),
Uta Hagen, Judy Holliday, Ethel Barrymore, Fred Astaire,
Ann Pennington, Lionel Barrymore, Lillian Gish, Fay
Bainter, Helen Hayes, Bobby Clark, Doris Humphrey,
Blanche Bates, Holbrook Blinn, Laurette Taylor, Rex
Harrison, Peggy Wood, Ed Wynn, E. H. Sothern, Julia
Marlowe, Moran and Mack, Fred Allen

New York, NY

UNION SQUARE THEATRE (other names: B. F. Keith's Union Square
Theatre, Bijou Dream, Acme), Union Square South
OPENING DATE: September 11, 1871
OPENING SHOW: Variety bill featuring Marie Bonfanti
ARCHITECT: H. M. Simons   TYPE OF BUILDING: Hotel
TYPE OF THEATRE: (b)   DEGREE OF RESTORATION: (c)
CLOSING DATE: 1936   CURRENT USE: Vacant
PERFORMANCE SPACES IN BUILDING: 1
LOCATION OF AUDITORIUM: Ground floor
STAGE DIMENSIONS AND EQUIPMENT: * Height and width of
proscenium, 35ft x 30 ft; Shape of proscenium arch,
rectangular; Distance from edge of stage to back wall
of stage, 34ft; Distance from edge of stage to curtain
line, 4ft 6in; Distance between side walls of stage, 49ft
5in; Depth under stage, 7ft; Dressing rooms (beneath
stage)
SEATING (3 levels)
SHAPE OF AUDITORIUM: Horseshoe-shaped
MAJOR TYPES OF ENTERTAINMENT:. Vaudeville, drama, burlesque,
movies
MAJOR STARS WHO APPEARED AT THEATRE: The Vokes Family,
Agnes Ethel, F. F. Mackay, Kate Holland, Claude
Burroughs, Kate Claxton, J.H. Stoddard, James O'Neill,
Charles Coughlan, Agnes Booth, Margaret Mather, Stuart
Robson, William H. Crane, George M. Cohan
ADDITIONAL INFORMATION: The Union Square was the first
Keith-Albee theatre in New York.

New York, NY

VICTORY THEATRE (other names: Republic, Belasco), 207 West
    42nd Street
  OPENING DATE: September 27, 1900
  OPENING SHOW: Sag Harbor
  ARCHITECTS: J. B. McElfatrick and Co.   TYPE OF THEATRE: (a)
  DEGREE OF RESTORATION: (d)   CURRENT USE: Film house
  PERFORMANCE SPACES IN BUILDING: 1
  LOCATION OF AUDITORIUM: Ground floor
  STAGE DIMENSIONS AND EQUIPMENT: * Height and width of
    proscenium, 29ft x 32ft; Shape of proscenium arch,
    rectangular; Distance from edge of stage to back wall
    of stage, 30ft; Distance from edge of stage to curtain
    line, 5ft; Distance between side walls of stage, 70ft;
    Depth under stage, 18ft;
  SEATING: 1st level, 450; 2nd level, 200; 3rd level, 300
  MAJOR TYPES OF ENTERTAINMENT: Drama, movies
  MAJOR STARS WHO APPEARED AT THEATRE: Mrs. Leslie Carter,
    Blanche Bates, David Warfield
  ADDITIONAL INFORMATION: The Republic, erected for Oscar
    Hammerstein, was the first theatre on 42nd Street. It
    was later turned over to David Belasco who named the
    theatre after himself.

New York, NY

WINTER GARDEN, 1634 Broadway
  OPENING DATE: March 20, 1911
  OPENING SHOW: Bow Sing   and   La Belle Paree
  ARCHITECT: William A. Swasey   STYLE OF ARCHITECTURE:
    Federal Revival   FACADE: Grey; brick, stone and terra
    cotta   TYPE OF THEATRE: (a)   DEGREE OF RESTORATION: (d)
    CURRENT USE: Legitimate theatre
  LOCATION OF AUDITORIUM: Ground floor
  STAGE DIMENSIONS AND EQUIPMENT: Height and width of
    proscenium, 24ft 3in x 44ft; Shape of proscenium arch,
    arched;   Distance from edge of stage to back wall of
    stage, 42ft; Distance between side walls of stage, 71ft;
    Distance from stage floor to fly loft, 29ft 6in; Depth
    under stage, 8ft 8in; Stage floor, flat; Dressing rooms,
    13
  DIMENSIONS OF AUDITORIUM: Distance stage to back wall
    of auditorium, 77ft; Orchestra pit, yes
  SEATING (3 levels): 1st level, 1032; 2nd level, 135; 3rd
    level, 347; boxes, 52
  SHAPE OF THE AUDITORIUM: Rectangular
  MAJOR TYPES OF ENTERTAINMENT: Drama, musical comedy, film,
    revues
  MAJOR STARS WHO APPEARED AT THEATRE: Al Jolson (1911),
    Eddie Cantor, Bert Lahr, Ray Bolger, Fanny Brice,
    Marilyn Miller, Irene Bordini, Josephine Baker, Bob
    Hope, Ed Wynn, Smith and Dale, Fred Astaire, Bobby
    Clark, Jack Benny, Mae West, Marie Dressler, Ethel
    Waters, Bea Lillie, Fred Allen, George Jessel, Milton

Berle, Eve Arden, Phil Silvers, Clifton Webb, Tammy
Grimes, Angela Lansbury (1966)
ADDITIONAL INFORMATION: As originally designed by
Swasey, the Winter Garden was once described as a
"roof garden on the ground floor."

Owego, NY

TIOGA THEATRE, 208 Main Street
  OPENING DATE: September 17, 1908
  OPENING SHOW: The Mummy and the Humming Bird
  ARCHITECT: Arland W. Johnson   FACADE: Yellow pressed
  brick   TYPE OF THEATRE: (a)   DEGREE OF RESTORATION: (d)
  CURRENT USE: Movie theatre
  STAGE DIMENSIONS AND EQUIPMENT: Height and width of
  proscenium, 10ft x 40ft; Shape of proscenium arch,
  rectangular; Distance from edge of stage to back wall
  of stage, 32ft; Distance between side walls of stage,
  64ft; Stage floor, flat; Scenery storage rooms, 1;
  Dressing rooms, 9 (under stage)
  DIMENSIONS OF AUDITORIUM: Distance between side walls
  of auditorium, 64ft; Distance stage to back wall of
  auditorium, 52ft
  SEATING (3 levels): 1st level, 520; 2nd level, 244;
  3rd level, 200
  SHAPE OF THE AUDITORIUM: Rectangular
  MAJOR TYPES OF ENTERTAINMENT: Drama, musical comedy,
  vaudeville, movies
  MAJOR STARS WHO APPEARED AT THEATRE: John Griffith, others

Penn Yan, NY

CORNWELL OPERA HOUSE (other name: Bush's Hall),
  113-119 Main Street
  OPENING DATE: 1874
  TYPE OF BUILDING: Commercial   FACADE: Red brick with
  wooden cornice   TYPE OF THEATRE: (b)
  DEGREE OF RESTORATION: (c)   CURRENT USE: Vacant,
  store on first floor
  LOCATION OF AUDITORIUM: Second floor
  MAJOR TYPES OF ENTERTAINMENT: Drama, lectures
  MAJOR STARS WHO APPEARED AT THEATRE: Charles Sumner,
  Frederick Douglass, Ralph Waldo Emerson, P. T. Barnum,
  Susan B. Anthony, Tom Thumb and wife, Commodore Nutt,
  Minnie Warren, others

Penn Yan, NY

SAMPSON THEATRE, East Elm Street
  OPENING DATE: October 11, 1910
  OPENING SHOW: The Cheater

FACADE: Buff-colored brick   TYPE OF THEATRE: (a)
DEGREE OF RESTORATION: (c)   CLOSING DATE: c. 1930
CURRENT USE: Tire storage
LOCATION OF AUDITORIUM: Ground floor
STAGE DIMENSIONS AND EQUIPMENT: Height and width of
    proscenium, 25ft x 32ft; Dressing rooms, 8 (basement)
SEATING (3 levels)
MAJOR TYPES OF ENTERTAINMENT: Drama, musical comedy,
    vaudeville, burlesque, minstrel shows, opera, movies
MAJOR STARS WHO APPEARED AT THEATRE: Georgia Minstrels,
    Jimmie Cole, Ray Bolger, Helen Keller
ADDITIONAL INFORMATION: When the building was purchased in
    1936 and converted into a car dealership, many of the
    theatrical features disappeared.

Poughkeepsie, NY

BARDAVON OPERA HOUSE (other name: Collingwood Opera
    House), 35 Market Street
OPENING DATE: February 1, 1869
OPENING SHOW: Benefit concert for James Collingwood
ARCHITECT: James Post   FACADE: Painted brick, white
    with blue trim   TYPE OF THEATRE: (a)   DEGREE OF
RESTORATION: (a)   CURRENT USE: Theatre
LOCATION OF AUDITORIUM: Ground floor
STAGE DIMENSIONS AND EQUIPMENT: Height and width of
    proscenium, 25ft x 34ft; Shape of proscenium arch,
    arched; Distance from edge of stage to back wall of
    stage, 27ft 7in; Distance from edge of stage to curtain
    line, 3ft 1in; Distance between side walls of stage,
    80ft; Depth under stage, 10ft; Distance from stage floor
    to fly loft, 25ft; Stage floor, flat; Scenery storage
    rooms, 0; Dressing rooms, 3 (under stage)
DIMENSIONS OF AUDITORIUM: Distance between side walls
    of auditorium, 80ft; Distance stage to back wall of
    auditorium, 27ft 1in; Capacity of orchestra pit, 15
SEATING (2 levels): 1st level, 632; 2nd level, 312
SHAPE OF THE AUDITORIUM: U-shaped
MAJOR TYPES OF ENTERTAINMENT: Drama, musical comedy,
    vaudeville, concerts, minstrel shows, movies, dance,
    opera, civic functions
MAJOR STARS WHO APPEARED AT THEATRE: Maude Adams,
    Margaret Anglin, George Arliss, the Barrymores, Edwin
    Booth, Bernhardt, Ole Bull, Billie Burke, Caruso, Pablo
    Casals, George M. Cohan, Fanny Davenport, Isadora Duncan,
    Edwin Forrest, Tom Thumb, Gilmore's Band, Nat Goodwin,
    Jasha Heifetz, Anna Held, Joseph Jefferson, Laura Keene,
    Clara Louise Kellogg, Lillie Langtry, Richard Mansfield,
    Robert Mantell, Modjeska, Clara Morris, Tony Pastor,
    Christine Nilsson, Paderewski, Serge Rachmaninoff,
    Arthur Rubinstein, Lillian Russell, Ruth St. Denis,
    Salvini, Mme. Schumann-Heinck, Otis Skinner, John Phillip
    Sousa, others
ADDITIONAL INFORMATION: When the Bardavon closed as a
    second-run movie theatre in 1975, it was scheduled for

demolition. Saved by a local citizens' group, it has
been restored and now offers an extensive schedule of
touring Broadway productions, concerts, dance recitals,
opera, and children's theatre from September to June.

Pultneyville, NY

GATES HALL (other names: Union Church, Union Hall),
    Corner of Lake Road and Route 21
    OPENING DATE: June 21, 1867   OPENING SHOW: An
    "entertainment" by the Pultneyville Lyceum STYLE OF
    ARCHITECTURE: Colonial   TYPE OF BUILDING:
    Meeting hall   FACADE: Wood, cream with brown trim
    TYPE OF THEATRE: (b)   DEGREE OF RESTORATION: (d)
    CURRENT USE: Performing arts center
    LOCATION OF AUDITORIUM: Ground floor
    STAGE DIMENSIONS AND EQUIPMENT: Height and width of
    proscenium, 11ft x 20ft 6in; Shape of proscenium arch,
    rectangular; Distance from edge of stage to back wall of
    stage, 21ft; Distance from edge of stage to curtain line,
    1ft; Distance between side walls of stage, 30ft; Stage
    floor, flat; Trap doors, 1; Scenery storage rooms, 2
    (basement of the hall); Dressing rooms, 2 (basement of
    the building)
    DIMENSIONS OF AUDITORIUM: Distance between side walls
    of auditorium, 30ft; Distance stage to back wall of
    auditorium, 27ft
    SEATING (2 levels): 1st level, 100; 2nd level, 60
    SHAPE OF THE AUDITORIUM: Rectangular
    MAJOR TYPES OF ENTERTAINMENT: Drama, light opera, lectures,
    musical comedy, civic functions
    ADDITIONAL INFORMATION: Long the social center of
    Pultneyville, the building first served as a church
    "open to any denomination claiming to be Christians."
    In 1859, it was converted to theatrical and social
    uses.   In the years that followed, it was used for
    public meetings to discuss slavery, women's rights,
    and the evils of alcohol; for preparations for the
    Civil War; and for memorial services for those killed
    in action.   The theatre became more important in 1867
    with the formation of the Pultneyville Lyceum and a more
    permanent stage was installed. In 1893, the community
    organized to preserve the building and it was remodeled
    into the current theatre/village hall.

Riverhead, NY

VAIL-LEAVITT MUSIC HALL (other names: Leavitt Music Hall/
    Lyceum, Vail Music Hall), Peconic Avenue
    OPENING DATE: 1881
    STYLE OF ARCHITECTURE: Victorian   TYPE OF BUILDING:
    Commercial   TYPE OF THEATRE: (b)   DEGREE OF
    RESTORATION: (c)   CLOSING DATE: c. 1920   CURRENT USE:
    Stores   LOCATION OF AUDITORIUM: Second floor

MAJOR TYPES OF ENTERTAINMENT: Drama, lectures, vaudeville,
  concerts, movies

Rye, NY

LYCEUM HALL, 31 Purchase Street
  OPENING DATE: November 1893
  TYPE OF BUILDING: Commercial   TYPE OF THEATRE: (b)
  DEGREE OF RESTORATION: (c)   CURRENT USE: Stores
  LOCATION OF AUDITORIUM: Second floor
  ADDITIONAL INFORMATION: The theatre proper was established
    in 1893 when the building was renovated. The hall was
    painted in a "sand finish" and was equipped with opera
    chairs. The stage was described as "not over elaborate,
    but [containing all of] the appointments of the more
    pretentious town halls."

Sackets Harbor, NY

USO HALL (other name: Minstrel Hall), 103 West Main Street
  OPENING DATE: Mid-19th century
  FACADE: Red brick   TYPE OF THEATRE: (a)   DEGREE OF
  RESTORATION: (c)   CURRENT USE: Vacant
  LOCATION OF AUDITORIUM: Ground floor

Seneca Falls, NY

JOHNSON OPERA HOUSE, 126 Fall Street
  OPENING DATE: 1871
  STYLE OF ARCHITECTURE: Federal   FACADE: Brick
  TYPE OF THEATRE: (c)   DEGREE OF RESTORATION: (c)
  CURRENT USE: Part of historic park
  ADDITIONAL INFORMATION: The structure was erected by
    the Wesleyan Methodists as a church in 1843. In 1871,
    the building was converted into a theatre, a facade
    added and an addition constructed at the rear of the
    building. Because of its significance as the site of
    the first women's rights convention, the National Park
    Service purchased it and now uses it as part of a
    Women's Rights National Historic Park.

Sing Sing, NY

OLIVE OPERA HOUSE (other name: Olive Hall),
    Central Avenue and Leonard Street
  OPENING DATE: 1868
  ARCHITECT: Hugh Herringshaw   STYLE OF ARCHITECTURE:
    Victorian   FACADE: Brick, painted white
  TYPE OF THEATRE: (b)   DEGREE OF RESTORATION: (c)
  CURRENT USE: Loft and art gallery

MAJOR TYPES OF ENTERTAINMENT: Drama, vaudeville,
  minstrel shows, medicine shows, concerts, lectures,
  boxing matches, burlesque, opera, dance
MAJOR STARS WHO APPEARED AT THEATRE: The Hi Henry
  Minstrels, Eddie Leonard, John L. Sullivan, Lillian
  Russell

Spencertown, NY

SPENCERTOWN ACADEMY, Route 203
OPENING DATE: 1847
STYLE OF ARCHITECTURE: Neo-Classical   TYPE OF BUILDING:
  School   FACADE: White wood   TYPE OF THEATRE: (b)
DEGREE OF RESTORATION: (d)   CURRENT USE: Performing
  arts center   LOCATION OF AUDITORIUM: Ground floor
STAGE DIMENSIONS AND EQUIPMENT: Height and width of
  proscenium, 9ft 1in x 16ft 8in; Shape of proscenium arch,
  rectangular; Distance from edge of stage to back wall of
  stage, 13ft 5in; Distance from edge of stage to curtain
  line, 1ft 6in; Distance between side walls of stage, 16ft
  8 in; Depth under stage, 1ft 9in; Stage floor, raked;
  Trap doors, 0; Scenery storage rooms, 1 (stage left);
  Dressing rooms, 1 (stage right)
DIMENSIONS OF AUDITORIUM: Distance between side walls of
  auditorium, 33ft 9in; Distance stage to back wall of
  auditorium, 38ft 6in
SEATING (1 level): 1st level, 175
SHAPE OF THE AUDITORIUM: Rectangular
MAJOR TYPES OF ENTERTAINMENT: Drama, opera, concerts,
  lectures, movies
MAJOR STARS WHO APPEARED AT THEATRE: Pete Seeger, Tom
  Paxton, Jean Redpath, Odetta, Mabel Mercer, Walter
  Hautzig, Burton Fine, Arnold Steinhardt, Jonothan Miller
ADDITIONAL INFORMATION: The building was first a private
  academy and then a public school until 1970. Instead
  of allowing the building to decay after it was closed,
  a citizens' group formed the Spencertown Academy
  Society to preserve the building and to sponsor
  activities. The Society has offered a concert series
  in the past and in the summer of 1983 first sponsored
  an Equity company presenting performances of plays by
  Dorothy Parker and Tennessee Williams.

Staten Island, NY

SNUG HARBOR MUSIC HALL/THEATRE, 1000 Richmond Terrace
OPENING DATE: 1892
OPENING SHOW: Staten Island Symphony concert
ARCHITECT: Robert W. Gibson   STYLE OF ARCHITECTURE:
  Beaux Arts   FACADE: White/grey limestone and marble
TYPE OF THEATRE: (a)   DEGREE OF RESTORATION: (b)
CLOSING DATE: 1960s   CURRENT USE: None

PERFORMANCE SPACES IN BUILDING: 1
LOCATION OF AUDITORIUM: Ground floor
STAGE DIMENSIONS AND EQUIPMENT: Height and width of
    proscenium, 33ft x 36ft; Shape of proscenium arch,
    rectangular; Distance from edge of stage to back wall
    of stage, 27ft; Distance from edge of stage to curtain
    line, 4ft; Distance between side walls of stage, 41ft;
    Depth under stage, 8ft; Stage floor, flat; Dressing
    rooms, 4 (in wings on second and third floors)
DIMENSIONS OF AUDITORIUM: Distance between side walls
    of auditorium, 62ft; Distance stage to back wall of
    auditorium, 71ft; Capacity of orchestra pit, 20
SEATING (2 levels): 1st level, 500; 2nd level, 150
SHAPE OF THE AUDITORIUM: U-shaped
MAJOR TYPES OF ENTERTAINMENT: Vaudeville, concerts, movies

Tarrytown, NY

THE MUSIC HALL (other name: Tarrytown Music Hall),
    11 Main Street
OPENING DATE: December 12, 1885
OPENING SHOW: Ike Wilson, ventriloquist
ARCHITECT: Phillip Edmunds   STYLE OF ARCHITECTURE:
    Queen Anne   FACADE: Red brick, stucco, terra cotta
TYPE OF THEATRE: (a)   DEGREE OF RESTORATION: (d)
CURRENT USE: Performing arts center
LOCATION OF AUDITORIUM: Ground floor
STAGE DIMENSIONS AND EQUIPMENT: Height and width of
    proscenium, 21ft 6in x 32ft; Shape of proscenium
    arch, rectangular; Distance from edge of stage to back
    wall of stage, 32ft; Distance from edge of stage to
    curtain line, 4ft; Distance between side walls of stage,
    63ft; Stage floor, raked; Trap doors, 0; Scenery storage
    rooms, 0; Dressing rooms, 11 (stage left)
DIMENSIONS OF AUDITORIUM: Distance between side walls of
    auditorium, 75ft;
SEATING (2 levels): 1st level, 452; 2nd level, 388
SHAPE OF THE AUDITORIUM: Rectangular
MAJOR TYPES OF ENTERTAINMENT: Drama, musical comedy,
    vaudeville, opera, concerts, lectures, minstrel shows,
    dance, movies, balls
MAJOR STARS WHO APPEARED AT THEATRE: Raphael Josefy, Jose
    Greco, Mae West, Theda Bara, Kim Hunter, Ginger Rogers,
    Ezio Flagello, Gwen Verdon
ADDITIONAL INFORMATION: The theatre was built in 1885 by
    William Wallace, a chocolate manufacturer. It is one of
    the oldest legitimate theatres in Westchester County and
    one of the first theatres in the county to convert to
    movies. The theatre underwent renovation in 1915, when a
    marquee was added, and again in 1922 when a proscenium
    was built, permanent seating installed, and the interior
    remodeled. Today, under the auspices of The Friends of
    the Mozartina Conservatory of Tarrytown, the theatre
    hosts a variety of productions.

Troy, NY

TROY SAVINGS BANK MUSIC HALL, 32 Second Street
   OPENING DATE: April 19, 1875
   OPENING SHOW: Concert, Theodore Thomas Orchestra
   ARCHITECT: George B. Post   STYLE OF ARCHITECTURE:
     Italian Renaissance   TYPE OF BUILDING: Bank
   FACADE: Grey granite   TYPE OF THEATRE: (b)
   DEGREE OF RESTORATION: (c)   CURRENT USE: Concert hall
   LOCATION OF AUDITORIUM: Second floor
   DIMENSIONS OF AUDITORIUM: Distance between side walls
     of auditorium, 106ft; Distance stage to back wall of
     auditorium, 110ft
   SEATING (3 levels): 1st level, 826; 2nd level, 188;
     3rd level, 98; boxes, 144
   SHAPE OF THE AUDITORIUM: U-shaped
   MAJOR TYPES OF ENTERTAINMENT: Opera, concerts
   MAJOR STARS WHO APPEARED AT THEATRE: Theodore Thomas
     Orchestra, Fritz Kreisler, Paderewski, Lucrezia Bori,
     Rosa Ponsell, Heifetz, Iturbi, Rachmaninoff, Leontyne
     Price, Duke Ellington
   ADDITIONAL INFORMATION: The Music Hall, which was virtually
     untouched during a 1949 renovation of the building, is
     renowned for the excellence of its acoustics.   The hall
     contains a concert pipe organ built in 1882 by J. H. and
     C. S. Odell & Co.

Westfield, NY

VIRGINIA HALL (other name: The Opera House),
     East Street at North Portage
   OPENING DATE: 1872
   STYLE OF ARCHITECTURE: Italianate   TYPE OF BUILDING:
     Commercial   FACADE: Red brick   TYPE OF THEATRE: (b)
   DEGREE OF RESTORATION: (c)   CLOSING DATE: c. 1912
   CURRENT USE: Rehearsal hall
   LOCATION OF AUDITORIUM: Third floor
   DIMENSIONS OF AUDITORIUM: Distance between side walls
     of auditorium, 54ft; Distance stage to back wall of
     auditorium, 44ft
   SEATING (1 level)
   SHAPE OF THE AUDITORIUM: Rectangular
   MAJOR TYPES OF ENTERTAINMENT: Drama, musical comedy,
     concerts, lectures, minstrel shows, vaudeville, dances,
     local variety shows, movies
   ADDITIONAL INFORMATION: The hall now serves as rehearsal
     space for Das Puppenspiel, a professional puppet troupe.

Worcester, NY

WIETING OPERA HOUSE (other name: Worcester Theatre),
     140 Main Street
   OPENING DATE: February 4, 1910
   OPENING SHOW: A Woman's Way

ARCHITECT: Linn Kinne   STYLE OF ARCHITECTURE:
   Colonial   TYPE OF BUILDING: Library, D.A.R. Hall
FACADE: Red brick   TYPE OF THEATRE: (a)
DEGREE OF RESTORATION: (b)   CURRENT USE: Library,
   clubhouse   LOCATION OF AUDITORIUM: Ground floor
STAGE DIMENSIONS AND EQUIPMENT: Height and width of
   proscenium, 20ft x 20ft; Shape of proscenium arch,
   square; Distance from edge of stage to back wall of
   stage, 22ft; Distance from edge of stage to curtain
   line, 5ft; Distance between side walls of stage, 26ft;
   Depth under stage, 3ft 6in; Stage floor, flat; Scenery
   storage rooms, 0; Dressing rooms, 2 (stage right)
DIMENSIONS OF AUDITORIUM: Distance between side walls
   of auditorium, 33ft; Distance stage to back wall of
   auditorium, 44ft
SEATING (2 levels): 1st level, 260; 2nd level, 167
MAJOR TYPES OF ENTERTAINMENT: Drama, minstrel shows,
   local variety shows, movies

41. INDIANOLA OPERA HOUSE. Indianola, Nebraska. Credit: James J. Sughroue.

42. MOORE OPERA HOUSE. Wood River, Nebraska. Credit: Mrs. C. E. Moyer.

43. PIPER'S OPERA HOUSE. Virginia City, Nevada. Used by permission of the Chesley Collection.

44. APOLLO THEATRE. New York, New York. Credit: Stephen Vallillo.

45. BROOKLYN ACADEMY OF MUSIC. Brooklyn, New York. Present BAM with original cornice. Used by permission of the Chesley Collection.

46. BROOKLYN ACADEMY OF MUSIC. Brooklyn, New York. Opera House Interior. Used by permission of the Chesley Collection.

47. CARNEGIE HALL. New York, New York. Used by permission of the Chesley Collection.

48. CARNEGIE HALL. New York, New York. Interior. Used by permission of the Chesley Collection.

50. NEW AMSTERDAM. New York, New York.
Credit: Stephen Vallillo.

49. HARRIS THEATRE. New York, New York. Credit:
Stephen Vallillo.

51. GATES HALL. Pultneyville, New York. Used by permission of the Chesley Collection.

52. TARRYTOWN MUSIC HALL. Tarrytown, New York. Credit: Stephen Vallillo.

53. THALIAN HALL. Wilmington, North Carolina. Exterior view of City Hall/Thalian Hall. Photograph by Steve Cofer.

54. THALIAN HALL. Wilmington, North Carolina. View of the stage and Proscenium from the
auditorium. Photograph by Jerry Blow.

55. SORG OPERA HOUSE. Middletown, Ohio. Exterior circa 1920. Used by permission of the Chesley Collection.

56. NEW MARKET THEATER. Portland, Oregon. Credit: Ted Van Arsdol.

57. Grooves at MARLIN'S OPERA HOUSE. Brookville, Pennsylvania. Used by permission of the Chesley Collection.

58. ACADEMY OF MUSIC. Philadelphia, Pennsylvania. Used by permission of the Chesley Collection.

59. METROPOLITAN OPERA HOUSE. Philadelphia, Pennsylvania. Used by permission of the Chesley Collection.

60. OLD MUSICAL FUND HALL. Philadelphia, Pennsylvania. Used by permission of the Chesley Collection.

61. TROCADERO THEATRE. Philadelphia, Pennsylvania. Used by permission of the Chesley Collection.

62. THE OPERA HOUSE. Chester, South Carolina. Credit: Jack Neeson.

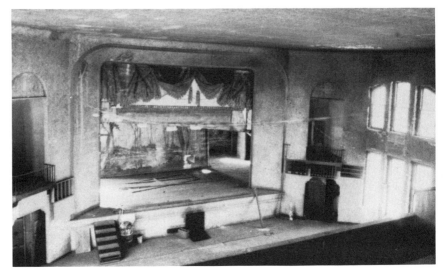

63. NEWBERRY OPERA HOUSE. Newberry, South Carolina. Credit: Jack Neeson.

64. OPERA HOUSE. Sumter, South Carolina. Credit: Jack Neeson.

65. ORPHEUM. Sioux Falls, South Dakota. Used by permission of the Chesley Collection.

66. MATTHEWS OPERA HOUSE. Spearfish, South Dakota. Used by permission of the Chesley Collection.

67. MOUNTAIN HOME MEMORIAL HALL. Johnson City, Tennessee. Used by permission of the Chesley Collection.

68. MOUNTAIN HOME MEMORIAL HALL. Johnson City, Tennessee. Used by permission of the Chesley Collection.

69. STAFFORD OPERA HOUSE. Columbus, Texas. Photo credit: The Gallery, Columbus, Texas.

70. THE GRAND 1894 OPERA HOUSE. Galveston, Texas. Constructed: 1894. Opening date: January 3, 1895. Photographer: Van Edwards. View of house right, orchestra level, view of fire curtain and boxes in 1986, after completion of restoration.

71. CHANDLER MUSIC HALL. Randolph, Vermont. Used by permission of the Chesley Collection.

72. TOWN HALL. Bethel, Vermont. Used by permission of the Chesley Collection.

73. ACADEMY OF MUSIC. Lynchburg, Virginia. Credit: Jack Neeson.

74. LIBERTY UNIVERSITY ACADEMY OF MUSIC. Lynchburg, Virginia. Opened: 1905. Rebuilt and improved after a fire, 1912. Interior as it appears in 1987. Photographer: Mark Bailey.

75. OLD OPERA HOUSE. Charles Town, West Virginia. Used by permission of the Chesley Collection.

76. AL RINGLING THEATRE. Baraboo, Wisconsin. Used by permission of the Chesley Collection.

77. CONCERT HALL. Beaver Dam, Wisconsin. Used by permission of the Chesley Collection.

78. PABST THEATRE. Milwaukee, Wisconsin. Used by permission of the Chesley Collection.

79. GRAND OPERA HOUSE. Oshkosh, Wisconsin. Used by permission of the Chesley Collection.

80. VIROQUA OPERA HOUSE. Viroqua, Wisconsin. Used by permission of the Chesley Collection.

North Carolina

Kernersville, NC

CUPID'S PARK (other name: Korner's Folly Theatre),
  South Main Street
OPENING DATE: 1897
ARCHITECT: Jule Gilmer Korner   STYLE OF ARCHITECTURE:
  Victorian Gothic   TYPE OF BUILDING: Private home
FACADE: Brick   TYPE OF THEATRE: (b)   DEGREE OF
RESTORATION: (b)   CURRENT USE: Theatre
PERFORMANCE SPACES IN BUILDING: 1
LOCATION OF AUDITORIUM: Fourth floor
STAGE DIMENSIONS AND EQUIPMENT: Distance from edge of stage
to back wall of stage, 18ft; Distance between side walls
of stage, 16ft; Depth under stage, 3ft; Stage floor, flat;
Trap doors, 1; Scenery storage rooms, 1 (behind and under
stage); Dressing rooms, 2 (second floor)
DIMENSIONS OF AUDITORIUM: Distance between side walls
  of auditorium, 20ft; Distance stage to back wall of
  auditorium, 18ft; Capacity of orchestra pit, 8
SEATING (1 level): 1st level, 75
MAJOR TYPES OF ENTERTAINMENT: Tableaux, pantomines, music
  recitals, short plays, drama, recitations, declamations
ADDITIONAL INFORMATION: A charming theatre built on the
  fourth floor of a private residence. The stage is hex-
  agonal. There is no proscenium arch, but an elaborately
  carved curtain rod that is about 10' high.

New Bern, NC

MASONIC THEATRE, Hancock and Johnson
  OPENING DATE: 1805/1809
  STYLE OF ARCHITECTURE: Federal   TYPE OF BUILDING:
    Lodge, movie theatre, jail   FACADE: Brick
  TYPE OF THEATRE: (b)   DEGREE OF RESTORATION: (a)
  CURRENT USE: Movies, rehearsals
  LOCATION OF AUDITORIUM: Ground floor
  STAGE DIMENSIONS AND EQUIPMENT: Height and width of

   proscenium, 20ft x 33ft; Shape of proscenium arch,
   rectangular; Distance from edge of stage to back wall of
   stage, 30ft; Distance from edge of stage to curtain line,
   33ft; Distance between side walls of stage, 35ft; Depth
   under stage, 8ft; Stage floor, flat
   DIMENSIONS OF AUDITORIUM: Distance between side walls
     of auditorium, 37ft; Distance stage to back wall of
     auditorium, 54ft; Orchestra pit, yes
   SEATING (2 levels)
   SHAPE OF THE AUDITORIUM: Rectangular
   MAJOR TYPES OF ENTERTAINMENT: Local and touring productions
   ADDITIONAL INFORMATION: A series of renovations have
     "modernized" the theatre's interior. The building is
     in good condition, but is without distinctive theatrical
     features. The building has been owned by the Masons
     since 1805. The exact opening date of the theatre is
     not known because records indicate theatrical activity
     in 1805, but the theatre was not formally dedicated
     until 1809.

Salisbury, NC

MERONEY'S OPERA HOUSE (other name: Center Theatre)
   OPENING DATE: 1909
   TYPE OF THEATRE: (a)   DEGREE OF RESTORATION: (a)
   CURRENT USE: Movie theatre
   LOCATION OF AUDITORIUM: First floor
   STAGE DIMENSIONS AND EQUIPMENT: Height and width of
     proscenium, 26ft x 32ft; Distance from edge of stage
     to back wall of stage, 26ft; Distance between side
     walls of stage, 61ft; Distance from stage floor to fly
     loft, 30ft; Depth under stage, 10ft; Stage floor, flat
   SEATING (3 levels): 1st level, 550; 2nd level, 350;
     3rd level, 250
   MAJOR TYPES OF ENTERTAINMENT: Local and touring productions
   MAJOR STARS WHO APPEARED AT THEATRE: Bernhardt, Sousa
   ADDITIONAL INFORMATION: The stage, balconies and dressing
     room are intact, but boxes are gone. A 1984 renovation/
     conversion to "twin theatres" has divided the auditorium.
     This is the second Meroney's Opera House on the site.

Wilmington, NC

THALIAN HALL (other names: The Wilmington Academy of Music,
   The Wilmington Opera House), 305 Princess Street
   OPENING DATE: October 12, 1858
   OPENING SHOW: The Honeymoon and The Loan of a Lover
   ARCHITECT: John Montague Trimble   STYLE OF ARCHITECTURE:
     Italianate Revival   TYPE OF BUILDING: Theatre, City
     hall   FACADE: White plaster   TYPE OF THEATRE: (a)
   DEGREE OF RESTORATION: (b)   CURRENT USE: Community center
   LOCATION OF AUDITORIUM: Ground floor
   STAGE DIMENSIONS AND EQUIPMENT: Height and width of
     proscenium, 20ft x 32ft; Shape of proscenium arch,

rectangular; Distance from edge of stage to back wall
of stage, 30ft 6in; Distance from edge of stage to
curtain line, 3ft; Distance between side walls of stage,
50ft; Distance from stage floor to fly loft, 20ft; Stage
floor, flat; Dressing rooms, 3 (basement)
DIMENSIONS OF AUDITORIUM: Distance between side walls
of auditorium, 50ft; Distance stage to back wall of
auditorium, 56ft; Capacity of orchestra pit, 12
SEATING (3 levels): 1st level, 334; 2nd level, 196;
3rd level, 200
SHAPE OF THE AUDITORIUM: Horseshoe-shaped
MAJOR TYPES OF ENTERTAINMENT: Drama, vaudeville, burlesque,
opera, minstrel shows, community recitals
MAJOR STARS WHO APPEARED AT THEATRE: Maude Adams, Marian
Anderson, Maurice Barrymore, Josh Billings, William
Jennings Bryan, Ole Bull, Emma Calve, William Cody, Lotta
Crabtree, Fanny Davenport, Kim Hunter, Fanny Janauschek,
Harry Lauder, Anna Held, Mrs. John Drew, others
ADDITIONAL INFORMATION: Significant restoration through-
out which will be completed in 1987. The theatre contains
the only known intact "thunder run" in the United States.

North Dakota

Fargo, ND

LITTLE COUNTRY THEATRE, North Dakota State University
  OPENING DATE: February 1914   OPENING SHOW: Two plays
  STYLE OF ARCHITECTURE: Romanesque   TYPE OF BUILDING:
    Administration building   FACADE: Brick
  TYPE OF THEATRE: (b)   DEGREE OF RESTORATION: (b)
  CLOSING DATE: 1968   CURRENT USE: Offices
  LOCATION OF AUDITORIUM: Second floor
  SEATING (1 level): 1st level, 200
  SHAPE OF THE AUDITORIUM: Rectangular
  MAJOR TYPES OF ENTERTAINMENT: Drama, vaudeville, pageants
  MAJOR STARS WHO APPEARED AT THEATRE: Paul Robeson, Marian
    Anderson, Cedric Hardwicke, Agnes Moorehead
  ADDITIONAL INFORMATION: The theatre was founded by E. G.
    Arvold and was an early attempt to carry the Little
    Theatre movement into a rural community.

Grand Forks, ND

MASONIC TEMPLE, 423 Bruce Avenue
  OPENING DATE: June 15, 1915
  OPENING SHOW: Dedication program
  ARCHITECT: Joseph Bell DeRemer   TYPE OF BUILDING: Masonic
    lodge   FACADE: Gray limestone   TYPE OF THEATRE: (b)
  DEGREE OF RESTORATION: (d)   CURRENT USE: Lodge
  LOCATION OF AUDITORIUM: Second floor
  STAGE DIMENSIONS AND EQUIPMENT: Height and width of
    proscenium, 21ft x 29ft 8in; Shape of proscenium
    arch, rectangular; Distance from edge of stage to back
    wall of stage, 47ft 6in; Distance from edge of stage to
    curtain line, 14ft; Distance between side walls of stage,
    62ft; Depth under stage, 6ft; Stage floor, flat; Trap
    doors, 1; Scenery storage rooms, 1 (stage left); Dressing
    rooms, 3 (along stage left corridor)
  DIMENSIONS OF AUDITORIUM: Distance between side walls
    of auditorium, 62ft; Distance stage to back wall of

auditorium, 68ft; Orchestra pit, none
SEATING (2 levels): 1st level, 500; 2nd level, 400
SHAPE OF THE AUDITORIUM: U-shaped
MAJOR TYPES OF ENTERTAINMENT: Lodge-related entertainments
and initiations

Valley City, ND

ACADEMY OF MUSIC, 154 East Main
OPENING DATE: c. 1885
TYPE OF BUILDING: Commercial   FACADE: Brick
TYPE OF THEATRE: (b)   DEGREE OF RESTORATION: (c)
CLOSING DATE: c. 1930   CURRENT USE: Apartments
LOCATION OF AUDITORIUM: Second floor
STAGE DIMENSIONS AND EQUIPMENT: * Height and width of
proscenium, 12ft x 18ft; Distance from edge of stage
to back wall, 20ft; Distance from edge of stage to
curtain line, 2ft 6in; Trap doors, 1
DIMENSIONS OF AUDITORIUM: Distance between side walls
of auditorium, 50ft
SEATING (1 level)
MAJOR TYPES OF ENTERTAINMENT: Drama, vaudeville, burlesque,
opera, magic shows
ADDITIONAL INFORMATION: The theatre was used as a lodge
hall from 1920 until its closing.

Wahpeton, ND

WAHPETON OPERA HOUSE (other name: Opera House),
Dakota Avenue and 4th Street
OPENING DATE: December 1894   OPENING SHOW: Amorita
TYPE OF BUILDING: Commercial   TYPE OF THEATRE: (b)
DEGREE OF RESTORATION: (d)   CURRENT USE: Furniture store
LOCATION OF AUDITORIUM: Second floor
DIMENSIONS OF AUDITORIUM: Distance between side walls
of auditorium, 50ft; Distance stage to back wall of
auditorium, 100ft
ADDITIONAL INFORMATION: The opera house, erected to replace
an earlier version which had burned, was modeled after
the Fargo Opera House.

Ohio

Celina, OH

CELINA TOWN HALL AND OPERA HOUSE, Main Street
  OPENING DATE: 1890
  ARCHITECTS: Kreusch and Fanger   TYPE OF BUILDING:
    Municipal   FACADE: Red brick   TYPE OF THEATRE: (b)
  DEGREE OF RESTORATION: (d)   CURRENT USE: City offices
  LOCATION OF AUDITORIUM: Second floor
  STAGE DIMENSIONS AND EQUIPMENT: * Height and width of
    proscenium, 16ft x 28ft; Shape of proscenium arch,
    rectangular; Distance from edge of stage to back wall
    of stage, 24ft; Distance from edge of stage to curtain
    line, 2ft; Distance between side walls of stage, 60ft;
    Depth under stage, 3ft 6in; Trap doors, 1
  DIMENSIONS OF AUDITORIUM: Capacity of orchestra pit, 5
  MAJOR TYPES OF ENTERTAINMENT: Drama

Chillicothe, OH

MAJESTIC THEATRE (other name: Majestic Opera House),
    45 East 2nd Street
  OPENING DATE: 1876
  ARCHITECT: John F. Cook   TYPE OF BUILDING: Masonic
    lodge   FACADE: Stucco with stone trim
  TYPE OF THEATRE: (b)   DEGREE OF RESTORATION: (d)
  CURRENT USE: Movie theatre
  LOCATION OF AUDITORIUM: First and second floors
  STAGE DIMENSIONS AND EQUIPMENT: Height and width of
    proscenium, 50ft x 30ft; Shape of proscenium arch,
    rectangular; Distance from edge of stage to back wall
    of stage, 38ft; Distance from edge of stage to curtain
    line, 8ft; Distance between side walls of stage, 50ft;
    Stage floor, flat; Trap doors, 1; Scenery storage rooms
    (both sides of stage); Dressing rooms, 5 (below stage;
    there is 1 star dressing room)
  DIMENSIONS OF AUDITORIUM: Distance between side walls
    of auditorium, 50ft; Distance stage to back wall of

auditorium, 80ft; Capacity of orchestra pit, 15
SEATING (2 levels): 1st level, 365; 2nd level, 255
SHAPE OF THE AUDITORIUM: U-shaped
MAJOR TYPES OF ENTERTAINMENT: Drama, musical comedy,
  vaudeville, burlesque, opera, movies
MAJOR STARS WHO APPEARED AT THEATRE: Mrs. Fiske, Richard
  Mansfield, James O'Neill, Eddie Foy, James T. Powers,
  Eleanor Robson, Elsie Janis, Henry Dixey, Viola Allen,
  Holbrook Blinn, Sophie Tucker, De Wolf Hopper, George
  Arliss, Mabel Taliaferro, Henrietta Crosman, and others
ADDITIONAL INFORMATION: The Majestic is situated on
  the site of an earlier theatre. It shares the building
  with a second auditorium, the Masonic Lodge Hall, which
  occupies the fourth floor. The theatre was sold in 1915
  to the Myers brothers who attempted vaudeville and stock
  presentations for a while before converting the theatre
  to a film house. The theatre was bought and restored by
  Harley Bennett in 1971.

Cincinnati, OH

CINCINNATI MUSIC HALL (Springer Auditorium), 1243 Elm Street
OPENING DATE: May 1878   OPENING SHOW: May festival
ARCHITECTS: Samuel Hannaford and Henry Proctor
STYLE OF ARCHITECTURE: Gothic Revival   TYPE OF BUILDING:
  Convention center   FACADE: Orange-red brick
TYPE OF THEATRE: (a)   DEGREE OF RESTORATION: (a)
CURRENT USE: Theatre
LOCATION OF AUDITORIUM: Ground floor
STAGE DIMENSIONS AND EQUIPMENT: Height and width of
  proscenium, 39ft x 49ft 9in; Shape of proscenium arch,
  arched; Distance from edge of stage to back wall of
  stage, 73ft; Distance from edge of stage to curtain
  line, 25ft; Distance between side walls of stage, 120ft;
  Distance from stage floor to fly loft, 42ft; Stage floor,
  flat; Trap doors, 0; Scenery storage rooms, 1 (north
  wing); Dressing rooms, 19 (south wing)
DIMENSIONS OF AUDITORIUM: Distance between side walls
  of auditorium, 120ft; Distance stage to back wall of
  auditorium, 120ft; Capacity of orchestra pit, 60
SEATING (3 levels): 1st level, 1,767; 2nd level, 964;
  3rd level, 839; boxes, 60
SHAPE OF THE AUDITORIUM: Horseshoe-shaped
MAJOR TYPES OF ENTERTAINMENT: Drama, musical comedy,
  opera, concerts, dance
ADDITIONAL INFORMATION: The building is actually three
  buildings under the same roof. In addition to the
  Springer Auditorium, the complex also contains the
  Music Hall Ballroom (for large receptions, fashion
  shows, reunions, dances and meetings), and Corbett
  Tower, an elegant reception room "upstairs."

Cincinnati, OH

EMERY THEATRE (other names: Emery Auditorium, Emery Hall),
  1112 Walnut Street
  OPENING DATE: January 6, 1912
  OPENING SHOW: Concert by Cincinnati Symphony Orchestra
  ARCHITECT: Samuel Hannaford   STYLE OF ARCHITECTURE:
    Tudor Gothic   TYPE OF BUILDING: University class
    building   FACADE: Red brick; terra cotta trim
  TYPE OF THEATRE: (a)   DEGREE OF RESTORATION: (b)
  CURRENT USE: Theatre
  LOCATION OF AUDITORIUM: Ground floor
  STAGE DIMENSIONS AND EQUIPMENT: Height and width of
    proscenium, 45ft x 54ft; Shape of proscenium arch,
    arched; Distance from edge of stage to back wall of
    stage, 37ft; Distance from edge of stage to curtain
    line, 6ft; Distance between side walls of stage, 82ft;
    Distance from stage floor to fly loft, 29ft; Depth
    under stage, 10ft; Stage floor, flat; Trap doors, 1;
    Scenery storage rooms, 0; Dressing rooms, 7 (5 at
    stage level, 2 above stage level)
  DIMENSIONS OF AUDITORIUM: Distance between side walls
    of auditorium, 82ft; Distance stage to back wall of
    auditorium, 79ft; Capacity of orchestra pit, 20
  SEATING (3 levels): 1st level, 821; 2nd level, 608;
    3rd level, 694; boxes, 84
  SHAPE OF THE AUDITORIUM: U-shaped
  MAJOR TYPES OF ENTERTAINMENT: Drama, musical comedy,
    concerts, annual Passion Play
  MAJOR STARS WHO APPEARED AT THEATRE: Pavlova, Ted Shawn,
    George Gershwin (1927), Igor Stravinsky (1925), Vladimir
    Horowitz (1928)
  ADDITIONAL INFORMATION: The theatre was the home of
    the Cincinnati Symphony Orchestra from 1912 until 1936
    under conductors Leopold Stokowski, Fritz Reiner and
    Eugene Goossens. The theatre is currently owned by the
    University of Cincinnati. It houses a 3/27 Wurlitzer
    Pipe Organ which was removed from the RKO Albee Theatre
    and is used each weekend to accompany movies.

Cincinnati, OH

HAMILTON COUNTY MEMORIAL HALL/BUILDING (other name: Memorial
  Hall), 1225 Elm Street
  OPENING DATE: 1908
  ARCHITECTS: Samuel Hannaford and Sons
  STYLE OF ARCHITECTURE: Beaux Arts Classical Revival
  TYPE OF BUILDING: Veterans' hall   FACADE: Stone
  TYPE OF THEATRE: (b)   DEGREE OF RESTORATION: (c)
  CURRENT USE: Civic events
  LOCATION OF AUDITORIUM: Second and third floors
  STAGE DIMENSIONS AND EQUIPMENT: Width of proscenium, 28ft
    6in; Distance from edge of stage to back wall of stage,
    14ft; Distance between side walls of stage, 29ft 6in;
    Stage floor, flat; Trap doors, 0

DIMENSIONS OF AUDITORIUM: Orchestra pit, yes
SEATING (2 levels): 1st level, 242; 2nd level, 375
SHAPE OF THE AUDITORIUM: U-shaped
MAJOR TYPES OF ENTERTAINMENT: Drama, vaudeville, burlesque,
  opera, concerts, lectures, dance, movies, civic functions
ADDITIONAL INFORMATION: The building was erected and was
  dedicated as a memorial to soldiers and was first used
  by veterans and their spouses. Sporadically, the hall
  was used by the neighboring Cincinnati College of Music
  and gradually the hall was booked by various touring
  companies. Today, the building serves as a center
  for the arts.

Cleveland, OH

BOHEMIAN NATIONAL HALL, 4939 Broadway Avenue
  OPENING DATE: October 1897
  ARCHITECTS: Mitermiler and Hrodek
  STYLE OF ARCHITECTURE: Romanesque and Renaissance
  TYPE OF BUILDING: Social hall   FACADE: Red and orange
    brick and stone   TYPE OF THEATRE: (b)   DEGREE OF
  RESTORATION: (a)   CURRENT USE: Social hall
  PERFORMANCE SPACES IN BUILDING: 2
  LOCATION OF AUDITORIUM: Second and third floors
  STAGE DIMENSIONS AND EQUIPMENT: Width of proscenium,
    33ft; Distance from edge of stage to back wall of stage,
    25ft; Distance from edge of stage to curtain line, 3ft;
    Distance between side walls of stage, 70ft; Trap doors,
    3; Scenery storage rooms, 1 (in back of stage); Dressing
    rooms, 8 (rear of stage and 3rd floor)
  MAJOR TYPES OF ENTERTAINMENT: Drama, opera

Cleveland, OH

OLYMPIA THEATRE, Broadway and East 55th Street
  OPENING DATE: 1911
  STYLE OF ARCHITECTURE: Classical   TYPE OF BUILDING:
    Apartments, stores   FACADE: Red brick
  TYPE OF THEATRE: (a)   DEGREE OF RESTORATION: (c)
  CLOSING DATE: 1980   CURRENT USE: Vacant
  LOCATION OF AUDITORIUM: Ground floor
  STAGE DIMENSIONS AND EQUIPMENT: Shape of proscenium arch,
    arched; Distance from edge of stage to back wall of
    stage, 31ft 6in: Distance between side walls of stage,
    63ft 11in; Stage floor, flat
  DIMENSIONS OF AUDITORIUM: Distance between side walls of
    auditorium, 72ft 2in; Orchestra pit, yes
  SEATING (2 levels)
  SHAPE OF THE AUDITORIUM: Rectangular
  MAJOR TYPES OF ENTERTAINMENT: Vaudeville, movies, concerts
  ADDITIONAL INFORMATION: When the Olympia opened, the
    neighborhood was (and to some extent still is) composed
    primarily of Polish and Bohemian immigrants. The
    theatre opened as a combination vaudeville and film

house and was part of B. F. Keith's vaudeville empire.
It had its own orchestra, the Olympia Concert Orchestra,
which accompanied both the vaudeville acts and the silent
films.   In 1914, the Olympia sponsored "farm nights,"
giving away an assortment of birds, beasts and fowl,
and during the Depression the theatre presented "dish
nights," when four-piece place settings were awarded to
certain patrons.

Clyde, OH

TERRY'S HALL (other name: Terry's Opera House),
   106-110 South Main Street
   OPENING DATE: c. 1874
   STYLE OF ARCHITECTURE: Victorian Classic   TYPE OF
   BUILDING: Commercial   FACADE: Red brick, now painted
   TYPE OF THEATRE: (b)   DEGREE OF RESTORATION: (c)
   CLOSING DATE: c. 1925   CURRENT USE: Storage
   LOCATION OF AUDITORIUM: Third floor
   STAGE DIMENSIONS AND EQUIPMENT: Height and width of
    proscenium, 10ft x 18ft; Shape of proscenium arch,
    arched; Distance from edge of stage to back wall of
    stage, 12ft; Distance from edge of stage to curtain
    line, 2ft; Distance between side walls of stage, 30ft;
    Depth under stage, 3ft; Stage floor, flat; Trap doors,
    0; Scenery storage rooms, 0; Dressing rooms, 0
   DIMENSIONS OF AUDITORIUM: Distance between side walls
    of auditorium, 30ft; Distance stage to back wall of
    auditorium, 50ft; Orchestra pit, none
   SEATING (1 level): 1st level, 200
   SHAPE OF THE AUDITORIUM: Rectangular
   MAJOR TYPES OF ENTERTAINMENT: Drama, vaudeville, lectures,
    civic functions
   ADDITIONAL INFORMATION: Clyde was the boyhood home of
    Sherwood Anderson and Terry's Opera House is the
    theatre and social hall of his Winesburg, Ohio.

Columbus, OH

SOUTHERN THEATRE (other names: Great Southern Theatre,
   Towne Cinema), 21 East Main Street
   OPENING DATE: September 21, 1896
   OPENING SHOW: In Gay New York
   CURRENT USE: Vacant
   STAGE DIMENSIONS AND EQUIPMENT: * Height amd width of
    proscenium, 34ft x 34ft; Distance from edge of stage
    to back wall of stage, 52ft; Distance from edge of
    stage to curtain line, 6ft; Distance between side walls
    of stage, 71ft; Depth under stage, 18ft; Trap doors, 8;
   DIMENSIONS OF AUDITORIUM: Capacity of orchestra pit, 10
   MAJOR TYPES OF ENTERTAINMENT: Drama, vaudeville, movies
   MAJOR STARS WHO APPEARED AT THEATRE: John Drew, Lillian
    Russell, Gilmore's Band, Victor Herbert, Maggie Cline,
    Mrs. Leslie Carter, Mrs. Patrick Campbell, William A.

Brady, Frances Ring, Elsie Janis, McIntyre and Heath,
Marilyn Miller, William Faversham, Pavlova, Al Jolson,
Maude Adams, Lenore Ulrich, Nazimova
ADDITIONAL INFORMATION: The theatre is incorporated into
the Southern Hotel.

Dayton, OH

VICTORY THEATRE (other names: See ADDITIONAL INFORMATION),
   138 North Main Street
   OPENING DATE: January 1, 1866
   OPENING SHOW: Virginius with Edwin Forrest
   ARCHITECT: John Rouzer, Contractor   STYLE OF ARCHITECTURE:
   Second Empire/Victorian Italianate   TYPE OF BUILDING:
   Commercial and offices   FACADE: Brick and limestone,
   painted pale cream   TYPE OF THEATRE: (a)
   DEGREE OF RESTORATION: (a)   CURRENT USE: Theatre
   LOCATION OF AUDITORIUM: Ground floor
   STAGE DIMENSIONS AND EQUIPMENT: Height and width of
   proscenium, 29ft x 37ft 5in; Shape of proscenium arch,
   rectangular; Distance from edge of stage to back wall
   of stage, 32ft; Distance from edge of stage to curtain
   line, 3ft; Distance between side walls of stage, 37ft
   5in; Distance from stage floor to fly loft, 25ft; Stage
   floor, flat; Trap doors, 2; Dressing rooms, 11 (3
   levels, entrance stage left)
   DIMENSIONS OF AUDITORIUM: Orchestra pit, yes
   SEATING (2 levels): 1st level, 613; 2nd level, 529
   SHAPE OF THE AUDITORIUM: Rectangular
   MAJOR TYPES OF ENTERTAINMENT: Drama, musical comedy, dance,
   concerts, movies
   MAJOR STARS WHO APPEARED AT THEATRE: Edwin Forrest, Maude
   Adams (1889, 1890s, 1907, 1912), John Drew (1890s), Otis
   Skinner, Madame Schumann-Heinke (1916), George M. Cohan,
   Ethel Barrymore, Tallulah Bankhead, Paderewski, and
   others
   ADDITIONAL INFORMATION: The theatre was also known by the
   following names: Turner's Opera House (1866), The Music
   Hall (1871), The Grand Opera House (1885), Victoria Opera
   House, and Victoria Theater (1901). It was named the
   Victory Theater in 1910.

Genoa, OH

GENOA OPERA HOUSE (other name: Town Hall Opera House),
   6th and Main Streets
   OPENING DATE: 1886   OPENING SHOW: The Three Wise Owls
   STYLE OF ARCHITECTURE: Victorian Gothic   TYPE OF
   BUILDING: Municipal   FACADE: Red brick and stone
   TYPE OF THEATRE: (b)   DEGREE OF RESTORATION: (a)
   CURRENT USE: Theatre, town hall
   LOCATION OF AUDITORIUM: Second floor
   STAGE DIMENSIONS AND EQUIPMENT: Shape of proscenium arch,
   arched; Stage floor, flat; Trap doors, 1; Scenery storage

rooms, 1 (third floor); Dressing rooms, 1 (first floor)
DIMENSIONS OF AUDITORIUM: Capacity of orchestra pit, 15
SEATING (2 levels)
SHAPE OF THE AUDITORIUM: U-shaped
MAJOR TYPES OF ENTERTAINMENT: Drama, vaudeville, opera,
  concerts, minstrel shows, civic functions
ADDITIONAL INFORMATION: The building has been restored and
  was prominantly displayed in 1985 during centennial
  celebrations when Rossini's Stabat Mater was produced
  there.

McConnelsville, OH

OPERA HOUSE THEATER (other name: Twin City Opera House),
  15 West Main Street
OPENING DATE: May 28, 1892   OPENING SHOW: The Mikado
ARCHITECT: H. C. Lindsay   FACADE: Red brick and sandstone
TYPE OF THEATRE: (a)   DEGREE OF RESTORATION: (d)
CURRENT USE: Theatre
LOCATION OF AUDITORIUM: Ground floor
STAGE DIMENSIONS AND EQUIPMENT: Height and width of
  proscenium, 30ft 4in x 35ft 2in; Shape of proscenium
  arch, arched; Distance from edge of stage to back wall
  of stage, 45ft; Distance from edge of stage to curtain
  line, 4ft; Distance between side walls of stage, 55ft;
  Depth under stage, 10ft; Stage floor, raked; Trap doors,
  1; Scenery storage rooms, (backstage); Dressing rooms, 0
DIMENSIONS OF AUDITORIUM: Distance between side walls
  of auditorium, 70ft; Distance stage to back wall of
  auditorium, 50ft; Capacity of orchestra pit, 30
SEATING (2 levels): 1st level, 300; 2nd level, 300
SHAPE OF THE AUDITORIUM: Horseshoe-shaped
MAJOR TYPES OF ENTERTAINMENT: Drama, musical comedy,
  opera, vaudeville, minstrel shows, medicine shows,
  concerts, lectures, movies, chautauquas, civic functions
MAJOR STARS WHO APPEARED AT THEATRE: William Jennings
  Bryan, Rev. Billy Sunday, J. A. Coburn's Minstrels,
  Ellery's Band
ADDITIONAL INFORMATION: Memories of the Opera House include
  the time "the stage caught fire and the orchestra played
  on, meanwhile the hose and reel wagon rolled up to the
  back door, [and] extinguished the fire as the show went
  on"; an unfortunate Little Eva in a travelling Uncle
  Tom's Cabin company who got stuck while ascending to
  heaven and resorted to "language ...not fitting for an
  angel"; and the old celluloid film burning during the
  process of being shown.

Middletown, OH

SORG OPERA HOUSE (other names: Colonial Theatre, Sorg
  Theatre, Sorg's Opera House), 57 South Main Street
OPENING DATE: September 12, 1891

OPENING SHOW: The Little Tycoon
ARCHITECT: Samuel Hannaford   STYLE OF ARCHITECTURE:
  Richardsonian Romanesque   TYPE OF BUILDING: Multiple
  use building   FACADE: Red and white limestone
TYPE OF THEATRE: (b)   DEGREE OF RESTORATION: (d)
CURRENT USE: Occasional live performance
LOCATION OF AUDITORIUM: Ground floor
STAGE DIMENSIONS AND EQUIPMENT: Height and width of
  proscenium, 34ft x 36ft; Shape of proscenium arch,
  arched; Distance from edge of stage to back wall of
  stage, 31ft 3in; Distance from edge of stage to curtain
  line, 5ft 3in; Distance between side walls of stage, 64ft
  3in; Stage floor, raked; Trap doors, 0; Scenery storage
  rooms, 1 (stage left); Dressing rooms, 3 (2 stage right,
  1 in basement)
DIMENSIONS OF AUDITORIUM: Distance between side walls
  of auditorium, 64ft; Distance stage to back wall of
  auditorium, 65ft; Orchestra pit, yes
SEATING (3 levels): 1st level, 520; 2nd level, 240;
  3rd level, 440
SHAPE OF THE AUDITORIUM: Horseshoe-shaped
MAJOR TYPES OF ENTERTAINMENT: Drama, musical comedy,
  vaudeville, operetta, concerts, lectures, minstrel
  shows, movies
MAJOR STARS WHO APPEARED AT THEATRE: Nora Bayes, John
  Phillip Sousa (1898, 1919), George Sidney (1905), Elsie
  Janis (1905), William Jennings Bryan (1906), Williams and
  Walker (1907), Mrs. Leslie Carter (1907), De Wolf Hopper
  (1910), Eva Tanguay (1910, 1926), Marie Dressler (1912),
  Sophie Tucker (1912), John McCormack (1916), Francis X.
  Bushman, Eddie Cantor, Will Rogers, Alice Roosevelt
  Longworth, Al Jolson
ADDITIONAL INFORMATION: During the early years of the
  century, the Sorg, which was on the mainline of the
  New York Central railroad, prospered as a road house.
  In 1918, the theatre changed its policy from road shows
  to movies and in 1929 a fixed screen was installed. In
  1983, the fixed screen, which had reduced the usable
  stage depth to 12 feet, was replaced with a moveable
  screen and the stage was made ready for the return of
  live theatre.

Nelsonville, OH

STUART'S OPERA HOUSE, Public Square
OPENING DATE: 1879
ARCHITECT: W. H. Vorhees   STYLE OF ARCHITECTURE:
  Italianate   TYPE OF BUILDING: Storage
  FACADE: Red brick with wood trim   TYPE OF THEATRE: (b)
DEGREE OF RESTORATION: (c)   CLOSING DATE: 1924
CURRENT USE: Storage
LOCATION OF AUDITORIUM: Second floor
STAGE DIMENSIONS AND EQUIPMENT: Height and width of
  proscenium, 16ft 8in x 28ft; Shape of proscenium
  arch, rectangular; Distance from edge of stage to

back wall of stage, 33ft; Distance from edge of stage to
curtain line, 8ft; Distance between side walls of stage,
61ft 5in; Distance from stage floor to fly loft, 21ft;
Stage floor, flat; Trap doors, 0; Scenery storage rooms,
1 (under stage, accessible by lift); Dressing rooms, 8
(rear of stage)
DIMENSIONS OF AUDITORIUM: Distance between side walls
  of auditorium, 60ft; Distance stage to back wall of
  auditorium, 57ft; Capacity of orchestra pit, 23
SEATING (3 levels): 1st level, 351; 2nd level, 156;
  boxes, 20
MAJOR TYPES OF ENTERTAINMENT: Drama
ADDITIONAL INFORMATION: In March of 1980, a fire
  destroyed the roof, the interior (minus the balcony)
  and storerooms. The theatre is presently being restored to its original interior.

Peninsula, OH

G.A.R. HALL, Route 303 and Riverview Road
  OPENING DATE: Dedicated 1888
  STYLE OF ARCHITECTURE: Victorian   TYPE OF BUILDING:
    Meeting house   FACADE: Gray wood   TYPE OF THEATRE: (b)
  DEGREE OF RESTORATION: (a)   CURRENT USE: Meeting hall
  LOCATION OF AUDITORIUM: Ground floor
  STAGE DIMENSIONS AND EQUIPMENT: Width of proscenium, 18ft;
    Shape of proscenium arch, arched; Distance from edge of
    stage to back wall of stage, 15ft; Distance between side
    walls of stage, 29ft; Stage floor, raked; Trap doors, 2;
  DIMENSIONS OF AUDITORIUM: Distance between side walls
    of auditorium, 29ft; Distance stage to back wall of
    auditorium, 42ft; Orchestra pit, none
  SHAPE OF THE AUDITORIUM: Rectangular
  MAJOR TYPES OF ENTERTAINMENT: Drama, vaudeville, burlesque
  ADDITIONAL INFORMATION: The hall, built in the mid-1880s,
    was originally used by veterans of the Grand Army of the
    Republic and their families. In 1963, it was purchased
    and restored by Robert L. Hunker and now serves as a
    meeting hall.

Put-in-Bay, OH

PUT-IN-BAY TOWN HALL, Catawba Avenue
  OPENING DATE: December 27, 1887   OPENING SHOW: Concert
    and ball featuring The Great Western Band
  ARCHITECT: George E. Gascoyne   TYPE OF BUILDING:
    Municipal FACADE: Red brick
  TYPE OF THEATRE: (b)   DEGREE OF RESTORATION: (d)
  CURRENT USE: Town hall
  LOCATION OF AUDITORIUM: Second floor
  STAGE DIMENSIONS AND EQUIPMENT: Height and width of
    proscenium, 18ft x 20ft; Shape of proscenium arch,
    arched; Distance from edge of stage to back wall of
    stage, 24ft; Distance from edge of stage to curtain

line, 3ft; Distance between side walls of stage, 44ft;
Depth under stage, 3ft; Stage floor, flat; Trap doors,
2; Scenery storage rooms, 1 (side of stage); Dressing
rooms, 1 (side of stage)
DIMENSIONS OF AUDITORIUM: Distance between side walls
of auditorium, 44ft; Distance stage to back wall of
auditorium, 75ft; Orchestra pit, none
SEATING (1 level)
SHAPE OF THE AUDITORIUM: Rectangular
MAJOR TYPES OF ENTERTAINMENT: Drama, musical comedy,
vaudeville, opera, concerts, lectures
ADDITIONAL INFORMATION: Put-in-Bay was also home to an
"Actors' Colony," which was composed of former vaudeville
performers.

Rising Sun, OH

RISING SUN OPERA HOUSE, Northeast corner of Main and
Vine Streets
OPENING DATE: c. 1899
TYPE OF BUILDING: Town hall   FACADE: Red brick
TYPE OF THEATRE: (b)   DEGREE OF RESTORATION: (a)
CURRENT USE: Theatre   LOCATION OF AUDITORIUM: Second floor
STAGE DIMENSIONS AND EQUIPMENT: Trap doors, 1; Scenery
storage rooms, 0; Dressing rooms, 2 (rear corners of the
stage)
DIMENSIONS OF AUDITORIUM: Orchestra pit, none
SEATING (2 levels): 1st level, 125; 2nd level, 50
SHAPE OF THE AUDITORIUM: Square
MAJOR TYPES OF ENTERTAINMENT: Drama, vaudeville
MAJOR STARS WHO APPEARED AT THEATRE: Lillian Gish (debut
performance)

Toledo, OH

LOEW'S VALENTINE THEATRE (other names: The Valentine,
Renaissance Valentine), 402-412 Adams; 405-419 St. Clair
OPENING DATE: December 25, 1895
OPENING SHOW: Rip Van Winkle with Joseph Jefferson
ARCHITECT: E. O. Fallis   STYLE OF ARCHITECTURE:
Sullivanesque   TYPE OF BUILDING: City offices
FACADE: Brown brick   TYPE OF THEATRE: (b)
DEGREE OF RESTORATION: (c)   CURRENT USE: City offices,
TV Station   LOCATION OF AUDITORIUM: Ground floor
SEATING (2 levels)
MAJOR TYPES OF ENTERTAINMENT: Drama, musical comedy,
opera, vaudeville, movies
MAJOR STARS WHO APPEARED AT THEATRE: Joseph Jefferson,
Lillian Russell, John Barrymore, Ethel Barrymore,
David Warfield, Eddie Foy, Richard Mansfield, Ed Wynn
ADDITIONAL INFORMATION: The theatre was billed as "the
greatest showplace west of the Alleghenies" when it
opened in 1895. In 1918, the Loew's Circuit assumed

the lease and converted the house to films, and in 1942 it was modernized by the firm of Rapp and Rapp. During WW II, the building housed the USO club and the Rainbow Room night club. It is now owned by the City of Toledo.

Oklahoma

Vinita, OK

GRAND THEATRE (other name: City Hall), City Hall
OPENING DATE: 1914
TYPE OF BUILDING: Offices   TYPE OF THEATRE: (a)
DEGREE OF RESTORATION: (c)   CLOSING DATE: 1930s
CURRENT USE: City hall
LOCATION OF AUDITORIUM: First floor
STAGE DIMENSIONS AND EQUIPMENT: Distance from edge of stage
    to back wall of stage, 34ft; Distance between side walls
    of stage, 70ft
MAJOR TYPES OF ENTERTAINMENT: Local and touring
    productions
ADDITIONAL INFORMATION: The theatre served as an office
    for the Grand River Dance Project and when the project
    was completed, it became the City Hall. It is still in
    use as offices.

Oregon

Portland, OR

NEW MARKET THEATRE, 50 Southwest 2nd Avenue
  OPENING DATE: March 25, 1875
  OPENING SHOW: Rip Van Winkle, James A. Herne Company
  ARCHITECTS: E. M. Burton and W. W. Piper   STYLE OF
  ARCHITECTURE: Italian Renaissance   TYPE OF BUILDING:
    Public market (1st floor)   FACADE: Brick, cast iron,
    stone, wood cornices   TYPE OF THEATRE: (b)
  DEGREE OF RESTORATION: (a)   CURRENT USE: Shops, offices,
    restaurant   LOCATION OF AUDITORIUM: Second floor
  STAGE DIMENSIONS AND EQUIPMENT: Height and width of
    proscenium, 26ft x 50ft; Distance from edge of stage
    to back wall, 30ft; Stage floor, raked
  DIMENSIONS OF AUDITORIUM: Distance between side walls
    of auditorium, 60ft; Distance stage to back wall of
    auditorium, 145ft
  MAJOR TYPES OF ENTERTAINMENT: Drama, opera, vaudeville,
    burlesque, minstrel shows, lectures
  MAJOR STARS WHO APPEARED AT THEATRE: Primrose and West
    Minstrels, Rose Eytinge, Henry Ward Beecher, Blanche
    Bates, David Belasco, James A. Herne, Commodore Nutt,
    Mrs. Scott Siddons, Frank Mayo, Maude Adams, William A.
    Brady, Sol Smith Russell, Fanny Janauschek, and others
  ADDITIONAL INFORMATION: The New Market Theatre, regarded
    by the Oregon Historical Society as "the most important
    historical building in the state," stands at the heart of
    Portland's historic district. In restoring the building,
    the original three floors were converted to six.

Roseburg, OR

ROSEBURG OPERA HOUSE, 105 South Jackson
  OPENING DATE: February 16, 1893   OPENING SHOW: Pasha
  STYLE OF ARCHITECTURE: Victorian   TYPE OF BUILDING:
    I.O.O.F. Lodge hall   FACADE: Original facade, red brick
  TYPE OF THEATRE: (b)   DEGREE OF RESTORATION: (c)

CLOSING DATE: 1909   CURRENT USE: Lodge, commercial
LOCATION OF AUDITORIUM: Ground floor
SHAPE OF THE AUDITORIUM: Rectangular
MAJOR TYPES OF ENTERTAINMENT: Drama, opera, vaudeville
ADDITIONAL INFORMATION: At the time of construction, the
  50'x 100' building had towers at both the northeast and
  northwest corners. In 1924, the towers were removed and
  a third story added.

Salem, OR

GRAND THEATRE (other name: Grand Opera House),
    High and Court Streets
OPENING DATE: November 30, 1900   OPENING SHOW: El Capitan
TYPE OF BUILDING: Business, lodge   TYPE OF THEATRE: (b)
DEGREE OF RESTORATION: (a)   CURRENT USE: Theatre, lodge
LOCATION OF AUDITORIUM: Ground floor
STAGE DIMENSIONS AND EQUIPMENT: Height and width of
  proscenium, 28ft x 32ft; Shape of proscenium arch,
  square; Distance from edge of stage to back wall of
  stage, 30ft; Distance from edge of stage to curtain
  line, 3ft; Distance between side walls of stage, 50ft;
  Depth under stage, 4ft; Stage floor, flat; Dressing
  rooms, 5 (under stage)
DIMENSIONS OF AUDITORIUM: Distance between side walls
  of auditorium, 50ft; Distance stage to back wall of
  auditorium, 50ft; Capacity of orchestra pit, 5
SEATING (2 levels): 1st level, 300; 2nd level, 180
SHAPE OF THE AUDITORIUM: Horseshoe-shaped
MAJOR TYPES OF ENTERTAINMENT: Drama, vaudeville, opera,
  movies
MAJOR STARS WHO APPEARED AT THEATRE: Will Rogers, William
  Frawley
ADDITIONAL INFORMATION: An early drawing of the theatre
  shows a tower in front which no longer exists. The
  Grand was converted to movies in the mid-1930s and was
  considerably renovated in 1937. Present occupant is Salem
  Theatre of Performing Arts, a community theatre group.

Salem, OR

REED OPERA HOUSE, 189 Liberty Street Northeast
OPENING DATE: October 9, 1869
OPENING SHOW: The Female Gambler and Our Yankee Gal
ARCHITECT: G. W. Rhodes   TYPE OF BUILDING: Commercial
FACADE: Red brick   TYPE OF THEATRE: (b)   CURRENT USE:
  Shops and offices   LOCATION OF AUDITORIUM: Second floor
STAGE DIMENSIONS AND EQUIPMENT: Distance from edge of stage
  to back wall of stage, 40ft; Distance between side walls
  of stage, 60ft
DIMENSIONS OF AUDITORIUM: Distance between side walls
  of auditorium, 60ft; Distance stage to back wall of
  auditorium, 70ft
MAJOR TYPES OF ENTERTAINMENT: Drama, opera, variety,

concerts, minstrel shows, dances
MAJOR STARS WHO APPEARED AT THEATRE: Frederick Warde, Louis
  James, Blanche Walsh, Robert Mantell, Ellen Beach Yaw,
  Eugenie Blair, Sousa's Band, Mr. and Mrs. F. M. Bates
ADDITIONAL INFORMATION: The theatre opened its doors ten
  months before construction was completed and remained
  Salem's social and cultural center until 1900 when the
  Grand Theatre opened. The last show at the Reed was
  The Great Barlow Minstrels on October 20, 1900.

Pennsylvania

Allentown, PA

SYMPHONY HALL (other names: Lyric Theatre, Central Market
    Hall), 23 North 6th Street
  OPENING DATE: October 10, 1899
  OPENING SHOW: Frederick the Great
  ARCHITECT: J. B. McElfatrick (1899 conversion)
  FACADE: Red brick and concrete   TYPE OF THEATRE: (b)
  DEGREE OF RESTORATION: (c)   CURRENT USE: Musical
    presentations   LOCATION OF AUDITORIUM: Ground floor
  STAGE DIMENSIONS AND EQUIPMENT: Height and width of
    proscenium, 38ft x 34ft; Shape of proscenium arch,
    rectangular; Distance from edge of stage to back wall
    of stage, 44ft; Distance from edge of stage to curtain
    line, 3ft; Distance between side walls of stage, 67ft;
    Depth under stage, 8ft; Stage floor, flat; Trap doors,
    1; Dressing rooms, 12 (rear of stage)
  DIMENSIONS OF AUDITORIUM: Distance between side walls
    of auditorium, 67ft; Distance stage to back wall of
    auditorium, 52ft; Orchestra pit, yes
  SEATING (3 levels): 1st level, 805; 2nd level, 400;
    3rd level, 200; boxes, 48
  SHAPE OF THE AUDITORIUM: Rectangular with lyre-shaped
    balcony
  MAJOR TYPES OF ENTERTAINMENT: Drama, opera, concerts,
    political gatherings
  MAJOR STARS WHO APPEARED AT THEATRE: Otis Skinner, Douglas
    Fairbanks, Judith Anderson, John Barrymore, Bernhardt,
    the Marx Brothers
  ADDITIONAL INFORMATION: For several years, the Lyric
    Theatre shared dominance of theatre in Allentown with
    the Academy of Music. After the Academy burned in 1903,
    the Lyric assumed the role of "the leading play-house and
    assemblage hall in the city." Ben Hur was once staged
    there using live horses on a treadmill.

Altoona, PA

MISHLER THEATRE, 1208-12 Avenue
  OPENING DATE: February 15, 1906
  OPENING SHOW: Merely Mary Ann with Eleanor Robson
  ARCHITECT: Albert Westover   FACADE: Red brick and
    Indiana limestone   TYPE OF THEATRE: (a)   DEGREE OF
  RESTORATION: (a)   CURRENT USE: Performing arts center
  LOCATION OF AUDITORIUM: Ground floor
  STAGE DIMENSIONS AND EQUIPMENT: Height and width of
    proscenium, 31ft x 38ft; Shape of proscenium arch,
    arched; Distance from edge of stage to back wall of
    stage, 37ft; Distance from edge of stage to curtain
    line, 3ft 6in; Distance between side walls of stage,
    71ft; Distance from stage floor to fly loft, 68ft;
    Depth under stage, 8ft 6in; Stage floor, flat; Trap
    doors, 1; Scenery storage rooms, 1 (under auditorium);
    Dressing rooms, 8 (below stage level)
  DIMENSIONS OF AUDITORIUM: Distance between side walls
    of auditorium, 72ft; Distance stage to back wall of
    auditorium, 56ft; Capacity of orchestra pit, 25
  SEATING (3 levels): 1st level, 499; 2nd level, 285;
    3rd level, 126
  SHAPE OF THE AUDITORIUM: Horseshoe-shaped
  MAJOR TYPES OF ENTERTAINMENT: Drama, musical comedy,
    vaudeville, burlesque, opera, concerts, lectures,
    dance, boxing matches
  MAJOR STARS WHO APPEARED AT THEATRE: Mme. Schumann-Heink,
    Fritz Kreisler, John Phillip Sousa, Isadora Duncan,
    Pavlova, Bernhardt, Ellen Terry, Mrs. Patrick Campbell,
    and others
  ADDITIONAL INFORMATION: The theatre was a major stopover
    for stars between 1906 and 1925. It was on the mainline
    of the Pennsylania Railroad and Mr. Mishler owned other
    theatres in Altoona, Johnstown and Trenton, N.J.

Blairsville, PA

EINSTEIN OPERA HOUSE, East Market Street
  OPENING DATE: 1904
  STYLE OF ARCHITECTURE: Romanesque Vernacular
  TYPE OF BUILDING: Commercial   FACADE: Brick with stone
    trim   TYPE OF THEATRE: (b)   DEGREE OF RESTORATION: (c)
  CLOSING DATE: 1920s   CURRENT USE: Storage, restaurant
  LOCATION OF AUDITORIUM: Second floor
  DIMENSIONS OF AUDITORIUM: Orchestra pit, yes
  SEATING (3 levels)
  MAJOR TYPES OF ENTERTAINMENT: Drama, musical comedy,
    opera, minstrel shows, local variety shows, lectures,
    concerts, movies, vaudeville, civic functions
  MAJOR STARS WHO APPEARED AT THEATRE: William Jennings Bryan
    (1907)

Brookville, PA

MARLIN'S OPERA HOUSE (other name: Brookville Opera House),
225-237 Main Street
OPENING DATE: November 1, 1886
OPENING SHOW: Monte Cristo
ARCHITECTS: Osman and Cousner   STYLE OF ARCHITECTURE:
Victorian Italianate   TYPE OF BUILDING: Stores and
offices   FACADE: Masonry; salmon-colored common brick
TYPE OF THEATRE: (b)   DEGREE OF RESTORATION: (c)
CLOSING DATE: c. 1902   CURRENT USE: Vacant
LOCATION OF AUDITORIUM: Second and third floors
STAGE DIMENSIONS AND EQUIPMENT: Height and width of
proscenium, 17ft 11in x 32ft; Shape of proscenium
arch, arched; Distance from edge of stage to back wall
of stage, 28ft; Distance from edge of stage to curtain
line, 1ft 6in; Distance between side walls of stage,
62ft; Stage floor, flat; Trap doors, 0; Dressing rooms,
4 (several levels, stage right and left)
DIMENSIONS OF AUDITORIUM: Distance between side walls
of auditorium, 62ft; Distance stage to back wall of
auditorium, 53ft; Capacity of orchestra pit, 8
SEATING (3 levels)
SHAPE OF THE AUDITORIUM: Rectangular
MAJOR TYPES OF ENTERTAINMENT: Drama, musical comedy,
lectures, civic functions
MAJOR STARS WHO APPEARED AT THEATRE: Belle Boyd, Fisk
Jubilee Singers
ADDITIONAL INFORMATION: The interior is finished in golds,
soft blues and reds. The seats are gone and the curtain
and lighting fixtures have been removed, but the 36-light
chandelier, footlights and gas fittings remain.

Easton, PA

ABEL'S OPERA HOUSE, 344 Northampton Street
OPENING DATE: 1872
OPENING SHOW: Hamlet with Mr. and Mrs. E. L. Davenport
STYLE OF ARCHITECTURE: Victorian   TYPE OF BUILDING:
Commercial   FACADE: Red brick   TYPE OF THEATRE: (b)
DEGREE OF RESTORATION: (c)   CLOSING DATE: 1915
CURRENT USE: Bridal gallery
LOCATION OF AUDITORIUM: Second floor rear
STAGE DIMENSIONS AND EQUIPMENT: * Height and width of
proscenium, 33ft x 33ft; Distance from edge of stage
to back wall of stage, 48ft; Distance from edge of
stage to curtain line, 4ft; Distance between side
walls of stage, 50ft; Depth under stage, 10ft; Trap
doors, 4; Scenery storage rooms, 1 (basement)
DIMENSIONS OF AUDITORIUM: Distance between side walls
of auditorium, 50ft; Distance stage to back wall of
auditorium, 120ft; Capacity of orchestra pit, 10
SEATING (3 levels)
MAJOR TYPES OF ENTERTAINMENT: Drama, musical comedy, opera,
vaudeville, movies

MAJOR STARS WHO APPEARED AT THEATRE: Mr. and Mrs. E. L.
    Davenport
ADDITIONAL INFORMATION: The building was almost totally
    destroyed by fire in 1930. Only the street level and
    mezzanine remain. Very little of the opera house is
    intact.

Easton, PA

CASINO, Northeast corner, Centre Square
    OPENING DATE: August 1908   OPENING SHOW: Vaudeville bill
    TYPE OF BUILDING: Commercial   FACADE: Clapboard
    TYPE OF THEATRE: (c)   DEGREE OF RESTORATION: (c)
    CLOSING DATE: Summer 1909   CURRENT USE: Vacant store
    MAJOR TYPES OF ENTERTAINMENT: Vaudeville
    MAJOR STARS WHO APPEARED AT THEATRE: The Four Nightingales,
        Janie O'Reiley, Groucho, Harpo, and Gummo Marx
    ADDITIONAL INFORMATION: The Casino was converted from a
        bowling alley in the Arcade Building.

Easton, PA

ODD FELLOWS HALL (other name: Masonic Hall), 44 South 3rd
        Street
    OPENING DATE: March 30, 1848   OPENING SHOW: The Argus
    STYLE OF ARCHITECTURE: Victorian   TYPE OF BUILDING:
        Commercial   FACADE: Grey stone and masonry
    TYPE OF THEATRE: (b)   DEGREE OF RESTORATION: (c)
    CLOSING DATE: 1871   CURRENT USE: Store and warehouse
    MAJOR TYPES OF ENTERTAINMENT: Drama, vaudeville, burlesque,
        local variety
    MAJOR STARS WHO APPEARED AT THEATRE: J. H. Powell Company,
        The Wallace Sisters, Washburn's Great Moral Show

Easton, PA

STATE THEATRE (other name: Neumeyer Theatre),
        453 Northampton Street
    OPENING DATE: August 10, 1910
    OPENING SHOW: Vaudeville bill
    STYLE OF ARCHITECTURE: Beaux Arts   TYPE OF BUILDING: Bank
    FACADE: Grey rough-faced granite   TYPE OF THEATRE: (a)
    DEGREE OF RESTORATION: (b)   CURRENT USE: Theatre
    LOCATION OF AUDITORIUM: Ground floor
    STAGE DIMENSIONS AND EQUIPMENT: Trap doors, 1; Scenery
        storage rooms (in basement); Dressing rooms, 12 (3 floors
        on each side of stage)
    DIMENSIONS OF AUDITORIUM: Distance between side walls
        of auditorium, 85ft; Distance stage to back wall of
        auditorium, 100ft; Orchestra pit, yes
    SEATING (3 levels)
    MAJOR TYPES OF ENTERTAINMENT: Vaudeville
    ADDITIONAL INFORMATION: In 1926, the theatre was enlarged,

the name was changed to the State, and it became part
of the Keith circuit.

Gettysburg, PA

OPERA HOUSE (other name: McClellan's Opera House),
    Northeast quadrant, Lincoln Square
    OPENING DATE: January 20, 1880
    OPENING SHOW: A "Musical and Dramatic Entertainment"
    TYPE OF BUILDING: Commercial   FACADE: Brick
    TYPE OF THEATRE: (b)   CLOSING DATE: Early 1890s
    CURRENT USE: Apartments
    LOCATION OF AUDITORIUM: Upper floors
    SEATING (2 levels)
    MAJOR TYPES OF ENTERTAINMENT: Drama, musical comedy, opera,
    minstrel shows, concerts, lectures, local variety shows,
    civic functions

Honesdale, PA

CAPITOL THEATRE (other name: Lyric Theatre), 1050 Main Street
    OPENING DATE: December 30, 1907
    OPENING SHOW: The Lion and the Mouse
    FACADE: Brick   TYPE OF THEATRE: (a)   DEGREE OF
    RESTORATION: (c)   CURRENT USE: Movie theatre
    LOCATION OF AUDITORIUM: Ground floor
    SEATING (2 levels)
    MAJOR TYPES OF ENTERTAINMENT: Drama, vaudeville, burlesque,
    movies, civic functions
    ADDITIONAL INFORMATION: The theatre was gutted by fire in
    1961. The theatre was rebuilt within the exterior walls,
    but without the balcony.

Honesdale, PA

LIBERTY HALL (other name: Masonic Hall), Corner of 9th
    and Main Streets
    OPENING DATE: 1860
    TYPE OF BUILDING: Lodge, offices   FACADE: Brick
    TYPE OF THEATRE: (b)   DEGREE OF RESTORATION: (d)
    CLOSING DATE: c. 1875   CURRENT USE: Lodge, offices
    MAJOR TYPES OF ENTERTAINMENT: Drama, vaudeville, burlesque,
    opera, boxing matches, wrestling matches, political
    rallies
    ADDITIONAL INFORMATION: The building was originally two
    stories tall, but a third story was added later. It was
    named Liberty Hall when rallies for the Union Cause were
    held there during the Civil War.

Jim Thorpe, PA

MAUCH CHUNK OPERA HOUSE (other name: Capitol Theatre),
    14 West Broadway
    OPENING DATE: August 10, 1881
    OPENING SHOW: Edgewood Folks
    ARCHITECT: Addison Hutton   STYLE OF ARCHITECTURE:
    Italianate   FACADE: Yellow brick
    TYPE OF THEATRE: (b)   DEGREE OF RESTORATION: (b)
    CURRENT USE: Being renovated
    MAJOR TYPES OF ENTERTAINMENT: Drama, musical comedy,
    vaudeville, concerts, lectures, opera

Lancaster, PA

FULTON OPERA HOUSE, (other name: Fulton Hall),
    12 North Prince Street
    OPENING DATE: 1852   OPENING SHOW: Concert by Ole Bull
    ARCHITECT: Samuel Sloan   FACADE: Brick
    TYPE OF THEATRE: (a)   DEGREE OF RESTORATION: (d)
    CURRENT USE: Theatre
    LOCATION OF AUDITORIUM: Ground floor
    STAGE DIMENSIONS AND EQUIPMENT: Height and width of
    proscenium, 28ft x 33ft; Shape of proscenium arch,
    arched; Distance from edge of stage to back wall of
    stage, 44ft 6in; Distance from edge of stage to curtain
    line, 3ft 6in; Distance between side walls of stage,
    53ft; Depth under stage, 7ft; Trap doors, 3; Scenery
    storage rooms, 1 (scene dock off stage left); Dressing
    rooms, 6 (under stage)
    DIMENSIONS OF AUDITORIUM: Distance between side walls
    of auditorium, 53ft; Capacity of orchestra pit, 15
    SEATING (2 levels): 1st level, 528; 2nd level, 381
    SHAPE OF THE AUDITORIUM: Rectangular
    MAJOR TYPES OF ENTERTAINMENT: Drama, musical comedy,
    vaudeville, concerts, dance, lectures
    MAJOR STARS WHO APPEARED AT THEATRE: Maude Adams, Viola
    Allen, Mary Anderson, Lawrence Barrett, the Barrymores,
    Bernhardt, Edwin Booth, J. B. Booth II, Billie Burke,
    Francis X. Bushman, Marie Cahill, George M. Cohan, Jane
    Cowl, Fanny Davenport, Mrs. John Drew, John Drew, Isadora
    Duncan, Douglas Fairbanks, William Faversham, Lew Fields,
    Mrs. Fiske, W. C. Fields, Eddie Foy, William Gillette,
    Edward Harrigan, W. S. Hart, Anna Held, De Wolf Hopper,
    Fanny Janauschek, Joseph Jefferson, Al Jolson, Lillie
    Langtry, Harry Lauder, Alfred Lunt, Robert B. Mantell,
    Julia Marlowe, Frank Mayo, Helena Modjeska, Marilyn
    Miller, Clara Morris, Nazimova, James O'Neill, Olga
    Nethersole, Pavlova, Blanche Ring, Lillian Russell,
    Fritzi Scheff, Otis Skinner, E. A. Sothern, Fred Stone,
    E. H. Sothern, John Phillip Sousa, Frances Starr, Eva
    Tanguay, Spencer Tracy, Mark Twain, Sophie Tucker, David
    Warfield, and others

`

Lock Haven, PA

OPERA HOUSE, 201-211 East Main Street
    OPENING DATE: November 1869
    ARCHITECT: Patrick Keefe   STYLE OF ARCHITECTURE:
      Italianate   TYPE OF BUILDING: Storerooms, meeting hall
    FACADE: Brick, now painted gray   TYPE OF THEATRE: (b)
    DEGREE OF RESTORATION: (c)   CURRENT USE: Apartments
    LOCATION OF AUDITORIUM: Second floor
    STAGE DIMENSIONS AND EQUIPMENT: * Height and width of
      proscenium, 28ft x 28ft; Distance from edge of stage
      to back wall of stage, 28ft; Distance from edge of
      stage to curtain line, 5ft; Distance between side walls
      of stage, 48ft; Depth under stage, 4ft; Trap doors, 3
    DIMENSIONS OF AUDITORIUM: Distance between side walls
      of auditorium, 50ft; Distance stage to back wall of
      auditorium, 100ft
    MAJOR TYPES OF ENTERTAINMENT: Drama, opera, lectures
    MAJOR STARS WHO APPEARED AT THEATRE: Mark Twain and others
    ADDITIONAL INFORMATION: The opera house shared the building
      with stores on the first floor and a meeting room on the
      third. Gas jets were added to the facade of the building
      in 1871, allowing the "OPERA HOUSE" sign to be lit on
      nights when a show was being presented.

Meadville, PA

ACADEMY (other name: Academy of Music), 275 Chestnut Street
    OPENING DATE: December 15, 1885
    OPENING SHOW: Francesca da Rimini with Lawrence Barrett
    ARCHITECT: J. M. Wood   FACADE: Philadelphia pressed brick
    TYPE OF THEATRE: (a)   DEGREE OF RESTORATION: (d)
    CURRENT USE: Movie theatre
    LOCATION OF AUDITORIUM: Ground floor
    STAGE DIMENSIONS AND EQUIPMENT: * Height and width
      of proscenium, 26ft x 28ft; Shape of proscenium
      arch, arched; Distance from edge of stage to back
      wall of stage, 33ft; Distance from edge of stage to
      curtain line, 3ft; Distance between side walls of
      stage, 52ft; Depth under stage, 7ft; Trap doors, 3;
      Dressing rooms, 9
    SEATING (3 levels): 1st level, 405; 2nd level, 200;
      3rd level, 240
    MAJOR TYPES OF ENTERTAINMENT: Drama, musical comedy,
      vaudeville, burlesque, opera, concerts, lectures,
      minstrel shows, movies, and "spectacular pieces"
    MAJOR STARS WHO APPEARED AT THEATRE: Margaret Mather,
      Richard Mansfield (1886), James O'Neill, Frederick
      Warde (1886), Fanny Davenport (1885), William Gillette
      (1886), Adelaide Moore (1886), Kate Claxton (1886),
      Haverly's Minstrels, Gus Williams, Effie Ellsler,
      Pat Rooney, Frank Mayo, Mrs. Fiske, Henrietta Crosman,
      E. H. Sothern, Julia Marlowe, Robert B. Mantell,
      John L. Sullivan, James J. Corbett

ADDITIONAL INFORMATION: The Academy was built to
  replace an earlier theatre, the Opera House, which
  had been destroyed by fire. The Academy also suffered
  fire damage in 1985 which resulted from a short circuit
  during electrical repair work.

Mount Gretna, PA

MOUNT GRETNA CHAUTAUQUA PLAYHOUSE (other name: Penn'a
  Chautauqua Auditorium)
  OPENING DATE: 1892
  ARCHITECT: John Cilley   TYPE OF THEATRE: (a)
  DEGREE OF RESTORATION: (d)   CURRENT USE: Theatre
  MAJOR TYPES OF ENTERTAINMENT: Drama, concerts
  MAJOR STARS WHO APPEARED AT THEATRE: Charlton Heston,
    Lionel Hampton, Dave Brubeck, George Shearing
  ADDITIONAL INFORMATION: The building was the original
    Assembly Auditorium of the Pennsylvania Chautauqua
    patterned after the Chautauqua in New York State. It
    consists of 26 wooden trusses "resting on their outer
    ends on chestnut posts and meeting at the roof apex.
    Outward thrust loads are contained by iron rods which
    meet at a collector ring in the center" (from the
    questionnaire). The building has been used as a theatre
    since 1925 and hosts a Shaw Festival, classical and jazz
    concerts and Sunday worship services.

Philadelphia, PA

ACADEMY OF MUSIC OF PHILADELPHIA, INC. (other name: American
  Academy of Music), Broad and Locust Streets
  OPENING DATE: January 26, 1857
  OPENING SHOW: Il Trovatore
  ARCHITECTS: Napoleon LeBrun and Gustav Runge
  STYLE OF ARCHITECTURE: Italian Byzantine   FACADE:
    Brick and sandstone   TYPE OF THEATRE: (a)
  DEGREE OF RESTORATION: (a)   CURRENT USE: Live performance
  LOCATION OF AUDITORIUM: Ground floor
  STAGE DIMENSIONS AND EQUIPMENT: Height and width of
    proscenium, 34ft x 48ft; Shape of proscenium arch,
    arched; Distance from edge of stage to back wall of
    stage, 70ft; Distance from edge of stage to curtain line,
    3ft; Distance between side walls of stage, 90ft; Distance
    from stage floor to fly loft, 34ft; Depth under stage,
    15ft; Stage floor, raked; Trap doors, 0; Scenery storage
    rooms, 2 (stage right and rear of stage); Dressing rooms,
    16 (3 floors, stage right; 2 floors, stage left)
  DIMENSIONS OF AUDITORIUM: Distance between side walls
    of auditorium, 90ft; Distance stage to back wall of
    auditorium, 102ft; Capacity of orchestra pit, 60
  SEATING (4 levels): 1st level, 1,307; 2nd level, 524;
    3rd level, 561; 4th level, 529
  SHAPE OF THE AUDITORIUM: Horseshoe-shaped
  MAJOR TYPES OF ENTERTAINMENT: Opera, concerts (symphony,

instrumental, vocal, jazz, rock), minstrel shows, dance, balls, magic lantern shows, movies, lectures, cattle shows, political events

MAJOR STARS WHO APPEARED AT THEATRE: Marcella Sembrich, Melba, Caruso, Adelina Patti, Christine Nilsson, Pasqualino Brignoli, Fritzi Scheff, Luciano Pavarotti, Anna Louise Cary, Leopold Stokowski, Italo Campanini, Jeanette MacDonald, Anton Rubinstein, Gustav Mahler, Tchaikovsky, Richard Strauss, Victor Herbert, Fritz Kreisler, Rachmaninoff, Toscanini, Duke Ellington, Cab Calloway, Alfred Lunt, Lynn Fontanne, Helen Hayes, Jascha Heifetz, Abbott and Costello, Paul Robeson, and others

ADDITIONAL INFORMATION: The hall, called "The Grand Old Lady of Locust Street," is renowned for its superb acoustics. It continues as a "hemp" house. During World War II, the theatre housed the Stage Door Canteen which featured such stars as Frank Sinatra, Lunt and Fontanne, Hedy Lamarr, Irene Castle and many of the great bands of the era. The hall was used for the recording of the soundtrack of Walt Disney's Fantasia and a football game was once played on the orchestra floor. Now the home of the Philadelphia Orchestra.

Philadelphia, PA

GIRARD AVENUE THEATRE, 625 Girard Avenue
OPENING DATE: March 30, 1891
OPENING SHOW: The Dead Heart with James O'Neill
FACADE: Brick   TYPE OF THEATRE: (a)
DEGREE OF RESTORATION: (c)   CURRENT USE: Supermarket
STAGE DIMENSIONS AND EQUIPMENT: * Height and width of proscenium, 30ft x 35ft; Distance from edge of stage to back wall of stage, 30ft; Distance from edge of stage to curtain line, 2ft; Distance between side walls of stage, 71ft; Depth under stage, 10ft; Dressing rooms, 11
SHAPE OF THE AUDITORIUM: Semi-circular
MAJOR TYPES OF ENTERTAINMENT: Drama, opera, movies
MAJOR STARS WHO APPEARED AT THEATRE: Mrs. John Drew, Amelia Bingham, Margaret Dale, James O'Neill

Philadelphia, PA

METROPOLITAN OPERA HOUSE (other names: Philadelphia Opera House, The Met), North Broad and Poplar Streets
OPENING DATE: November 17, 1908   OPENING SHOW: Carmen
ARCHITECT: W. H. McElfatrick   STYLE OF ARCHITECTURE: Neo-Classical   FACADE: Cream-colored brick and stone
TYPE OF THEATRE: (a)   DEGREE OF RESTORATION: (c)
CURRENT USE: Church   LOCATION OF AUDITORIUM: Ground floor
STAGE DIMENSIONS AND EQUIPMENT: Height and width of proscenium, 40ft x 51ft 3in; Distance from edge of stage to back wall of stage, 66ft 5in; Distance from edge of stage to curtain line, 5ft; Distance between side walls

of stage, 116ft; Depth under stage, 12ft; Dressing
    rooms, 20
DIMENSIONS OF AUDITORIUM: Distance between side walls
    of auditorium, 120ft; Distance stage to back wall of
    auditorium, 150ft; Capacity of orchestra pit, 160
SEATING: 1st level, 726; 2nd level, 616; 3rd level,
    904; 4th level, 750; Boxes, 486
SHAPE OF THE AUDITORIUM: U-shaped
MAJOR TYPES OF ENTERTAINMENT: Drama, musical comedy,
    vaudeville, opera, concerts, ballroom dancing,
    movies, boxing, basketball
MAJOR STARS WHO APPEARED AT THEATRE: Pavlova, Ballet
    Russe, Harry Lauder (1911, 1913), Weber and Fields
    (1912), Lillian Russell (1912), De Wolf Hopper, John
    Phillip Sousa (1916), Bernhardt (1916), Laurette Taylor
    (1918), George M. Cohan (1918), Tetrazinni, Mrs. Fiske
    (1918), Ed Wynn, Mae Desmond, Will Rogers (1927), Isadora
    Duncan (1929), George Arliss, and others
ADDITIONAL INFORMATION: In 1926, Max Reinhardt presented
    The Miracle at the theatre and George White's Scandals
    appeared there in 1935. The Metropolitan Opera House was
    built and opened by impresario Oscar Hammerstein, who
    had already ventured into grand opera with the opening
    of the Manhattan Opera House in New York. Bricks from
    the Harrah mansion, which had previously occupied the
    site of the theatre, went into the construction of the
    Metropolitan Opera House which boasted not only superb
    acoustics, but excellent sightlines from each seat. The
    theatre, which at one time boasted a mammoth Moller
    organ, was damaged by fire in 1948. All dimensions and
    seating capacity are from the Theatre Collection at the
    Philadelphia Free Library and an article, "The Metropol-
    itan Opera House - Philadelphia," Marquee, Third Quarter
    1979 by Irvin R. Glazer.

Philadelphia, PA

OLD MUSICAL FUND HALL (other names: Musical Fund Society
    Hall, Musical Fund Hall), 810 Locust Street
OPENING DATE: June 16, 1824
OPENING SHOW: Concert, Marie Malibran
ARCHITECT: William Strickland
STYLE OF ARCHITECTURE: Eclectic, Greek Revival influence
FACADE: Tan brick   DEGREE OF RESTORATION: (c)
CURRENT USE: Facade fronts condominium
MAJOR TYPES OF ENTERTAINMENT: Opera, concerts, lectures,
    dances, political events, boxing matches
MAJOR STARS WHO APPEARED AT THEATRE: Jenny Lind, Adelina
    Patti, Ole Bull, Henry Ward Beecher, William Makepeace
    Thackeray, 1856 Republican Convention
ADDITIONAL INFORMATION: When Musical Fund Hall was
    erected, it was designed to be a church, but was sold
    to the Musical Fund Society instead and converted into a
    concert hall. The auditorium was described as "a marvel

of acoustics."   In 1847, the facade was remodeled by
Napoleon LeBrun and in 1891 the building was renovated
and a Victorian look achieved.   Use of the hall dimin-
ished after the opening of the Academy of Music.   Today
only the facade remains.   The remainder of the building
was demolished and a condominium erected in its place.
The facade fronts the condominium.   For further information, see Irvin R. Glazer, Philadelphia Theatres, A-Z:
A   Comprehensive,   Descriptive Record of 813 Theatres
Constructed Since 1724 (Westport, CT: Greenwood Press,
1984).

Philadelphia, PA

TROCADERO THEATRE (other names: See ADDITIONAL INFORMATION),
   1003-1005 Arch Street (10th and Arch)
   OPENING DATE: August 29, 1870
   OPENING SHOW: Simmons and Slocum's Minstrels
   ARCHITECT: Edwin F. Durang   FACADE: Brick
   TYPE OF THEATRE: (a)   DEGREE OF RESTORATION: (d)
   CURRENT USE: Disco   LOCATION OF AUDITORIUM: Ground floor
   STAGE DIMENSIONS AND EQUIPMENT: * Height and width of
   proscenium, 33ft x 33ft; Distance from edge of stage to
   back wall of stage, 33ft; Distance from edge of stage to
   curtain line, 5ft; Distance between side walls of stage,
   60ft; Dressing rooms, 8
   DIMENSIONS OF AUDITORIUM: Distance between side walls
   of auditorium, 48ft; Distance stage to back wall of
   auditorium, 170ft
   SEATING (3 levels): 1st level, 509; 2nd level, 297;
   3rd level, 350, boxes, 52
   SHAPE OF THE AUDITORIUM: Horseshoe-shaped
   MAJOR TYPES OF ENTERTAINMENT: Drama, burlesque, minstrel
   shows, movies
   MAJOR STARS WHO APPEARED AT THEATRE: Sally Rand, Georgia
   Southern, Ann Corio, Agnes Booth, John Drew, Ada Rehan,
   Harrigan and Hart, Lotta Crabtree, Pat Rooney, Weber
   and Fields
   ADDITIONAL INFORMATION: The theatre was variously known as
   Sweatman's Arch Street Opera House, the Arch Street Opera
   House, The Park, The Continental, The Casino, and "The
   Troc."

Philadelphia, PA

WALNUT STREET THEATRE (other names: The New Circus, Olympic,
   American), 9th and Walnut Streets
   OPENING DATE: February 2, 1809
   OPENING SHOW: Equestrian exhibition
   ARCHITECT: John Haviland (1828 Renovation)   STYLE OF
   ARCHITECTURE: Neo-Classical   FACADE: White marble,
   cement TYPE OF THEATRE: (a)   DEGREE OF RESTORATION: (a)
   CURRENT USE: Theatre   LOCATION OF AUDITORIUM: Ground floor
   STAGE DIMENSIONS AND EQUIPMENT: Height and width of

proscenium, 24ft x 38ft; Shape of proscenium arch,
arched; Distance from edge of stage to back wall of
stage, 41ft; Distance between side walls of stage,
60ft 6in; Distance from stage floor to fly loft, 28ft;
Depth under stage, 10ft 4in; Stage floor, flat; Trap
doors, 26; Scenery storage rooms, 1 (953 Front Street);
Dressing rooms, 12 (3 levels behind stage)
DIMENSIONS OF AUDITORIUM: Capacity of orchestra pit, 40
SEATING (2 levels): 1st level, 558; 2nd level, 494
MAJOR TYPES OF ENTERTAINMENT: Drama, musical comedy,
vaudeville, burlesque, minstrel shows, dance, concerts,
lectures, opera, circus, movies
MAJOR STARS WHO APPEARED AT THEATRE: Edwin Forrest (his
stage debut), Mrs. John Drew, Edwin Booth, Joseph
Jefferson, Chauncey Olcott, J. S. Clarke, Charlotte
Cushman, Bernhardt, the Barrymores, George M. Cohan,
Fanny Janauschek, George Arliss, the Marx Brothers,
Edmund Kean, Rachel, Junius Brutus Booth, Robert
Mantell, Nat Goodwin, Lillie Langtry, Julia Marlowe,
Helena Modjeska, Mrs. Fiske, Otis Skinner, Richard
Mansfield, Walter Hampden, Helen Hayes, and others
ADDITIONAL INFORMATION: The Walnut Street Theatre is
"the oldest theatre in continuous operation in the
English-speaking world." It opened as the New Circus,
with the first play, **The Rivals**, being presented in
1812. The facade has been restored based upon the 1828
John Haviland reconstruction and the interior has been
modernized.   The theatre now houses the Walnut Street
Theatre Company.

Phoenixville, PA

COLONIAL THEATRE, 227 Bridge Street
OPENING DATE: September 5, 1903
OPENING SHOW: **The Beauty Doctor**
STYLE OF ARCHITECTURE: Empire   FACADE: Stone
TYPE OF THEATRE: (a)   DEGREE OF RESTORATION: (b)
CURRENT USE: Theatre
LOCATION OF AUDITORIUM: Ground floor
STAGE DIMENSIONS AND EQUIPMENT: Height and width of
proscenium, 29ft x 34ft 6in; Shape of proscenium arch,
rectangular; Distance from edge of stage to back wall of
stage, 26ft; Distance between side walls of stage, 55ft;
Depth under stage, 8ft; Stage floor, flat; Trap doors, 1;
Scenery storage rooms, 0; Dressing rooms, 6 (under stage)
DIMENSIONS OF AUDITORIUM: Distance between side walls
of auditorium, 55ft; Capacity of orchestra pit, 15
SEATING (3 levels): 1st level, 524; 2nd level, 92;
3rd level, 113
SHAPE OF THE AUDITORIUM: Rectangular with horseshoe-shaped
balcony
MAJOR TYPES OF ENTERTAINMENT: Drama, musical comedy,
vaudeville, revues, movies, magic shows, concerts,
minstrel shows
MAJOR STARS WHO APPEARED AT THEATRE: Fred E. Wright,

Adelaide Thurston, Henry Horton, Thurston, the
Magician, Houdini
ADDITIONAL INFORMATION: The theatre now houses the
Chester County Center for the Performing Arts and
presents movies daily and a monthly vaudeville show.
The stage shows contain a silent film and are accompanied by the theatre's prize possession, a 25-rank,
Kimball theater organ. The organ, which was twice
damaged and restored, once played at the State Theatre
in Philadelphia. The organ rests on an elevator in the
pit and can be raised and lowered for performances. At
present, a 31-rank Kimball awaits installation and there
are plans to present concerts with the two organs playing
simultaneously.

Reading, PA

RAJAH THEATRE (other name: New Academy of Music), 136
    North 6th Street
  OPENING DATE: October 1886
  OPENING SHOW: L'Article 47
  STYLE OF ARCHITECTURE: Middle Eastern   TYPE OF
  THEATRE: (a)   LOCATION OF AUDITORIUM: Ground floor
  STAGE DIMENSIONS AND EQUIPMENT: Height and width of
    proscenium, 30ft x 45ft; Distance from edge of stage
    to back wall of stage, 32ft 8in; Distance from edge of
    stage to curtain line, 2ft; Distance between side walls
    of stage, 74ft; Dressing rooms, 15
  SEATING: 1st level, 1,147; 2nd level, 186;
    3rd level, 708; boxes, 42
  MAJOR TYPES OF ENTERTAINMENT: Drama, musical comedy,
    concerts, opera, dance, movies

Ridgway, PA

RIDGWAY OPERA HOUSE, Main Street
  OPENING DATE: April 20, 1897   OPENING SHOW: A Texas Steer
  ARCHITECTS: Walter P. Murphy and H. C. Park
  TYPE OF THEATRE: (a)   DEGREE OF RESTORATION: (c)
  CURRENT USE: Store   LOCATION OF AUDITORIUM: Ground floor
  STAGE DIMENSIONS AND EQUIPMENT: Height and width of
    proscenium, 27ft x 33ft 6in; Distance from edge of
    stage to back wall of stage, 41ft; Distance from edge
    of stage to curtain line, 4ft; Distance between side
    walls of stage, 64ft 6in; Distance from stage floor to
    fly loft, 25ft; Depth under stage, 10ft; Trap doors, 6;
    Scenery storage rooms, 2 (1 each side of the stage);
    Dressing rooms, 12 (in basement)
  SEATING (2 levels)
  MAJOR TYPES OF ENTERTAINMENT: Drama, musical comedy, opera,
    operettas, concerts
  ADDITIONAL INFORMATION: For the grand opening, special
    trains were scheduled from neighboring towns. Original
    equipment in the theatre included 26 drops and a $1,500

Chickering piano. The opera house was the victim of
arson in 1905, requiring the structure be rebuilt.
The rebuilt Opera House reopened on October 5, 1906
with William A. Brady's The Pit.

Scranton, PA

THE POLI (other names: The Ritz, Comerford, Ritz Cinema),
    220 Wyoming Avenue
  OPENING DATE: 1906
  STYLE OF ARCHITECTURE: Victorian with Greek motif
  TYPE OF BUILDING: Commercial   FACADE: Gray stone
  TYPE OF THEATRE: (a)   DEGREE OF RESTORATION: (d)
  CURRENT USE: Movie theatre
  LOCATION OF AUDITORIUM: Ground floor
  MAJOR TYPES OF ENTERTAINMENT: Drama, musical comedy,
    opera, vaudeville, movies
  MAJOR STARS WHO APPEARED AT THEATRE: Joan Crawford, Eddie
    Leonard, James O'Neill, Amadeo Baldi
  ADDITIONAL INFORMATION: Initially opened and operated by
    S. Z. Poli, the theatre was sold in 1925 and was renamed
    the Comerford. In 1930, it was acquired by the Publix-
    Paramount Corporation and renamed the Ritz. Today, in
    a drasticallly altered condition, it is part of a mall.

Towanda, PA

HALE'S OPERA HOUSE (other name: Keystone Theatre),
    Corner of Main and Washington Streets
  OPENING DATE: September 1, 1887
  OPENING SHOW: Queen Elizabeth   FACADE: Red brick
  TYPE OF THEATRE: (a)   DEGREE OF RESTORATION: (a)
  CURRENT USE: Movie theatre
  LOCATION OF AUDITORIUM: Ground floor
  MAJOR TYPES OF ENTERTAINMENT: Drama, musical comedy,
    minstrel shows, concerts, local variety shows, civic
    functions
  MAJOR STARS WHO APPEARED AT THEATRE: Frank Mayo, Fanny
    and Harry Davenport, Edna Wallace Hopper, Lou Telegen,
    Blanche Ring, Blackstone (the Magician), May Robson,
    Robert Mantell, Helena Modjeska, John L. Sullivan
  ADDITIONAL INFORMATION: When Hale's Opera House opened,
    the theatre was on the second floor and was reached by
    climbing a wide flight of stairs. When the building was
    converted into a movie theatre in 1913, the theatre was
    moved downstairs. At this time, a pipe organ (no details
    available) was installed.

Warren, PA

LIBRARY THEATRE (other names: Library Hall, Struthers Library
    Theatre), 302 Third Avenue West
  OPENING DATE: December 3, 1883   OPENING SHOW: Iolanthe

ARCHITECT: D. K. Dean   TYPE OF BUILDING: Commercial
FACADE: Red brick   TYPE OF THEATRE: (b)   DEGREE OF
RESTORATION: (a)   CURRENT USE: Performing arts center
LOCATION OF AUDITORIUM: Ground floor
STAGE DIMENSIONS AND EQUIPMENT: Height and width of
  proscenium, 27ft x 34ft; Shape of proscenium arch,
  arched; Distance from edge of stage to back wall of
  stage, 27ft; Distance from edge of stage to curtain
  line, 4ft; Distance between side walls of stage, 69ft;
  Depth under stage, 7ft; Stage floor, raked; Trap doors,
  0; Scenery storage rooms, 1 (dressing room wing to rear);
  Dressing rooms, 7 (in addition at rear of building)
DIMENSIONS OF AUDITORIUM: Distance between side walls
  of auditorium, 64ft; Distance stage to back wall
  of auditorium, 82ft; Capacity of orchestra pit, 20
SEATING (2 levels): 1st level, 581; 2nd level, 414
SHAPE OF THE AUDITORIUM: Rectangular
MAJOR TYPES OF ENTERTAINMENT: Drama, musical comedy,
  vaudeville, opera, minstrel shows, magic shows,
  concerts, lectures, dance, movies, civic functions
MAJOR STARS WHO APPEARED AT THEATRE: Lew Dockstader's
  Minstrels, Otis Skinner, John Phillip Sousa, Victor
  Herbert, Cecil B. DeMille, Harry Lauder, Helena
  Modjeska, George Arliss, Mrs. Fiske, Tyrone Power,
  Sr., Irene Castle, Geraldine Farrar, Francis X.
  Bushman, Duke Ellington, and others
ADDITIONAL INFORMATION: The library building which contains
  the Library Theatre was donated to the town of Warren by
  industrialist, Thomas Struthers. The theatre was totally
  renovated in 1919 at a cost of $80,000, equipment for
  "any type of entertainment" was added, and an addition
  at the rear of the building provided more new dressing
  rooms. The grand reopening was held November 10, 1919
  and featured musical selections by the theatre orchestra
  and the play, My Lady Friends.   Ten years later, the
  theatre was converted to movies and continued to show
  films until September 1980. During recent renovation
  (begun in 1981), velvet drapes, ruffled curtains, a
  vaudeville drop, and original scenery were discovered.
  A silk curtain also remains. The building is held in
  trust by a seven-member citizens board.

Warren, PA

ROSCOE HALL, 416 Pennsylvania Avenue West
  OPENING DATE: February 3, 1869
  OPENING SHOW: Fireman's Ball to celebrate opening
  TYPE OF BUILDING: Commercial   FACADE: Dark red brick
  TYPE OF THEATRE: (b)   DEGREE OF RESTORATION: (c)
  CLOSING DATE: c. 1885   CURRENT USE: Club rooms for Sons
  of Italy   LOCATION OF AUDITORIUM: Third floor
STAGE DIMENSIONS AND EQUIPMENT: Width of proscenium, 30ft;
  Distance from edge of stage to back wall of stage, 15ft;
  Distance between side walls of stage, 50ft
DIMENSIONS OF AUDITORIUM: Distance between side walls
  of auditorium, 50ft; Distance stage to back wall of

auditorium, 65ft; Orchestra pit, none
SEATING (2 levels)
SHAPE OF THE AUDITORIUM: Rectangular
MAJOR TYPES OF ENTERTAINMENT: Drama, musical comedy,
   minstrel shows, concerts, lectures, civic functions
MAJOR STARS WHO APPEARED AT THEATRE: Blind Tom
ADDITIONAL INFORMATION: When the theatre opened, it was
   equipped with "scenery and a drop curtain ornamented
   with an imaginative painting in which the Rocky Mountains and the Allegheny River, Indians and raftsmen
   were curiously mingled." The first drama of record,
   The Amateur Millionaire, or What Came of an Oil Strike
   with an afterpiece (School for Scamps) was presented
   on April 15, 1869. During the 1880s, the hall fell
   into disrepute and was seldom used as a theatre after
   1883. It was variously used as a National Guard Armory,
   a roller skating rink and a clubhouse.

Williamsport, PA

ULMAN OPERA HOUSE, 2 East Third Street
OPENING DATE: May 4, 1868   OPENING SHOW: Lady of Lyons
TYPE OF BUILDING: Office building   FACADE: Red brick
TYPE OF THEATRE: (b)   DEGREE OF RESTORATION: (a)
CLOSING DATE: 1874   CURRENT USE: Apartments
LOCATION OF AUDITORIUM: Second and third floors
MAJOR TYPES OF ENTERTAINMENT: Drama, vaudeville
MAJOR STARS WHO APPEARED AT THEATRE: Frank Mordaunt,
   Annie Waite, Chestnut Street Company
ADDITIONAL INFORMATION: Built in 1868 in a then-thriving
   lumber center, the Ulman Opera House likewise prospered
   until a newer theatre, the Academy of Music, was opened
   in 1870. After several years of competing with the
   Academy, the Ulman Opera House closed in 1874. The
   building is currently owned by Founders Federal Savings
   and Loan Assn., but it is reported that it soon will be
   sold.

Rhode Island

NEWPORT CASINO THEATRE (other name: Van Alen Casino Theatre),
194 Bellevue Avenue
OPENING DATE: August 1880
ARCHITECTS: McKim, Mead and White   STYLE OF
ARCHITECTURE: Shingle Victorian   TYPE OF BUILDING:
Gentlemen's club   FACADE: Wood; wood shingle
TYPE OF THEATRE: (b)   DEGREE OF RESTORATION: (d)
CURRENT USE: Performances
LOCATION OF AUDITORIUM: Ground floor
STAGE DIMENSIONS AND EQUIPMENT: Height and width of
proscenium, 26ft x 30ft; Shape of proscenium arch,
arched; Distance from edge of stage to back wall of
stage, 26ft; Distance from edge of stage to curtain
line, 3ft 6in; Distance between side walls of stage,
60ft; Depth under stage, 15ft; Stage floor, raked;
Trap doors, 0; Scenery storage rooms, 1 (rear of
stage); Dressing rooms, 8 (rear of stage, upstairs
and downstairs)
DIMENSIONS OF AUDITORIUM: Distance between side walls
of auditorium, 42ft; Distance stage to back wall of
auditorium, 60ft; Capacity of orchestra pit, 30
SEATING: 1st level, 306; 2nd level, 60; boxes, 44
SHAPE OF THE AUDITORIUM: Rectangular
MAJOR TYPES OF ENTERTAINMENT: Drama, musical comedy,
opera, dance, concerts, lectures, balls
MAJOR STARS WHO APPEARED AT THEATRE: Oscar Wilde, Tallulah
Bankhead, Danilova, Basil Rathbone, Will Rogers, Estelle
Taylor, Charlton Heston, Joan Blondell
ADDITIONAL INFORMATION: The theatre was erected as an
adjunct to the Casino. With the advent of World War I,
the theatre closed. In 1927, it reopened as a theatre
festival and for eight summers it attracted the "most
famous of American actors and actresses to its stage."
It closed again during the depression, but later reopened
for touring summer companies and it continued in this way
until 1959. Four years later, the property was converted

into the Tennis Hall of Fame, and in 1966 the Newport
Players Guild leased the theatre for use as a performing
arts center. Under their auspices, the theatre presently
houses plays, a children's theatre series, films, workshops and benefit productions. The theatre is furnished
with modern equipment.

Providence, RI

SHAKESPEARE HALL (other name: Sprague-Knight Building),
   128 Dorrance Street
  OPENING DATE: October 29, 1838
  OPENING SHOW: A Soldier's Daughter and A Pleasant Neighbor
  ARCHITECT: James Bucklin   STYLE OF ARCHITECTURE:
   Greek Revival (originally)   FACADE: Stucco
  TYPE OF THEATRE: (a)   DEGREE OF RESTORATION: (d)
  CLOSING DATE: 1844   CURRENT USE: Commercial
  LOCATION OF AUDITORIUM: Ground floor
  MAJOR TYPES OF ENTERTAINMENT: Drama
  ADDITIONAL INFORMATION: The opening performance
   at Shakespeare Hall (on October 29, 1838) was
   enthusiastically received, according to the records,
   and was preceded by "an elegant prologue" written by
   Providence's premier poetess, Sarah Helen Whitman.
   The theatre's success was shortlived, however, despite
   appearances by well-known actors of the period. Under
   attack by one of its neighbors, the Second Baptist
   Church, Shakespeare Hall closed in 1844. Later in the
   same year, the building reopened as a planetarium under
   the direction of Dr. Dionysus Lardner only to be gutted
   by fire in October 1844. Utilizing the remaining walls,
   the current building was constructed and adapted to
   commercial uses.

South Carolina

Abbeville, SC

ABBEVILLE OPERA HOUSE, Town Square
  OPENING DATE: October 18, 1908
  OPENING SHOW: The Great Divide
  TYPE OF BUILDING: Municipal building   FACADE: Red brick
  TYPE OF THEATRE: (b)   DEGREE OF RESTORATION: (a)
  CURRENT USE: Summer theatre
  PERFORMANCE SPACES IN BUILDING: 1
  STAGE DIMENSIONS AND EQUIPMENT: Height and width of
    proscenium, 55ft x 31ft 7in; Shape of proscenium arch,
    rectangular; Distance from edge of stage to back wall
    of stage, 66ft 6in; Distance from edge of stage to
    curtain line, 4ft; Distance between side walls of stage,
    71ft 10in; Distance from stage floor to fly loft, 75ft;
    Depth under stage, 30ft; Stage floor, flat; Trap doors,
    1; Scenery storage rooms, 6 (various locations); Dressing
    rooms, 16 (4 floors of dressing rooms)
  DIMENSIONS OF AUDITORIUM: Distance between side walls of
    auditorium, 71ft 10in; Distance stage to back wall of
    auditorium, 70ft; Orchestra pit, yes
  SEATING (3 levels): 1st level, 218; 2nd level, 150;
    3rd level, 100
  SHAPE OF THE AUDITORIUM: Slightly U-shaped
  MAJOR TYPES OF ENTERTAINMENT: Drama, vaudeville, burlesque,
  MAJOR STARS WHO APPEARED AT THEATRE: Jimmy Durante,
    Fanny Brice, Ziegfeld's Follies and George White's
    Scandals
  ADDITIONAL INFORMATION: Currently houses a professional
    summer stock company that presents a 36-week, five-play
    season each year.

Camden, SC

CAMDEN OPERA HOUSE, Corner of Broad and Rutledge Streets
  OPENING DATE: 1885

STYLE OF ARCHITECTURE: Empire   TYPE OF BUILDING: City
  chambers   FACADE: Brick and mortar
TYPE OF THEATRE: (b)   CLOSING DATE: c. 1964
CURRENT USE: Store   LOCATION OF AUDITORIUM: Second floor
MAJOR TYPES OF ENTERTAINMENT: Drama, vaudeville, opera
ADDITIONAL INFORMATION: The actual opera house section
  of the building was torn down, and the only remaining
  portion of the original structure is the clock and bell
  tower.

Charleston, SC

MCCRADY'S TAVERN AND LONG ROOM, 153 East Bay Street
  OPENING DATE: 1778
  ARCHITECT: Edward McCrady, builder   TYPE OF BUILDING:
    Banquet room, plays, recitals   FACADE: Wood
  TYPE OF THEATRE: (b)   DEGREE OF RESTORATION: (a)
  CURRENT USE: Social events
  LOCATION OF AUDITORIUM: Second floor
  STAGE DIMENSIONS AND EQUIPMENT: Height and width of
    proscenium, 8ft 6in x 16ft; Shape of proscenium arch,
    rectangular; Distance from edge of stage to back wall
    of stage, 20ft; Distance from edge of stage to curtain
    line, 1ft 6in; Distance between side walls of stage,
    30ft; Depth under stage, 0ft; Stage floor, raked
  DIMENSIONS OF AUDITORIUM: Distance between side walls
    of auditorium, 30ft; Distance stage to back wall of
    auditorium, 60ft
  SHAPE OF THE AUDITORIUM: Rectangular
  MAJOR TYPES OF ENTERTAINMENT: Local productions and
    "entertainments"
  MAJOR STARS WHO APPEARED AT THEATRE: George Washington
    once attended a dinner here.
  ADDITIONAL INFORMATION: The theatre may be "oldest extant
    English Theatre in America". The Long Room is on the
    second floor of an extension building added to the rear
    of McCrady's original 1757 Tavern. The theatre was used
    until 1791. A room above stage may have been a green
    room or a dressing room. A small door in stage left
    wall may have led to the prompter's box.

Chester, SC

THE OPERA HOUSE, 100 West End Street
  OPENING DATE: September 1891
  OPENING SHOW: Barlow's Brothers Minstrels
  ARCHITECT: Frank Munson   STYLE OF ARCHITECTURE:
    Romanesque Revivial   TYPE OF BUILDING: City hall
  FACADE: Unpainted brick, terra cotta   TYPE OF THEATRE: (b)
  DEGREE OF RESTORATION: (c)   CLOSING DATE: 1929
  CURRENT USE: Offices
  PERFORMANCE SPACES IN BUILDING: 1
  STAGE DIMENSIONS AND EQUIPMENT: Height and width of

proscenium, 25ft x 28ft; Distance from edge of stage to
back wall of stage, 25ft; Distance from edge of stage to
curtain line, 5ft; Distance between side walls of stage,
55ft; Distance from stage floor to fly loft, 30ft; Depth
under stage, 10ft; Trap doors, 1
DIMENSIONS OF AUDITORIUM: Orchestra pit, yes
SHAPE OF THE AUDITORIUM: Horseshoe-shaped
MAJOR TYPES OF ENTERTAINMENT: Drama, burlesque, opera,
    vaudeville
MAJOR STARS WHO APPEARED AT THEATRE: Babe LaTeur, Martha
    Scott, William Jennings Bryan, W. Rainey Bennett, the
    Metropolitan Orchestra, Princesss Shining Star and
    Company, Edgar Bergen, John B. Ratto
ADDITIONAL INFORMATION: The theatre was destroyed by fire,
    but the building still exists.

Lancaster, SC

MACKEY OPERA HOUSE (other name: Opera House), Gay Street
    OPENING DATE: 1907
    STYLE OF ARCHITECTURE: Romanesque
    TYPE OF BUILDING: Community use   FACADE: Red brick
    TYPE OF THEATRE: (b)   CURRENT USE: Bank
    PERFORMANCE SPACES IN BUILDING: 1
    LOCATION OF AUDITORIUM: Second floor
    STAGE DIMENSIONS AND EQUIPMENT: Height and width of
        proscenium, 16ft x 26ft
    SEATING (2 levels): 1st level, 400; 2nd level, 200
    MAJOR TYPES OF ENTERTAINMENT: Local and touring productions
    ADDITIONAL INFORMATION: Building now houses a bank and
        condition of the theatre is unknown.

Marion, SC

MARION OPERA HOUSE (other name: Town Hall and Opera House),
    Corner West Godbold and West Court
    OPENING DATE: c. 1910
    STYLE OF ARCHITECTURE: Vernacular   TYPE OF BUILDING:
        Offices and meetings   FACADE: Red brick
    TYPE OF THEATRE: (b)   DEGREE OF RESTORATION: (a)
    CURRENT USE: Theatre   PERFORMANCE SPACES IN BUILDING: 1
    LOCATION OF AUDITORIUM: Second floor
    STAGE DIMENSIONS AND EQUIPMENT: Height and width of
        proscenium, 26ft x 19ft; Shape of proscenium arch,
        rectangular; Distance from edge of stage to curtain
        line, 27ft; Distance between side walls of stage,
        46ft; Depth under stage, 4ft; Stage floor, flat;
        Scenery storage rooms, 1 (rear of auditorium);
        Dressing rooms, 2 (south side of stage)
    DIMENSIONS OF AUDITORIUM: Distance between side walls
        of auditorium, 45ft; Distance stage to back wall of
        auditorium, 57ft; Orchestra pit, none
    SEATING (1 level): 1st level, 278
    SHAPE OF THE AUDITORIUM: U-shaped

MAJOR TYPES OF ENTERTAINMENT: Drama, vaudeville
ADDITIONAL INFORMATION: The opera house is used for
   productions, public meetings and for Chamber of
   Commerce offices and general public functions.

Newberry, SC

NEWBERRY OPERA HOUSE AND COURTHOUSE (other name: City Opera
   House), Boyce and Nance Streets
OPENING DATE: February 22, 1882
OPENING SHOW: Speeches, poetry, and music
ARCHITECT: Osborne Wells, builder   STYLE OF ARCHITECTURE:
   Victorian Gothic   TYPE OF BUILDING: Municipal
FACADE: Red brick   TYPE OF THEATRE: (b)
DEGREE OF RESTORATION: (b)   CURRENT USE: Vacant
PERFORMANCE SPACES IN BUILDING: 1
LOCATION OF AUDITORIUM: Second and third floors
STAGE DIMENSIONS AND EQUIPMENT: Height and width of
   proscenium, 20ft x 25ft; Shape of proscenium arch,
   arched; Distance from edge of stage to back wall of
   stage, 30ft; Distance from edge of stage to curtain
   line, 4ft; Distance between side walls of stage, 51ft;
   Distance from stage floor to fly loft, 23ft; Depth under
   stage, 10ft; Stage floor, raked; Scenery storage rooms, 1
DIMENSIONS OF AUDITORIUM: Orchestra pit, yes
MAJOR TYPES OF ENTERTAINMENT: Local and traveling
   companies
MAJOR STARS WHO APPEARED AT THEATRE: Lionel Barrymore
ADDITIONAL INFORMATION: The following stage equipment
   still exists: a variable speed windlass for raising
   and lowering stage curtain; a rolled, painted act
   curtain; a "forest drop"; treadmill trap; and phantom
   trap. The building was "re-arranged" in 1930s for sound
   movies, but other than that it is basically "untouched".

Sumter, SC

OPERA HOUSE (other names: City Hall, Sumter Theatre,
   Academy of Music), 21 North Main Street
OPENING DATE: 1893
ARCHITECT: J. C. Turner, Augusta, GA
STYLE OF ARCHITECTURE: Richardson Romanesque
FACADE: Cumberland buff stone   TYPE OF THEATRE: (b)
DEGREE OF RESTORATION: (b)   CLOSING DATE: 1981
CURRENT USE: Vacant   PERFORMANCE SPACES IN BUILDING: 1
LOCATION OF AUDITORIUM: Second to fourth floors
STAGE DIMENSIONS AND EQUIPMENT: Height and width of
   proscenium, 22ft x 28ft; Distance from edge of stage to
   back wall of stage, 38ft; Distance from edge of stage to
   curtain line, 4ft; Distance between side walls of stage,
   42ft; Distance from stage floor to fly loft, 38ft 8in;
   Depth under stage, 4ft; Stage floor, flat; Trap doors, 4
SEATING (2 levels): 1st level, 575; 2nd level, 225
SHAPE OF THE AUDITORIUM: U-shaped

MAJOR TYPES OF ENTERTAINMENT: Concerts, opera
MAJOR STARS WHO APPEARED AT THEATRE: Clara Louise Kellogg
ADDITIONAL INFORMATION: The theatre is above City Hall.
  Backstage space was eliminated. The theatre is now
  vacant, but restoration is in progress.

South Dakota

Dell Rapids, SD

GRAND OPERA HOUSE (other name: Old Grand Opera House),
    Fourth Street
    OPENING DATE: November 5, 1888   OPENING SHOW: Lynwood
    ARCHITECTS: Paulson and Bentson   TYPE OF BUILDING: Cafe
    FACADE: Pink quartzite   TYPE OF THEATRE: (a)
    DEGREE OF RESTORATION: (c)   CURRENT USE: Hardware store
    LOCATION OF AUDITORIUM: Second floor
    STAGE DIMENSIONS AND EQUIPMENT: Height and width of
      proscenium, 13ft 2in x 18ft 10in; Shape of proscenium
      arch, rectangular; Distance from edge of stage to back
      wall of stage, 24ft; Distance from edge of stage to
      curtain line, 4ft; Distance between side walls of stage,
      32ft 2in; Depth under stage, 3ft 3in; Stage floor, flat;
      Trap doors, 1; Scenery storage rooms, 1 (stage left),
      Dressing rooms, 2 (1 on each side of stage)
    DIMENSIONS OF AUDITORIUM: Distance between side walls
      of auditorium, 43ft; Distance stage to back wall of
      auditorium, 63ft; Orchestra pit, none
    SEATING (2 levels): 1st level, 250; 2nd level, 200
    SHAPE OF THE AUDITORIUM: Rectangular
    MAJOR TYPES OF ENTERTAINMENT: Drama, opera, lectures,
      movies
    MAJOR STARS WHO APPEARED AT THEATRE: Willard Simms
    ADDITIONAL INFORMATION: The theatre remains relatively
      unchanged since it was last used as a movie theatre. A
      non-profit group, The Old Opera House Players Inc., has
      been organized to save and restore the theatre with the
      intention of again presenting live entertainment there.

Flandreau, SD

CRYSTAL THEATRE (other name: P. R. Matson's Opera House),
    215 2nd E (Plain Avenue)
  OPENING DATE: December 1913
  TYPE OF BUILDING: Photography studio

FACADE: Red brick   TYPE OF THEATRE: (a)   DEGREE OF
RESTORATION: (d)   CURRENT USE: Movie theatre
LOCATION OF AUDITORIUM: Ground floor
STAGE DIMENSIONS AND EQUIPMENT: Height and width of
  proscenium, 16ft x 21ft; Distance from edge of stage
  to back wall of stage, 12ft; Distance from edge of stage
  to curtain line, 4ft; Distance between side walls of
  stage, 40ft; Depth under stage, 4ft; Stage floor, flat;
  Trap doors, 0; Scenery storage rooms (in basement);
  Dressing rooms (in basement)
DIMENSIONS OF AUDITORIUM: Distance between side walls
  of auditorium, 32ft; Distance stage to back wall of
  auditorium, 100ft; Orchestra pit, none
SEATING (2 levels): 1st level, 322; 2nd level, 50
SHAPE OF THE AUDITORIUM: Rectangular; horseshoe-
  shaped balcony
MAJOR TYPES OF ENTERTAINMENT: Drama, opera, movies
MAJOR STARS WHO APPEARED AT THEATRE: Mary Pickford
ADDITIONAL INFORMATION: The theatre has been in
  continuous use since 1913 and has never been
  renovated with the exception of the replacement
  of some of the original opera chairs following
  a fire in 1927.

Hot Springs, SD

VA MEDICAL CENTER AUDITORIUM, VA Medical Center
  OPENING DATE: 1915
  FACADE: Pink sandstone   TYPE OF THEATRE: (b)
  DEGREE OF RESTORATION: (c)   CURRENT USE: Theatre
  LOCATION OF AUDITORIUM: Ground floor
  STAGE DIMENSIONS AND EQUIPMENT: Height and width of
    proscenium, 14ft x 19ft 6in; Shape of proscenium arch,
    rectangular; Distance from edge of stage to back wall
    of stage, 15ft 4in; Distance from edge of stage to
    curtain line, 14ft 2in; Distance between side walls of
    stage, 28ft; Depth under stage, 3ft 6in; Trap doors, 0;
    Scenery storage rooms, 0; Dressing rooms, 1 (stage left)
  DIMENSIONS OF AUDITORIUM: Distance between side walls of
    auditorium, 43ft 6in; Distance stage to back wall of
    auditorium, 52ft; Orchestra pit, none
  SEATING (2 levels): 1st level, 230; 2nd level, 95
  SHAPE OF THE AUDITORIUM: Rectangular
  MAJOR TYPES OF ENTERTAINMENT: Drama

Lead, SD

HOMESTAKE OPERA HOUSE, P. O. Box 694
  OPENING DATE: August 31, 1914
  OPENING SHOW: Il Trovatore, The Bohemian Girl, and Martha
  ARCHITECTS: Walter R. Shattuck and Harry H. Hussey
  TYPE OF BUILDING: Recreation complex   FACADE: Red-brown
    brick with white limestone trim   TYPE OF THEATRE: (b)

DEGREE OF RESTORATION: (c)   CLOSING DATE: April 2, 1984
CURRENT USE: Vacant due to fire
LOCATION OF AUDITORIUM: Ground floor
SEATING (2 levels): 1st level, 566; 2nd level, 450
SHAPE OF THE AUDITORIUM: Horseshoe-shaped
MAJOR TYPES OF ENTERTAINMENT: Drama, musical comedy,
  opera, vaudeville, minstrel shows, concerts, lectures,
  dance, movies, boxing, wrestling matches
MAJOR STARS WHO APPEARED AT THEATRE: Clint and Bessie
  Robbins, Boyd B. Trousdale Company, Arington's
  Comedians, Chase-Lister Company, Sanford Dodge and
  Company, Gaskill and MacVitty, Schuster Musical Comedy
  Company, Arden Dramatic Company, Richards and Pringles'
  Minstrels
ADDITIONAL INFORMATION: The theatre was seriously
  damaged by fire in April 1984 and, at first, there was
  talk of demolishing the remaining structure. Currently,
  however, there are no plans for razing the building, but
  it is uncertain whether a theatre will ever operate in
  the building again. The roof has been replaced and the
  building cleaned up, but no other decisions have been
  made. Items which survived the fire, including brass
  railings, chandeliers, cherub statues, and candelabra,
  have been stored.

Madison, SD

  PRAIRIE VILLAGE OPERA HOUSE (other names: Socialist Hall,
    Social Hall), RR 1, Box 256
  OPENING DATE: 1912   FACADE: Embossed metal
  TYPE OF THEATRE: (a)   DEGREE OF RESTORATION: (a)
  CURRENT USE: Summer theatre
  LOCATION OF AUDITORIUM: Ground floor
  STAGE DIMENSIONS AND EQUIPMENT: Height and width of
    proscenium, 25ft x 36ft; Shape of proscenium arch,
    arched; Distance from edge of stage to back wall of
    stage, 21ft; Distance between side walls of stage,
    36ft; Depth under stage, 4ft; Stage floor, flat;
    Trap doors, 1; Scenery storage rooms, 2 (attached
    to rear of theatre); Dressing rooms, 2 (rear of
    theatre)
  DIMENSIONS OF AUDITORIUM: Distance between side walls
    of auditorium, 49ft; Distance stage to back wall of
    auditorium, 55ft; Orchestra pit, none
  SEATING (2 levels): 1st level, 220; 2nd level, 76
  SHAPE OF THE AUDITORIUM: Rectangular; U-shaped balcony
  MAJOR TYPES OF ENTERTAINMENT: Drama, musical comedy,
    vaudeville, burlesque, opera, lectures
  MAJOR STARS WHO APPEARED AT THEATRE: Lawrence Welk (stage
    debut in 1924), Booker T. Washington
  ADDITIONAL INFORMATION: The opera house is part of Prairie
    Village, a living museum. It was originally erected in
    Oldham, SD and was moved in 1970 to become part of the
    restored village. Original fly-loft, dressing rooms and

storage areas were removed in 1946. The theatre
currently has a thrust stage and is used by the
Repertory Theatre of SDSU.

Pierre, SD

GRAND OPERA HOUSE (other names: Grand Theatre, Studio 109),
    109 South Pierre Street
  OPENING DATE: November 25, 1906
  OPENING SHOW: Quincy Adams Sawyer
  ARCHITECTS: Jeffers and Henry   STYLE OF ARCHITECTURE:
    Classical Revival   TYPE OF BUILDING: Apartments, offices
  FACADE: Brown brick   TYPE OF THEATRE: (b)
  DEGREE OF RESTORATION: (d)   CURRENT USE: Theatre
  LOCATION OF AUDITORIUM: Ground floor
  STAGE DIMENSIONS AND EQUIPMENT: * Height and width
    of proscenium, 22ft x 32ft; Shape of proscenium arch,
    rectangular; Distance from edge of stage to back wall
    of stage, 21ft; Dressing rooms, 10
  SEATING (3 levels): 1st level, 600; 2nd level, 400;
    3rd level, 200
  SHAPE OF THE AUDITORIUM: U-shaped
  MAJOR TYPES OF ENTERTAINMENT: Drama, movies, musical comedy
  ADDITIONAL INFORMATION: The theatre is currently the home
    of the Pierre Players, a local company.

Rapid City, SD

ELKS THEATRE, 512 6th Street
  OPENING DATE: May 12, 1911
  FACADE: Brown brick   TYPE OF THEATRE: (b)
  DEGREE OF RESTORATION: (d)   CURRENT USE: Movie theatre
  LOCATION OF AUDITORIUM: Ground floor
  STAGE DIMENSIONS AND EQUIPMENT: Height and width of
    proscenium, 39ft x 65ft; Shape of proscenium arch,
    rectangular; Distance from edge of stage to back wall
    of stage, 25ft; Distance from edge of stage to curtain
    line, 12ft; Distance between side walls of stage, 78ft;
    Distance from stage floor to fly loft, 28ft; Depth under
    stage, 16ft; Stage floor, flat; Trap doors, 2; Dressing
    rooms, 2 (basement)
  DIMENSIONS OF AUDITORIUM: Distance between side walls
    of auditorium, 84ft; Distance stage to back wall of
    auditorium, 110ft
  SEATING (2 levels): 1st level, 470; 2nd level, 241
  SHAPE OF THE AUDITORIUM: U-shaped
  MAJOR TYPES OF ENTERTAINMENT: Drama, vaudeville, burlesque,
    movies

Sioux Falls, SD

ORPHEUM THEATRE OF SIOUX FALLS (other name: Sioux Falls
    Community Playhouse), 315 North Phillips

OPENING DATE: 1913
FACADE: Green spattered terra cotta
TYPE OF THEATRE: (a)   DEGREE OF RESTORATION: (a)
CURRENT USE: Theatre
LOCATION OF AUDITORIUM: Ground floor
STAGE DIMENSIONS AND EQUIPMENT: Height and width of
  proscenium, 19ft 6in x 32ft 9in; Shape of proscenium
  arch, arched; Distance from edge of stage to back wall
  of stage, 29ft; Distance from edge of stage to curtain
  line, 3ft; Distance between side walls of stage, 50ft;
  Depth under stage, 9ft; Stage floor, flat; Trap doors,
  1; Scenery storage rooms, 5 (under stage); Dressing
  rooms, 2 (basement of exterior shop)
DIMENSIONS OF AUDITORIUM: Distance between side walls
  of auditorium, 50ft; Distance stage to back wall of
  auditorium, 85ft; Capacity of orchestra pit, 10
SEATING (2 levels): 1st level, 300; 2nd level, 392
SHAPE OF THE AUDITORIUM: Rectangular
MAJOR TYPES OF ENTERTAINMENT: Drama, vaudeville
MAJOR STARS WHO APPEARED AT THEATRE: Stan Laurel,
  Ruth Gordon, Lyle Talbott

Tennessee

Johnson City, TN

MOUNTAIN HOME MEMORIAL HALL, Mountain Home
  OPENING DATE: 1905   STYLE OF ARCHITECTURE: Beaux Arts
  TYPE OF BUILDING: Meeting hall   TYPE OF THEATRE: (c)
  DEGREE OF RESTORATION: (a)
  LOCATION OF AUDITORIUM: First floor
  MAJOR TYPES OF ENTERTAINMENT: Local productions
  ADDITIONAL INFORMATION: This stunning example of Beaux
    Arts architecture is located in a Veterans' Admin-
    istration Hospital complex. It was completely restored
    in 1981. The theatre is similar to the St. James in New
    York. The building is on the National Register.

Knoxville, TN

LAMAR HOUSE-BIJOU THEATRE, 803 Gay Street, Southwest
  OPENING DATE: March 8, 1909
  ARCHITECT: Oakley of Montgomery, Alabama
  TYPE OF BUILDING: Movie theatre   TYPE OF THEATRE: (b)
  DEGREE OF RESTORATION: (a)
  LOCATION OF AUDITORIUM: First floor
  STAGE DIMENSIONS AND& EQUIPMENT: Height and width of
    proscenium, 28ft x 34ft 8in; Distance from edge of
    stage to back wall, 35ft; Distance between side walls
    of stage, 68ft 8in; Stage floor, flat
  DIMENSIONS OF AUDITORIUM: Orchestra pit, yes
  SEATING (3 levels)
  SHAPE OF THE AUDITORIUM: Rectangular
  MAJOR TYPES OF ENTERTAINMENT: Local and touring productions
  ADDITIONAL INFORMATION: The theatre was a former Keith
  Circuit house and has an elegant Baroque interior. Some
  of the original theatre elements remain.

Pulaski, TN

PULASKI OPERA HOUSE (other name: Antoinette Hall),
    East side of Town Square
    OPENING DATE: December 25, 1868
    OPENING SHOW: Presentation by local group, Ben Johnson Club
    ARCHITECT: M. D. LeMayne   STYLE OF ARCHITECTURE:
    French Second Empire   TYPE OF BUILDING: Commercial
    FACADE: Brick   TYPE OF THEATRE: (b)   DEGREE OF
    RESTORATION: (c)   CLOSING DATE: 1930s   CURRENT USE:
    Vacant   LOCATION OF AUDITORIUM: Second floor
    STAGE DIMENSIONS AND EQUIPMENT: Height and width of
    proscenium, 16ft x 25ft; Shape of proscenium arch,
    arched; Distance from edge of stage to back wall of
    stage, 25ft; Distance from edge of stage to curtain
    line, 5ft; Distance between side walls of stage, 40ft;
    Stage floor, raked; Trap doors, 1
    DIMENSIONS OF AUDITORIUM: Distance between side walls
    of auditorium, 40ft; Distance stage to back wall of
    auditorium, 25ft; Orchestra pit, none
    SEATING (2 levels)
    SHAPE OF THE AUDITORIUM: Rectangular
    MAJOR TYPES OF ENTERTAINMENT: Vaudeville, minstrel
    shows, political rallies
    ADDITIONAL INFORMATION: A restoration drive to repair a
    mansard roof was conducted in 1985.

South Pittsburg, TN

OPERA HOUSE (other names: New Opera House, Wilson Theatre),
    Cedar Avenue between 1st and 2nd Streets
    OPENING DATE: Pre-1910   STYLE OF ARCHITECTURE: Commercial
    TYPE OF BUILDING: Commercial   FACADE: Brick
    TYPE OF THEATRE: (b)   DEGREE OF RESTORATION: (c)
    CURRENT USE: Commercial
    LOCATION OF AUDITORIUM: Second floor
    STAGE DIMENSIONS AND EQUIPMENT: Height and width of
    proscenium, 16ft x 30ft; Distance from edge of stage
    to back wall of stage, 25ft; Distance from edge of stage
    to curtain line, 2ft; Distance between side walls of
    stage, 50ft; Distance from stage floor to fly loft, 16ft
    MAJOR TYPES OF ENTERTAINMENT: Local and touring
    productions, minstrel shows
    MAJOR STARS WHO APPEARED AT THEATRE: Booker T. Washington,
    Oscar Seagle
    ADDITIONAL INFORMATION: The Opera House was part of a
    business venture called the Opera House Block and still
    bears an inscription on its facade which identifies it
    as such.

Texas

Austin, TX

MILLET OPERA HOUSE, 110 East 9th Street
OPENING DATE: 1878
ARCHITECT: Frederick E. Ruffini   TYPE OF BUILDING:
  Lodge, storage   FACADE: Stone   TYPE OF THEATRE: (a)
DEGREE OF RESTORATION: (c)   CLOSING DATE: 1911
CURRENT USE: Storage   LOCATION OF AUDITORIUM: First floor
SEATING (2 levels)
MAJOR TYPES OF ENTERTAINMENT: Local and touring productions
MAJOR STARS WHO APPEARED AT THEATRE: Edwin Booth in
  Othello, 1888; and James O'Neill in The Count of Monte
  Cristo, 1892; William Jennings Bryan, John L. Sullivan
ADDITIONAL INFORMATION: Little remains of the theatre due
  to several remodelings. The building now is used for
  storage by the Austin Independent School District.

Austin, TX

PARAMOUNT THEATRE (other name: Majestic Theatre), 713
  Congress Avenue
OPENING DATE: October 11, 1915
ARCHITECT: John Eberson   STYLE OF ARCHITECTURE:
  Neo-Classical   TYPE OF BUILDING: Movie theatre
TYPE OF THEATRE: (a)   DEGREE OF RESTORATION: (d)
CURRENT USE: Theatre
LOCATION OF AUDITORIUM: First floor
STAGE DIMENSIONS AND EQUIPMENT: Height and width of
  proscenium, 32ft x 32ft; Shape of proscenium arch,
  square; Distance from edge of stage to back wall of
  stage, 34ft; Distance between side walls of stage,
  34ft; Dressing rooms, 6
DIMENSIONS OF AUDITORIUM: Capacity of orchestra pit, 25
MAJOR TYPES OF ENTERTAINMENT: Drama, vaudeville,
  musicals, movies
MAJOR STARS WHO APPEARED AT THEATRE: Helen Hayes,
  Katherine Hepburn, Pavlova, Orson Welles, Sarah

Bernhardt, the Barrymores, John Phillip Sousa,
George M. Cohan,
ADDITIONAL INFORMATION: Built at a cost of $150,000 by
Ernest Nalle, it was originally named the Majestic
Theatre.

Columbus, TX

STAFFORD OPERA HOUSE, Milan at Spring
OPENING DATE: 1886
OPENING SHOW: As In A Looking Glass with Lillian Russell
ARCHITECT: Nicholas J. Clayton   STYLE OF ARCHITECTURE:
Second Empire   TYPE OF BUILDING: Bank and commercial
FACADE: Red brick   TYPE OF THEATRE: (b)   DEGREE OF
RESTORATION: (a)   CLOSING DATE: 1916   CURRENT USE:
Theatre   LOCATION OF AUDITORIUM: Second floor
STAGE DIMENSIONS AND EQUIPMENT: Height and width of
proscenium, 16ft x 30ft; Distance from edge of stage to
back wall of stage, 30ft; Distance from edge of stage to
curtain line, 3ft; Depth under stage, 3ft; Trap doors, 2
SEATING (2 levels): 1st level, 600; 2nd level, 400
MAJOR TYPES OF ENTERTAINMENT: Local and touring productions
MAJOR STARS WHO APPEARED AT THEATRE: Lillian Russell,
Joseph Jefferson, Emma Abbott, Al Jolson, Houdini
ADDITIONAL INFORMATION: Restoration is underway. The
Facade has some cast iron details.

Galveston, TX

GRAND OPERA HOUSE (other names: State, Martini),
2020 Post Office Street
OPENING DATE: January 3, 1895
ARCHITECT: Frank Cox of New Orleans
STYLE OF ARCHITECTURE: Romanesque Revival   TYPE OF
BUILDING: Movie theatre   TYPE OF THEATRE: (a)
DEGREE OF RESTORATION: (a)   CURRENT USE: Theatre
LOCATION OF AUDITORIUM: First floor
STAGE DIMENSIONS AND EQUIPMENT: * Height and width of
proscenium, 30ft x 38ft; Shape of proscenium arch,
rectangular; Distance from edge of stage to back wall
of stage, 36ft; Distance from edge of stage to curtain
line, 1ft 6in; Distance between side walls of stage,
59ft; Distance from stage floor to fly loft, 50ft; Depth
under stage, 10ft; Stage floor, flat; Trap doors, 1;
Dressing rooms, 3
DIMENSIONS OF AUDITORIUM: Capacity of orchestra pit, 45
SEATING (3 levels): 1st level, 500; level, 250;
3rd level, 250; boxes, 72
MAJOR TYPES OF ENTERTAINMENT: Drama, movies
MAJOR STARS WHO APPEARED AT THEATRE: Pavlova, Paderewski,
Sarah Bernhardt, George M. Cohan, Sousa, William Jennings
Bryan, and the Barrymores
ADDITIONAL INFORMATION: The theatre was built as part of
an adjoining hotel complex.

Granbury, TX

GRANBURY OPERA HOUSE, 116 East Pearl
OPENING DATE: March 1886
FACADE: Limestone with pressed-tin decoration
TYPE OF THEATRE: (b)   DEGREE OF RESTORATION: (a)
CURRENT USE: Theatre   LOCATION OF AUDITORIUM: First floor
STAGE DIMENSIONS AND EQUIPMENT: Height and width of
  proscenium, 23ft x 26ft; Shape of proscenium arch,
  arched; Distance from edge of stage to back wall of
  stage, 18ft; Distance from edge of stage to curtain
  line, 7ft; Distance between side walls of stage, 50ft;
  Distance from stage floor to fly loft, 28ft; Depth under
  stage, 3ft; Stage floor, flat; Scenery storage rooms, 1
  (rear of stage); Dressing rooms, 2 (rear of stage)
DIMENSIONS OF AUDITORIUM: Distance between side walls
  of auditorium, 50ft; Distance stage to back wall of
  auditorium, 50ft; Orchestra pit, yes
SEATING (2 levels): 1st level, 220; 2nd level, 83
SHAPE OF THE AUDITORIUM: Rectangular
MAJOR TYPES OF ENTERTAINMENT: Local and traveling
  companies, drama, vaudeville, burlesque, opera

Uvalde, TX

GRAND OPERA HOUSE (other name: Uvalde Grand Opera House),
  100 West North Street
OPENING DATE: May 18, 1893
OPENING SHOW: Commencement excercise program
ARCHITECT: B. F. Trister, Jr.   STYLE OF ARCHITECTURE:
  Victorian Commercial   FACADE: Beige brick and gray trim
TYPE OF THEATRE: (a)   DEGREE OF RESTORATION: (a)
CURRENT USE: Community theatre
LOCATION OF AUDITORIUM: Second floor
STAGE DIMENSIONS AND EQUIPMENT: Height and width of
  proscenium, 17ft 8in x 34ft; Shape of proscenium arch,
  arched; Distance from edge of stage to back wall of
  stage, 22ft; Distance from edge of stage to curtain
  line, 4ft 6in; Distance between side walls of stage,
  58ft; Distance from stage floor to fly loft, 18ft;
  Stage floor, flat; Dressing rooms, 2 (basement)
DIMENSIONS OF AUDITORIUM: Capacity of orchestra pit, 7
MAJOR TYPES OF ENTERTAINMENT: Drama, vaudeville
MAJOR STARS WHO APPEARED AT THEATRE: Kingston Trio
  (September, 1984)

Utah

Beaver, UT

BEAVER OPERA HOUSE, 55 East Center Street
  OPENING DATE: March 1909
  ARCHITECTS: Liljenberg and Maeser   STYLE OF
  ARCHITECTURE: Classical Revival   TYPE OF BUILDING:
    Church, storage, civic center   FACADE: Stone
  TYPE OF THEATRE: (a)   DEGREE OF RESTORATION: (b)
  CLOSING DATE: 1929   CURRENT USE: Senior citizens'
    recreation center   LOCATION OF AUDITORIUM: First floor
  SEATING (1 level)
  SHAPE OF THE AUDITORIUM: Rectangular
  MAJOR TYPES OF ENTERTAINMENT: Local and touring productions
  MAJOR STARS WHO APPEARED AT THEATRE: Ralph Cloniger, Luke
    Cosgrave, Shelby Roach, Walter Christensen
  ADDITIONAL INFORMATION: All theatre elements have been
    removed.

Heber City, UT

HEBER AMUSEMENT HALL (other name: Wasatch Stake Tabernacle),
    100 West Street
  OPENING DATE: 1908
  ARCHITECT: Mr. Watkins, Provo, Utah   TYPE OF BUILDING:
    Community center   FACADE: Stone   TYPE OF THEATRE: (b)
  DEGREE OF RESTORATION: (b)   CURRENT USE: Theatre and
    community center   LOCATION OF AUDITORIUM: First floor
  MAJOR TYPES OF ENTERTAINMENT: Local productions
  ADDITIONAL INFORMATION: The theatre is part of a complex
    for local dramatics. It was built in a "T-shape"
    consisting of two rectangular rooms. The first was
    126ft x 61ft and the second was 61ft x 40ft 8in. A
    large ballroom is situated above the theatre.

Koosharem, UT

KOOSHAREM AUMSEMENT HALL
  OPENING DATE: 1914
  ARCHITECT: Erected by community members
  STYLE OF ARCHITECTURE: Frame   TYPE OF BUILDING: Community
    center   FACADE: Wood   TYPE OF THEATRE: (c)
  DEGREE OF RESTORATION: (d)   CURRENT USE: Community events
  LOCATION OF AUDITORIUM: First floor
  MAJOR TYPES OF ENTERTAINMENT: Local productions, lectures,
    dances, parties
  ADDITIONAL INFORMATION: This small Mormon community has
    used the amusement hall, which consists of a gymnasium,
    stage, kitchen, and basement, for community events
    including plays, dances, funerals, and miscellaneous
    programs. The two-story wood frame building is in good
    condition.

Logan, UT

LYRIC THEATRE, 28 West Center
  OPENING DATE: October 14, 1913
  OPENING SHOW: The Wolf and the Lure
  ARCHITECT: G. W. Thatcher   STYLE OF ARCHITECTURE:
    Victorian   FACADE: Plaster and wood
  TYPE OF THEATRE: (a)   DEGREE OF RESTORATION: (b)
  CURRENT USE: Theatre   LOCATION OF AUDITORIUM: First floor
  STAGE DIMENSIONS AND EQUIPMENT: Height and width of
    proscenium, 16ft x 21ft 5in; Shape of proscenium arch,
    arched; Distance from edge of stage to back wall of
    stage, 18ft 5in; Distance from edge of stage to curtain
    line, 5ft 6in; Distance between side walls of stage,
    36ft 9in; Distance from stage floor to fly loft, 40ft;
    Depth under stage, 8ft; Stage floor, flat; Trap doors,
    1; Scenery storage rooms, 1 (stage left); Dressing rooms,
    2 (in basement)
  DIMENSIONS OF AUDITORIUM: Distance between side walls
    of auditorium, 36ft 9in; Distance stage to back wall of
    auditorium, 100ft; Capacity of orchestra pit, 12
  SEATING (2 levels): 1st level, 273; 2nd level, 115
  SHAPE OF THE AUDITORIUM: Rectangular
  MAJOR TYPES OF ENTERTAINMENT: Drama, vaudeville, opera
  MAJOR STARS WHO APPEARED AT THEATRE: John E. Kellerd,
    Stewart Walker, Lucy Gates

Richfield, UT

RICHFIELD OPERA HOUSE (other name: Lyric)
  OPENING DATE: 1881
  ARCHITECTS: Hansen and Thurber, builders   STYLE OF
  ARCHITECTURE: Western   TYPE OF BUILDING: Commercial
  FACADE: Wood   TYPE OF THEATRE: (b)   DEGREE OF
  RESTORATION: (c)   CURRENT USE: Vacant
  LOCATION OF AUDITORIUM: First floor

SHAPE OF THE AUDITORIUM: Rectangular
MAJOR TYPES OF ENTERTAINMENT: Local and traveling
  productions, movies
ADDITIONAL INFORMATION: The theatre is vacant, but there
  is interest in restoration. The first performance took
  place in 1884 when a stage was added to the dance hall.
  The auditorium has been enlarged twice.

Salt Lake City, UT

CAPITOL THEATRE (other name: Orpheum), 46 West Second South
  OPENING DATE: August 1, 1913
  ARCHITECT: G. Albert Lansburgh   STYLE OF ARCHITECTURE:
    Italian Renaissance   TYPE OF BUILDING: Movie theatre
  FACADE: Brick   TYPE OF THEATRE: (a)   DEGREE OF
  RESTORATION: (a)   CURRENT USE: Movie theatre
  LOCATION OF AUDITORIUM: First floor
  STAGE DIMENSIONS AND EQUIPMENT: Height and width of
    proscenium, 45ft x 45ft; Shape of proscenium arch,
    rectangular; Distance from edge of stage to back wall
    of stage, 50ft; Distance between side walls of stage,
    96ft; Stage floor, flat
  DIMENSIONS OF AUDITORIUM: Capacity of orchestra pit, 110
  SEATING (4 levels)
  SHAPE OF THE AUDITORIUM: Horseshoe-shaped
  MAJOR TYPES OF ENTERTAINMENT: Drama, dance, movies
  ADDITIONAL INFORMATION: This is the second theatre in
    Salt Lake City to bear this name. The auditorium has
    been restored and the stage house has been enlarged to
    accommodate dance. Stage dimensions presented are the
    present ones. The Capitol is now a performing arts
    center and is listed on the National Register.

Salt Lake City, UT

PROMISED VALLEY PLAYHOUSE (other names: State Street
    Theatre, Orpheum, Wilkes Playhouse, Roxy, Lake, Lyric),
    132 South State Street
  OPENING DATE: December 25, 1905
  OPENING SHOW: Vaudeville and burlesque
  STYLE OF ARCHITECTURE: Classical   TYPE OF BUILDING:
    Movie theatre   FACADE: Stone   TYPE OF THEATRE: (a)
  DEGREE OF RESTORATION: (a)   CURRENT USE: Theatre
  LOCATION OF AUDITORIUM: First floor
  STAGE DIMENSIONS AND EQUIPMENT: Height and width of
    proscenium, 22ft x 38ft; Distance from edge of stage
    to back wall of stage, 32ft; Distance from edge of stage
    to curtain line, 29ft; Distance between side walls of
    stage, 80ft; Distance from stage floor to fly loft, 44ft;
    Depth under stage, 13ft; Trap doors, 1
  SEATING (2 levels): 1st level, 640; 2nd level, 581
  MAJOR TYPES OF ENTERTAINMENT: Local and touring productions

ADDITIONAL INFORMATION: The theatre has been carefully
   restored by the Mormons and now is home of the play,
   Promised Valley. The theatre is also a cultural center.
   It was known as the Orpheum before a "new" Orpheum was
   opened in 1913. The second Orpheum later became the
   Capitol.

Vermont

Barre, VT

BARRE OPERA HOUSE (other name: Barre Theatre), North Main at
    Prospect Street
OPENING DATE: August 23, 1899
OPENING SHOW: Charles Klein's Two Little Vagrants
ARCHITECT: George G. Adams   STYLE OF ARCHITECTURE:
    Palladian   TYPE OF BUILDING: Municipal   FACADE:
    Yellow brick with granite trim   TYPE OF THEATRE: (b)
DEGREE OF RESTORATION: (a)   CLOSING DATE: 1943
CURRENT USE: Performing arts
LOCATION OF AUDITORIUM: Second floor
STAGE DIMENSIONS AND EQUIPMENT: Height and width of
    proscenium, 22ft x 32ft; Shape of proscenium arch,
    rectangular; Distance from edge of stage to back wall
    of stage, 33ft 10in; Distance from edge of stage to
    curtain line, 3ft 10in; Distance between side walls
    of stage, 64ft 6in; Depth under stage, 3ft 6in; Stage
    floor, flat; Trap doors, 2; Scenery storage rooms, 2
    (off fly gallery); Dressing rooms, 5 (beneath stage)
DIMENSIONS OF AUDITORIUM: Distance between side walls
    of auditorium, 70ft; Capacity of orchestra pit, 15
SEATING (2 levels): 1st level, 434; 2nd level, 200;
    boxes, 16
SHAPE OF THE AUDITORIUM: U-shaped
MAJOR TYPES OF ENTERTAINMENT: Drama, musical comedy,
    vaudeville, burlesque, opera, concerts, lectures,
    movies, boxing, wrestling matches
MAJOR STARS WHO APPEARED AT THEATRE: Edward Harrigan
    (1900), Marian Manola (1900), George M. Cohan, Sarah
    Cowell Le Moyne (1901), Roland Reed (1901), Gertrude
    Coghlan (1902), James O'Neill (1902), John Phillip
    Sousa, Helen Keller, Eugene Debs, Tom Mix and horse
ADDITIONAL INFORMATION: The current building was erected
    to replace a previous opera house which had burned. The
    wooden floor of the hall rises to the rear in stages and
    three-tiered boxes flank the proscenium arch. A balcony
    trimmed with carved garlands "extends around the entire

rear of the room in the shape of a horseshoe"
and the auditorium has a pressed metal ceiling.

Bennington, VT

HARTE THEATRE
OPENING DATE: 1915
TYPE OF THEATRE: (a)   DEGREE OF RESTORATION: (d)
CURRENT USE: Movie theatre
LOCATION OF AUDITORIUM: Ground floor
STAGE DIMENSIONS AND EQUIPMENT: Shape of proscenium arch,
  rectangular; Stage floor, flat
DIMENSIONS OF AUDITORIUM: Orchestra pit, yes
SEATING: (2 levels)
MAJOR TYPES OF ENTERTAINMENT: Drama, vaudeville, movies
ADDITIONAL INFORMATION: The theatre opened as a combination
  film/vaudeville house. It was remodeled in 1950.

Bethel, VT

TOWN HALL, Main Street
OPENING DATE: January 1893   OPENING SHOW: Dedication Ball
ARCHITECT: George Guernsey   STYLE OF ARCHITECTURE:
  Romanesque   TYPE OF BUILDING: Municipal
FACADE: Red brick   TYPE OF THEATRE: (b)
DEGREE OF RESTORATION: (c)   CURRENT USE: Meeting rooms
STAGE DIMENSIONS AND EQUIPMENT: Height and width of
  proscenium, 13ft x 22ft; Shape of proscenium arch,
  arched; Distance from edge of stage to back wall of
  stage, 18ft 6in; Distance from edge of stage to curtain
  line, 2ft 6in; Distance between side walls of stage,
  30ft; Stage floor, flat; Trap doors, 1; Scenery storage
  rooms (above and to rear of stage); Dressing rooms, 2
  (under stage)
DIMENSIONS OF AUDITORIUM: Distance between side walls
  of auditorium, 42ft; Distance stage to back wall of
  auditorium, 47ft; Orchestra pit, none
SEATING (2 levels)
SHAPE OF THE AUDITORIUM: Rectangular
MAJOR TYPES OF ENTERTAINMENT: Drama, musical comedy,
  vaudeville, lectures, movies, local variety shows

Burlington, VT

HOWARD OPERA HOUSE, Bank at Church Street
OPENING DATE: February 24, 1879
OPENING SHOW: Lucia Di Lammermoor
ARCHITECT: Stephen D. Hatch   STYLE OF ARCHITECTURE:
  Romanesque   FACADE: Red brick with Nova Scotia stones
TYPE OF THEATRE: (b)   DEGREE OF RESTORATION: (c)
CLOSING DATE: November 30, 1904   CURRENT USE:
  Department store   LOCATION OF AUDITORIUM: Second floor
STAGE DIMENSIONS AND EQUIPMENT: Height and width of

proscenium, 32ft x 32ft; Shape of proscenium arch, square; Distance from edge of stage to back wall of stage, 30ft; Distance between side walls of stage, 76ft; Depth under stage, 7ft; Stage floor, raked; Trap doors, 2; Dressing rooms, 4 (beneath stage)
DIMENSIONS OF AUDITORIUM: Distance between side walls of auditorium, 76ft; Distance stage to back wall of auditorium, 129ft; Capacity of orchestra pit, 25
SEATING (2 levels): 1st level, 700; 2nd level, 360
SHAPE OF THE AUDITORIUM: U-shaped
MAJOR TYPES OF ENTERTAINMENT: Drama, musical comedy
MAJOR STARS WHO APPEARED AT THEATRE: Clara Louise Kellogg (1879), Joseph Jefferson (1879), W. J. Florence (1880), Mary Anderson (1880), William Warren II (1880), Fanny Janauschek (1881), Denman Thompson (1881); James O'Neill (1881), Lester Wallack (1881), George L. Fox (1882), Frank Chanfrau (1882), Lotta Crabtree (1882), Lawrence Barrett (1882), Hortense Rhea (1882), Lillie Langtry (1883), Dion Boucicault (1885), Helena Modjeska (1886), Genevieve Ward (1886), Robert Mantell (1888), E. H. Sothern (1891), Frank Mayo (1891), Wilson Barrett (1893), Clara Morris (1893), De Wolf Hopper (1896), John E. Toole (1897), James A. Herne (1900), Edward Harrigan (1900), J. H. Stoddard (1902)

Derby Line, VT (Rock Island, Quebec)

HASKELL FREE LIBRARY AND OPERA HOUSE, Caswell Avenue, Derby Line
OPENING DATE: 1904
OPENING SHOW: The Isle of Rock by the Columbian Minstrels
ARCHITECT: James Ball   TYPE OF BUILDING: Library
FACADE: Granite and brick   TYPE OF THEATRE: (a)
DEGREE OF RESTORATION: (d)   CURRENT USE: Theatre
STAGE DIMENSIONS AND EQUIPMENT: Height and width of proscenium, 20ft x 26ft; Shape of proscenium arch, arched; Distance from edge of stage to back wall of stage, 24ft; Distance from edge of stage to curtain line, 2ft; Distance between side walls of stage, 50ft; Depth under stage, 4ft; Stage floor, flat; Trap doors, 0; Scenery storage rooms (stage right); Dressing rooms, 4 (stage left)
DIMENSIONS OF AUDITORIUM: Distance between side walls of auditorium, 44ft; distance stage to back wall of auditorium, 23ft; Orchestra pit, none
SEATING (2 levels): 1st level, 270; 2nd level, 136
SHAPE OF THE AUDITORIUM: Square; U-shaped balcony
MAJOR TYPES OF ENTERTAINMENT: Drama, musical comedy, concerts, minstrel shows, lectures
MAJOR STARS WHO APPEARED AT THEATRE: William Jennings Bryan, Guy Brothers Minstrels, Sunny South Minstrels, Sir Hubert Wilkins, Sir Dudley Stamp, Bread and Puppet Theatre
ADDITIONAL INFORMATION: Designed as a scale model of the Boston Opera House, the theatre rests squarely on the

international border between the United States and
Canada. The entrance to the theatre is in the United
States, as are most of the seats, but the stage and
a few of the seats are in Canada.

Enosburg Falls, VT.

ENOSBURG OPERA HOUSE, 31 Depot Street
  OPENING DATE: 1892
  STYLE OF ARCHITECTURE: Queen Anne   TYPE OF THEATRE: (a)
  DEGREE OF RESTORATION: (a)   CURRENT USE: Summer theatre
  LOCATION OF AUDITORIUM: Second floor
  STAGE DIMENSIONS AND EQUIPMENT: Height and width of
    proscenium, 15ft x 25ft; Shape of proscenium arch,
    arched; Distance from edge of stage to back wall of
    stage, 30ft 2in; Distance from edge of stage to curtain
    line, 4ft 6in; Distance between side walls of stage,
    46ft 6in; Stage floor, flat; Trap doors, 1; Scenery
    storage rooms, 1 (basement); Dressing rooms, 2 (basement)
  DIMENSIONS OF AUDITORIUM: Distance between side walls
    of auditorium, 46ft 6in; Distance stage to back wall
    of auditorium, 47ft 2in; Orchestra pit, none
  SEATING (1 level): 1st level, 264
  MAJOR TYPES OF ENTERTAINMENT: Drama, vaudeville, musical
    comedy, concerts, medicine shows, civic functions
  MAJOR STARS WHO APPEARED AT THEATRE: John Phillip Sousa
  ADDITIONAL INFORMATION: The Enosburg Opera House was a
    gift to the town by the B. J. Kendall Company, a firm
    which manufactured patent medicines. The building housed
    travelling shows, as well as Kendall Company sponsored
    medicine shows.

Hyde Park, VT

HYDE PARK OPERA HOUSE, Main Street
  OPENING DATE: 1910
  STYLE OF ARCHITECTURE: Neo-Classical
  FACADE: White wood   TYPE OF THEATRE: (a)
  DEGREE OF RESTORATION: (a)   CURRENT USE: Theatre
  STAGE DIMENSIONS AND EQUIPMENT: Height and width of
    proscenium, 20ft x 22ft; Shape of proscenium arch,
    square; Distance from edge of stage to back wall of
    stage, 18ft; Distance from edge of stage to curtain
    line, 3ft; Depth under stage, 25ft; Stage floor, flat;
    Trap doors, 1; Scenery storage rooms, 1 (above
    auditorium); Dressing rooms, 6 (basement)
  DIMENSIONS OF AUDITORIUM: Orchestra pit, none
  SHAPE OF THE AUDITORIUM: Square
  MAJOR TYPES OF ENTERTAINMENT: Drama, musical comedy
  ADDITIONAL INFORMATION: The theatre is currently occupied
    by the Lamoille County Players. In 1952, local officials
    considered selling the property so that the building
    could be demolished to make room for a bowling alley;

but it was, instead, rented to the Players and restored
by them. An early act curtain with a painted image of
the Natural Bridge in Virginia remains.

Londonderry, VT

LONDONDERRY TOWN HALL (other name: Londonderry Town House),
    Middletown Road
  OPENING DATE: 1860
  TYPE OF BUILDING: Community hall   FACADE: Clapboard
  TYPE OF THEATRE: (b)   DEGREE OF RESTORATION: (d)
  CURRENT USE: Theatre, municipal building
  LOCATION OF AUDITORIUM: Ground floor
  MAJOR TYPES OF ENTERTAINMENT: Drama, lectures, concerts,
    civic functions
  ADDITIONAL INFORMATION: The town hall was built in 1860,
    but the theatre portion was constructed after 1889. In
    that year, according to town records, a theatrical group
    was given permission to erect an addition to the back of
    the town hall to create a stage area. At a later date,
    a dining area was added under the theatre. The stage
    curtain, "View on the Rhine," was restored in 1976. It
    is inscribed, "Cha's Huiest Studio, TROY, N.Y. 1890?".

Montpelier, VT

BLANCHARD OPERA HOUSE, 73 Main Street
  OPENING DATE: August 24, 1885
  OPENING SHOW: Augustin Daly's 7-20-8
  ARCHITECT: George H. Guernsey
  STYLE OF ARCHITECTURE: Victorian   FACADE: Dark red brick
  TYPE OF THEATRE: (b)   DEGREE OF RESTORATION: (c)
  CLOSING DATE: April 1, 1910   CURRENT USE: Apartments,
    offices, shops   LOCATION OF AUDITORIUM: Second floor
  STAGE DIMENSIONS AND EQUIPMENT: Height and width of
    proscenium, 25ft x 33ft; Shape of proscenium arch,
    rectangular; Distance from edge of stage to back wall
    of stage, 45ft; Distance between side walls of stage,
    61ft 8in; Dressing rooms, 6 (2 under stage, 4 on sides)
  DIMENSIONS OF AUDITORIUM: Distance between side walls
    of auditorium, 62ft; Distance stage to back wall of
    auditorium, 73ft
  SEATING: 1st level, 600; 2nd level, 160
  SHAPE OF THE AUDITORIUM: U-shaped
  MAJOR TYPES OF ENTERTAINMENT: Drama, musical comedy,
    minstrel shows
  MAJOR STARS WHO APPEARED AT THEATRE: John T. Raymond
    (1885), Denman Thompson (1885), Henry E. Dixey (1888),
    Hortense Rhea (1890), Edward Harrigan (1900), Nance
    O'Neil (1905)

Randolph, VT

CHANDLER MUSIC HALL (other name: Chandler Music Hall and
   Cultural Center), 71-73 Main Street
   OPENING DATE: August 20, 1907   OPENING SHOW: Concert
   ARCHITECT: Ernest N. Boyden   FACADE: Concrete block
   TYPE OF THEATRE: (a)   DEGREE OF RESTORATION: (a)
   CURRENT USE: Concert hall, theatre
   LOCATION OF AUDITORIUM: Ground floor
   STAGE DIMENSIONS AND EQUIPMENT: Height and width of
      proscenium, 19ft x 32ft; Shape of proscenium arch,
      rectangular; Distance from edge of stage to back wall
      of stage, 24ft; Distance from edge of stage to curtain
      line, 3ft; Distance between side walls of stage, 58ft;
      Depth under stage, 12ft; Stage floor, raked; Trap doors,
      1; Scenery storage rooms, 1 (basement of cultural
      center); Dressing rooms, 8 (under stage: 4 group;
      4 single)
   DIMENSIONS OF AUDITORIUM: Distance between side walls
      of auditorium, 58ft 6in; Distance stage to back wall
      of auditorium, 50ft; Capacity of orchestra pit, 25
   SEATING: 1st level, 438; 2nd level; 120; 3rd level,
      55; boxes, 12
   SHAPE OF THE AUDITORIUM: Modified horseshoe
   MAJOR TYPES OF ENTERTAINMENT: Drama, musical comedy,
      vaudeville, opera, concerts, movies, lectures,
      political meetings, civic functions
   MAJOR STARS WHO APPEARED AT THEATRE: Denman Thompson
      (an appearance billed as his last performance in The
      Old Homestead), Margery Wilson, Elsie Ferguson, Margaret
      Wycherly, John Phillip Sousa
   ADDITIONAL INFORMATION: The music hall has been de-
      scribed as "a jewel from yesteryear when live theater,
      orchestral and vaudeville performances, and silent movies
      were presented there usually to large audiences" and is
      reputed to be the only "free-standing" opera house
      (built exclusively as an opera house; not above a store
      or town hall) in the state.   The building adjacent to
      the music hall has been converted into a cultural center.

Rutland, VT

PARAMOUNT THEATRE (other name: The Playhouse), 30 Center
   Street
   OPENING DATE: January 1914
   FACADE: Tan brick   TYPE OF THEATRE: (a)
   DEGREE OF RESTORATION: (c)   CURRENT USE: Vacant
   ADDITIONAL INFORMATION: The building is currently unused.
      A bond issue to restore the building was defeated in the
      spring of 1986.

Rutland, VT

RUTLAND OPERA HOUSE, 18-20 Merchants' Row
  OPENING DATE: October 10, 1881
  OPENING SHOW: The Mighty Dollar
  ARCHITECT: Jean J. R. Randall   STYLE OF ARCHITECTURE:
    Victorian   FACADE: Red brick with red mortar
  TYPE OF THEATRE: (b)   DEGREE OF RESTORATION: (c)
  CLOSING DATE: March 4, 1915   CURRENT USE: The shell houses
    shopping mall   LOCATION OF AUDITORIUM: Second floor
  STAGE DIMENSIONS AND EQUIPMENT: Height and width of
    proscenium, 20ft x 23ft; Shape of proscenium arch,
    rectangular; Distance from edge of stage to back wall
    of stage, 25ft; Distance from edge of stage to curtain
    line, 5ft; Distance between side walls of stage, 56ft;
    Depth under stage, 5ft; Trap doors, 1
  DIMENSIONS OF AUDITORIUM: Capacity of orchestra pit, 10
  SEATING (2 levels)
  SHAPE OF THE AUDITORIUM: U-shaped
  MAJOR TYPES OF ENTERTAINMENT: Drama, musical comedy,
    minstrel shows
  MAJOR STARS WHO APPEARED AT THEATRE: Denman Thompson,
    Sarah Cowell Le Moyne

Vergennes, VT

VERGENNES OPERA HOUSE (other names: Vergennes City Hall,
    Vergennes Theater), 120 Main Street
  OPENING DATE: 1900
  TYPE OF BUILDING: Municipal   FACADE: Brick
  TYPE OF THEATRE: (b)   DEGREE OF RESTORATION: (c)
  CLOSING DATE: 1974   CURRENT USE: Vacant
  LOCATION OF AUDITORIUM: Second floor
  STAGE DIMENSIONS AND EQUIPMENT: Height and width of
    proscenium, 16ft x 40ft; Shape of proscenium arch,
    arched; Distance from edge of stage to back wall of
    stage, 40ft; Distance from edge of stage to curtain
    line, 3ft; Stage floor, flat; Scenery storage rooms
    (beneath stage)
  DIMENSIONS OF AUDITORIUM: Distance between side walls
    of auditorium, 60ft; Distance stage to back wall of
    auditorium, 60ft; Orchestra pit, none
  SEATING (2 levels): 1st level, 300; 2nd level, 200
  SHAPE OF THE AUDITORIUM: Square
  MAJOR TYPES OF ENTERTAINMENT: Drama, musical comedy,
    vaudeville, burlesque, opera

Woodstock, VT

TOWN HALL THEATRE (other name: Opera House), 29 the Green
  OPENING DATE: October 12, 1900
  OPENING SHOW: The Sunshine of Paradise Alley
  ARCHITECT: Arthur H. Smith   STYLE OF ARCHITECTURE: New
    England Colonial   TYPE OF BUILDING: Town hall

FACADE: Red brick   TYPE OF THEATRE: (b)
DEGREE OF RESTORATION: (a)   CURRENT USE: Theatre
LOCATION OF AUDITORIUM: Second floor
STAGE DIMENSIONS AND EQUIPMENT: Distance from edge of stage
    to back wall of stage, 25ft; Distance between side walls
    of stage, 50ft
DIMENSIONS OF AUDITORIUM: Distance between side walls
    of auditorium, 50ft; Distance stage to back wall of
    auditorium, 57ft; Orchestra pit, yes
SEATING (2 levels): 1st level, 400; 2nd level, 50
SHAPE OF THE AUDITORIUM: Rectangular
MAJOR TYPES OF ENTERTAINMENT: Drama, vauedville, opera
ADDITIONAL INFORMATION: The theatre was planned as
    "a modern theatre or opera house with sloping floor,
    curved seats, sunk[en] orchestra, with splendid modern
    drop curtain, scenery and stage appointments.... The
    acoustics of the room are good and from every seat in
    the house an equally fine view of the stage can be
    obtained." (INTER-STATE JOURNAL AND ADVERTISER, Mid-
    summer, 1900).

Virginia

Abingdon, VA

BARTER THEATRE (other names: Abindon Opera House, Town
    Hall, Temperance Hall), Main Street at Goodman Place
    OPENING DATE: 1833   OPENING SHOW: Unknown (1876)
    ARCHITECT: Built under David Preston's leadership
    STYLE OF ARCHITECTURE: Neo-Classical   TYPE OF BUILDING:
    Church, hospital   FACADE: Red brick some white
    TYPE OF THEATRE: (c)   DEGREE OF RESTORATION: (a)
    CURRENT USE: Theatre   PERFORMANCE SPACES IN BUILDING: 1
    LOCATION OF AUDITORIUM: First floor
    STAGE DIMENSIONS AND EQUIPMENT: Height and width of
    proscenium, 12ft x 28ft 3in; Shape of proscenium arch,
    rectangular; Distance from edge of stage to back wall
    of stage, 27ft 6in; Distance from edge of stage to
    curtain line, 5ft 6in; Distance between side walls of
    stage, 48ft; Distance from stage floor to fly loft,
    20ft; Depth under stage, 9ft; Stage floor, flat; Trap
    doors, 2; Scenery storage rooms, 1 (scene dock, rear
    of building); Dressing rooms 2 (basement)
    DIMENSIONS OF AUDITORIUM: Distance between side walls
    of auditorium, 48ft; Distance stage to back wall of
    auditorium, 50ft; Capacity of orchestra pit, 15
    SEATING (2 levels): 1st level, 310; 2nd level, 70
    SHAPE OF THE AUDITORIUM: Rectangular with continental
    seating
    MAJOR TYPES OF ENTERTAINMENT: Drama, contemporary and
    classic comedies
    ADDITIONAL INFORMATION: Built as a Town Hall in 1833,
    the building housed the first theatrical performance
    in 1876. In 1933, it became known as Barter Theatre
    for its practice of accepting bartered food in lieu of
    admission costs. In 1953, the theatre was refurbished
    with $75,000 worth of materials from the soon-to-be-
    demolished Empire Theatre in New York City. The Barter
    Theatre is the State Theatre of Virginia.

Charlottesville, VA

LEVY OPERA HOUSE/TOWN HALL (other name: Opera House),
    High and Park Streets
    OPENING DATE: December 1852
    STYLE OF ARCHITECTURE: Classical   TYPE OF BUILDING:
    Shop, church, school   FACADE: Brick
    TYPE OF THEATRE: (a)   DEGREE OF RESTORATION: (c)
    CLOSING DATE: 1912   CURRENT USE: Apartments
    PERFORMANCE SPACES IN BUILDING: 1
    LOCATION OF AUDITORIUM: First floor
    STAGE DIMENSIONS AND EQUIPMENT: Height and width of
    proscenium, 20ft x 30ft; Distance from edge of stage
    to back wall of stage, 28ft; Distance from edge of
    stage to curtain line, 4ft; Distance between side walls
    of stage, 48ft; Distance from stage floor to fly loft,
    50ft; Stage floor, flat; Trap doors, 1; Dressing rooms,
    2 (basement)
    DIMENSIONS OF AUDITORIUM: Distance between side walls
    of auditorium, 40ft; Distance stage to back wall of
    auditorium, 40ft
    SEATING (2 levels)
    SHAPE OF THE AUDITORIUM: Square
    MAJOR TYPES OF ENTERTAINMENT: Local and traveling
    productions, concerts, minstrel shows
    ADDITIONAL INFORMATION: No trace of theatre survives.
    It is difficult to determine earliest measurements.
    Levy, the owner in 1888 enlarged "a narrow cramped
    stage." Theatre had a movable bridge. The theatre
    was remodeled in 1914 and again during the 1980s.

Harrisonburg, VA

NEW VIRGINIA (other name: Virginia), South Main Street
    OPENING DATE: 1913
    STYLE OF ARCHITECTURE: Commercial
    TYPE OF BUILDING: Movie theatre   FACADE: Red brick
    TYPE OF THEATRE: (a)   DEGREE OF RESTORATION: (c)
    CLOSING DATE: December 1985   CURRENT USE: Vacant
    LOCATION OF AUDITORIUM: First floor
    STAGE DIMENSIONS AND EQUIPMENT: Distance from edge of stage
    to back wall of stage, 33ft; Distance between side walls
    of stage, 68ft
    SEATING (2 levels)
    SHAPE OF THE AUDITORIUM: Rectangular
    MAJOR TYPES OF ENTERTAINMENT: Local and touring productions
    ADDITIONAL INFORMATION: The Virginia closed in 1985 when
    its owner opened several mall cinemas and no new lessee
    appeared. The theatre has an unusually tall stagehouse
    that stands out against the adjacent buildings.

Lynchburg, VA

ACADEMY OF MUSIC, 6th and Main Street

OPENING DATE: February 1, 1905
OPENING SHOW: The Show Girl
ARCHITECTS: Edward S. Frye and Aubrey Chesterman
STYLE OF ARCHITECTURE: Beaux Arts   FACADE: Stone
TYPE OF THEATRE: (a)   DEGREE OF RESTORATION: (b)
CLOSING DATE: Late 1950s
STAGE DIMENSIONS AND EQUIPMENT: Height and width of
   proscenium, 35ft x 35ft; Shape of proscenium arch,
   square; Distance from edge of stage to back wall of
   stage, 37ft; Distance from edge of stage to curtain
   line, 3ft; Distance between side walls of stage,
   78ft; Stage floor, flat; Trap doors, 3; Dressing
   rooms, 8 (understage)
DIMENSIONS OF AUDITORIUM: Distance between side walls
   of auditorium, 65ft; Distance stage to back wall, 56ft
SEATING (3 levels): 1st level, 410; level, 334;
   3rd level, 196
MAJOR TYPES OF ENTERTAINMENT: Local and touring productions
ADDITIONAL INFORMATION: Restoration of the building is in
   progress. Six boxes were removed when the theatre was
   converted to movies.

Norfolk, VA

WELLS THEATRE, 108 Tazwell Street
OPENING DATE: 1913   OPENING SHOW: The Merry Countess
ARCHITECTS: E. C. Horn and Sons (New York)
STYLE OF ARCHITECTURE: Beaux Arts Classic
FACADE: Concrete and steel
TYPE OF THEATRE: (a)   DEGREE OF RESTORATION: (b)
CURRENT USE: Theatre   PERFORMANCE SPACES IN BUILDING: 1
STAGE DIMENSIONS AND EQUIPMENT: Height and width of
   proscenium, 28ft x 36ft; Shape of proscenium arch,
   rectangular; Distance from edge of stage to back wall
   of stage, 47ft; Distance from edge of stage to curtain
   line, 12ft; Depth under stage, 7ft; Stage floor, flat;
   Trap doors, 3; Dressing rooms, 3 (second level stage
   left)
SEATING (3 levels)
SHAPE OF THE AUDITORIUM: U-shaped
MAJOR TYPES OF ENTERTAINMENT: Drama, movies, musicals
MAJOR STARS WHO APPEARED AT THEATRE: Will Rogers, Billie
   Burke, Douglas Fairbanks, Sousa, Maude Adams, Otis
   Skinner, John Drew, Fred and Adele Astaire
ADDITIONAL INFORMATION: The theatre was built as one of
   the Wells Brothers' chain of thirty four theatres along
   the Atlantic. From 1960 to 1979, the proscenium arch
   was cemented shut and a restaurant was situated on the
   theatre's huge stage.

Pocahontas, VA

OPERA HOUSE
OPENING DATE: 1895

STYLE OF ARCHITECTURE: Vernacular   FACADE: Brick
TYPE OF THEATRE: (a)   DEGREE OF RESTORATION: (a)
CURRENT USE: Dinner theatre
LOCATION OF AUDITORIUM: First floor
STAGE DIMENSIONS AND EQUIPMENT: * Height and width of
   proscenium, 15ft x 30ft; Distance from edge of stage
   to back wall of stage, 25ft; Distance from edge of
   stage to curtain line, 3ft; Distance between side
   walls of stage, 47ft; Depth under stage, 8ft; Trap
   doors, 3; Scenery storage rooms, 1
SHAPE OF THE AUDITORIUM: Rectangular
MAJOR TYPES OF ENTERTAINMENT: Local and touring companies
ADDITIONAL INFORMATION: Theatre is now a dinner theatre.

Richmond, VA

EMPIRE THEATRE (other name: Strand), 118 West Broad Street
   OPENING DATE: December 1911   OPENING SHOW: Vaudeville
   STYLE OF ARCHITECTURE: Beaux Arts   TYPE OF BUILDING:
   Movie theatre   FACADE: Brick   TYPE OF THEATRE: (a)
   DEGREE OF RESTORATION: (a)   CURRENT USE: Theater
   LOCATION OF AUDITORIUM: First floor
   STAGE DIMENSIONS AND EQUIPMENT: Height and width of
   proscenium, 30ft x 33ft; Distance from edge of stage
   to back wall of stage, 31ft 9in; Distance between side
   walls of stage, 58ft 6in; Stage floor, flat
   DIMENSIONS OF AUDITORIUM: Capacity of orchestra pit, 15
   SEATING (3 levels)
   MAJOR TYPES OF ENTERTAINMENT: Local and traveling shows
   MAJOR STARS WHO APPEARED AT THEATRE: Kit Carson, Otis
   Skinner, Mary Pickford
   ADDITIONAL INFORMATION: A 1976 renovation enlarged the
   orchestra pit capacity to 45. The original fire curtain
   has been rediscovered. The theatre is part of a downtown
   restoration project.

Washington

Everett, WA

EVERETT THEATRE, 2911 Colby Avenue
  OPENING DATE: 1901
  ARCHITECTS: Bebb and Mendel   STYLE OF ARCHITECTURE:
    Renaissance Revival   FACADE: Buff-colored brick
    (1923 facade)   TYPE OF THEATRE: (a)   DEGREE OF
  RESTORATION: (d)   CURRENT USE: Movie theatre
  LOCATION OF AUDITORIUM: Ground floor
  STAGE DIMENSIONS AND EQUIPMENT: * Height and width of
    proscenium, 30ft x 28ft; Distance from edge of stage
    to back wall of stage, 36ft; Distance between side
    walls of stage, 66ft
  MAJOR TYPES OF ENTERTAINMENT: Drama, musical comedy, movies
  ADDITIONAL INFORMATION: The Everett was severely damaged
    by fire on December 11, 1923 and was rebuilt under the
    supervision of a designer named Leather. Further
    modifications were made in 1952.

Seattle, WA

MOORE THEATRE (other names: Moore Egyptian, Orpheum),
    2nd and Virginia Streets
  OPENING DATE: 1907
  ARCHITECT: E. W. Houghton   TYPE OF BUILDING: Hotel
  FACADE: Concrete, ceramic glazed brick
  TYPE OF THEATRE: (a)   DEGREE OF RESTORATION: (d)
  CURRENT USE: Theatre
  STAGE DIMENSIONS AND EQUIPMENT: Distance between side
    walls of stage, 71ft; Dressing rooms, 14 (back stage
    and below stage)
  DIMENSIONS OF AUDITORIUM: Capacity of orchestra pit, 23
  SEATING (3 levels): 1st level, 779; 2nd level, 662;
    3rd level, 509
  MAJOR TYPES OF ENTERTAINMENT: Drama, musical comedy,
    vaudeville, dance, concerts. revues, movies, boxing
    matches, revival meetings

MAJOR STARS WHO APPEARED AT THEATRE: Ballet Russe de
   Monte Carlo, Josef Hoffman, Sergei Rachmaninoff, The
   Weavers, Julie Harris, Mickey Rooney, Dizzy Gillespie,
   Marie Dressler, Victor Moore, Ethel Barrymore, John Drew,
   Billie Burke, Pavlova, Feodor Chaliapin, and others
ADDITIONAL INFORMATION: The Moore Theatre shares a
   building with a hotel which was erected to accommodate
   anticipated crowds coming to the Alaska Yukon Pacific
   Exposition in 1909. The hotel opened in April 1909,
   with the theatre opening several months later. The
   theatre was first managed by James Cort and in the
   1920s was part of the Orpheum circuit.

Yakima, WA

SWITZER OPERA HOUSE, 25 North Front Street
   OPENING DATE: 1889
   ARCHITECT: Abram F. Switzer   TYPE OF BUILDING:
      Brewing company   FACADE: Brick   TYPE OF THEATRE: (a)
   DEGREE OF RESTORATION: (c)   CLOSING DATE: c. 1897
   CURRENT USE: Vacant
   LOCATION OF AUDITORIUM: Second floor
   MAJOR TYPES OF ENTERTAINMENT: Drama, vaudeville
   ADDITIONAL INFORMATION: The theatre had a level floor
      and a small stage with only three sets (parlor, kitchen
      and garden). The opening of larger, more modern theatres
      doomed the theatre in 1897. A later attempt to revive
      it, with plans for renovation and presentation of
      "refined and educational vaudeville," proved futile.

West Virginia

Charles Town, WV

THE OLD OPERA HOUSE (other name: The New Opera House, 1910),
    Liberty and George Streets
  OPENING DATE: February 11, 1911
  OPENING SHOW: Talent Show by Daughters of the Confederacy
  ARCHITECT: T. E. Mullett   STYLE OF ARCHITECTURE:
    Conventional   TYPE OF BUILDING: Theatre and bar
  FACADE: Brick   TYPE OF THEATRE: (a)   DEGREE OF
  RESTORATION: (a)   CURRENT USE: Community theatre
  STAGE DIMENSIONS AND EQUIPMENT: Height and width of
    proscenium, 16ft x 25ft; Shape of proscenium arch,
    rectangular; Distance from edge of stage to back wall
    of stage, 30ft; Distance from edge of stage to curtain
    line, 3ft; Distance between side walls of stage, 8ft;
    Distance from stage floor to fly loft, 45ft; Depth under
    stage, 15ft; Stage floor, flat; Scenery storage rooms, 1
    (basement); Dressing rooms, 5 (adjacent to building)
  DIMENSIONS OF AUDITORIUM: Distance between side walls
    of auditorium, 40ft; Distance stage to back wall of
    auditorium, 60ft; Capacity of orchestra pit, 14
  SEATING (2 levels)
  SHAPE OF THE AUDITORIUM: U-shaped
  MAJOR TYPES OF ENTERTAINMENT: All types including movies
  ADDITIONAL INFORMATION: Home of Old Opera House Acting
    Company, a community theatre that produces two musicals,
    four plays, and two dinner theatres annually.

Martinsburg, WV

APOLLO THEATRE (other name: Thorn)
  OPENING DATE: 1913   STYLE OF ARCHITECTURE: Commercial
  FACADE: Brick   TYPE OF THEATRE: (a)   DEGREE OF
  RESTORATION: (a)   CURRENT USE: Civic theatre
  LOCATION OF AUDITORIUM: First floor
  MAJOR TYPES OF ENTERTAINMENT: Drama, vaudeville, and
    movies

Wisconsin

Baraboo, WI

AL RINGLING THEATRE, 136 Fourth Avenue
OPENING DATE: November 17, 1915
OPENING SHOW: Lady Luxury
ARCHITECTS: Rapp and Rapp   FACADE: Stone, cement,
  polished marble   TYPE OF THEATRE: (a)   DEGREE OF
RESTORATION: (a)   CURRENT USE: Movie theatre
LOCATION OF AUDITORIUM: Ground floor
STAGE DIMENSIONS AND EQUIPMENT: Height and width of
  proscenium, 22ft x 37ft; Shape of proscenium arch,
  rectangular; Distance from edge of stage to back wall
  of stage, 30ft; Distance between side walls of stage,
  74ft; Dressing rooms, 11 (below stage)
DIMENSIONS OF AUDITORIUM: Capacity of orchestra pit, 17
SEATING (2 levels): 1st level, 772; 2nd level, 102
MAJOR TYPES OF ENTERTAINMENT: Drama, musical comedy,
  opera, vaudeville, concerts, movies
MAJOR STARS WHO APPEARED AT THEATRE: Warner Baxter,
  Lionel Barrymore, Olga Petrova, Maude Adams, May
  Robson, Irene Fenwick, Fiske O'Hara, John Barrymore,
  Charlotte Greenwood
ADDITIONAL INFORMATION: Al Ringling, of the famed Ringling
  Brothers, allegedly built the theatre "to keep himself
  from utter idleness" during his retirement. The theatre
  has been variously described as "America's prettiest
  playhouse" and a "red plush, gold lined jewel box." The
  original Wurlitzer pipe organ was replaced in 1928 by a
  new three manual Barton pipe organ.

Beaver Dam, WI

CONCERT HALL, 105-107 Front Street
  OPENING DATE: c. 1863
  TYPE OF BUILDING: Commercial   FACADE: Brick
  TYPE OF THEATRE: (b)   DEGREE OF RESTORATION: (c)
  CURRENT USE: Stores   LOCATION OF AUDITORIUM: Third floor

STAGE DIMENSIONS AND EQUIPMENT: Height and width of
    proscenium, 12ft x 20ft; Distance from edge of stage
    to back wall of stage, 18ft; Distance from edge of
    stage to curtain line, 7ft; Depth under stage, 4ft
DIMENSIONS OF AUDITORIUM: Distance stage to back wall
    of auditorium, 90ft
MAJOR TYPES OF ENTERTAINMENT: Drama, lectures, concerts,
    minstrel shows, dances, medicine shows, political
    rallies, civic functions
MAJOR STARS WHO APPEARED AT THEATRE: P. T. Barnum, Tom
    Thumb, Lavinia Warren, Commodore Nutt, Artemus Ward,
    Mark Twain, the Black Patti, Blind Tom, John T. Kelly,
    James Whitcomb Riley, Primrose and West, and others
ADDITIONAL INFORMATION: This theatre is the subject of
    the book, Town Hall Tonight, by Harlowe R. Hoyt.

Columbus, WI

COLUMBUS CITY HALL AUDITORIUM (other name: City Hall Opera
    House), Dickason Boulevard and West James Street
OPENING DATE: March 1893   OPENING SHOW: Lost in the Hills
ARCHITECT: T. D. Allen   TYPE OF BUILDING: City hall
FACADE: Cream brick with red sandstone trim
TYPE OF THEATRE: (b)   DEGREE OF RESTORATION: (b)
CLOSING DATE: Late 1930s   CURRENT USE: Vacant
LOCATION OF AUDITORIUM: Second floor
STAGE DIMENSIONS AND EQUIPMENT: Height and width of
    proscenium, 13ft 2in x 25ft 3in; Shape of proscenium
    arch, rectangular; Distance from edge of stage to back
    wall of stage, 26ft 3in; Distance from edge of stage to
    curtain line, 4ft; Distance between side walls of stage,
    42ft 6in; Depth under stage, 4ft 5in; Stage floor, flat;
    Trap doors, 3; Scenery storage rooms, 1 (fourth floor
    attic); Dressing rooms, 3 (both sides of stage)
DIMENSIONS OF AUDITORIUM: Distance between side walls of
    auditorium, 56ft 6in; Distance stage to back wall of
    auditorium, 52ft; Orchestra pit, yes
SEATING (2 levels): 1st level, 442; 2nd level, 186
MAJOR TYPES OF ENTERTAINMENT: Drama, vaudeville, minstrel
    shows, operettas, concerts, lectures, movies, local
    variety shows, civic functions
MAJOR STARS WHO APPEARED AT THEATRE: William Quentmeyer,
    Erle Smith, partner of Bunny Berigan (Smith and Berigan)
ADDITIONAL INFORMATION: First floor and exterior have
    been restored and restoration of the remainder will
    be accomplished as money permits.

Fifield, WI

FIFIELD TOWN HALL (other name: Old Opera House),
    Main State Highway 13 and Pine Street
OPENING DATE: 1894   TYPE OF BUILDING: Town hall
FACADE: White wood with dark green trim
TYPE OF THEATRE: (b)   DEGREE OF RESTORATION: (a)

CLOSING DATE: 1923   CURRENT USE: Display area in a museum
LOCATION OF AUDITORIUM: Second floor
STAGE DIMENSIONS AND EQUIPMENT: Height and width of
  proscenium, 10ft 4in x 15ft 2in; Shape of proscenium
  arch, square; Distance from edge of stage to back wall
  of stage, 16ft; Distance between side walls of stage,
  30ft 10in; Stage floor, raked; Trap doors, 0; Scenery
  storage rooms, 1 (rear of theatre); Dressing rooms, 1
SEATING (1 level): 1st level, 125
SHAPE OF THE AUDITORIUM: Oblong
MAJOR TYPES OF ENTERTAINMENT: Drama, vaudeville, opera,
  chautauquas, medicine shows, lectures, local variety
  shows
ADDITIONAL INFORMATION: The theatre was used until 1923
  when a new gym/theatre was built in the local school.

Kewaunee, WI

KEWAUNEE OPERA HOUSE (other name: Bohemian Cesam Sokol),
  Milwaukee and Harrison Streets
OPENING DATE: c. 1900
TYPE OF BUILDING: Commercial   FACADE: Red brick
TYPE OF THEATRE: (a)   DEGREE OF RESTORATION: (c)
CLOSING DATE: c. 1950   CURRENT USE: Store, apartments
LOCATION OF AUDITORIUM: Ground floor
STAGE DIMENSIONS AND EQUIPMENT: Height and width of
  proscenium, 14ft x 14ft; Shape of proscenium arch,
  arched; Distance from edge of stage to back wall of
  stage, 24ft; Distance from edge of stage to curtain
  line, 8ft; Depth under stage, 4ft; Stage floor, flat;
  Trap doors, 0; Dressing rooms, 5 (under stage)
SEATING (2 levels): 1st level, 300; 2nd level, 100
SHAPE OF THE AUDITORIUM: Square
MAJOR TYPES OF ENTERTAINMENT: Drama, local variety shows,
  dance, movies
ADDITIONAL INFORMATION: The lower floor is used as an
  electrical showroom and the balcony and projection
  room have been converted into apartments.

Menomonie, WI

MABEL TAINTER MEMORIAL THEATER (other name: Tainter Theater),
  205 Main Street
OPENING DATE: Formally July 3, 1890
OPENING SHOW: Erminie, September 17, 1890
ARCHITECT: Harvey Ellis   STYLE OF ARCHITECTURE:
  Romanesque   TYPE OF BUILDING: Library, meeting rooms
FACADE: Dunville sandstone   TYPE OF THEATRE: (b)
DEGREE OF RESTORATION: (a)   CURRENT USE: Theatre, library,
LOCATION OF AUDITORIUM: Ground floor
STAGE DIMENSIONS AND EQUIPMENT: Height and width of
  proscenium, 38ft 3in x 26ft 5in; Shape of proscenium
  arch, arched; Distance from edge of stage to back wall
  of stage, 20ft; Distance from edge of stage to curtain

line, 3ft; Distance between side walls of stage, 24ft
6in; Depth under stage, 14ft; Stage floor, flat; Trap
doors, 3; Scenery storage rooms, 1 (scenery loft,
backstage); Dressing rooms, 7 (backstage, basement,
and 3rd floor)
DIMENSIONS OF AUDITORIUM: Distance between side walls
  of auditorium, 51ft; Distance stage to back wall of
  auditorium, 37ft; Capacity of orchestra pit, 8
SEATING (2 levels): 1st level, 204; 2nd level, 109
SHAPE OF THE AUDITORIUM: Fan-shaped
MAJOR TYPES OF ENTERTAINMENT: Drama, lectures
MAJOR STARS WHO APPEARED AT THEATRE: George Arliss,
  Joseph Jefferson, Helen Keller, Roald Amundson, The
  Hyer Sisters, Frank and John Winninger Companies,
  Edward Arnold, Frances Dee
ADDITIONAL INFORMATION: The Mabel Tainter Memorial
  Building was erected by Captain and Mrs. Andrew
  Tainter as a memorial to their daughter who had died
  of appendicitis at the age of nineteen. In 1959, the
  Mabel Tainter Memorial Building Preservation Association
  was organized and preservation work began slowly on the
  building which has been described as an excellent example
  of "the Gilded Age." Among the first restoration projects
  was "the huge water-powered" Steere and Turner pipe organ
  which had been silent for 20 years. The organ, installed
  when the theatre was built, contains 1597 pipes and 25
  stops.

Milton, WI

GOODRICH HALL, 4 South Janesville Street
OPENING DATE: Pre-1885
STYLE OF ARCHITECTURE: Frame Vernacular
TYPE OF BUILDING: Creamery   FACADE: Frame painted
  dark color   TYPE OF THEATRE: (b)   DEGREE OF
RESTORATION: (c)   CURRENT USE: Apartment house
SEATING (1 level): 1st level, 400
MAJOR TYPES OF ENTERTAINMENT: Drama, musical comedy,
  poetry readings
ADDITIONAL INFORMATION: When the building was converted to
  apartments, the stage area was still visible in different
  rooms. In between its use as a theatre and converstion
  into apartments, the area was layered over with hardwood
  and used as a roller skating rink.

Milwaukee, WI

PABST THEATRE, 144 East Wells Street
OPENING DATE: November 9, 1895   OPENING SHOW: Zwei Wappen
ARCHITECT: Otto Strack   STYLE OF ARCHITECTURE: Victorian
FACADE: Brick, sandstone   TYPE OF THEATRE: (a)
DEGREE OF RESTORATION: (a)   CURRENT USE: Theatre
LOCATION OF AUDITORIUM: Ground floor
STAGE DIMENSIONS AND EQUIPMENT: Height and width of

proscenium, 21ft x 35ft; Shape of proscenium arch,
arched; Distance from edge of stage to back wall of
stage, 38ft; Distance between side walls of stage,
72ft; Stage floor, flat; Trap doors, 6; Scenery storage
rooms, 1 (trap room used for storage); Dressing rooms,
13 (stage level, above stage, and off trap room)
DIMENSIONS OF AUDITORIUM: Capacity of orchestra pit, 40
SEATING (3 levels): 1st level, 592; 2nd level, 397;
3rd level, 399
MAJOR STARS WHO APPEARED AT THEATRE: Caruso, Bill
"Bojangles" Robinson, Fritz Kreisler, Bernhardt,
Jascha Heifetz, Pavlova, Vladimir Horowitz, Pablo
Casals, Harry Lauder, Josef Hoffman, John Phillip
Sousa, Jan Paderewski, Ernestine Schumann-Heink, Julie
Harris, Marlene Dietrich, Peter Ustinov, Lynn Fontanne,
Alfred Lunt, Helen Hayes, Katherine Hepburn, and others
ADDITIONAL INFORMATION: The theatre was built by the
Pabst Brewing interests to replace the Stadt Theatre
which had burned. It was remodeled in 1928 and many
of original features were changed. The crystal chande-
lier, boxes and half of the grand staircase were removed;
the center aisle was eliminated; and the deep reds of
the interior were eliminated in favor of lighter, softer
colors. In 1953, the theatre was sold to the Pabst
Foundation and in 1960, to the City of Milwaukee.
During the 1970s, the theatre was restored to its 1895
appearance and on September 23, 1976 the Pabst reopened.

Mineral Point, WI

HIGH STREET CIVIC CENTER (other names: Municipal Theatre,
Opera House, Point Theatre), 139 High Street
OPENING DATE: Winter, 1915
OPENING SHOW: The Misleading Lady
ARCHITECTS: Claude and Storck   FACADE: Dark red brick
TYPE OF THEATRE: (a)   DEGREE OF RESTORATION: (d)
CURRENT USE: Theatre
LOCATION OF AUDITORIUM: Ground floor
STAGE DIMENSIONS AND EQUIPMENT: Height and width of
proscenium, 24ft x 26ft; Shape of proscenium arch,
arched; Distance from edge of stage to back wall of
stage, 28ft 2in; Distance from edge of stage to
curtain line, 4ft; Distance between side walls of
stage, 51ft; Depth under stage, 9ft 2in; Stage floor,
flat; Trap doors, 1; Scenery storage rooms, 1 (storage
gallery above stage left; Dressing rooms, 7 (under stage)
DIMENSIONS OF AUDITORIUM: Distance between side walls
of auditorium, 51ft; Distance stage to back wall of
auditorium, 28ft 2in; Capacity of orchestra pit, 20
SEATING (2 levels): 1st level, 210; 2nd level, 220
SHAPE OF THE AUDITORIUM: Horseshoe-shaped
MAJOR TYPES OF ENTERTAINMENT: Drama, musical comedy,
vaudeville, movies, dance
MAJOR STARS WHO APPEARED AT THEATRE: Gene Autry, Maynard
Ferguson

Oshkosh, WI

GRAND OPERA HOUSE, 100 High Street
  OPENING DATE: August 9, 1883
  OPENING SHOW: The Bohemian Girl
  ARCHITECT: William Waters   STYLE OF ARCHITECTURE:
    Romanesque   FACADE: Cream city brick
  TYPE OF THEATRE: (a)   DEGREE OF RESTORATION: (b)
  CURRENT USE: Theatre   LOCATION OF AUDITORIUM: Ground floor
  STAGE DIMENSIONS AND EQUIPMENT: Height and width of
    proscenium, 27ft 6in x 27ft 6in; Shape of proscenium
    arch, arched; Distance from edge of stage to back wall
    of stage, 44ft; Distance from edge of stage to curtain
    line, 12ft; Distance between side walls of stage, 57ft;
    Depth under stage, 8ft 6in; Stage floor, flat; Trap
    doors, 1; Scenery storage rooms, 2 (lower level);
    Dressing rooms, 6 (lower level)
  DIMENSIONS OF AUDITORIUM: Distance between side walls
    of auditorium, 57ft 6in; Distance stage to back wall
    of auditorium, 44ft; Orchestra pit, yes
  SEATING (4 levels): 1st level, 188; 2nd level, 164;
    3rd level, 170; 4th level, 182
  SHAPE OF THE AUDITORIUM: U-shaped
  MAJOR TYPES OF ENTERTAINMENT: Drama, musical comedy,
    vaudeville, burlesque, opera, dance, concerts
  MAJOR STARS WHO APPEARED AT THEATRE: Mark Twain, John
    Phillip Sousa, Caruso, Sarah Bernhardt, Maude Adams,
    Harry Lauder, Houdini, Pavlova, William Howard Taft,
    Galli-Curci
  ADDITIONAL INFORMATION: After extensive restoration, the
    opera house reopened (October 1986) with a production of
    The Bohemian Girl, the same show which opened the theatre
    in 1883.

Racine, WI

BIJOU THEATRE, 245 Main Street (Main and 3rd Streets)
  OPENING DATE: 1906   OPENING SHOW: Vaudeville bill
  STYLE OF ARCHITECTURE: Classic Revival
  TYPE OF BUILDING: Hotel, offices   FACADE: Red brick
  TYPE OF THEATRE: (a)   DEGREE OF RESTORATION: (a)
  CURRENT USE: Offices
  LOCATION OF AUDITORIUM: Ground floor
  MAJOR TYPES OF ENTERTAINMENT: Drama, vaudeville, movies
  MAJOR STARS WHO APPEARED AT THEATRE: Brandy and Wilson,
    originators of the "Brandy Step"
  ADDITIONAL INFORMATION: This theatre is generally
    referred to as the "first" Bijou. It was opened as
    a vaudeville house by W. C. Tiede, an early Racine
    showman. The theatre was the site of Racine's first
    movie showing (The Great Train Robbery). The exterior
    of the building has been recently restored to its
    original appearance by the Johnson Wax Development
    Corporation.

Racine, WI

BIJOU THEATRE (other names: State, Badger), 423 Main Street
OPENING DATE: c. 1908
CLOSING DATE: 1951   CURRENT USE: Offices, stores
MAJOR TYPES OF ENTERTAINMENT: Vaudeville, movies
ADDITIONAL INFORMATION: At the time of its closing,
    the "second" Bijou was under the management of Warner
    Brothers.   At one time, it had been owned by the Fox
    Midwestco Theater interests.

Spooner, WI

SPOONER OPERA HOUSE, 202 Walnut
OPENING DATE: 1902
TYPE OF BUILDING: Municipal building
FACADE: Originally red brick; now white stucco
TYPE OF THEATRE: (b)   DEGREE OF RESTORATION: (d)
CURRENT USE: City offices
LOCATION OF AUDITORIUM: Second floor
SHAPE OF THE AUDITORIUM: Rectangular
MAJOR TYPES OF ENTERTAINMENT: Drama, medicine shows,
    local variety shows
ADDITIONAL INFORMATION: The stage and original equipment
    no longer exist.

Stoughton, WI

CITY HALL AUDITORIUM, 5th and Main
OPENING DATE: February 22, 1901
OPENING SHOW: Doctor's Warm Reception
ARCHITECT): F. H. Kemp   TYPE OF BUILDING: City hall
FACADE: Red brick, sandstone   TYPE OF THEATRE: (b)
DEGREE OF RESTORATION: (b)   CLOSING DATE: 1953
CURRENT USE: Vacant; open for tours
LOCATION OF AUDITORIUM: Second and third floors
STAGE DIMENSIONS AND EQUIPMENT: Height and width of
    proscenium, 20ft x 30ft; Shape of proscenium arch,
    arched; Distance from edge of stage to back wall
    of stage,   26ft; Distance from edge of stage to
    curtain line, 8ft; Distance between side walls of
    stage, 36ft; Depth under stage, 8ft; Stage floor,
    flat; Scenery storage rooms, 2 (backstage); Dressing
    rooms, 2 (backstage)
DIMENSIONS OF AUDITORIUM: Distance between side walls
    of auditorium, 50ft; Distance stage to back wall of
    auditorium, 53ft; Capacity of orchestra pit, 12
SEATING (2 levels): 1st level, 400; 2nd level, 350
SHAPE OF THE AUDITORIUM: Square; horseshoe-shaped balcony
MAJOR TYPES OF ENTERTAINMENT: Drama, musical comedy,
    vaudeville, minstrel shows, temperence lectures, movies

Viroqua, WI

VIROQUA OPERA HOUSE, 122 North Main
  OPENING DATE: 1891
  TYPE OF BUILDING: Commercial   FACADE: Red brick with
    light stone trim   TYPE OF THEATRE: (b)
  DEGREE OF RESTORATION: (c)   CLOSING DATE: Mid-1930s
  CURRENT USE: Stores and apartments
  LOCATION OF AUDITORIUM: Second floor
  MAJOR TYPES OF ENTERTAINMENT: Drama, vaudeville, minstrel
    shows, dances
  ADDITIONAL INFORMATION: The hall ran east to west across
    the second floor of the building. The balcony was on the
    south and the stage was situated on the northern side of
    the building. Seating was on wooden chairs. The ceiling
    consisted of cast-metal blocks and the rafters were
    described as "decorative."

Watertown, WI

CONCORDIA OPERA HOUSE, 117 North 1st Street (North 1st
    and Madison Streets)
  OPENING DATE: June 23, 1888
  OPENING SHOW: Schiller's Glocke
  ARCHITECT: William Waters   STYLE OF ARCHITECTURE: "Modern
    American"   FACADE: Cream-colored Watertown brick
  TYPE OF THEATRE: (b)   DEGREE OF RESTORATION: (d)
  CURRENT USE: Elks Lodge
  LOCATION OF AUDITORIUM: Ground floor
  STAGE DIMENSIONS AND EQUIPMENT: Width of proscenium, 24ft;
    Distance from edge of stage to back wall of stage, 24ft
  SEATING (2 levels)
  MAJOR TYPES OF ENTERTAINMENT: Drama, vaudeville, opera,
    concerts, minstrel shows
  ADDITIONAL INFORMATION: When the theatre opened, THE
    WATERTOWN REPUBLICAN reported that the "appointments
    of the stage are of the most modern construction....
    With the splendid drop curtain before them and the other
    surroundings the audience might well imagine themselves
    in a first-class metropolitan theatre."   When the local
    Elks bought the building in January 1916, they exten-
    sively remodeled the theatre, removing the balcony and
    the "improved" opera chairs located there.

Westby, WI

WESTBY OPERA HOUSE (other name: Bekkedal-Unseth Building),
    100 North Main Street
  OPENING DATE: c. 1901
  TYPE OF BUILDING: Offices, bank   FACADE: Sienna brick
  TYPE OF THEATRE: (b)   DEGREE OF RESTORATION: (c)
  CLOSING DATE: 1940   CURRENT USE: Apartments
  LOCATION OF AUDITORIUM: Second floor
  DIMENSIONS OF AUDITORIUM: Distance between side walls of

auditorium, 40ft; Distance stage to back wall of
auditorium, 70ft
SEATING (1 level)
SHAPE OF THE AUDITORIUM: Rectangular
MAJOR TYPES OF ENTERTAINMENT: Drama, musical comedy,
concerts, dances, local variety shows

Wood, WI

WARD MEMORIAL HALL, Mitchell Boulevard
OPENING DATE: March 15, 1882
ARCHITECT: Henry C. Koch   STYLE OF ARCHITECTURE:
Victorian   TYPE OF BUILDING: Recreation hall
FACADE: Red and cream city brick; painted wood
TYPE OF THEATRE: (a)   DEGREE OF RESTORATION: (c)
CLOSING DATE: 1954   CURRENT USE: Rehearsal hall
LOCATION OF AUDITORIUM: Ground floor
STAGE DIMENSIONS AND EQUIPMENT: Height and width of
proscenium, 24ft 10in x 27ft 2in; Shape of proscenium
arch, arched; Distance from edge of stage to back wall
of stage, 25ft 6in; Distance from edge of stage to
curtain line, 2ft 1in; Distance between side walls of
stage, 50ft 6in; Distance from stage floor to fly loft,
24ft 10in; Depth under stage, 9ft 3in; Stage floor, flat;
Trap doors, 0; Scenery storage rooms, 1 (back-stage
west); Dressing rooms, 3
DIMENSIONS OF AUDITORIUM: Distance between side walls
of auditorium, 44ft 8in; Distance stage to back wall
of auditorium, 56ft; Capacity of orchestra pit, 19
SEATING (2 levels): 1st level, 326; 2nd level, 260;
boxes, 54
SHAPE OF THE AUDITORIUM: U-shaped
MAJOR TYPES OF ENTERTAINMENT: Drama, vaudeville, concerts,
lectures, movies
ADDITIONAL INFORMATION: The hall was named for Horatio
Ward, an early philanthropist. During renovation in
1898, the floor was sloped and many of the present
interior features were added. The theatre reopened
in January of the following year with a presentation
by the Alhambra company of Milwaukee. The theatre is
located on the grounds of the Veteran's Administration
Home.

Wyoming

Cody, WY

TEMPLE THEATRE, 12th and Runway
OPENING DATE: 1912
ARCHITECTS: Link and Haire   TYPE OF BUILDING: Masonic
   temple, civic center   FACADE: Tan brick with brown
   trim   TYPE OF THEATRE: (b)   DEGREE OF
RESTORATION: (d)   CURRENT USE: Masonic temple
LOCATION OF AUDITORIUM: Second floor
SEATING (2 levels)
SHAPE OF THE AUDITORIUM: Rectangular
MAJOR TYPES OF ENTERTAINMENT: Drama, concerts, local
   variety shows, lectures, movies, wrestling matches
ADDITIONAL INFORMATION: The building was erected in 1912
   at a cost of $20,000, but the walls were blown down the
   following year. The building was reconstructed at a cost
   of $40,000.

THEATRES REPORTED/
CONFIRMED

In a number of cases, theatres have been reported by various sources, but questionnaires sent to them have remained unanswered. These theatres are identified with the symbol [R], which indicates that neither the existence nor any data listed for these theatres has been verified.

In other cases, the existence of a particular theatre has been verified, but no additional documentation was conveyed to us. These theatres are identified by the symbol [C], indicating that they are still standing, but have not been documented. The reader should also be aware that not all theatres listed in this section are included in the Chesley Collection.

ALABAMA (AL)

Tuscaloosa, AL   BRICE INSTITUTE THEATRE, 1860.
                        Theatre in an asylum. [C]

ARIZONA (AZ)

Prescott   ELK'S OPERA HOUSE, 1904.
                        Now a movie theatre. [R]

Tombstone   CAN CAN SALOON. [R]

Tombstone   CRYSTAL PALACE. [R]

ARKANSAS (AK)

Arkansas City   OPERA HOUSE, 1880. Storage now. [R]

Eureka Springs   Reported theatre. [R]

Fayetteville   OZARK THEATRE, 1905.
                       For sale (1983). [R]

Fort Smith   NEW THEATRE BUILDING, 1905.
                       Now a pawn shop. [R]

CALIFORNIA   (CA)

Arcata   ARDEN (MINOR) THEATRE, 1914. Named for
                       Minor family. Designed by Franklin
                       Georgeson. Used for movies and live
                       theatre. [C]

Bay Field   HUNTER'S POINT OPERA HOUSE. [R]

Bodie   MINER'S UNION HALL, 1878.
                       A Bodie area museum now. [R]

Cordelia   CORDELIA THEATRE, 1902.
                       Abandoned hall over bar and
                       grocery. [R]

Eureka   INGOMAR THEATRE, 1892. On F Street
                       between Second and Third. Built by
                       William Carson, prominant Eureka
                       lumberman. Closed in 1920 due to
                       competition from films. Proscenium
                       and ceiling remain. Local group is
                       currently trying to promote the
                       restoration of the theatre. [C]

Eureka   SWEAZEY THEATRE, 1890. Built by Eureka
                       Mayor Richard Sweazey. Later named the
                       State. Facade was renovated in 1920.
                       Part of proscenium arch, stairs, and
                       railing to balcony, upper balcony and
                       projection room are intact. Now being
                       used as Daly's Department Store. [C]

Gridley   Reported Theatre. [R]

Guinda   GUINDA HALL, 1908.
                       Houses local productions. [R]

Hollywood   LAS PALMAS. [R]

Livermore   BELL THEATRE, 1913. In Schenone
                       Building. Designed by Italo Zannolini of
                       San Francisco. Later known as the State.
                       Now a mall with small shops. [C]

Locke   STAR THEATRE, 1915. Chinese community
                       theatre for plays in that language. [C]

Los Angeles	PAN ANDREAS THEATRE. [R]
Los Angeles	PHILHARMONIE AUDITORIUM, 1905. Restoration planned. [C]
Lower Lake	OLD BRICK HALL, 1868. Used for entertainment, dances and Native Sons of the Golden West. [C]
Petaluma	HILL OPERA HOUSE, 1902. Now the Phoenix, a movie house. [R]
Petaluma	OPERA HOUSE, 1870. Commercial building now. [R]
Plymouth	CHAUTAUQUA SETTLEMENT THEATRE. [R]
Red Bluff	RED BLUFF OPERA HOUSE, 1908. Gutted by fire in 1946. Part of the original opera house still stands and is now a doctor's office. [C]
Redwood City	ALHAMBRA THEATRE, 1896. Now a Masonic Lodge. [R]
Riverside	LORING OPERA HOUSE, 1890. Poor condition. [R]
Roseville	MCRAE OPERA HOUSE, 1908. Used by local newspaper now. [R]
Rumsey	TOWN HALL, 1906. One-story hall with stage and some original scenery. [C]
Sacramento	TURN VERIEN THEATRE, 1854. Not to be confused with 1925 Turn Verien Hall which is in use now. [R]
San Francisco	EMBASSY THEATRE, 1907. Rebuilt after 1906 earthquake. [R]
Santa Monica	Theatre in Veterans' Administration Complex. [R]
Santa Monica	MAYFAIR MUSIC HALL, 1911. The former Santa Monica Opera House bacame a music hall. [R]
Santa Rosa	SCOTTISH RITE TEMPLE (Theatre). [R]
Sierra City	BUSCH HALL. [R]
Smith's Flat	Reported Theatre, c. 1858. Dance hall/theatre and rooming house. [R]

Sutter Creek   LEVAGGI'S OPERA HOUSE. Now an antique
                      shop. [R]

Thornton   Reported Theatre. [R]

Tomales   CHURCH WITH MANY FLOWERS. Theatre in
                      barn on Church property. [R]

Walnut Grove   THE HALL, 1860. Now storage. [R]

Willits   COLONIAL THEATRE, 1914. In Schieve Block
                      (215 South Main Street). First floor now
                      vacant, but rooms above are rented. [C]

Winters   SEAMAN'S OPERA HOUSE, 1876. Built by B.
                      R. Sackett, an area ranch owner. Opera
                      house was on second floor and was the
                      site of local civic, political, social
                      and theatrical events. Now storage. [C]

COLORADO (CO)

Colorado Springs   Theatre in a sanitorium. [R]

Colorado Springs   BROADMOOR HOTEL THEATRE, 1909. [R]

Crested Butte   PRINCESS THEATRE. Now used as a movie
                      theater. [R]

Fort Collins   FORT COLLINS OPERA HOUSE, 1881. Now
                      closed. [R]

Fort Garland   SOLDIER'S THEATRE, 1858. Small platform
                      stage in barracks. [R]

Ouray   GOLD BELT THEATRE, 1889. Most of
                      building has been destroyed or
                      vandalized. [R]

Ouray   KNIGHTS OF PYTHIAS HALL, 1886. Hall is
                      used for plays and dances. [R]

Rico   Reported Theatre. [R]

Salida   SALIDA OPERA HOUSE, 1889. Now a movie
                      house and known as the Empress. [R]

Trinidad   WEST THEATRE, 1904. Now movies. [R]

CONNECTICUT (CT)

Bridgewater   BRIDGEWATER TOWN HALL, 1904. [R]

Brookfield	BROOKFIELD TOWN HALL, 1886. [R]
Deep River	DEEP RIVER TOWN HALL, 1892. [R]
Haddam	ST. JOHN OPERA HOUSE. [R]
Hazardville	HAZARDVILLE INSTITUTE, 1869. [R]
Manchester	CHENEY SILK MILLS, 1850. [R]
Milford	CONNECTICUT STAGE, 1902. [R]
New Hartford	NEW HARTFORD TOWN HALL, 1855. [R]
New Haven	WOOLSEY HALL, 1903. On the campus of Yale University. [R]
New London	ORPHEUM THEATRE, 1882. [R]
North Haven	NORTH HAVEN TOWN HALL, 1886. [R]
Norwich	SLATER HALL (Slater Academy), 1887. [R]
South Canaan	SOUTH CANAAN MEETING HOUSE, 1804. [R]
Thomaston	TOWN HALL/OPERA HOUSE, 1884. A brick and stone building with theatre on the second floor. [R]
Watertown	WATERTOWN CINEMA, 1909. [R]
Westport	WESTPORT COUNTRY PLAYHOUSE, 1895. [C]

DISTRICT OF COLUMBIA (DC)

Washington	HOWARD THEATRE, 1914. [R]

FLORIDA (FL)

Bay Pines	Reported Theatre. [R]

GEORGIA (GA)

Blakely	POWELL OPERA HOUSE, 1904. Vacant now. [R]
Brunswick	RITZ THEATRE, 1891. Formerly the Grand Opera House and now part of an historic district. [R]

Camilla	Reported Theatre. [R]
Forsyth	Reported Theatre. [R]
Macon	RIALTO THEATRE, 1905. Only the facade remains of the former theatre. [R]
Milledgeville	Reported Theatre. [R]

IDAHO (ID)

Glenns Ferry	GORBY OPERA HOUSE, 1914. [R]

ILLINOIS (IL)

Beardstown	BEARDSTOWN OPERA HOUSE, 1872. [R]
Bowen	BOWEN OPERA HOUSE, 1896. Little change in exterior, but theatre interior is gone. [R]
Bushnell	BUSHNELL OPERA HOUSE, 1883. Italianate brick and stone facade. Reported intact in 1983. [R]
Camp Point	BAILEY'S OPERA HOUSE, 1903. Upstairs theatre in Opera House block. [R]
Canton	CANTON OPERA HOUSE, 1891. 1893 fire left only the stone and brick facade which was extant in 1983. [R]
Champagne	VIRGINIA THEATRE. [R]
Chicago	OAK THEATRE, 1884. [R]
Farmersville	FARMERSVILLE OPERA HOUSE. [R]
Freeport	GRAND OPERA HOUSE, 1889. Building now houses apartments. Damaged by fire in 1912 and again in 1981. [R]
Hillsboro	HILLSBORO OPERA HOUSE, 1887. Roof of two-story building collapsed in 1977. Damage was repaired and building now houses various stores. [R]
McHenry	OPERA HOUSE, c. 1915. [C]

Metamora	METAMORA COURT HOUSE, 1844. An upstairs hall which was converted into an opera house. [R]
Peotone	PEOTONE OPERA HOUSE, 1900. Restored second floor opera house last reported functioning as a dinner theatre. [R]
Webster	WEBSTER OPERA HOUSE, 1900. An upstairs opera house over a general store containing original benches and a unique painted roll-drop. [R]
NOTE:	According to a 1981 survey by Western Illinois University College of Fine Arts and the Illinois Arts Council, more than 60 undocumented opera houses still exist throughout the state.

INDIANA (IN)

Aurora	GRAND OPERA HOUSE, 1878. Upstairs theatre with some original equipment. Little of opera house remains. [C]
Bloomfield	BLOOMFIELD OPERA HOUSE, 1884. Originally Moss Opera House. [C]
Dunreith	OPERA HOUSE, 1872. [C]
Elkhart	BUCKLEN OPERA HOUSE, 1884. On National Register. A 1977 roof collapse caused extensive damage. [C]
Evansville	ALHAMBRA, 1913. [C]
Greencastle	OPERA HOUSE, 1883. Little of theatre remains. Interior was damaged by fire in September 1985. [C]
Hagerstown	ODD FELLOWS HALL, 1883. Now the home of the Historical Society and used as a museum. [C]
Hartford City	VAN CLEVE THEATRE. Originally a second floor house. Second floor was removed a number of years ago. [C]
Indianapolis	ATHENAEUM, 1894. Built by the Athenaeum Turners. [C]
Knightstown	ALHAMBRA THEATRE, 1897. [R]

Martinsville	INDIANA THEATRE, 1898. Initially the Grace Opera House. Also operated as a movie theatre. [R]
Plainfield	KNIGHTS OF PYTHIAS OPERA HOUSE, 1886. [R]
Straughn	STRAUGHN OPERA HOUSE, 1872. [C]
Topeka	SYCAMORE LITERARY HALL, 1883. [R]
Zionsville	TOWN HALL, 1902. Originally an upstairs theatre over town hall. [C]

IOWA (IA)

Derby	DERBY OPERA HOUSE, 1900. Small, brick theatre. [R]
Iowa City	ENGLERT, 1913. [C]
Iowa City	GRAND OPERA HOUSE, 1877. [R]
Iowa Falls	THE MET, 1889. [R]
LeMars	DALTON OPERA HOUSE, 1893. Cut lime-stone building, first-level facade of castiron. Little of theatre remains. [R]
Washington	GRAHAM OPERA HOUSE, 1893. Theatre altered in 1916. Currently movie theatre. [R]

KANSAS (KS)

Claflin	Reported Theatre. [R]
Emporia	FOX THEATRE. Pseudo-Spanish stucco building in use as a commercial theatre. [R]
Emporia	OPERA HOUSE. [R]
Eureka	OPERA HOUSE, 1880. Former second floor theater is now divided into apartments. [R]
Frankfort	FRANKFORT OPERA HOUSE, 1889. [R]

KENTUCKY (KY)

Ashland	ASHLAND OPERA HOUSE, 1887. Now a furniture store. [C]
Ashland	MODERN/LYRIC THEATRE, 1913. Funeral parlor converted to theatre and now a fabric store. [R]
Berea	WILDERNESS ROAD TICKET OFFICE, 1876. Theatre reported by Landmark Commission. [C]
Bowling Green	POTTER OPERA HOUSE, 1866. Now a bank. [C]
Bradstown	BROADWAY GRAND OPERA HOUSE, 1908. Now an auto body shop. [C]
Campbellsville	OPERA HOUSE, 1905. Now apartments. [C]
Campbellsville	OPERA HOUSE, 1913. Built in Gowdy Block after 1911 fire and may have become part of the Alhambra Movie House. Now a business. [R]
Carlisle	COMMERCIAL BUILDING, 1914. Theatre converted to a mortuary. [C]
Covington	ODD FELLOWS HALL, 1857. Now vacant. [C]
Cynthiania	ROHS OPERA HOUSE, 1885. Now houses movies. [C]
Frankfort	CAPITOL THEATRE, 1883. Threatened with demolition. [R]
Frankfort	GRAND THEATRE, 1900. [R]
Franklin	Reported Theatre, 1908. Now a hardware store. [C]
Franklin	WADE'S HALL-OPERA HOUSE. Now vacant. [C]
Hopkinsville	HOLLAND OPERA HOUSE, 1882. Auditorium was removed in 1974. [C]
Horse Cave	HORSE CAVE THEATRE, 1911. Now houses a summer repertory company. [C]
La Grange	ODD FELLOWS HALL-OPERA HOUSE, 1879. [C]
Maysville	WASHINGTON OPERA HOUSE, 1899. Built as part of a firehouse and still houses productions by Maysville Players. [C]

Oldham	SAUER BROTHERS OPERA HOUSE-ODD FELLOWS HALL, 1879. Used by Lodge now. [C]
Paducah	MARBLE HALL, 1873. Now a business. [C]
Shelbyville	LAYSON HALL, 1850. Theatre space over businesses, but condition of theatre is unknown. [C]
Stanford	STANFORD OPERA HOUSE, 1900. Theatre used for square dancing now. [C]
Walton	Reported Theatre. Threatened with demolition. [R]
Winchester	OPERA HOUSE-MUSIC HALL, 1877. Now a business. [C]
Winchester	TOWN HALL, 1901. Theatre in town hall complex. [C]

LOUISIANA (LA)

New Orleans	CIVIC THEATRE, 1906. Formerly the Lafayette and now closed. [R]

MAINE (ME)

Belfast	HAYFORD HALL, 1869. Greek Revival and Italianate building. Has not been used for roughly twenty-five years. Condition unknown. [R]
Biddeford	BIDDEFORD CITY HALL AND OPERA HOUSE, 1895. Theatre in third-story wing. 860 seats, horseshoe balcony. [R]
Brunswick	TOWN HALL, 1910. [R]
Camden	CAMDEN OPERA HOUSE, 1894. [R]
Gardiner	JOHNSON OPERA HOUSE, 1864. Third floor theatre in poor condition and used for storage. [R]
Lakewood	LAKEWOOD THEATRE, 1882. Opened as Spiritualist meeting hall and converted

	to theatre in 1898. Rebuilt and enlarged in 1925-26. [R]
Lewiston	CITY HALL THEATRE, 1892. Second and third floor theatre. Now occupied by municipal offices. [R]
Lewiston	MYSTIC THEATRE, 1896. Second floor theatre also know as Mystic Hall. Once contained offices of William P. Gray who controlled 150 theatres in Maine and New Hampshire. [R]
Lincolnville Center	TRANQUILITY GRANGE, 1908. Used for local entertainment. One-story building which has been used as church and Grange hall. [R]
Rockport	OPERA HOUSE, 1892. Wood frame building. [R]
Rockport	UNION HALL, 1858. Second floor room still used as meeting hall. Seats approximately 400. [R]
Stonington	OPERA HOUSE, 1912. [C]

MARYLAND (MD)

Baltimore	BIJOU, 1904. Now vacant. [R]
Baltimore	EASTERN, 1909. Now a flea market. [R]
Baltimore	GAYETY, 1905. Now shows X-rated films. [R]
Baltimore	HIPPODROME, 1914. Now a movie house. [R]
Baltimore	MAYFAIR, 1870. Now a movie house. [R]
Baltimore	NEW THEATRE, 1910. Now a movie house. [R]
Baltimore	PARKWAY, 1915. Now vacant. [R]
Baltimore	TOWN, 1911. Now a movie house. [R]
Baltimore	WAVERLY, 1909. Now a Goodwill Store. [R]

MASSACHUSETTS (MA)

Boston	SAN JUAN HILL CYCLORAMA, 1895. [R]
Cambridge	MEMORIAL HALL, 1868. Theatre on campus of Harvard University. [R]
Clinton	TOWN HALL OPERA HOUSE, 1908. Received national attention in 1978 when President Carter held town meeting there. [R]
Gardner	GARDNER THEATRE, 1900. [R]
Great Barrington	MAHAWIE THEATRE, 1903. Currently a movie theatre. [C]
Leominster	TOWN HALL-OPERA HOUSE, pre-1910. [R]
Milford	MUSIC HALL, pre-1910. [R]
Newburyport	CITY HALL, pre-1910. [R]
Provincetown	TOWN HALL, pre-1910. [R]
Taunton	TAUNTON THEATRE, pre-1904. [R]
Waltham	PARK THEATRE, pre-1904. [R]
Ware	CASINO THEATRE, c. 1906. [R]
Worcester	MECHANICS HALL, 1857. This Victorian hall once hosted performers of the stature of Caruso and Paderewsi and such famous speakers as Dickens, Emerson and Thoreau. The 1,600-seat hall has been fully restored. [C]

MICHIGAN (MI)

Ann Arbor	HILL AUDITORIUM, 1912. [R]
Bath	BATH COMMUNITY HALL, 1881. [C]
Bay City	COLUMBIA OPERA HOUSE, pre-1904. [R]
Bayview	LECTURE HALL, c. 1870. [R]
Burt	BURT OPERA HOUSE, 1891. One-story brick building currently used as a town hall. [R]
Concord	OPERA HOUSE, c. 1885. [R]
Decatur	DECATUR TOWNSHIP HALL, 1901. [R]

Detroit	HYLAND, 1915. [R]
Detroit	ANDREWS SOCIETY HALL, 1907-12. [R]
Fayette State Park	OPERA HOUSE, 1868. Second floor theatre in wood structure. [R]
Flint	FENTON OPERA HOUSE, 1880. Commercial building with theatre upstairs. Moved from Fenton to Crossroads Village. [R]
Fowler	STURGIS OPERA HOUSE, c. 1904. Upper floors of commercial block. Not used as theatre for many years. [R]
Iron River	IRON RIVER TOWN HALL, c. 1914. [C]
Leslie	UNION HALL BUILDING, 1871. [C]
Manchester	ARBITER'S HALL, 1881. [R]
Marshall	WAGNER HALL, 1870. Upstairs hall also called Mitchell Hall. [C]
Muir	MUIR TOWN HALL, 1894. [R]
Rockford	OPERA HOUSE, 1896. Closed for over sixty years. Condition unknown. [R]
Stockbridge	STOCKBRIDGE TOWN HALL, 1893. First floor theatre with town offices in basement. [R]
Vassar	MILLER'S OPERA HOUSE, 1879. At one time atached to Jewell Hotel. Originally seated 750. [R]

MINNESOTA (MN)

Anoka	COLONIAL HALL AND MASONIC LODGE, pre-1914. [R]
Cokato	TEMPERENCE HALL, 1896. Built by Finnish community as a meeting hall. Hall was equipped with small stage. Nominated for National Register. [R]
Fergus Falls	LYCEUM, pre-1910. [R]
Hibbing	SONS OF ITALY HALL. On National Register. [R]
Jasper	BAUMAN HALL, c. 1890. Theatre originally

	above hotel in North Sioux Falls. In 1907, the stone building was dismantled and then reassembled in Jasper. [R]
Kenyon	KENYON OPERA HOUSE, pre-1915. [R]
Lake Benton	OPERA HOUSE, 1896. [R]
Linwood Township	CRESCENT GRANGE HALL, pre-1915. [R]
Litchfield	G.A.R. HALL, pre-1915. [R]
Marshall	MASONIC TEMPLE, pre-1915. [R]
Montgomery	HILLTOP HALL, pre-1915. [R]
Nininger Township	GOOD TEMPLERS HALL, pre-1915. [R]
Pine Island	OPERA HOUSE, 1895. [R]
Rothsy	ODD FELLOWS' HALL, pre-1915. [R]
Shakopee	Reported Theatre. [R]
Spring Valley	PARSONS HALL, c. 1910. [R]

MISSOURI (MO)

Clarksville	OPERA HOUSE, 1850. [R]
Kansas City	WILLIS WOOD THEATRE, pre-1910. [R]
St. Louis	GOLDEN ROD, 1909. Floating theatre moored here and houses productions. [R]
Springfield	LANDERS THEATRE, 1907. Former Orpheum Circuit theatre now houses community productions. [R]
Tarkio	MULE BARN THEATRE, 1893. [R]

MONTANA (MT)

Fort Peck	FORT PECK THEATRE. [C]
Red Lodge	FINNISH OPERA HOUSE, 1897. [R]

NEBRASKA (NE)

Brownsville	OPERA HOUSE, pre-1915. [C]
Chadron	P. B. NELSON OPERA HOUSE, 1889. On second story of brick building. [C]
David City	THORPE OPERA HOUSE, 1890. Restored second floor opera house. [C]
Diller	ANNE C. DILLER OPERA HOUSE, 1913. Three-story brick building. Opera house on upper levels. [C]
Madison	HEINZ OPERA HOUSE, c. 1894. Ground floor of two-story brick structure. [C]
Ravenna	OPERA HOUSE, 1890. [C]
Ravenna	PASTINE THEATRE, c. 1900. [R]
Table Rock	OPERA HOUSE, 1893. Three-story brick building now used as a museum. [C]
Tecumseh	OPERA HOUSE, pre-1915. [C]

NEVADA (NV)

Austin	Reported Theatre. [R]
Carson City	Reported Theatre. [R]
Dayton	ODEON HALL, 1862. Now a museum. [R]
Elko	Reported Theatre. [R]
Eureka	OPERA HOUSE, 1879. Theatre reported to be a "little jewel of an opera house" with a horseshoe balcony and raked stage. Advertising curtain and old movie projection equipment still intact. [R]
Pioche	THOMPSON'S OPERA HOUSE. Wood structure similar to Piper's Opera House. [R]

NEW HAMPSHIRE (NH)

Claremont	OPERA HOUSE, 1897. [R]

Dover	OPERA HOUSE, c. 1900. [R]
Lisbon	OPERA HOUSE, c. 1910. In town hall. [R]
Newport	OPERA HOUSE, 1886. On second floor of courthouse. [R]
Washington	TOWN HALL, c. 1850. Town Hall and school with a second floor theatre. [R]
Woodsville	OPERA HOUSE, 1886. [R]

NEW JERSEY (NJ)

Asbury Park	SAVOY THEATRE, 1911. [R]
Califon	CALIFON THEATRE, 1888. [R]
Carlstadt	DRAMATIC HALL DISTRICT, c. 1861. [R]
Dover	BAKER OPERA HOUSE, 1884. Now called the Bennett Building. [C]
Dover	NEW BAKER THEATRE, 1906. [C]
Englewood	THE LYCEUM, 1888. [R]
Englishtown	ENGLISHTOWN MUSIC HALL, 1891. [R]
Franklin	Reported Theatre, 1914. [R]
Lambertville	HOLCOMBE HALL, c. 1860. Originally named Corgell Hall. [R]
Madison	LYRIC HALL, 1898. [R]
Ocean Grove	AUDITORIUM, 1894. Victorian, wood structure with large auditorium. [R]
Woodstown	WOODSTOWN OPERA HOUSE, 1885. [R]

NEW MEXICO (NM)

Gallup	KITCHEN'S OPERA HOUSE. Used for storage now. [R]

Mogollon   MOGOLLON THEATRE, pre-1912. Wood frame
                        structure converted to movies in 1912 and
                        is now dilapated. [R]

San Miguel   DANCE HALL, pre-1900. Community hall.
    del Vado   [R]

NEW YORK (NY)

Flushing   FLUSHING TOWN HALL, 1862. [R]

Geneva   GENEVA THEATRE, 1894. Also known as
                        Smith's Opera House. [C]

Glens Falls   EMPIRE, 1899. [R]

Middletown   Reported Theatre, pre-1915. [R]

New York   ALHAMBRA THEATRE (126th Street),
                        1905. [C]

Pine Lake   SHERMAN THEATRE, 1910. [R]

NORTH CAROLINA (NC)

New Bern   THE ATHENS, 1911. Opened as a
                        combination house. Remodeled many
                        times. [R]

NORTH DAKOTA (ND)

Leith   LEITH OPERA HOUSE. [R]

OHIO

Cedarville   CEDARVILLE OPERA HOUSE. [R]

Chestertown   CHESTERTOWN OPERA HOUSE. [R]

Cleveland   ENGINEERS AUDITORIUM, 1910. [C]

Cleveland   METROPOLITAN THEATRE, 1913. Also known
                        as WHK Auditorium. In process of being

	renovated. [C]
Dayton	Reported Theatre in V.A. complex. [R]
Granville	OPERA HOUSE. [R]
Hayesville	OPERA HOUSE, 1886. [R]
Hillsboro	BELL OPERA HOUSE, pre-1915. [R]
Mason	MASON OPERA HOUSE. [R]
Milan	Reported Theatre, 1888. [R]
Mount Vernon	WOODWARD OPERA HOUSE, 1852. [R]
Port Clinton	TOWN HALL. [R]
Reamples	Reported Theatre. [R]

OKLAHOMA (OK)

Krebs	Reported Theatre, now a warehouse. [R]
Muskogee	THE RITZ, 1905. Formerly the Hinton Theatre. [R]
Talhequah	OPERA HOUSE. [R]

OREGON (OR)

Elgin	ELGIN OPERA HOUSE, 1910. [R]
Oregon City	OPERA HOUSE, 1873. [R]

PENNSYLVANIA (PA)

Brookville	MCCRACKEN'S HALL, 1871. Theatre on top floor of City Hall. [R]
Easton	NEW CORRELL FAMILY THEATRE, 1906. Also called the Lyric Family Theatre. [C]
Easton	PASTIME THEATRE, 1909. [C]

Harmony	ACADEMY OF MUSIC. [R]
Harrisburg	COLONIAL THEATRE, 1912. Building collapsed, but facade remains and is attached to a commercial structure. [C]
Lebanon	ACADEMY OF MUSIC, 1901. [R]
Lebanon	FAMILY THEATRE. [C]
New Kingston	OPERA HOUSE. [R]
Philadelphia	WANAMAKER'S. Three auditoriums – Egyptian Hall, The Grand Court, and Greek Hall – in a famous department store. [C]
Sayre	OPERA HOUSE. [R]
Sharon	OPERA HOUSE, 1873. [R]
Tarentum	NIXON THEATRE, 1906. [R]
Tidioute	GRANDIN OPERA HOUSE, 1872. [R]
Waynesboro	Reported Theatre, 1900. [R]

RHODE ISLAND (RI)

Newport	BRICKMARKET, 1761. Upper floor served as theatre in late 18th century. [R]

SOUTH CAROLINA (SC)

Alcolu	ALCOLU THEATRE/ALDERMAN THEATRE, 1914. Theatre built above a store which hosted plays and graduations. In poor condition. [R]

SOUTH DAKOTA (SD)

Doland	RILEY OPERA HOUSE, 1913. [C]
Madison	OLDHAM OPERA HOUSE, c. 1890. Opened as Socialist Hall. The building was moved from its original location to Prairie Village, outside of Madison. [C]

Rockam   ROCKAM COMMUNITY HALL. [R]

Spearfish   MATTHEWS OPERA HOUSE, 1906. [C]

Watertown   GOSS OPERA HOUSE, 1906. [C]

Yankton   LYRIC THEATRE, c. 1889. [R]

Yankton   RODGERS OPERA HOUSE, 1900. Also known as
                Hess Theatre and Dakota Theatre. [R]

Zell   ZELL COMMUNITY CENTER. [R]

TENNESSEE (TN)

Memphis   FRONT STREET THEATRE, 1911. [R]

TEXAS (TX)

Devine   DEVINE OPERA HOUSE, 1906. [R]

Jefferson   JEFFERSON OPERA HOUSE. [R]

Kerrville   PAMPELL'S HALL AND OPERA HOUSE, 1898.
                [R]

UTAH (UT)

Midway   MIDWAY AMUSEMENT HALL, 1898. Now used as
                a church welfare center and cannery. [R]

Payson   PAYSON OPERA HOUSE, 1882. [R]

VERMONT (VT)

Hardwick   HARDWICK MEMORIAL BUILDING, 1911. [R]

Hardwick   HARDWICK TOWN HALL/OPERA HOUSE, 1865. [R]

VIRGINIA (VA)

Lynchburg	OPERA HOUSE, 1879. Became the Trenton in 1914 and has been vacant since 1970s. [R]
Richmond	MASONIC HALL. [R]

WEST VIRGINIA (WV)

Sheppardstown	OPERA HOUSE. [R]
Sheppardstown	REYNOLDS HALL. [R]
Wheeling	COURT THEATRE, 1900. [R]

WISCONSIN (WI)

Argyle	STAR THEATRE, 1878. [R]
Dodgeville	SPANG'S OPERA HOUSE, c. 1883. [R]
Green Bay	VIC THEATRE, 1899. [C]
Racine	UPTOWN THEATRE. Formerly the Majestic. [R]
Rosendale	GRANGE HALL, 1870. [C]
Sheboygan	VAN DER VAURT THEATRE. [R]
Stevens Point	FOX THEATRE, 1894. [R]

WYOMING (WY)

Rock Springs	FOX THEATRE. [R]

Bibliography

Botto, Louis. AT THIS THEATRE. New York: Dodd, Mead & Company, 1984.

Cahn, Julius. JULIUS CAHN'S OFFICIAL THEATRICAL GUIDE. New York: Publication Office, Empire Theatre Building, 1899-1914.

Cain, Jerrilee. ILLINOIS OPERA HOUSE: A TIME OF GLORY. Western Illinois University Library Archives and Collections.

DIAGRAMS OF LEADING THEATRES, OPERA HOUSES, CONCERT HALLS, AND ATHLETIC FIELDS. New York: The City News Publishing Co., 1922.

Dimmick, Ruth Crosby. OUR THEATRES TO-DAY AND YESTERDAY. New York: The H. K. Fly Company, 1913.

Ernst, Alice Henson. TROUPING IN THE OREGON COUNTRY. Portland, Oregon: Oregon Historical Society, 1961.

Frick, John W. NEW YORK'S FIRST THEATRICAL CENTER: THE RIALTO AT UNION SQUARE. Ann Arbor, Michigan: UMI Research Press, 1985.

Gladson, Gene. INDIANAPOLIS THEATERS FROM A TO Z. Indianapolis, Indiana: Gladson Publications, 1976.

Havens, John F. DESCRIPTION OF COMMUNITY THEATRES IN THE UNITED STATES. Washington, D.C.: U. S. Department of Health, Education and Welfare, 1968.

HAWKINSVILLE CITY HALL AND AUDITORIUM. Eastman, Georgia: Heart of Georgia, 1975.

Henderson, Mary C. THE CITY AND THE THEATRE. Clifton, New Jersey: James T. White & Company, 1973.

HISTORIC PRESERVATION. Bi-monthly magazine of The National
    Trust for Historic Preservation. 1949-1986.

Hoyt, Harlowe R. TOWN HALL TONIGHT. Englewood Cliffs, New
    Jersey: Prentice-Hall, Inc., 1955.

Johnson, Charlie H. Jr. THE CENTRAL CITY OPERA HOUSE: A
    100 YEAR HISTORY. Colorado Springs, Colorado: Little
    London Press, 1980.

Johnson, Stephen Burge. THE ROOF GARDENS OF BROADWAY
    THEATRES, 1883-1942. Ann Arbor, Michigan: UMI Research
    Press, 1985.

LANSING'S PICTORIAL DIAGRAMS OF LEADING OPERA HOUSES,
    THEATRES, ETC. IN THE UNITED STATES. Boston: Lansing
    & Co. Publishers, 1880.

LIBRARY THEATRE. Warren, Pennsylvania: Published by the
    theatre, 1983.

McDonald, Donna, ed. DIRECTORY, HISTORICAL SOCIETIES AND
    AGENCIES IN THE UNITED STATES AND CANADA. Nashville,
    Tennessee: American Association for State and Local
    History, 1978.

McGowan, Martha. GROWING UP IN BROOKLYN. THE BROOKLYN
    ACADEMY OF MUSIC: MIRROR OF A CHANGING BOROUGH. Brooklyn:
    Brooklyn Academy of Music, 1983.

MARQUEE. Quarterly Journal of the Theatre Historical
    Society. 1969-1986.

MORTON THEATRE. Athens, Georgia: Published by the
    theatre.

NATIONAL REGISTER OF HISTORIC PLACES. Washington, D.C.:
    United States Department of the Interior, 1976.

Naylor, David. AMERICAN PICTURE PALACES: THE ARCHITECTURE
    OF FANTASY. New York: Van Nostrand Reinhold Company, 1981.

ODD FELLOWS AUDITORIUM. Atlanta, Georgia: Published by the
    theatre.

Olszewski, George J. RESTORATION OF FORD'S THEATRE.
    Washington, D.C.: United States Department of the
    Interior, 1963.

Perlman, Daniel H. THE AUDITORIUM BUILDING. Chicago:
    Roosevelt University, 1976.

Sheridan, Phil. THOSE WONDERFUL OLD DOWNTOWN THEATERS.
    Columbus, Ohio: Phil Sheridan, 1978.

Skidmore, Owings and Merrill. ORCHESTRA HALL: A CHRONICLE OF ITS ARCHITECTURE AND ACOUSTICS. Chicago: Skidmore, Owings & Merrill, 1980.

SOUTHERN THEATRE. Quarterly Magazine of the Southeastern Theatre Conference. 1963-1986.

SOUVENIR PROGRAM, RAMSDELL THEATRE. Manistee, Michigan: Manistee Civic Players, 1978.

STUBS: THE SEATING PLAN GUIDE. New York: Lenore Tobin, 1955.

SURVEY OF THEATRES BUILT BEFORE 1940 IN CONNECTICUT. Connecticut Trust for Historic Preservation, 1983.

TALMANAC: RESTORING THE AUDITORIUM. Chicago: Talman Federal Savings & Loan Association.

Tidworth, Simon. THEATRES: AN ARCHITECTURAL AND CULTURAL HISTORY. New York: Praeger Publishers, 1973.

Tompkins, Eugene, and Kilby, Quincy. THE HISTORY OF THE BOSTON THEATRE, 1854-1901. New York: Benjamin Blom, 1969.

Toms, Donald D., and Stone, William J. THE HOMESTAKE OPERA HOUSE AND RECREATION BUILDING. Lead, South Dakota: Lead City Fine Arts Association, 1985.

Tyson, Henry H. DIAGRAMS OF NEW YORK AND BROOKLYN THEATRES. New York: Willis McDonald Co. Printers, 1887.

Van Name, Fred. THE GOODSPEED OPERA HOUSE. East Haddam, Connecticut: Goodspeed Opera House Foundation, Inc., 1963.

Ward, Carlton. NATIONAL LIST OF HISTORIC THEATRE BUILDINGS. Washington, D.C.: League of Historic American Theatres, 1983

Young, Toni. THE GRAND EXPERIENCE. Watkins Glen, New York: The American Life Foundation, 1976.

Theatre Index

Subject Index

About the Editors

JOHN W. FRICK teaches in the Department of Drama at the University of Virginia. He is the author of *New York's First Theatrical Center: The Rialto at Union Square* and has contributed articles to *The Drama Review*, *Marquee*, and *Broadside*.

CARLTON WARD is affiliated with Jackson State University.